River Tove

Ox
Bridge

To
Towcester

To
Silverstone

Leeson House
(Vicarage)

School

(Barford)

(Redford)

Foot path

(Slack)

Manor

(Richardson)

New Inn

(Chapman)   (Abberley)

Abthorpe

Stocking frame

To Bucknell's Wood

Sketch

Slapton / Abthorpe

Nineteen - thirties

Scale approx in miles

0                                    $\frac{1}{4}$

STRENUOUS LIVES

THREE GENERATIONS IN PEACE AND WAR

JOHN HAYNES

HAIN HAYNE HAINES HAYNES

Germanic Hagano = by-name orig. hawthorn

Mid. High German   Hagen = hawthorn or hedge

Mid. English   Heghen = enclosure

(Oxford Dictionary of Names)

Published by John Haynes, 5, The Old Stables,
Tanybwlch, Rhydyfelin, Ceredigion, SY 23 4 PY

Printed by Cambrian Printers
January 2007

ISBN: 978-0-9555916-0-0

CONTENTS

page

Maps

Family trees

Chapters

ILLUSTRATIONS

PREFACE

"There's no point in writing a memoir unless you're famous," exclaimed my father's second wife, when I told her of my plan to do just that; echoed by a lady columnist in one of the quality broadsheets, "Why do we want to read about obscure people who have no claim upon our attention?" Why indeed, especially when no less a writer than Germaine Greer claims she never reads autobiographies because they are simply exercises in self-justification! My defence is that the lives of the 'obscure', that is ordinary people, looked at over several generations may be of great interest and provide an addition to social history, especially where the records allow them to speak in their own voices. With the distorting lens of supposed 'class struggle' removed we find that despite past hardships the quotient of happiness was much the same, providing a correction to the common view summed up in the question not, 'How did they live?' but 'How could they live!', arising from the delusion that there was no social progress and all was darkly Dickensian in Britain until after the Second World War. It is also widely believed that previously, no one from the 'working class' could obtain a higher education, or indeed, medical treatment; exemplified by the recent complaint (by a respected military historian) that in a reconstruction of the evacuations from Dunkirk by the BBC, the actors playing the troops were too fit and well fed and had their own teeth; and by another commentator, that before the War 'the poor' never ate white bread! I have been very conscious of Jack Priestley's injunction, "Not to tell fairy tales about the Thirties", but despite the Great Slump, it was not entirely a tale of hunger marches from Jarrow and soup kitchens in the Rhondda: most of the time, and in most places, people still managed to enjoy their 'cakes and ale'. It can also be said that 'class' terminology has been redundant since at least the time of the Second World War. In any case, the ranks of British society have always been permeable.

My second line of defence is filial piety. My father once told me that he thought I should write an account of how I became a geologist, because it would be of interest; and shortly before he died he said, "You must do it!" At the same time he had hopes of writing his own account of his life in business, in particular of his early days as a salesman, but although he told me a great deal about it he never managed to put anything down on paper. I have therefore described my parents' lives and background as the preamble to my own. This volume covers the lives of three generations, including my childhood in the Thirties and my youth during the Second World War. It ends when I leave to begin University and eventually train as a geologist. In so far as it hints at my eventual course in life the reader may well conclude, that considering my personal history and geography, it was quite logical that I should end up working in that field.

A great many people have helped me in my quest to tell it as it was, and I am very grateful, especially to my relations, for information and for correcting my misapprehensions. Acknowledgements are given in the notes to the chapters.

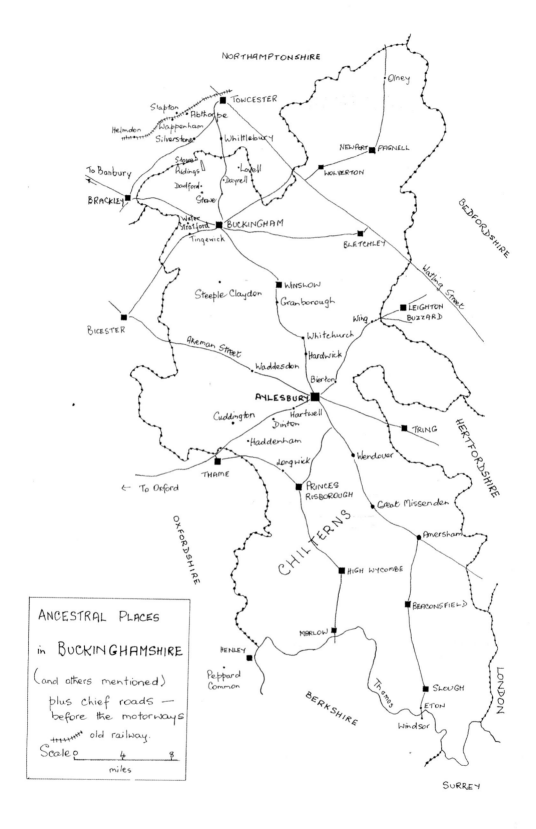

NORTHAMPTONSHIRE

Slapton
Abthorpe
Helmdon
Wappenham
Silverstone
Whittlebury
Towcester
Olney
Newport Pagnell
Wolverton
Stowe Ridings
Dadford
Dayrell
Lovell
Stowe
To Banbury
BRACKLEY
Water Stratford
BUCKINGHAM
Tingewick
BLETCHLEY
Watling Street
BEDFORDSHIRE
Steeple Claydon
WINSLOW
Granborough
Wing
LEIGHTON BUZZARD
BICESTER
Akeman Street
Whitchurch
Hardwick
Waddesdon
Bierton
AYLESBURY
Cuddington
Hartwell
Dinton
Haddenham
Longwick
Wendover
TRING
HERTFORDSHIRE
THAME
← To Oxford
PRINCES RISBOROUGH
Great Missenden
OXFORDSHIRE
Amersham
CHILTERNS
HIGH WYCOMBE
BEACONSFIELD
MARLOW
HENLEY
Peppard Common
BERKSHIRE
Thames
SLOUGH
ETON
Windsor
LONDON
SURREY

ANCESTRAL PLACES

in BUCKINGHAMSHIRE

(and others mentioned)
plus chief roads —
before the motorways
+++ old railway.
Scale o ———4———8
miles

CHAPTER 1

LANDMARKS

For most of my childhood and youth we lived in different places on the Buckinghamshire/Northamptonshire border; near the midpoint of the upland heights made by the Great and Inferior Oolite, Jurassic limestone that runs across the country from the Dorset to the Yorkshire coast. This countryside was then relatively remote from busy urban centers and is still quite well wooded.

From the window in the gable room in my late uncle's farm, Woodlands, Stowe Ridings, where I lived in my late teens, one looks south past the Wolfe monument and the north front of Stowe House. In those days there were scattered oaks in the field by the farmhouse and an avenue of very tall English elms by the lake in Dadford. These framed the distant view across the Ouse valley to the Oxford Clay lands around the Claydon villages beyond; leading the eye to another limestone ridge (known as the Corallian because of its contained coral and shells) making higher ground near Whitchurch. It was here that my Mother's maternal ancestors, the Brooks, were farming at the time of the Civil War. At times of very good visibility one can see further, across the Vale of Aylesbury to the dim, blue-green billow of the Chiltern chalk downs, some twenty-five miles away. (See map.)

In the Vale are isolated outliers of the highest Jurassic limestone (the Portland Stone—the most widely used of all the Jurassic building stones). These make patches of higher ground marking the site of Aylesbury and the village of Cuddington where my mother's paternal ancestors were farm labourers during the Napoleonic Wars (and no doubt much earlier). When I was born in Aylesbury, in 1929, the town was still largely confined to the higher ground of the Portland outcrop but since then has spread out in all directions over the low ground of the Hartwell Clay.

At that time, Aylesbury could still be described as a small market town showing signs of its eighteenth century prosperity (as by Pevsner even as late as 1960). Since then, the town has been transformed and many of its 'seventeenth and eighteenth century buildings, perhaps not individually of outstanding merit but giving to the town character, variety and a human scale' have fallen to the bulldozer (see notes 1 & 2).

I was, therefore, a child of the 'scarplands' with their oak woods and thorn brakes and of the clay vales with their slow, brown rivers placid beneath pollard willows; and also, of a small market town built on a human scale. Of course, this background was only instinctively and intuitively absorbed in childhood but became an essential substratum.

THE BROOKS

Three generations of farmers: The earliest records of my mother's maternal ancestors reveal three generations of farmers living near Whitchurch and Hardwick, north of Aylesbury on the Buckingham road. The first record is of three children born to Thomas and Mary Brooks in the late 1650's at the time of the Cromwellian Commonwealth, so the parents clearly grew up in the reign of Charles 1 and during the Civil War. Only their first-born son, William (1655-1715) lived beyond teenage, through the reigns of four monarchs, Charles II, James II, William and Mary and Queen Anne, into the first year of the accession of George I.

William and his wife Ann had sixteen children. Most of them died in childhood but four boys and four girls lived into adulthood (being mentioned in their mother's will, of 1729) three of the boys at least, into the seventies. (Incidentally, this shows how misleading average death rates are when considering how long people lived in the old days: if child and childbirth mortality are removed from the statistics we find that large numbers reached the biblical three score and ten, as is attested by the gravestones in most country churchyards.)

Joseph Brooks (1686-1760) was the fourth child of William and Ann, in the direct line. He was described as a yeoman farmer of Whitchurch on the occasion of his marriage to Elizabeth Cheshire at Hoggeston, a nearby village; (his younger brother James also became a yeoman farmer at Kingsbury and one of the four constables of Aylesbury). Joseph and Elizabeth had seven children, four surviving to adulthood and their second son James (1717-1792) in the direct line, was born three years after his grandfather William died, three years into the Georgian era.

Two generations of bakers: Following a pattern that had become typical in the eighteenth century in response to the agricultural revolution and the expansion of trade which drew the younger sons of farmers into the country towns, James Brooks became a baker in Aylesbury and in 1739 married Elizabeth Saunders in St. Mary's Church. Elizabeth "dyed in childbed" and their child failed to survive. James' second marriage was to Rebecca Mills in nearby Bierton in 1742 and they had six children. Of these only their son James lived to manhood and he died the year before his father.

James Brooks junior (1746-1791) followed his father's trade as a baker in Aylesbury and in 1771 married Eleanor Horwood, again like his parents in nearby Bierton. James and Eleanor had eleven children, five dying in infancy but the others surviving into adulthood and married life. It was their eleventh child, Amos born just after his father's early death at forty-five, who was to become the grandfather of my grandmother Lillie Brooks.

Brooks line:

(All born in Mid Bucks)

THOMAS c.1630-1713 = MARY d. 1687

WILLIAM 1655-1715   RICHARD 1656-1673   MARY 1659-1671

WILLIAM c1655-1715 = ANN d. 1729
(Farmer of Hardwick,)

THOMAS 1676-1713 MARY 1679- ANN 1681- WILLIAM 1684-1755 JOSEPH c1686- 1760 JANE 1690- SARAH 1693-
ELIZABETH 1697- JAMES 1693-1772 (4 others dying in childhood)

J OSEPH c1686 -15/12/1760 = ELIZABETH CHESHIRE d. c1767
(Yeoman farmer, Whitchurch,)   Married at nearby village, Hoggeston, 3/11/1709

THOMAS 1710-?   ? ?   JAMES 1717-1792   MICHAEL 1719-?   JOHN 1722-?   CHARLES 1723-? (2 others dying in childhood)

JAMES 1717-1792 = ELIZABETH SAUNDERS 1717-1741
(Baker in Aylesbury)   Married at St. Mary's Church, Aylesbury 17/2/1739

SAUNDERS 1741   (mother 'dyed in childbed')

= REBECCA MILLS 1723-1756
(Daughter of John Mills and Alice Gilpin)
Married at St. Mary's Church, Aylesbury 15/2/1742

ALICE 1743-59 ANSTACE 1745- JAMES 1746-1791 ELIZABETH 1747/7 JOHN 1748/9 ABIGAIL 1751/1

JAMES 6/9/ 1746-1791= ELEANOR HORWOOD 3/4/ 1752-1823
(Baker in Aylesbury)   (Daughter of Benjamin Horwood and Martha Barney)
Married at Bierton nr Aylesbury, 17/10/1771

JOHN MILLS 1772/2 PATTY 1773/5 BECKY 1775- JOSEPH 1776-1849 JAMES 1778/9 WILLIAM 1780- ANSTIS 1782 JAMES
1784-1857 THOMAS 1785- MICHAEL 1788- AMOS 1792-1857

AMOS 23/4/ 1792- 1857 = CATHERINE EVITT? c.1793-1865
(Shoemaker in Aylesbury)

ELIZABETH 1813- BENJAMIN 1814- HARRIET 1817-1846 BITHIAN 1819 SIMEON 1823- JOEL 1825- JAMES 1829-1900
ANN 1836/6

JAMES 1829-1900 = MARTHA BONNICK 6/9/1827 - 1909
(Shoemaker in Aylesbury)   (Daughter of Richard Bonnick and Martha or Harriet Reeve)
Married at St. Mary's Church, Aylesbury 1/8/1847

GEORGE 1849- HARRIET 1851- JAMES 1853- AMOS 1855- MARY (Polly) 1857- ELIZABETH 1859- MARTHA(Pat) 1859-
1948 ALICE MAUDE 1861- WALTER 1864-1934 MINNIE 1867 LAURA 1870- LILLIE 1872-1960

(See Watson line)

Two generations of shoemakers:

> I'll make thee shoes and make them well,
> Will last thee years and years.
> I'll make thee shoes and make them well,
> Of leather, thread and tears.
>
> Shoemaker's lament

'Making shoes by hand is an extremely hard, slow, backbreaking process. It takes about forty hours to make each pair. …. It is labour intensive and requires a special personality. Shoemakers are solid, quiet citizens with an earthy view of the world' (see note 3).

Amos Brooks (1792-1857) is recorded as a shoemaker at Castle Street (1817) and Whitehall Street (1841). At this time Aylesbury had a population of about 6000 and there were a number of shoemakers and bootmakers, especially in Temple Street, formerly called Cobbler's Row. (See note 4). His marriage certificate has not been found but they had eight children, five surviving infancy into marriage. The influence of John Wesley and the Methodist revival is clear in the names of one of the girls, Bithian and of the boys, Benjamin, Simeon and Joel; and the youngest brother (and seventh child) was given his grandfather's name James.

James Brooks 3rd (1829-1890) like his brother Joel, followed the trade of his father and is first recorded as a cordwainer of Aylesbury at his parents' address in Whitehall Street in 1841, before his marriage to Martha Bonnick in 1847 and at No.11, Buckingham Arms Yard in 1871 and 1881. The houses down on the left side (later called Cambridge Place) are gone now and replaced by an office block but I remember as a boy taking a short cut through Buckingham Arms Yard to Kingsbury Square (or Weatherheads famous bookshop) and being struck by an unusual architectural feature—each pair of houses had an opposite pair of steps descending to a basement floor in a recess, often with washing hanging up. Grandmother was born in one of these houses on the 8th November 1872, the last of twelve children. James, tall and fair, and Martha, a short dark woman (photos 1-1), successfully brought up all twelve of their children to adulthood and marriage (though Elizabeth, one of a pair of twins was killed by lightning on her wedding day, closing the curtains in a thunder storm). This success was a reflection of their industry and care as well as the rising standards of the "Age of Reform". (Population in Britain doubled in the first part of the nineteenth century and their third child, also called James, born in 1854, and his wife Hannah had twenty-three children, of which fifteen lived to adulthood.)

Photographs 1-1 Brooks and Watson Side

Top left-: Great-Grandmother Martha Brooks (née Bonnick). The shoemaker's daughter with firm views on Home Rule for Ireland.
Top right-: Grandmother Lillie Watson (née Brooks) who strongly admired Disraeli.
Bottom left-: Mother at three years old, hair still auburn, taken to the photographic studio straight from playing in the street. Bottom right-: Grandfather Bert Watson, noted singer, coarse fisherman and darts player.

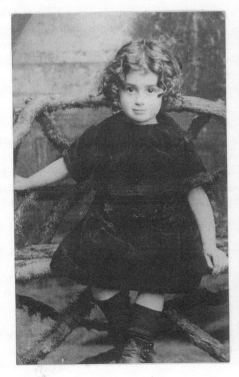

James 3rd, in the tradition of dissenting shoemakers who spent long hours bent over the last making shoes for better off people (who often failed to pay their bills), was a liberal and strong supporter of Gladstone. In this husband and wife were agreed, because despite being married in St. Mary's Church which probably means that Martha was originally an Anglican, Grandmother was christened in the Wesleyan Chapel and she remembered, when a girl, her mother standing at the corner of Kingsbury Square and Buckingham Street (see note 2, V and N, photo 40a) haranguing passers-by on the necessity of home rule for Ireland. This was also in the radical tradition of Aylesbury, going back through the turbulent John Wilkes, of Prebendal House, to John Hampden and opposition to the ship tax prior to the Civil War.

Grandmother also remembered, as a girl, being told by her father to go and tell Grinell's the tanner's behind the Red Lion in Temple Street, that the latest batch of leather was unfit for shoe making (in no uncertain terms). The Misses Grinell kept the shop unaltered until the 1920's (see note 2, V and N, photo 81b). I also have a tiny photo, cut from a larger one that shows my Great-grandfather, bearded and wearing a stovepipe hat, outside the old Primitive Methodist Chapel that once stood at the end of New Street; and there is a sweep standing a little way behind him with all his brushes.

Only four months after Grandmother was born, on the morning of March 24th, 1873, a large crowd of emigrants gathered at the Aylesbury railway station that served the London, Midland and Scottish branch line. They were accompanied by their relatives who had come to see them off on the train bound for London via Cheddington for the East India Docks where they would board the *SS Ramsey* for the passage to Brisbane, Australia. The emigrants included Grandmother's eldest brother, my Great-Uncle George Brooks (23) with his wife Clara and infant son Alfred, together with her sister, Great-Aunt Mary ("Polly"16) and brother, Great-Uncle Amos (17). No doubt Martha was there with grandmother as a babe in arms to see them off. She would never see any of them, except Mary, again. Perhaps the care of her new baby helped her to deal with the wrenching loss of her older children.

What factors led to such a large number of emigrants, over two hundred, from Buckinghamshire at this time, especially as most of them would never have seen the sea, to face up to the hazards of a three-month voyage round the Cape of Good Hope in the cramped confines of a clipper ship? Only two months previously the SS *Northfleet*, bound for Tasmania with emigrants, had gone down in the English Channel with the loss of three hundred lives.

The early years of the eighteen seventies when Grandmother was born were a time of deep agricultural depression, caused by a combination of poor harvests and increased competition from the Americas and Eastern Europe. The population boom made it harder for unskilled labourers to find work, especially in the southern counties away from the burgeoning industrial areas of the north. The successful efforts of Joseph Arch in Warwickshire and Edward Richardson, "The Aylesbury Agitator", in Bucks, to organize the agricultural labourers into unions and increase wage rates, actually worsened the problem because it led to loss of jobs and to the farmers (pressed to pay their rents) laying off more men in the winter (see note 5).

It so happened that the new state of Queensland in Australia (founded in 1859) was experiencing a labour shortage at this time, caused by a series of gold rushes and was actively searching for new immigrants, with free passages offered for accredited agricultural workers. Richardson turned from union work to assist the Queensland government agent in Bucks. He suggested that the best plan was to get a large group together and for him to accompany them to Australia, giving the whole party more confidence. Advertisements were put out for three hundred agricultural workers and meetings were held in the bigger villages. By this means over two hundred people were finally assembled for the voyage.

The Brooks family members comprised four of only seven emigrants actually from Aylesbury. This was because free passage was for accredited agricultural workers only. Amos was working in the Nestles Milk factory prior to leaving but it appears that both he and his brother George were attracted by the opportunities open in Queensland and the possibility of acquiring land there. This comes out in their letters home. I shall quote extensively from these below, not only because of their intrinsic interest and because the letter written by George about the voyage and arrival was described in the *The Aylesbury Agitator* as "by far the most comprehensive and colourful account" but because they reveal aspects of my grandmother's family background which have come down to influence me through my mother. My grandmother's influence was also direct during my early teens.

Voyage to Australia: One of the reasons the Brooks family elected to go out on the *SS Ramsey* was probably that it had been especially converted from a former bulk oil carrier into an emigrant ship fitted with 'Allen's Patent Berths' that gave each family separate accommodation. Unmarried women were also given separate quarters under the care of a matron (and intruders kept out with the threat of being clapped in irons).

It appears to have been a reasonably happy voyage with good order and harmony maintained over the ninety–one days at sea, the key-note being sounded at the outset, when, as The Daily News for 31st March, 1873 put it, "Before the ship was clear of the basin, groups of girls struck up a melody on the quarter deck, while further 'forrard' a young (agricultural) unionist produced a violin and drew lively music out of its strings." Although four infants under two died on the voyage there were four births and the ship remained free of infectious diseases. There was entertainment of readings, recitations and music every weeknight and three religious services on Sundays. Edward Richardson gave lectures on Natural history and Geography and also composed ballads about the voyage.

Inevitably, as George describes it, when the ship ran into rough weather, "the effects of the ship's motion could be seen on most of the strangers; they were almost all sick and groaned, and cried and retched in the most frightful manner". However, they all recovered, George himself not being sick. But off the Canaries they ran into very severe weather, "The sea was like very high mountains, and the water came over the sides of the ship in tons, drenching everyone that stood on the upper deck".

They were becalmed for a week on the Equator, where it was "Terribly hot; and I don't think we moved an inch during that time". The passengers were affected by "prickly heat" and this was where some of the infants and one of the crew died. However, they caught the SE Trades and made the Cape in three weeks. When they sailed into the Roaring Forties, "It was a sight to stand on the forecastle and watch the mountains of water come rolling after us. One night in particular it was terrible. A tremendous wave dashed right over amidships and carried part of the bulwark away, and the jib and topsails were also carried away; the water came down the hatches into the lower deck and swamped some in their beds. But still, we were assured that there was no danger, for it was not half as bad as it might have been" (see note 6).

When at last they reached Australia and sailed into Moreton Bay, It was, "Glorious to see dry ground once more, and when we came to anchor in the bay what cheers went up from the old *Ramsey"*. Sailing twenty miles up the river to Brisbane, along the route there were, "Trees growing down to the water's edge; now and then a small village, the cottages being built in a good style (although of wood) and placed in delightful situations; to see the orange groves and banana plantations, the cotton and sugar fields, the pineapples, and the sugar and water melons growing round the houses was beautiful".

From Brisbane, the Brooks family with about a hundred others were taken about fifty miles upstream, to Ipswich, and finally after a fortnight George got a job on a sheep and cattle station some four hundred miles into the outback (at £30 a year with rations). This is how he described the sheep station at Wallan:

"Mr. Ferrett's station is six hundred square miles in extent. There is a great number of men and women employed on it. There are about 4,000 cattle, tame and wild, and about 75,000 sheep, and the horses cannot be counted for most of them are wild..... As for the country, it is a beautiful place; anything will grow here almost. I know what Mr. Richardson will say about it, and he will be quite right.... I am a shepherd at last. You will laugh at this....just as if I knew a lot about shepherding; but all I have to do is to take the sheep out of a morning, and go into the forest with them (it is all forest here). Then I can sit down and read a book or watch the kangaroos, the opposums and the lizards. .... Then there are the birds; the eagles screaming in the air, the parrots and cockatoos chattering in the trees, the magpies singing all the while.... There are a good many snakes here, but I have not seen one yet. I have seen plenty of lizards, in shape just like a crocodile, and all colours, but they are the most harmless things in the world.... And by the side of the rivers and lagoons you see great tall cranes stalking about....

"It is lovely looking country; if you could look some nice summer day from Aylesbury towards Aston Hills, and fancy there was no enclosure in between, but that it was all covered with trees, you would have some idea of some parts of this country, but you miss something and a good something it is. You look upwards at the sky. It is hazy at the best of times in England but here the sky is glorious and transparent."

Georges's enthusiastic description of his situation on the sheep station was to be echoed by my brother, David when he went out to New South Wales sponsored by the "Big Brother

Movement" in 1951 at the age of seventeen. Although he didn't know about our Great Uncle's letter then, his description of his life on a sheep and cattle station in the Hunter Valley and of the birds in letters home, was very similar.

The reaction of Great Uncle Amos, also seventeen, was rather different. He left the Immigration Depot in Ipswich, without informing Richardson, to take a job in a tin mine at two pounds ten a week but it proved too much for him. He then tried two more jobs in the next two weeks and travelled 150 miles before eventually finding work on a sheep station. However, he didn't like the conditions and reacted strongly:

> "Believe me, the object of the Government in bringing people out here is to knock the wages down. They want to overstock the country with men, so they can have them at their own price.... I like Richardson very well, but I think he had better turn schoolmaster again, and keep to his union. If the poor men like him at home, they hate him here. If the farmers hate him at home, they like him here because they think he will bring out men for little wages for them.... I do not say that a man cannot do as well here as he can at home; he might do better and he might do worse. The country is as bad as England, and everybody here is ready to cut his neighbour's throat if he thought he could get a pound by it. .... I shall not stop in this country long."

In this outburst, nicely composed and well balanced, we hear, perhaps, his mother's voice, that would be raised later on the windy corner of Kingsbury Square and Buckingham Road on behalf of Irish home rule and certainly, the authentic voice of radical dissent as expressed by that archetypal pleb, the cobbler and mender of "souls", in *Coriolanus*. However, Amos did "stop" and two years later when he met Richardson in Brisbane he told him he wouldn't go back home even if his ticket was paid for! He went on to have six children and descendants scattered over Australia.

As he wrote in a letter home from Aramac (in 1891 after the death of his father):
> "I am doing very well. I always have more work than I can manage and I get the best price in Queensland for my work. I have taken up some land from the government, 1280 acres, and I think I shall do well out of it as it is some of the best land in Australia".

His nostalgia for the Sabbath pieties of his home town, is revealed in the following extract:
> "The church is open today for the first time in two years. Just think of that. Aramac and Muttaburra, sixty miles away, are to share a parson. We are to   have him a fortnight and they a fortnight. I often think of the old days at home …Sunday school and chapel three times a day. I am nearly always singing the good old hymns we used to sing."

He was also upset by his sister Polly, who had apparently, 'taken to drink':
> "He (George) and I are very angry at Polly's conduct. She was a trouble to us out here and we thought that when she went home she would reform but it does not appear to be the case. I am afraid she will die in the gutter."

Amos may have worried unnecessarily about his sister because she appears to have returned to Australia where she had three children in Roma, Queensland. However, it brings out very well the strict, teetotal, religious background and atmosphere of the Brooks family in Aylesbury into which Grandmother was born. This may now seem to us excessively narrow but there is no doubt that at a time of economic hardship, this culture of God-fearing self-help, hard work and chapel-based sociability, helped Martha and James bring up their twelve children, when there was little welfare or 'benefit' available. The letters of both George and Amos are strikingly well written, considering they both left school at twelve years old. This indicates a book-loving household and also a strong drive towards self-education, encouraged by the Sunday school, where of course the children came under the beneficent influence of the prose style of the King James Bible and the "good old hymns" of Charles and John Wesley.

Despite the lack of opportunity in Aylesbury at the time of the emigration of the older Brooks siblings, in the later nineteenth century the town was becoming a centre of the information industry with the establishment of printing works. Grandmother's brother Walter, her nearest brother and ninth in the family, worked as a compositor and reader in Hazell, Watson and Viney's (see note 2, photo 52a, V & A) and was responsible for taking a colour printing machine out to Australia; and at the time of the 1881 Census, her sister Maud (20) worked as a 'female compositor' and her sister Minnie (15) as a printer's reader. Co-incidentally, three of her cousins, children of Joel Brooks, were also working in printing at the time of the Census, Sarah (16) as a binder, Joseph (14) as a printer's clerk and Bethia (12) as a photograph printer, possibly also in Hazell's.

In her teens, Grandmother went to work at McCorquodale's, a printing firm in the small railway town of Wolverton, some twenty-five miles away in northeast Bucks. George McCorquodale had brought his firm down from Newton Le Willows in 1878 to take advantage of the demand for printing by the London and Northwestern Railway Company; it was also where the Royal trains were maintained. While she worked there she lived with her nearest elder sister, Laura (eleventh in the family and married to Richard Williams, who played cricket for Bucks).

I only became aware of Grandmother's involvement in printing on the occasion of my mother's seventieth birthday when I took her to see Cowper's house in Olney. Neither of us had been to that corner of northeast Bucks before. It was one of those days when the elements conspired to match a silvery-gray sky with the shining loops of the river Ouse, the gray-green willows and the gray stones of the buildings. The town center was almost empty and we were the only visitors to the house. After we had been round we sat on a bench in the long garden, where Cowper's hare had 'limped forth to feed' and I mentioned to Mother that it was her mother that had first introduced me to *John Gilpin* when I was a boy.

On the way home we passed McCorquodale's in Wolverton and Mother told me that Grandmother had worked there from the age of seventeen when she lived with her sister Laura at no. 4 The Square. Apparently, on one occasion she was asked to take round a group of visitors that included an Indian Prince and a titled lady who, complimenting her afterwards, surprised to find that she had left school at twelve, said what a pity it was that she hadn't been able to go on to a good education. Mother then said, "She always had her head stuck in a book," and also recalled how she had loved doing the Times crossword puzzle. Eventually, Grandmother left work to marry Albert Watson of Granville Place, Aylesbury, near St. Mary's Church, and went on to have ten children of her own (see photos 1-1 top right and bottom right).

THE WATSONS

From the labouring life to the drink trade: The earliest records of my mother's paternal ancestors are of Tom Watson (born 1798) listed in the 1841 Census as a farm labourer of Baverstock Lane, Cuddington and of his wife Mary (born 1797). Cuddington is a village on rising ground towards the Oxford road on the south bank of the river Thame (a tributary of the Thames) about four miles from Aylesbury.

Tom and Mary had six children, four boys and two girls. The fifth child, Richard (1834-?) was my mother's grandfather. A short, dark man, he became a tailor and married Elizabeth Gutteridge (baptized on the 11th of March, 1834), a tall fair girl (I believe from Dinton) a village south of the Oxford Road—where Edward Richardson, the 'Aylesbury Agitator', was briefly schoolmaster and was driven to his activities on behalf of the rural poor. Richard and Eliza had seven children, my grandfather, Albert (born on the 1st of June 1873, in Aylesbury) being the seventh and last. Two of his three older brothers died in childhood and he was much cherished by his two surviving sisters, Annie and Jenny.

As well as being a tailor, Richard was at different times a publican. At first, sometime in the 1860s, he was landlord of *The Bottle and Glass,* a beautiful thatched pub at Gibralter, on the Oxford Road between Dinton and Haddenham (photos 1-2). Later, apparently after the birth of Albert in Aylesbury, he was landlord of *The Whitehorse* at Longwick near Princes Risborough, in the shadow of the Chilterns; see photos 1-3 top, where he is standing with Eliza at the entrance and Grandfather, then a young lad, is looking over the garden gate.

As a youth, Grandfather (always known as Bert) was apprenticed to Giles and Thresher's the fine painters and decorators. This firm did a great deal of work in the big houses in the Vale, especially in the mansions of the Rothschilds, the biggest landowners in the district. Through this work with the firm he found he could earn extra money waiting at tables at banquets, being tipped as much as a golden guinea, and later, when it was found that he could entertain, he was asked to sing at places like Waddesdon, Halton and Mentmore.

The marriage of Bert Watson and Lillie Brooks must have come about through an attraction of opposites; of the rather shy, book loving, quiet daughter of strict, God-fearing, teetotal parents to the outgoing, highly sociable, son of a publican, full of fun, quips and jokes. According to Father who got on well with his father-in-law, Bert was the best darts player he ever played against, an indication of the time Grandfather had spent in pubs! However, Grandmother left home at quite an early age and was probably already independent of her parents in thought like her elder sister Polly who so shocked her brother Amos by 'taking to drink' out in Australia. She became conservative in contrast to her parents' liberalism (full of admiration for Disraeli) and in any case, to begin with Grandfather was in a 'respectable trade'.

The couple had ten children, all being raised to adulthood and marriage except for one, Jack (1910) who died in infancy. There were three other boys and six girls, beginning with Val, the eldest boy (1894) and ending with Kit (1916) see photos 1-4. Mother, Jess, was the eighth child, born on the night of the great gale of September 9th 1908, when Grandfather was caught out on his motorbike in the Chilterns and was delayed by falling trees and had difficulty in getting back in time. The earliest photo of Mother (photos 1-1, lower left) was taken near her third birthday when her elder sister Blanche (third child and mother of my cousin James Robins) took her to the photographers, straight from playing with friends and as her mother and father later complained 'not dressed for it'. It is none the worse for that, showing her in her button boots and velvet dress. Her curly hair was auburn then but soon turned black. Most of her brothers and sisters were dark like grandmother, Trix, (Beatrice) the seventh child, particularly so with slightly frizzy, curly black hair, that led, in those less sensitive days, to the nickname, 'Wog' (Gollywog). She was indeed, always known to us as Aunt Wog. In contrast, her brother Alec, the fourth child, and her sister Kit were fair. Kit was remarkably like my Mother except in this respect. Her colouring was one of the reasons my mother identified with the "Celtic" element in our British inheritance (see note 7).

Note added in proof: after the manuscript had gone to the printers I managed to obtain a copy of the certificate recording the marriage of my maternal Grandparents, which took place on the sixth of August, 1895, in the Register office, Aylesbury, witnessed by Grandfather's brother, William Phillip and a lady friend. As their first child, Val, was born in 1895, this means that they 'had to get married', underlining the point made above about Grandmother becoming independent of her strict parents at an early age. (Indeed, Val may have been born before they got married.)

Photographs 1-2 Ancestral Watson Places

Top-: Mother showing Ann the cottage on the green, Cuddington, where her Great-Uncle Jack, 'the village poet', once lived.

Bottom-: Jessica and Sian my two eldest daughters outside the Bottle and Glass in Gibralter, on the Oxford Road between Dinton and Haddenham, where their Great-great grandfather was landlord sometime in the 1860s.

Watson line:

(All born in Mid Bucks except 'Young Bert' and 5th generation)

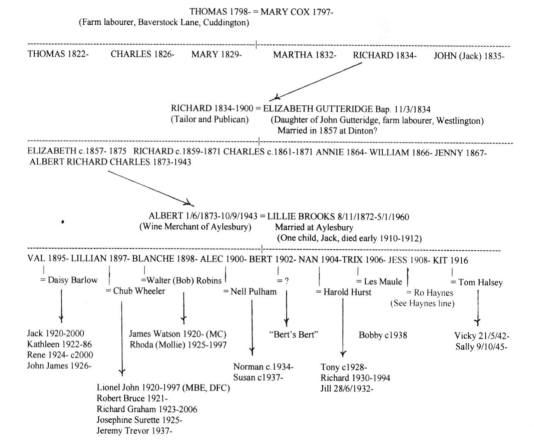

THOMAS 1798- = MARY COX 1797-
(Farm labourer, Baverstock Lane, Cuddington)

THOMAS 1822-   CHARLES 1826-   MARY 1829-   MARTHA 1832-   RICHARD 1834-   JOHN (Jack) 1835-

RICHARD 1834-1900 = ELIZABETH GUTTERIDGE Bap. 11/3/1834
(Tailor and Publican)   (Daughter of John Gutteridge, farm labourer, Westlington)
Married in 1857 at Dinton?

ELIZABETH c.1857- 1875   RICHARD c.1859-1871 CHARLES c.1861-1871 ANNIE 1864- WILLIAM 1866- JENNY 1867-
ALBERT RICHARD CHARLES 1873-1943

ALBERT 1/6/1873-10/9/1943 = LILLIE BROOKS 8/11/1872-5/1/1960
(Wine Merchant of Aylesbury)   Married at Aylesbury
(One child, Jack, died early 1910-1912)

VAL 1895- LILLIAN 1897- BLANCHE 1898- ALEC 1900- BERT 1902- NAN 1904- TRIX 1906- JESS 1908- KIT 1916

= Daisy Barlow   =Walter (Bob) Robins   = ?   = Les Maule   = Tom Halsey
= Chub Wheeler   = Nell Pulham   = Harold Hurst   = Ro Haynes
(See Haynes line)

Jack 1920-2000   James Watson 1920- (MC)   "Bert's Bert"   Bobby c1938   Vicky 21/5/42-
Kathleen 1922-86   Rhoda (Mollie) 1925-1997   Sally 9/10/45-
Rene 1924- c2000
John James 1926-   Norman c.1934-   Tony c1928-
Susan c1937-   Richard 1930-1994
Jill 28/6/1932-

Lionel John 1920-1997 (MBE, DFC)
Robert Bruce 1921-
Richard Graham 1923-2006
Josephine Surette 1925-
Jeremy Trevor 1937-

14

MOTHER'S EARLY MEMORIES

Childhood: When Grandfather and Grandmother got married they lived round the corner from Buckingham Arms Yard at 34, New Street. Mother was born there and at three years old went to St. John's Church School in Cambridge Street (although christened in the Wesleyan Chapel in Buckingham Road). As her first memories go back to this time I will let her speak for herself, with my own comments in brackets:

"My first memories are of when I was three and sent to St. John's Church School and learnt to count with an abacus. Then in the next class when I was learning to read, I remember feeling so pleased when I came to the letter J and it said Jess was a collie dog, because my name is Jess. There was this lovely picture of a collie dog at the top of the page.

"I was also taught to tell the time when I was about four. The teacher put the hands of a clock at five to four and asked if anyone knew what the time was. I put my hand up and said, 'It's five to four Miss Locke'. 'That's good, Jessie' she said. This annoyed me, because I hate being called Jessie, it's so soppy! Since growing up I've found that my feelings were justified. Watching 'Dad's Army' I heard the old Scot say to someone, 'You're a proper Jessie'. No wonder I always disliked it, because it means someone soppy in Scotland!

"One winter's day, while I was still a little girl in St. John's, there was a sudden snowstorm and my brother Alec, who was home early from the Grammar School, was sent to bring me home. He came with my grandmother's cape, which he wrapped round me. He then put me up on his shoulders to carry me home. This pleased me because he was my favourite brother.

"Just before my eighth birthday, I was given a certificate by the headmistress that says, 'For four excellences in Scripture, to Jessie, marked by Miss Hobley, 1916'; written on the back is a lovely text about Jesus. We used to have half an hour of Scripture every morning and the Parson used to come once a year to examine us.

"One Christmas my two closest sisters, Nance and Trix, and I were given a blackboard. When we played with it in the garden, mother and father used to laugh because every time they looked out of the window, if I was schoolteacher, it would be a Scripture lesson.

"There was one funny game we used to play with our playmates round the streets. The one who was 'in' would lean against a lamppost, shut their eyes and put one hand out behind them. One of the other children would then come up and touch the palm of their hand and say, 'Tiddly-widdly which way has that one gone'. The one 'in' would then, without looking, point at one of the children and tell them to go to a particular place and back. One evening, the boy 'in' pointed at me and told me to run down High Street, round Walton Road, up Walton Street, through the Square and down Cambridge Street to New Street again. I immediately set off running but it's quite a long way, it must be about a mile, and by the time I got back all the children had gone home!

"One of my father's associates was a Scotsman called Merrilees who came to Aylesbury to take over the Red Lion Hotel in Kingsbury Square. He had a little girl named Betty and he asked father if he had any little girls of her age she could play with. So I used to go and play with Betty in the old Red Lion. We used to go upstairs where it was all polished linoleum and play tig all round these glass cases full of stuffed fish. It's a wonder we didn't cause a lot of damage! I have wonderful memories of playing there. It had a gallery all round the yard outside.

"One of the boys about my age I played with was Carlo. He belonged to a lovely Italian family called Cordani. His father, Paul used to make ice-cream in the summer and fish and chips in the winter. I used to go with Carlo down to the railway station down Great Western Street to get the ice. We went down Friar's Passage, which is a cobbled alley, pushing a trolley to fetch the big barrel of ice that was used to make the ice cream, helping him on the way back to push the trolley up what to us seemed a very steep slope.

"On the way to the station we passed Seaton's Stables. I have always loved horses and one of my friends when I was about eight was Alf Haynes. His father helped Dick Seaton break in horses and sometimes they would bring little ponies down New Street and let me ride on one (see note 8).

"I was generally healthy when I was young apart from the usual childhood diseases. I did have a bad attack of quinsy when I was a girl and poor mother had to blow flowers of sulphur off a spoon into the back of my throat until I was better.

"Another time when I became seriously ill was during a visit by our cousin Grace Gulliver who had come to see my older sister Blanche. I was playing in the garden and mother thought I was being rude by constantly coming up to the open window and looking in; but I suddenly disappeared and when she looked out I had fainted. The doctor was sent for and it was found that I had scarlet fever. I was taken in a horse drawn vehicle to the Isolation Hospital, what is now the famous Stoke Mandeville Hospital. In those days it was a single brick building and a wooden hut for the diptheria patients. There was obviously quite an epidemic in Aylesbury because there were lots and lots of boys and girls that I knew in school there. As we got better we had great fun having pillow fights and other games."

Mother's recollections of her father: By the time Mother was born her father had already had a number of different jobs:

"As a young man my father was apprenticed to Giles and Thresher, an Aylesbury firm where he learned the trade of painting and decorating. When my mother was expecting her fifth baby, father took a job with a well-off family called Johnson on an estate. One morning the manager ordered him to go with some other men to help them hang a gate. My father said, 'I didn't come here to hang any bloody gates', and immediately left the job. By this time my poor mother had a babe in arms, my brother Bert ('Young Bert') who was given the second name Tolmus after the name of the place they were living in then, in Hertfordshire. All the rest of us were born in Aylesbury.

"When they came back to Aylesbury, father went to work as a travelling salesman for his brother-in–law, Sam Gulliver, the wine merchant, who had a big warehouse between Kingsbury Square and Buckingham Street. Uncle Sam married my father's older sister, Nancy, who we always called Aunt Annie; we were always impressed with how beautifully she dressed. Uncle Sam was in partnership with a gentleman in South Africa, in the sherry trade. For a while they were very comfortably off, living at Downe Hall in Essex, which had once been the home of Matthew Prior, (see note 9). They also had a Town flat in Argyll Street. Unfortunately, Uncle Sam and his partner got into difficulties and went bankrupt. However, Uncle Sam soon built up the business again; (it was said that he made a million and lost it twice).

"Another relation I remember on my father's side was Uncle Jack (a Great- Uncle). One day when I was a little girl, he walked in from Cuddington to see us. I remember how his white hair curled round his cap. He was known in Cuddington as the 'Village Poet' and he was well known for walking round the village followed by his string of Aylesbury ducks! (See photos 1-2 top.)

"By the time I was born at 34, New Street, father was a traveller for another two firms, the Taunton Cider Company and the Imperial Wine Service in Mark Lane in the City, making calls over a wide area on his motorbike. Sometimes he would come home on Saturdays having drunk rather a lot with his associates and friends and when he wrote up his weekly report he would show his employers his feelings with one or two choice phrases. He would always ask me to take the letter to the Post Office because my older sister, Trix, was afraid of the dark and used to frighten herself reading books like 'Dracula'; it was always me that had to get rid of spiders and daddy-long-legs! Before I went, mother would whisper, 'Don't you dare post it but bring it back to me'. I would run off and like the wind through Upper Hundreds where on Saturday nights there was often shouting and swearing, and sometimes fights, going all the way to the Post Office and then running back to quietly give my mother the letter. It never occurred to me to simply wait outside our house for a while before going back in. I suppose if I'd told my father that I'd been to the Post Office when I hadn't it would have been on my conscience.

"One Saturday, father had been up to London and came back after having too much to drink. On the way from the station he somehow got involved in a fight and was knocked down in the mud (with a broken jaw). He was so disgusted with himself that he gave up drinking there and then. Mother was very pleased, she had always been uneasy about father's job, but as he said, 'While I'm in the Drink Trade we won't starve'.

17

"Father was also a volunteer fireman. In those days, before the fire brigade was run by the Council, they were paid a shilling a fire. My mother told me that my youngest brother, Bert, before electric bells were installed in the firemen's houses, used to have to run all round the town and blow a little trumpet under each fireman's window, for this he was paid tuppence. When the bells were installed, my mother told me, she used to stuff an old pair of bloomers round the clappers so the noise wouldn't wake us children up. Father sometimes forgot to look to see if the bell was clear, and he said one night, 'Good God woman, you'll get me sacked'. However, he afterwards did become Captain of the fire brigade, after Dick Seaton. When dad retired, Charlie Ivatts took over. There was almost a strike, because the men thought he was too inexperienced, and wanted Bob Robins, my brother-in-law, to be Captain instead. Some men did resign over it (see photos 1-3).

"Father as well as being secretary of the Allotment Society was also secretary and later chairman of the Angling Association. He really loved fishing and he often used to fish out at Hartwell Pits. I remember feeling very proud on my way to school when Macfisheries had a pike that my father had caught, exhibited on a slab of ice in the shop, with a notice to say, 'Caught by Bert Watson, Weight 22 lbs'."

Photographs 1-3 Watson Activities

Top-: Richard Watson and Eliza (née Gutteridge) at the entrance to the Whitehorse, Longwick, late 1870s, Albert Richard (Bert) then a boy looking over the side gate.

Bottom-: Aylesbury Volunteer Fire Brigade receiving a presentation on the Old Recreation Ground about 1925/26. Front row from left are: Councillor Atkins, Dick Seaton, Landlord of the Crown Hotel, then Captain and who provided the horses from his stables, with Grandfather (then Lieutenant) on the right. Cousin James' father, Bob Robins, is fourth right in the back row with his friend Ted Kent, third right, who kept a sweet shop in Cambridge Street as well as running a painting and decorating business. The chap with an early example of a 'Hitler' type moustache may have been Small, while others included Southam and Norris. Some of the men are wearing their campaign medals earned by service in the Bucks Hussars, but James' father would not wear his, or attend reunions either and tried to persuade him not to join his old regiment at the outbreak of World War 2, apparently because of his experiences in World War 1.

James' early memories include attending the Sunday morning parade to watch his father, when they practiced running out the hoses and connecting them to the hydrants in Bourbon Street, as well as the ritual of polishing the brass helmets. The horses were stabled where later the Bucks Motor Co. was established, in Great Western Street, which ran on through to Friarage Passage and the Comrades Club that had two rusty, German field-guns in its forecourt.

The Great War: Mother was six years old when the Great War broke out, and by that time her parents had moved further down the street:

"Although I was born in 34, New Street, I spent most of my early life at 89, New Street (a three-storey house on the right side going down towards Buckingham Road). We were there during the Great War, and I lived there until I got married.

"After the war had broken out in 1914, my mother used to send me to a little Newsagents in Cambridge Street, to get a paper and I used to be horrified, looking at the pictures while carrying it home, of our poor soldiers in France: in the mud in the trenches, and on the barbed-wire, really dreadful. My eldest brother Val was in the landings at Gallipoli in the Dardenelles, his best friend was killed beside him, and my little sister, Kit who was born on January the 1st 1916, was named Kitty Suvla after the landing in Suvla Bay.

"My eldest sister, Lil (Chubbie) went out to France in the WAACS (Women's Auxiliary Army) and worked in Army Records in Rouen. She also acted and sang in shows that were put on to entertain the troops. Her fiancé, Cyril ('Chub') Wheeler, was also in the army out in France. Many people knew him, because he went to the old Grammar School in Aylesbury and afterwards worked in Hazell's. He also played for the Aylesbury Football Club. In the war he was batman to Lionel Crouch, a well-known local figure. In a book about Lionel Crouch, my brother-in-law is mentioned in a letter that his commanding officer sent home from France, 'Wheeler has just bought in a bunch of wild flowers, they are smashing'. Sadly, there is also a letter quoted which Chub wrote to Lionel Crouch's parents after his CO was killed by a sniper and he had carried his body back to the lines.

"Chub became a prisoner of war after being left for dead in a shell hole. He was picked up by a German patrol and a surgeon dug a bullet or piece of shrapnel out of his skull and saved his life. Thinking the food would be better, Chub told his captors that he had been a farm worker and so he was sent to work on a farm for the duration of the war.

Photographs 1-4 The Watson Family before and after the Great War

Top photo-: In the garden of 89, New Street, just before the outbreak of World War 1. From the right in the front row are, 'Young Bert', Grandfather 'Old Bert', Trix = 'Wog', Nan, Mother = Jess, Grandmother, Alec; in the back row, Lillian = 'Chubbie', Val, Blanche.

Bottom photo-: In the garden after the War, about 1919/1920. Front row right to left, Trix, Chubbie, Grandfather with Kitty Suvla between his knees (born in 1916 and named after the landing in Suvla Bay in the Dardenelles, in which Val was involved), Grandmother, Alec, Jess; back row, Young Bert, Nan, Blanche, Val.

"We had a lot of air raids and Mum and Dad used to take us children to an aunt (Aunt Annie and Uncle Sam Gulliver) who lived quite close at the top of Buckingham Road (no 41) as she had a basement where it was considered we would be safer. We were on our way there one night after the alarm had gone off, when my father suddenly remembered his bed-ridden mother had been left behind in the top bedroom, which he had forgotten; so poor Dad had to go back and sit with Grannie while we went on down to Auntie's! Fortunately, nothing happened that night, but one evening my father called us upstairs to look out of the top floor window to see the glow in the sky when the zeppelin was brought down at Cuffley, in Hertfordshire," (this was the night of September 2nd 1916, just before her 8th birthday, see note 10).

"When the war was over I remember getting home from school one day and thinking, 'Mother's got a fire alight. That's funny mother lighting a fire.'" She said to me, 'Aren't you going to kiss your brother?' and there was this strange man, to me, a little girl of ten, because it was my eldest brother Val. We hadn't seen him during the whole four years of the war. He was one of those young men who stood up all night with their straw boaters on the back of their heads that August, waiting to volunteer to join up; and now there he was reading the newspaper by the fire. I kissed him, still unable to take in that he was my brother!

"My eldest sister's fiancé, Chub, returned from Germany and went back to his old job at Hazell's printing works in Aylesbury. After they got married they lived in Bierton. When their first baby was born (christened Lionel in memory of Lionel Crouch) I ran all the way from Aylesbury to see the baby because I had become an aunt! My father and mother became worried when I didn't return before dark but assumed that my sister had kept me there for the night. In those days it was all fields and allotments from Bierton almost to the workhouse on one side and the prison on the other. I ran home with my heart throbbing because I was running so fast and it was so dark; I was eleven years old at the time. A little while after this the government brought in a scheme to settle ex-servicemen on small-holdings. As my brother-in-law was keen on farming and was great friends with the Bells who were farmers in Bierton (as well as having wartime experience in Germany) he was able to take advantage of this and took a farm at Water Stratford near Buckingham. It was a lovely old place called Manor Farm because it had been a Manor House and it had a priest hole. We greatly enjoyed going there as children for holidays. Later on they moved to a bigger farm, called Blackpit, in Stowe Ridings on the Robart's estate."

Schooldays: When Mother had been at St. John's Church school about five years, her mother decided to send her to the Council School:

"When I was about eight years old, Mother decided to send me to the Queens Park Council School because she thought the education there was probably better. I was put to sit next to a lovely girl called Ena Wakefield. We're now both in our seventies and have been friends ever since.

"During the war the school was turned into a hospital for the poor soldiers that had been wounded. Standards 1 and 2 went to the old Church House in St. Mary's Square, while the other forms went to the old Co-op. As I started in Standard 2, St. Mary's Square was not far to walk. We went back to the school at Queens Park (over the canal) at the end of the war when I was in Standard 5. Our form mistress was a Miss Dyson. In all my schooldays I had never been punished until I was in Standard 5. I realize now, growing older that the poor woman was probably sick. While I was in this class I was sent to the headmistress thirteen times. We were given two strokes of the cane on both hands. When Miss Lodge used to ask, 'Why have you been sent to me?' I didn't know. You only had to turn your head to be sent. Another old pupil has since told me that the same thing happened to her in that class. She never had the cane after she left it and neither did I. Funnily enough, it wasn't long before Miss Dyson left. I think Miss Lodge became suspicious with all these children being sent to her and none of them knowing why!

"All this was rather sad, considering that later on, whenever Miss Lodge wanted someone to take a message to the Education Office she usually asked me to take it. When I was in the Infant School at St. John's, where there were a lot of children from Upper Hundreds, a poorer quarter of the town, they used to call me 'Teachers Pet', because I was always chosen to take the registers round and do any jobs the teacher wanted done. Oh dear!

"It was at about this time when I was eleven that I got a certificate for playing the piano. Mother had bought me a good German piano from two elderly ladies she knew. I then had lessons given by a lady called Miss Nunn. I had to go up to London to appear at the London College of Music and managed to get a first class certificate, signed by J. Bath, Doctor of Music, in July 1920.

"When I was about thirteen and in Standard 7, we older girls had to go out across the playground on Monday mornings to a separate building to have lessons in cookery, washing and ironing, housewifery, and all to do with running the household. We did these subjects with Miss White through the three terms and at the end of the year she judged us on our work. She brought a silk blouse of her own, which I washed and ironed, and she said that it had never looked so good since the day she had bought it. However, although she considered that I was top of the class in cookery, washing and ironing and housewifery, she was not going to give me the prize because I talked too much. Too much gift of the gab, another disappointment!

"Each class had to put on a play at Christmas time and when I was in Standard 7, I was chosen together with my friends Ena and Mabel to play three robbers that were trying to steal a bird in a golden cage. My father, who was a very good actor, warned me, 'You are supposed to be a very rough, uncouth sort of fellah, and you wouldn't use a handkerchief, remember, you'd wipe your nose on your sleeve'. I had lots of boyfriends at the time and one lent me his cap, one his gaiters and one his stiff collar, so we could dress like men. I remember stomping across the stage and the whole school roaring with laughter when I wiped my nose on my sleeve. When we had finished our play, there was time left over so Miss Lodge asked the audience which one they would like to see again, and with one voice the whole school shouted, 'The Robbers'!

"I cried myself to sleep, the day I had to leave school because I had come to love it. My friend Ena and I were stock takers and looked after the library books. I used to play the piano for the children to march in, usually Colonel Bogy. My friend Elsie Prior also did this because she was very good on the piano. We used to share the piano playing for the other classes' singing and dancing lessons, which was very nice.

Family Life: As mentioned earlier, Grandfather was a noted singer in his youth and as Mother progressed with the piano she learned to accompany him in his songs:

"As well as acting, my father used to sing in public and play the spoons. He could also tap dance, doing a double act with my brother Alec. On one occasion I had to practise the piano accompaniment to a song he was going to sing at a concert up in London. It was rather difficult to play as it was in four sharps; and was called 'The Parson and the Man'. However, another gentleman from Hazell, Watson and Viney's was also appearing in this concert and it was eventually decided that his accompanist would play for father too. I was most upset because mother had promised me a new dress, but perhaps it was for the best as I should have been very, very nervous. My brother Alec was a very good pianist and could play any tune he heard by ear (a talent shared by Kit). He was also a very funny boy and constantly made the rest of the family laugh, as you can guess if you have ever watched and heard 'Old Mother Riley', because later Alec wrote jokes for him and for Billy Bennet. He also composed a lovely song for Ella Shields, the coloured singer. So in our house, we were either pushing each other off the piano stool, or capping each other's jokes. Alec was also a keen angler like my father and later he wrote humorous stories under the nom-de-plume 'Grey Ling' in the 'Midland Angler'. He invented an imaginary stooge called Phil and wrote the stories from the point of view that it was the fish that caught the man!"

"We used to have wonderful Christmases and one I remember especially was when Alec became engaged to a girl called Nell from London and brought her to spend it with us. Like most people in those days we used to play charades. Alec put our sister Nance in a chair and proceeded to act out a word to do with dentistry by putting a nut in her mouth and then extracting the supposed tooth with the nutcrackers. I've forgotten the word now but not how we laughed!

"My father had taken the trouble to decorate all the rooms with holly and balloons. So we decided to play with the balloons. The front window was one goal and the piano the other. Perched up on high chairs or down on stools we tried to score goals. Of course, the balloons kept bursting on the holly until my father threw it out into the hall but there were not many balloons left by then. On Boxing Day, Nance and I went to see if there was a shop that was still open, selling any, without success.

Afterwards, Nell who was an only child said she had never known a Christmas like it in her life. She laughed so much the tears ran down her face." (See note 11).

The flavour of these times is well brought out by one of Alec's songs, preserved by my cousin Sally, *Songs of the Family*:

> I'll sing me songs of Mother
> I'll sing me songs of Dad
> Of Sister and of Brother
> I'm in a mood that's glad.
>
> Who used to stroke my curly head
> Why Mother, my Mother
> Bath me on Fridays and send me to bed
> Why Mother, my Mother
> Chase me around with long thin canes
> Told me I'd got all the brains
> Woke me up to catch my trains
> Why Mother, my Mother.
>
> Who used to give me pots to clean
> Why Father, my Father
> When I came in, say 'Where a ye been'
> Why Father, my Father
> Owe me pennies for months and months
> Pay me at last but only once
> Clump my head and call me bonce
> Why Father, my Father.
>
> Who'd give me a penny and then throw fits
> Why Val, old Val
> For carting sand from 'Artle Pits
> Why Val, old Val
> And make me run to Wheelers and back
> For a bushel of corn and peas in a sack
> And who used to get me to scratch his back
> Why Val, old Val.
>
> Who brings me Quarrendon memories
> Why Lil, my Lil
> Of intensive search for blackberries
> Why Lil, my Lil
> Who pulled my hair and made me mad
> I called her something pretty bad
> Who said, 'ah! ah! Now I'll tell Dad'
> Why Lil, my Lil. (She never did—bless her.)

25

Who brought to me my loving wife
Why Blanche, old Blanche
To help me through a weary life
Why Blanche, old Blanche
Who reads these words, just like me
The accent where it ought to be
Who gave me potted meat for tea
Why Blanche, old Blanche.

Who made me laugh, and gave me a rap
Why Bert, our Bert
When sniffing hard and lifting my cap
Why Bert, our Bert
Who used to love his bread and cheese
And used to hate the morning breeze
Who raised the roof with many a sneeze
Why Bert, our Bert.

Who swigged the whisky on the stairs
Why Nan, our Nan
Who pinched my riding pants, one 'pairs'
Why Nan, our Nan
Who swore I was her only King
Loved me more than anything
(Now hears the Harold Angel sing)
Why Nan, our Nan.

Who keeps the old D.D. from ruin (Dominion Dairy)
Why Wog, our Wog
The only one who knows what's she's doin
Why Wog, our Wog
Who greets me always, never a frown
One eye black and one eye brown
Wins the sweeps and 'Pride of the Town'
Why Wog, our Wog.

Who also swears to love me true
Why Jess, our Jess
And finds me locks and keyholes to do
Why Jess, our Jess
Gets me on to push the pram
Who smiles (I'm lost) I say 'yes Mam'
And for the world don't care a (bit)
Why Jess, our Jess.

Who's heard of the Pub, 'The Crooked Billet'
Why Kit, our Kit
And also heard of Cyril 'Spillet'
Why Kit, our Kit
Made me laugh in Dad's old coats
Sits besides the piano and gloats
When I play those queer last notes
Why Kit, our Kit.

Who writes and thinks of everyone
Why Alec, our Alec
Who's got a pen and uses one
Why Alec, our Alec
Who'll come and pass the time away
As soon as he gets a holiday
And be as welcome as the snow in May
Why Alec, our Alec.

I've sung the songs of Mother
I've sung the songs of Dad
Of Sister and of Brother
And in my heart I'm glad.

Going out to work: In those days, the school leaving age was fourteen, but as Mother's birthday was in September, and she reached that age after the new school year had started, she had to stay in school a while longer:

"As my fourteenth birthday was in September (1922) I had to stay in school until Christmas. Then, reluctantly, I had to leave. At first I stayed and helped my mother until the daughter of a neighbour, who admired the way I did the housework, asked mother if I could go back with her to their home in Streatham, in London. She had just had a miscarriage and needed help with a little girl called Beccy. So I went up to London with them but I was terribly homesick and I badly missed all my friends in our local Sunday School. I also had recurrent nightmares. I dreamt that a man with a knife broke in through the pantry window to attack us! I became so upset that I wrote to mother and got her to write to Mrs Miles and say she needed me back at home.

"Our Sunday School teacher was a sweet girl called Winnie Hunt, the daughter of Mr. Hunt, (head of the printing firm Hunt Barnard's). There was something on almost every night of the week for us youngsters (there were about three hundred pupils altogether). As well as billiards the games included table tennis, which I was quite good at; only the two Winifreds could beat me at it (Winnie Hunt and another friend called Winifred) or at tennis, which we used to play at the 'Nook', a garden that belonged to the Hunt family (situated between Buckingham Road and Fleet Street).

"So we really had a wonderful time as young people, especially at the Sunday School concerts. There were so many of us that those of us over fourteen had our own school in a smaller room called the Institute. I remember being very pleased to get a boy called Eric Herman, who was rather fond of me, to sing a duet at one of the concerts. His father had a clothing shop in the High Street and was interned during the war, being of German origin, and his mother had to struggle to bring up five children.

"I was very pleased to get back home and I went to work down the Dominion Dairy. There were lots of former school friends there and we worked in the office together and had a lot of fun. We had to write labels to put on the butter boxes; a lot of it came in tubs from Russia (and New Zealand). A man with a horse and trap used to go round Aylesbury selling five of these lovely boxes for 1/3d (6p) when they were empty. One of my jobs at home was to chop up these boxes for firewood. Another job that I had to do at home, which I liked, was cleaning and polishing the shoes for everyone!

"I stayed in the Dominion Dairy for a year or two then I left there to work in Narbeth's a drapery shop in the High Street. I worked upstairs in the under-ware department run by a nice lady called Miss Hall who was related to the people who had the Bakery and Confectioner's in Great Western Street. She told me that I was no good as a saleswoman but wonderful in the way I could brush her hair and cure her headaches! You see, I couldn't push things onto people because I don't like people doing it to me, it puts me off!

"After a time another girl friend of mine, called Frieda Waters, asked me if I would like to work in one of her father's shops. He was a town councillor and owned three shops in the High Street. I was glad to do this because I was very happy in the little shop he had there, next to the Old Crown Yard, where you could hear the horses and traps coming in. It was here that one day, an old farmer, called (I think) Eldridge, from out Western Turville way, who used to come into this little shop on the corner of the Yard, said to me,' Oh my lass, your hair is like a raven's wing'. That was a lovely compliment wasn't it?

"It was while I was working at the Dominion Dairy, when I was fourteen or fifteen that I met a Grimsby family called Haynes that had moved down to Aylesbury. Mr. Haynes, who had been a trawler skipper, took the wine shop at the top of Walton Street and also bought the butcher's shop next door, where Woolworth's is now. I met one of the daughters, Irene, who came to my Sunday School and on Boxing Day (? 1923) I invited her to tea. In the evening there was a knock on the door and it was her brother Roland who had come to escort Irene home."

These (spontaneous, unrehearsed) reminiscences of my mother are largely based on recordings I made at the time of her seventy-fourth birthday. They are given almost verbatim but with some re-arrangement and addition of events described to me at other times. They illustrate the continuing clarity of her mind at that age and her ability to recall childhood scenes. They show that she was a popular girl with a wide circle of friends, good in school and at games and in demand at parties with her skill on the piano. What is not so evident is a certain stubborn, willful diffidence. There were times when she played truant from school and sat in a tree in Dunsham Lane, 'to be on my own' and she sometimes day-dreamed of running away to join the gypsies. When the time came to sit 'The Scholarship' examination for the Grammar School she and her friend Ena decided they wouldn't try so they could stay together with their other friends. Later, when she had singing lessons, her tutor, a German lady, impressed with her voice (a silvery soprano) arranged an audition for her in High Wycombe but she backed out at the last moment. She had an inveterate reluctance to rise in social station despite being able to converse easily and amicably at any level. As they said in those days 'she knew her place' but as with her father, woe-betide anyone who tried to take advantage of it.

SOURCES/NOTES—CHAPTER 1

I am greatly indebted to my cousin James Robins MC for his labours in the archives that have brought out the details of the family history of the Brooks and Watson lines, and also for copies of some of the Amos Brooks letters.

1) Pevsner, N. 1960. *Buckinghamshire,* in: *The Buildings of England,* Penguin.

2) Viney, E. and Nightingale, P. 1976. *Old Aylesbury,* White Crescent Press Ltd., London. (An excellent photographic record with numbered photos cited in text).

3) Llewellyn, R. 1997. *Made to Last,* The Independent, (27/9/97).

4) Meade, W.R. 1996. *Aylesbury—a personal memoir from the 1920's,* Bucks Print, Aylesbury (contains maps and fine sketches of many of the streets mentioned).

5) Millburn, J.R. and Jarrot, K. 1988. *The Aylesbury Agitator,* Central Printing Section, Bucks County Council, County hall, Aylesbury (includes extensive quotes from George Brooks' letters home, originally printed in the Bucks Advertiser).

6) This reminds me of my own voyage as an emigrant out to Canada some three quarters of a century later on the Cunard liner *Ascania*. I can guess at George's feelings because we ran into a severe, force 11 gale, south of Iceland and for two days simply held our position, after 'taking it green'. There is nothing like the awed exhilaration of a great gale at sea, especially when you have left the past behind and the future is unknown but full of promise; though I hasten to add I am not quite such a storm petrel as my brother David, who is still disappointed that he hasn't experienced a 'real storm' in the Bay of Biscay!

7) Although 'Celtic' and 'Anglo-Saxon' are both inaccurate and anachronistic terms, if applied outside the context of early mediaeval Britain, it's true that a Romano-British enclave held out in the Chilterns until the late sixth century. It was only after the battle of

Biedcanford (Bedford) in 571 that the Germanic tribes moving down the Ouse valley linked up with their settlements in the upper Thames valley (K. Rutherford Davis, 1982. *Britons and Saxons—the Chiltern Region 400-700.* Phillimore and Co. Ltd). No doubt the amalgamation of these groups with the remaining Romano-British, to produce the Early English, led to the diversity of physical types in the Vale.

8) The family of Alf Haynes was not related but it is of interest that my cousin, James, lived next door to them as a child in No. 3 Willow Road (before moving to No. 7 where my brother David was born). Alf was the eldest of four sons and there were two daughters. The father was a butcher who kept pigs and made sausages in the cellar of an adjacent tumbledown cottage. These were hawked round villages in a Model T Ford van and James remembers going out with him in the van to Ellesborough (near Chequers). He also supplied a hearse for funerals drawn by two black horses bedecked with plumes of black feathers.

9) Mother had a battered but treasured copy of Mathew Prior's poems. Another, coincidental connection with Downe House is that David, the first husband of James' wife Audrey, was 25th in line of succession to Viscount Downe.

10) This was the biggest air-raid of the war, with sixteen zeppelins in the attack. The one brought down near Cuffley was the first to be shot down by machinegun fire and the airman, Lt. W. Leefe-Robinson of No. 39 Squadron, was awarded the VC for it. He set fire to it in the air and as it was wooden it burned for over two hours on the ground. This information is given in Anne Williamson's book, *The Patriot's Progress* (in a discussion of an incident in Henry Williamson's novel, *The Golden Virgin,* in which 'Lily Cornford' is killed in a zeppelin attack); quoted from Capt. Joseph Morris, *The German Air Raids on Great Britain 1914-18.* Sampson Low, London.

11) These parties which Mother remembered so clearly, continued well into the time when Kit, the youngest daughter, was in her teens. James remembers the smell of Christmas cigars, brandy and magnums of champagne, singing round the piano and games of postman's knock. Nell (Pulham) was introduced to Alec by his sister Blanche, who worked with Nell at the same drapery shop in Islington.

CHAPTER 2

SEAMARKS

"The most dangerous job in Britain is trawler fishing.... Fishermen are at least fifty times more likely to have a fatal accident than the average worker." (See note 1.)

"These men are tough and wiry and of a very high standard of intelligence in fishing matters.... Men who are active there today (Grimsby) carry names that can be traced back generations to those rugged and dauntless pioneers who may have been deficient in the three R's but who, in the hard school of experience, mastered the way of ships, sailed through calm and troubled waters and gained a thorough knowledge of the habits of fish.... They were intolerant of physical weakness and were not only hard taskmasters to others but to themselves.... A desire for comfort was considered a weakness and discomfort something to take a pride in." (See note 2.)

THE HAYNES AND COOPER LINES

Early days of fishing from Grimsby:

"Grim was a right fine fisherman and worked much upon the sea taking there from many a good fish with net and hook. He caught great cod and porpoise, herring, mackerel and plaice.... And he made great baskets, one for himself, and for his sons, three more, therein to carry and sell up the country wholesale."

Lay of Havelock the Dane

Whatever may be the true history of Grim and his son, Prince Havelock, and their exploits as fishermen, by mediaeval times the industry was well established in Grimsby. Grimsby men not only worked the local fishing grounds but also ranged north to Iceland, landing there to salt cod on shore before returning to Grimsby where it was offered for sale to buyers from as far away as London. The port also acted as a distribution center for Icelanders, who likewise landed salted cod, salmon fishers from Scotland and herring fishers from the Low Countries; and there are records of smoke houses going back to the reign of Richard II. (See note 3.)

This early prosperity faded with the silting up of Grimsby Haven in the seventeenth century and by the eighteenth century, the port that had provided Edward III with eleven ships for the siege of Calais in 1346 was derelict. In an attempt at revival the Grimsby Haven Company was set up in 1796 and a great effort was made to dredge out a new dock, entirely by hand, which opened in 1800. However, the new dock, although then the biggest excavated dock in the country, did not attract much trade, despite a bounty being offered on every cargo of fish. However, two whalers, the *Binny* (a prize taken from the Spanish fleet during the Napoleonic Wars) and the *Earl Faucenberg,* sailed out of Grimsby for the Davis Straits, until 1821, when this episode of Greenland whaling came to an end.

The creation of the modern docks: The fortunes of the port were turned round by the far-sighted decision of the directors of the Manchester, Sheffield and Lincoln Railway, to petition parliament for permission to extend their lines to Grimsby, realizing that Grimsby would again become an attractive distribution center if it were provided with a fast link to the industrial towns of the north as well as London.

Royal Assent was given to the Grimsby Docks Bill in 1845, the first train running in 1848. The old Grimsby Haven Company was subsumed within the new Great Grimsby Royal Dock Company and a new 'Royal Dock' excavated with the foundation stone being laid by Prince Albert in 1849. With six hundred navvies at work it was completed in two years; with an Italianate dock tower (312 ft high) to control the hydraulic mechanism for the lock gates, which dominates the country around and has provided the first welcome sign of home for generations of fishermen. One of the prime movers behind these developments was Lord Yarborough, the new railway line running over his land, and other backers included families such as the Claytons (connected with the Tennysons).

The railway companies also set up the Deep Sea Fishing Company. This Company had its own shipyard, and in 1854, when the docks were officially opened by Queen Victoria, was operating nine fishing smacks, including four trawlers and five cod liners (one of which was steam powered). The slight predominance of cod-liners over trawlers shows that fishing with baited hooks was still the preferred method. There were two 'whelkers' in the port at this time, catching whelks in baskets (like lobsters) for bait.

An aggressive policy was pursued by the Manchester, Sheffield and Lincoln Railway Company, to attract fishermen to operate their vessels from Grimsby, rather than just to deliver their catches there. Their representatives visited Hull and different ports in the south, to as far away as Brixham in Devon, offering special inducements, including remission of dock dues and free transport on the railway for three years and also free tickets on the train for salesmen.

The first to accept the offer (in 1855) was John Howard together with the Mudds of Manningtree in Essex, who were already landing fish in Grimsby. Increasing numbers of fishing boats were soon seen as a 'nuisance' to other vessels in the Royal Dock, which led to the completion of the first fish dock of six acres in 1856; and within a year twenty two vessels were working out of it, including four more sailing trawlers and eight more cod-liners. This rapid growth led to the creation of the second fish dock of twelve acres in 1860 and there were one hundred and twelve vessels by 1863. The new arrivals included 'well-smacks' from the Thames, cod-liners with a special tank amidships, aerated with sea water via holes bored through the bulkhead, in which the fish could be kept alive until the vessel returned to port and then transferred to a floating chest in the dock (see note 4). Father's paternal and maternal ancestors were amongst those who transferred from Greenwich.

Haynes line:

JOSEPH GEORGE 1831- = MARY ANN QUILLINGHAM 1831- (of Lambeth)
(Fisherman of East Greenwich)   Married c.1851

CHARLES 1852-1932 ? THOMAS 1857- ? ? ? HENRY 1865- CATHERINE 1868- ELIZABETH 1870-
FREDERICK 1873- SARAH 1876-

CHARLES = FANNY CLACKSTON (of Scarborough)
b. 24/9/1852, E. Greenwich d. 6/7/1932, Lincoln   b.16/12/1852 d. 14/4/1929 Grimsby
(Fisherman/Skipper, Grimsby)   (Daughter of John Clackston, a fisherman, and Betsy Toby)
Married in Grimsby, 31/8/1874

JOHN (Jack) 1876-1936   GEORGE 1877   ALMA 1879   CELIA c.1881/2   VIOLET c.1883/4   FANNY 1885-86
| | | | |
= Florence Cooper   = Edith   = Stericker   = Bert Mason   = Day
                =Draper
        Stanley   ?   3 boys+ 2 girls   ?

JOHN (Lucky Jack) = FLORENCE COOPER (of Cleethorpes)
b. 8/1/1876, Grimsby d. 18/4/1936, Cleethorpes   b.7/10/77 d. 14/2/1956
(Master Mariner/Trawler Skipper, Grimsby)   (Daughter of David Cooper, a fisherman, and Sarah Barker)
Married in Clee Church, Cleethorpes, 26/9/1898

		(1st child)	2nd	3rd	4th
NORA, .29/1/ 00	Bill Whitbread	Doreen	Mavis		
JACK, 13/5/ 02	Ethel Frow				
CHARLES, 24/1/ 04	Mabel Johnson	Pam			
FRANK, 19/4/ 07	Kath Leggett				
ROLAND, 19/10/ 08	Jess Watson	John 21/4/29	Ann 16/9/31	David 28/4/33	Max 1/1/35
IRENE, 3/6/ 11	Cecil Ward				
FLOSS, 3/8/ 13	Eric Garnett+	Fiona 29/4/42	Nigel 27/6/39	Dianne 12/3/47	
NORMAN, 3/5/ 15					

+ Floss married Jack Modena in 1969, after Eric's death in 1965

ROLAND = JESS WATSON (of Aylesbury)
b. 19/10/1908, Grimsby d. 1/8/1994, Grimsby   b. 9/9/1908 d. 2/2/1993 Tregaron, Wales
(Salesman Print/Advertising Director)   (Daughter of Bert Watson, Wine Merchant, and Lillie Brooks)
Married at Aylesbury, October, 1928
Divorced 6/5/1952, made Absolute, 7/7/1952

JOHN ROLAND   ANN PATRICIA   DAVID TREVOR   MAX KNEAL
b. 21/4/29, at 39, Chiltern St b. 16/9/31, at Towyn, Old Stoke Rd b.28/4/33, at 7, Willow Rd b. 1/1/35, at 26, Havelock St.
All in Aylesbury

Second marriage = Edith Marshall, in Hampstead, 2/8/1952
b. 12/10/1919, Hampstead d. 27/5/ 2001, Grimsby
No issue
Second marriage Jess = James McHale, Steeplejack b. Ballina,
County Mayo. Marriage c 1956, divorce c 1970. No issue.

'Greenwich men first': When the parishioners of Greenwich petitioned the government for a new church in 1710, they claimed that nine-tenths of the men were seamen. Be that as it may, by the time my paternal great-grandfather (Charles John) was born at 5, Queen Street on the 24th September 1852, a high proportion were in the Navy, on merchant ships and fishing smacks, or working as Thames lightermen; and his father (Joseph George) is variously cited as fisherman or seaman on birth and marriage certificates. Joseph George was also born in East Greenwich in 1831, and his wife Mary (Quillingham) in Lambeth, in the same year. Charles John was their eldest son, and born when they were twenty-one, which probably indicates that their marriage was in 1851, the year of the Great Exhibition.

Greenwich is described as a fishing port in the Domesday Book and for centuries the Greenwich men had engaged in deep-sea fishing, ranging north to the Faroes and Iceland. They were well known in the east coast ports and were naturally amongst those invited to operate from Grimsby rather than simply land fish there. The Greenwich fishermen were also known for their navigation skills, which were taught during a seven-year apprenticeship. The apprentice had to be able to 'box the compass' (repeat the thirty two points forwards and backwards) by the first Sunday on board. The rule was 'no compass, no plum duff'!

An interesting difference in fishing style existed at that time between the men from Barking Creek, who employed 'fleeting' with the smacks fishing together under the command of an 'Admiral' who oversaw the transfer of the catches to a fast sailing lugger to take the fish to Billingsgate, and the Greenwich men who preferred to fish alone, (each his own 'Admiral') choosing their own course and fishing ground.

As an added inducement, the Greenwich fishermen were offered the use of the steam powered cod-liner, *John Ellis*, by the Deep-sea Trawling Company but it proved too noisy and was converted back to sail (in the event steam power did not take over until the end of the century, though steamers were used to tow smacks out to the Humber mouth and for docking).

The importance of the contribution made by the Greenwich fishermen, to the success of the new fish docks, was shown by their long held right of precedence over all other boats when going out of the dock gates. As Mrs Norledge, wife of one of the dock officials put it, "When the dock gate opened, Captain McBride, the first dockmaster, could be heard shouting, 'Greenwich men first'. She also recalled, "I have seen the dock crowded with smacks, ready for sea which would draw in close to make a waterway for a few Greenwich smacks to pass first. Compliments were plentiful, which the Greenwich man would receive with a bow; the old captain—-eye steady, hand on tiller, hat raised and a smile of triumph on his lips, would make for the open sea" (see note 5).

At first the Greenwich men returned periodically to Greenwich but eventually their families also moved to Grimsby. By the time Father told me of his boyhood memories of visits from Grandfather's Greenwich cousins all connection of our family with Greenwich had gone—-'Kentish Men' had become 'Lincolnshire Yellowbellies.'

The heyday of the sailing smacks: At the time of the 1881 Census both my paternal great grandfathers were at sea, Charles Haynes (then aged 28) as Master of the *Ann Guzzwell*, a sailing smack with a crew of three, including his brother Tom (23) as mate. The third hand was John Dove (20) a fisherman from Hull and the cook/apprentice was James Herrison (16) from Stafford. As trawling smacks normally carried a crew of five, it is possible that the apprentice /deckhand, was not available on this trip.

It is not known how long Charles had been Skipper of the *Ann Guzzwell* at this time, or indeed, when he arrived in Grimsby. It's possible that he came as an apprentice after the main flotilla of 'well-smacks' came up from Greenwich in 1863, following the enlargement of the fish dock to 12 acres in 1860. He was presumably already well established in Grimsby when, on the 31st of August, 1874, he married Florence (Fanny), born in Scarborough, on the 16th of December, 1852, see photos 2-1. Fanny was the daughter of a fisherman, John Clackston and his wife Betsy Toby, who may have come down in the 1850s, when the Alwards migrated to Grimsby with their trawlers because there were better facilities on offer. Scarborough is also more exposed to easterly gales.

By the time of the 1881 Census, when Charles and Fanny were living at 45 Humber Street, they already had three of their eventual five children and John ('Jack'), the eldest, born at a previous address (3 Worsley Buildings, on the 8th of January, 1876) was nearly five, and already at school, his brother George, three, and his sister Alma, one. Two further daughters, Celia and Violet were born later. They also had a young housemaid of fifteen living in, called Eileen Shaddick, from Westminster, London.

In the January of 1881, Father's maternal grandfather, David Cooper (1837-1914) was also at sea, as captain of the *Rambler,* with a crew of eight. According to Father, his Granddad Cooper was one of the first Grimsby fishermen to long-line (with baited hooks) for cod on the Grand Banks off Newfoundland, and the number of the crew, which could be up to ten or so on cod-liners, is consistent with this. The mate William Yarlott, (23), was from Greenwich, and there were two able seamen, Benjamin Sheppard, (54), and William Henry Shutton, (21), both from London, as well as a young able seaman, George Shatton, (19), from Hertford. There were also four apprentices, two from Gravesend, Kent, Edward Freshwater, (19), and Robert Snelling, (18). One was from London, Charles Henry Taunlett, (16), and one from Grimsby, William Douglas (15). This roll-call, like that for the *Ann Guzzwell,* shows the diverse origins of the Grimsby fishermen.

David Cooper, then forty-four was living with his wife Sarah at 99, Weelsby Street, with three older children, Sarah (16), David (14) and William (12) all born previously in Greenwich, together with Florence Emily, a child of three, born in Grimsby. (John Charles, a fisherman's son would eventually marry Florence Emily, a fisherman's and sea captain's daughter). Her older sister, Sarah is described as a domestic, so was presumably home helping her mother, and both boys were still in school (so may have been in the Grammar School). Two further daughters, Lydia (Lillie) and Mercia, were to be born later.

David Cooper arrived in Grimsby by a circuitous route. He was born in Suffolk, in 1837 in 'Stalim'? the son of a shoemaker, Joseph Cooper, and went to sea, possibly as an apprentice from Greenwich, because he married Sarah Ann, who was a Greenwich girl, in 1862, in Deptford, when he was twenty-five and she was seventeen. Sarah Ann was the daughter of James Barker, a coal porter, who had married her mother, Lydia Rider, also in Deptford, in 1828.   *? colporter = hawker*   ✗

Clearly, David and Sarah migrated to Grimsby sometime between the birth of their third child in 1868 and the arrival of Florence, during the decade in which the main transfer of Greenwich men to Grimsby took place. By 1873, only a year before Charles and Fanny were married, the number of fishermen in Grimsby had dramatically increased to 3400 (together with over 400 shipwrights and 400 smoke houses that employed a large number of women). There was now 'a great fleet of more than five hundred brown sailed trawlers and cod-liners and smaller craft' (mostly ketch-rigged smacks—see note 6). These made a fine sight leaving and arriving in the Humber and many fishing families lived in Sterling Street where the houses had balconies especially built so the boats could be seen coming in. It was now the general practice to pack fish in ice at sea and the Grimsby Ice Company also had 'ice-barques' coming in two or three times a week from Norway to restock the icehouse which held 2-300 tons through the summer.

The *Ann Guzzwell* was built in 1869 and named after the wife of one of the early

Cooper line:

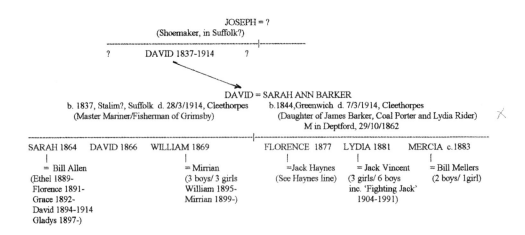

JOSEPH = ?
(Shoemaker, in Suffolk?)

?   DAVID 1837-1914   ?

DAVID = SARAH ANN BARKER

b. 1837, Stalim?, Suffolk d. 28/3/1914, Cleethorpes   b.1844,Greenwich d. 7/3/1914, Cleethorpes   ✗
(Master Mariner/Fisherman of Grimsby)   (Daughter of James Barker, Coal Porter and Lydia Rider)
M in Deptford, 29/10/1862

SARAH 1864	DAVID 1866	WILLIAM 1869	FLORENCE 1877	LYDIA 1881	MERCIA c.1883
= Bill Allen		= Mirrian	=Jack Haynes	= Jack Vincent	= Bill Mellers
(Ethel 1889-		(3 boys/ 3 girls	(See Haynes line)	(3 girls/ 6 boys	(2 boys/ 1girl)
Florence 1891-		William 1895-		inc. 'Fighting Jack'	
Grace 1892-		Mirrian 1899-)		1904-1991)	
David 1894-1914					
Gladys 1897-)					

fishermen. (The Guzzwells came up to Grimsby with the Brixham contingent and it's possible that Great-grandfather, Charles, skippered her for John Guzzwell senior, a retired smack owner at the time of the 1881 Census, on a share basis.) She was 66ft 9ins in length and 59.46 tons, about middle of the range of size of smacks (which doubled in size during the later years of the century—see notes 7, 8). A crew of five was normal for this size of smack with more on the larger ones. In the early days the main target areas were the Dogger Bank, a hundred miles away off the Yorkshire coast where cod were plentiful, and the Silver Pits to the south of it, muddy depressions some forty to fifty fathoms deep and attractive to sole and plaice, especially in winter. Navigation was by compass and sun and stars, together with the lead sounding line. Some smacks-men could find their way to the grounds by 'dead reckoning' and soundings alone (plus the fisherman's sixth sense).

The kind of catch that could be made by a smack such as the *Ann Guzzwell* is indicated by details given for the similar, sixty ton smack *Angelus*. (See note 9.) In 1869 this vessel made 274 hauls during the year, which gave 5610 baskets of fish weighing 96 tons. The catch included what were then considered 'prime fish': cod, soles, brill and halibut and, remarkable to us now, what was described as 'offal': plaice and haddock which sold at lower prices (and popular in poorer districts).

In the April of that same year, the *Angelus* took a pooled consignment of about forty tons of fish from a number of smacks, directly to Billingsgate to avoid the freight charges. Sold over three days this made a profit after expenses of £37, not including the offal. This suggests a profit of up to a £100 a year or so for the *Angelus* alone, from the figures given above. Of course, this needs to be multiplied by at least 70 times or more to put it into a modern perspective. Cod-liners with a storage well ('well-smacks') bringing in their catch in first class condition, hooked in the mouth only and undamaged, could command higher prices and the *James Fildes* brought in a record catch of 800 cod in 1865, that sold in Billingsgate for £300 (£21,000).

In the early days most trawling smacks were sailed by single owners and the profits were shared on the basis of eighths, the skipper taking 5 (plus six eighths of one share) while the mate and third hand each had one share (plus one eighth of one share). If the skipper sailed for an owner his portion dropped to one share (plus three eighths of one share) together with a wage of about £3 a month. The owner took 4 shares (plus three eighths of one share). The apprentice cooks and deckhands were paid a weekly wage of about fifteen shillings (75p) unless the skippers/owners paid for their lodgings and food when ashore. It was then reduced to pocket money.

On the cod-liners, more generally run by companies, the skipper received 9% gross, the mate about twenty-three shillings a week (£1.15p), the third hand about twenty-one shillings and the apprentices sixteen shillings (80p). Crews also shared in the 'offal' and in the proceeds of the cod liver oil, which was prepared on board. It will be appreciated that on these wages and returns it took considerable dedication for a youngster to work his way up to be the owner of a smack, costing some £1000 to £1500 to buy and fit out, and harder as the vessels became larger and more expensive.

Grandfather, John ('Jack'), left school when he was twelve in 1888 and became cook/apprentice on his father's smack. His duties were considerable: he had to cook the food, keep up a continuous supply of tea and look after the water supply (kept in barrels in the stern); keep the utensils and cabin clean and the decks clear of fish scales and offal; help the deckhand (fourth hand) trim the lamps, prepare flares and prime the pumps; take the helm when the trawl was being shot (hence the need to be able to 'box the compass') and coil away the trawl warp neatly afterwards.

Although Grandfather had been out on his father's boat as a child he found it difficult to adapt to the hardships of life on the smack that first winter and ran away. He got as far as Greenwich where he found refuge with an aunt but he was brought back, 'soundly thrashed', and put back to sea. Life at sea was becoming more arduous because the number of smacks reached a maximum of 815 in 1887 and increasing competition with Danish, German and Dutch fishermen led to increased fishing in distant waters. As my father put it, when talking of the early days, "It wasn't just a week or a fortnight when they went away fleeting. They would go away in groups, you see, and these smacks would stay on the fishing grounds for up to two months. All the fish was salted down and transferred to fast sailing boats, with the letters and other things, to be taken to Grimsby to be processed and packed, and sent abroad mostly". It will be easily understood why fleeting was never popular with the men. However, smacks trawling alone were not away so long but were completely out of contact. The cod-liners could be away longer; their typical routine was to work the Dogger Bank from October until Christmas, fish near shore until April and then spend April to September around Iceland and the Faroes.

Fortunately, by Grandfather's time the 'Fisher-lads Institution' had been set up (in 1879) to provide training during periods ashore, in fishing methods and seamanship, and in 1883, examinations were brought in for the different stages that led finally to the Skipper's ticket. (The Institute eventually became the famous Grimsby Nautical College.) As apprentice/deckhand, Grandfather had to be able to: keep watch, handle the small boat, splice ropes and braid the cod end, mend nets, take soundings and keep the fish room clean. As third hand, he had to be able to: manage the gear and shoot the trawl (a large bag-like net kept open with a beam) and also help the skipper navigate by knowing the position of all the capes and bays, lighthouses and navigation buoys (both land and sea marks) and follow the rules of the road at sea. As mate, he had to be able to: prepare, pack and store the fish properly. As Skipper he had to be able to: take overall responsibility for the whole working of the boat, the state of the rigging, gear, lights and pumps, to chart the course and know the position of the vessel at all times. On the cod-liners, the apprentice cook also had to help bait the lines (with whelks or river lampreys) and as deckhand, to gut and salt the fish as well as to pay out and haul in the long-lines as well as the shorter, hand lines used near shore. Essentially, the deckhand was equivalent to an ordinary seaman and the third hand to an able seaman.

Grandfather was a quick learner and with his interest aroused he was able to adapt to the smack-man's life, acquiring his mate's ticket at eighteen and his Skipper's ticket at twenty-two.

In the early days, most apprentices were Skipper's sons or relatives but at the time Grandfather was a boy, in the late 1870s and in the1880s, the rapid expansion of the trawling fleet had led to a labour shortage and increasing numbers of boys were being brought in from foundling homes, reform schools and prisons. Most of these boys were without any inkling of life at sea and many (some of them hardened criminals) had no tolerance for its necessary discipline. Inevitably, boys ran away, harsh punishments were handed out and some were returned to prison with the hope that the more incorrigible would be chastened and ready to return (one group of them in chains from Lincoln Prison which led to a national outcry).

With the hindsight of more than a hundred years' social progress it is easy to feel 'indignation' at the way these lads were returned to the 'living hell' on the smacks, but the life was no harder than for the Skipper's sons or the rest of the crew. Certainly the food was a lot better than in the institutions they had come from: fresh fish for breakfast every day and for the first week, roast beef and potatoes followed by suet duff for dinner, with salt beef or horse meat for dinner on the rest of the voyage with suet pudding and treacle, plus 1lb of bread daily. They were also provided with suitable clothing. The inexperienced apprentices faced dangers when ashore. Those receiving wages had to find their own food and lodging when in port. The boom in fishing had led to the ramshackle growth of Grimsby with a population of about 30,000 by 1880, producing an unsanitary sprawl with little provision for sport and recreation. Inevitably, some apprentices with money in their pockets for the first time lodged in the cheapest doss houses and spent it in the numerous pubs and brothels, often having to be hauled out to catch the morning tide. However, most smack owners and skippers were decent men who tried to do the best for the material and moral welfare of their charges. Many of them were strict teetotalers and members of the 'Blue Ribbon Army'. One well known example, Thomas Campbell, was a Primitive Methodist and held regular Sunday services on board and ashore when fishing Icelandic waters. He also built up an Apprentice Boys' choir and 'Tommy Campbell's Orphans' were famous for their renditions into the 1900s.

Although it was particularly dangerous for the inexperienced apprentice, who might be pulled overboard when attempting to get a bucket of water or fall from the rigging, the figures show that during the decade that Grandfather went to sea, the 1880s, the average loss of life from Grimsby was approximately 20 apprentices a year, compared with 120 fishermen lost each year, not much out of proportion with the number on the average smack. Clearly it was a very dangerous calling for all concerned, especially working on deck with the trawl, but the figures also illustrate how often the smacks foundered or were stranded with the loss of all hands. (See note 8.)

Some idea of the tragic scale of the losses can be gained from consideration of the figures for lost Grimsby smacks over the ten-year period 1879 to 1889. These show the particular dangers of the East Coast, with its shoals and sand banks, in an easterly gale. In the dark with rain or flying snow, without very good local knowledge, there was no really safe haven to aim for between the North Foreland and Flamborough Head, except Spurn and the Humber; and as was said, 'If you missed it, it was suicide'.

1879 was a bad year with fifteen losses. In 1880, six were lost in a great gale with north-east winds up to force 11. Ten were lost the following year and then in March 1883, five were lost in shoal waters on the Dogger Bank, when a north-west gale of hurricane force suddenly followed several days when the fleet was becalmed (over two hundred men and boys from the East Coast fishing fleets were lost altogether which prompted the enquiry that led with other regulations to mandatory examinations for Skippers). Then in December of the same year, three more went down. In 1884, fourteen were lost and in 1885, another nine, these included the *Ann Guzzwell* on which Great- grandfather, Charles, had been skipper only three years earlier. Over the years 1887 and 1888, twenty-one went down. In 1889, during the first year Grandfather, Jack, spent at sea, nine more were lost (and there were eighty losses on the East Coast as a whole). These figures give an average of nine losses a year from Grimsby during this period, quite apart from individual fishermen being swept overboard or dying in other accidents. Very few fishermen were saved when their smacks went down, encumbered by their heavy gear and usually unable to swim (there was a widely held superstition that it tempted fate to do so and, in any case, they didn't last long in Arctic waters, even with a lifebelt, in the rare case that there were any on board).

There were particular dangers in long-lining for cod in places like the Grand Banks, notorious for sudden fogs. The long–lines were made up of connected 'pieces', each piece 120 yards in length, with 52 hooks on short 'snoods'. These lines were paid out from little flat-bottomed boats, called dories and laid out on the sea-bed for up to ten miles with a marker buoy at every mile. If a blanket fog came down, the dories easily became separated from the mother ship and all too often the occupants were never seen again.

This catalogue of disasters conjures up a sad picture of wives and families down at the dockside desperate for news of missing men folk, praying and hoping against hope that they would return. There were some dramatic escapes. A number of vessels got caught in the Arctic ice for several weeks and managed to escape and the steam cod-liner *Sando* that sailed for Icelandic waters in November 1889, was trapped until March 1890. She was caught in a severe gale and badly damaged with the wheelhouse (and helmsman) carried away but managed to limp into an Iceland fjord where gradually she became mantled with ice and 'even the fishermen's clothing froze'. The men were given up for lost in Grimsby and the families began to suffer financial hardship but eventually the news got through from Iceland and a sister ship was sent to the rescue. It took two days for the *Sando* to be freed from the ice and several more, because of bad weather, before they could leave. The two vessels returned via Bergen in Norway, where provisions were taken on board and on the way to Grimsby they fished for four days near the Faroes and made a good catch of halibut, so they didn't come home empty-handed.

The rise of the steam trawlers: In 1882, there were only two steam trawlers operating from Grimsby, compared with 623 sailing smacks, and the smacks continued to increase in number until 1887. The early steamers were too underpowered to fish further than the Dogger Bank and, of course needed large amounts of coal. However, by the time Grandfather went to sea, James Alward had introduced the highly successful *Aries* and *Zodiac*. These more powerful steam trawlers could range into northern waters. They had the advantage of greater speed in all weathers, with greater size and safety, and steam winches that could handle larger beam trawls, up to 50 feet wide, as well as fish to 200 fathoms, hauling in the net with a wire warp in 30 minutes. They quite out- classed smacks, such as that of Great-grandfather, Charles, which had a 12 foot beam trawl and could only fish to 50 fathoms, in which the net was hauled in by a rope warp and took three hours; and by the end of the century, these new, larger trawlers almost completely replaced them.

The fall in numbers of sailing smacks was even more dramatic than their rise earlier. By 1903 there were 476 steam trawlers and only 34 smacks left. This rapid change was assisted by severe losses of smacks, especially in the great gales of 1890 and 1895. The smack owners then re-invested in the safer more profitable steam trawlers, which became even more efficient with the invention of otter boards to keep the mouth of the net open. These were named after their first successful use in the Scarborough trawler *Otter.* They dispensed with the clumsy beam and allowed nets up to 80 feet wide and over 100 feet long.

Although safer than the sailing smacks, thirteen steam trawlers were lost in the period up to 1900, during the period they were replacing the smacks, including the *Zodiac* in 1889, and six or seven each year up to 1914, which emphasizes that the dangers can be mitigated but not eliminated. In case it should be thought that the smacks weren't seaworthy, it must be pointed out that they were built to ride the gales, rarely foundering well out to sea but were generally lost after hitting a reef or shoals, or after becoming stranded. A large number were still operating up to eighty years after they were first launched. (See note 10.)

Although the introduction of the steam trawlers was extremely profitable (the tonnage of fish landed was trebled to 135,000 tons a year by little more than half as many ships during this period, and the population expanded to 75,000) it had a devastating effect on the single owner smacks-men and the smaller companies. They were unable to sell their boats, many became bankrupt and considerable numbers of fishermen and skippers were put 'on the beach' without work. It also meant that the ownership of the trawlers was concentrated in fewer and fewer hands.

The 'Peculiar Knowledge': Grandfather, Jack, received his training and obtained his skipper's ticket (in February 1899) during this period of turbulence in the industry and successfully stayed afloat by making the transition to the steam trawlers. He gradually acquired what was called the 'peculiar knowledge' of the Grimsby fisherman: concerning the habits of fish in relation to water depths, bottom sediments, tides and currents, seasonal changes, such as the winter occurrence of soles in the Silver Pits, and signs given by the colours of the sea and the movements of birds; to the extent that he became known as 'Lucky Jack', a skipper who could often return with fish when others failed to make a catch. Luck seems also to have attended most of his voyages in that they appear to have ended safely, but there was one occasion when his trawler sprang a leak, battered by a storm while he was fishing the Silver Pits, and was in danger of foundering. However, he managed to get it into Boston harbour late on Christmas Eve. This meant that he and his crew didn't get home to Grimsby until late on Christmas Day and is, probably, why this particular incident was remembered in the family when others were forgotten. (See photos 2-1 and 2-2.)

Jack (John Charles) and Florence Emily were married in Clee Church in September 1898, when he was twenty-two and she was not quite twenty-one, six months before he obtained his skipper's ticket in February 1899. At this time they were living at 126, Barcroft Street, Cleethorpes, with the Cooper parents, although by the time of the 1901 Census they had moved to no.115. Their first daughter, Nora, was born in the first year of the new century (1900) and their first son, John (also 'Jack'), in 1902; followed by two further sons, Charles (1904) and Frank (1907) and then Father, Roland, in 1908.

During this time, Grandfather established himself as a successful fisherman, in demand as a skipper by the trawler companies. While working for Bacons, he was approached by Alf Bannister who persuaded him to join him on the basis of a third share in a new trawler to be worked off as a mortgage. Shortly afterwards, Alec Black (later Sir Alec) tried to get him to change his mind and join him, offering him a considerable amount of money on the nail as an inducement, but as Father said, " Dad wouldn't, (couldn't) change his mind because he had shaken hands on the deal with Alf, that's how it was in those days".

The new trawler was built at Selby and it was intended that Grandmother, Florence Emily, would launch it, but because she had just had a new baby, Frank, her eldest daughter, Nora, then seven years old, was allowed to do it instead, christening the new vessel *Othello* (on the twenty-seventh of July, 1907). She was allowed to keep the engraved scissors she used to cut the ribbon and these have been passed down to my eldest daughter, Jessica. Exactly fifty years later, in 1957, Father's second wife, Edith, was to launch the Ross *Jaguar* also at Selby. (See photos 2-2.)

Photographs 2-1 Haynes Line

Top left-: Grandfather 'Lucky Jack' Haynes, who put to sea at twelve, ran away, was soundly thrashed, was sent back and went on to become a successful trawler skipper.

Top right-: Father Roland Haynes, at twelve years old, in the bum-freezer jacket required when attending St. James School, Grimsby.

Bottom-: Great-grandmother Florence 'Fanny' Haynes, (née Clackston) daughter of a Scarborough fisherman and reputed to have the 'second sight'.

FATHER'S EARLY MEMORIES

When Father, Roland, was born (on the nineteenth of October, 1908) the family were living at 17, Park Drive, a street laid out to mark the boundary between Grimsby, which occupied the Grant Thorold Estate, and Cleethorpes, which occupied land in the Manor of Itterby, owned by Sydney Sussex College, Cambridge. This meant that technically, my father was born in Cleethorpes, but as they moved into Grimsby when he was only eighteen months old, he always regarded himself as a Grimbarian.

His father, 'Lucky Jack', and his family background: Although Father was born in Cleethorpes, his first memories are of the house in Hainton Avenue, the continuation of Freeman Street, that Grandfather bought subsequently. What follows is in his words:

"It was a nice, neat little villa, no 17, in Park Drive, with a view of the new park but they already had Nora, Jack, Charles and Frank and as it only had three bedrooms, after my arrival they found another new house in a terrace in Hainton Avenue. It had four bedrooms with a bathroom and a separate loo upstairs. Downstairs, there was a front room, a middle room, a breakfast room and a kitchen with a big walk-in pantry. A covered area at the back had a scullery, a washhouse, and a coalhouse, opening into it, as well as another loo; a good old family house. It wasn't long before Dad (his father) had the two back bedrooms knocked into one to make a dormitory with four beds for us boys, five when Norman arrived (1915). The girls, including Irene (1911) and Floss (1913) had a big bedroom on the second floor.

"When father had paid for the new house and new furniture he explained to mother that all he had left was eleven hundred pounds in the bank, which meant they had to be careful. This shows he had been a very careful man all the years he had been a skipper, about fourteen years by the time we went into the new house. He had very few vices, didn't spend money on a lot of nonsense. With a large family and self-employed what he earned was all he had, though he did have an insurance policy with the 'Hearts of Oak'. They never bought anything on credit. Everything had to be paid for in cash, even when they were first married. He was a keen, hardworking young fisherman, 'Lightning Jack Haynes' they used to call him then, because he was such a fast worker. No one could beat him mending the nets. When you pull the net up it often snags a rock, or this and that, making a big tear so you lose the fish. As there are usually only two trawls on the boat at a time it is important to get nets repaired quickly. One day Dad noticed a new member of the crew busily mending the nets, very quickly and expertly. He went straight down from the bridge and sat next to him and joined in the work until he had proved to his own satisfaction that he could do it faster. This used to amuse the crew, but he was a good leader of men and the members of his crew always stayed with him. They would do little things for him and he looked after them in return." (A surviving logbook, his Board of Trade 'Continuous Certificate of Discharge,' records, in his own hand, that he was 5ft 6in in height, with brown hair and brown eyes and a tattoo of a sailor on his left arm.)

"Dad was very observant and after he had sailed with his father and other skippers he became very familiar with all the places they went to fish as well as mastering navigation and the operation of the boat. He was also very good with the engines when he went on to a steam trawler. Eventually, his skill in finding fish led to him being called 'Lucky Jack'.

"Dad was never short of money, because as a successful skipper he was always in a job, but he was never overpaid. It was amazing what a skipper had to lay out. He had to pay for his own food on the trawler out of the poundage he got from the profits on turnover. It was a long time before skippers got a salary with a share of the profits, without having to bear the costs of the overheads. So there was every incentive to get cracking. But he was very generous, always buying mother things, at which she would say, 'Take it back Jack, I don't want another fur coat and I don't need anymore jewelry'. She was very good too, you see, she was a strict Baptist, and so they went on very steadily.

"Father and mother had eight children: Nora, Jack, Charles, Frank, me, Irene, Floss and Norman, taking no account of miscarriages. Mother was well looked after, always had a maid and was given every attention when she had her children. Dad made sure there were a good doctor and nurse in attendance. So mother always said she didn't mind how many children she had.

"When I was a child, mother had a maid called Ethel. She was the last one mother had because when Nora left school, a little private school, she took the place of the maid. There was no question of a career for her in those days. Ethel was an orphan, very good. She cuffed my head a few times for pinching cakes and biscuits, or for doing what I shouldn't have done. One day I picked up a bread knife, to cut myself a slice of bread, when she wasn't there, and she came in and startled me so that I cut my finger. There was blood everywhere but she wasn't bothered about that. She gave me good hammering before dressing my finger. 'I'll tell your mother', she said. But she never did. She never ratted on us. She eventually left to marry a policeman and Nora took over.

"Father was very good at administering summary justice. If we were quarrelling he would come in and hand out a spanking all round. 'Punishment first and questions afterwards' was his motto. This was understandable, when you consider that he was only home for a night or two at a time and he wasn't going to have it spoilt by quarrelling kids.

"Mother's parents, Grand-dad and Grannie Cooper, died when I was quite small, (both in the same month, March, 1914). Grand-dad was a skipper and his career ran parallel to that of father's father. Mother had two brothers, William and David, and three sisters, Sarah, Lily and Mercia. Aunt Sarah was married to Bill Allen (the son of a sail-maker from Manningtree, in Essex) and tragically, their son, my cousin David, was drowned at sea (on the SS. *Ocang,* when he was only nineteen, in the same year as the grandparents died, at the very beginning of the war, December 1914).

"Father's mother (Fanny) was a fisherman's daughter too, from Scarborough. She was a very capable, educated girl and played the piano and the organ. She was very imaginative and used to tell us wonderful stories and recite poetry, keeping us all enthralled; and I know there is grave doubt about this today, but she had the gift of 'second sight'. So she was in great demand at parties and weddings, playing and singing and telling fortunes by reading the cards. Whether this is genuine or not, we don't know, do we?

"Father was the eldest in his family, followed by George and then three girls, Alma, Celia and Violet. Uncle George was extremely good with engines on the trawlers but he went blind while still quite young. There weren't the facilities then that there are today and his wife, faithless, left him and took their child, a son (Stanley), away to Hull and had nothing more to do with him. Father paid a woman to look after George and was very good to him all his life. One of my childhood memories is of going with him on a Sunday to see Uncle George and him slipping a pound note into his brother's hand and also giving a couple of quid to the good lady looking after him. He was also very good to his sisters, Alma and Violet, and I needn't tell you how many times he helped his mother and father when they were poorly off in later life.

"You can see that with his growing family and commitments, especially when he went into partnership with Alf Bannister and had to pay off his share, he was under a lot of pressure to earn more. He worked out that fishing the Dogger Bank and Silver Pits, he could get in two trips a week: by leaving early on Monday and reaching the fishing grounds by the afternoon, fishing all night and the next day, returning overnight to land the catch in Grimsby on the Wednesday, then sailing again on Thursday morning, fishing overnight and through Friday, returning in time to land the second catch for the market on Saturday. This would give two nights in over the weekend and Sunday at home, which suited father, who was a great family man; though it was really only a night and a half, because on the Monday the taxi would be at the door at 3 am.

Photographs 2-2 'Lucky Jack' and his two eldest daughters

Top-: Two of Father's sisters on the promenade, Cleethorpes, in the early 1930s. Nora, the eldest is on the right, with Irene next to her.

Bottom-: This shows 'Lucky Jack', fourth from left, with his crew on the *SS Othello*. This photo was published as a postcard in 1917, during World War 1, probably to show that despite U-boats and mines the 'seadogs' were still bringing home the fish. The *Othello* was launched by Nora, in 1907, when she was seven years old. The photo must have been taken earlier in the War before *Othello* was taken over for mine sweeping. In 1917 Grandfather was successively skipper of the *Andlo* and the *Kalso*.

Fishing in the 'North Sea.

"So at this period of his life, father concentrated on these 'quick trips' and peculiar as it might seem for a successful skipper, avoided the Iceland and Faroes run. However, I think it nearly killed him and finally the crew wouldn't have any more of it. His health began to suffer because he had a tendency to asthma and colds often led to bronchial attacks. It was the devil's own job to get him to look after himself. He had to be tied down not to go to sea. If there were any rows in the family between mother and father, it was always because he neglected himself and she couldn't make him look after himself. But you see, he had this drive to look after a large family and you got no money in those days if you didn't go to work. The settling day wouldn't include you, if you weren't on your boat.

"One of my earliest memories is of being woken while it was still dark, by the noise of the car that had come to take father to the docks. I went to the top of the stairs as he went out. It was a blustery night and the wind was blowing. I can see him now as he pulled his bag onto his shoulder before going out of the door. His boat was sailing on the morning tide, you see."

The Great War: Father's first memory of the Great War appears to be of a trip to sea with his brother Frank on Grandfather's trawler:

"One of my earliest and outstanding memories of that time is because my father was fond of taking us to sea with him when we were quite young. He would let me, and Frank, have his cabin, while he slept somewhere else, or we slept on the floor between the bunks. We never really got over sea-sickness but being boys we enjoyed it. He took us all in turns and I went about half a dozen times.

"We were back in the docks after being at sea with father and he had caught a lot of prawns. These had been boiled and we were outside on deck peeling off the red shells when someone came on board and said to father, 'You are back just in time because war has been declared'. It was August 1914 and I was six and Frank was eight and we had only just got back from sea—-a trip with father, you see.

"During the war the Navy took all the best trawlers for mine sweeping and that meant that they took the *Othello*. But, of course, fishing went on despite all the dangers of mines and U-boats and father took command of other trawlers. The difficulty now, was that the trawlers were only allowed to fish certain protected areas. Father, like a lot of the skippers couldn't bear to be told where to fish. He took his own line and, inevitably, was caught twice and heavily fined, then finally banned. After this he became a pilot on the Humber. Anyhow, he got through the war alright and at the end was made an honorary lieutenant in the RNVR. I had a photo of him once, in his naval hat and buttoned up uniform. (See note 11.)

"Father taught all of us to box and it was over these years that he taught me and Frank. He was a very fine boxer as a young man and he really taught us very expertly. I can see him now, kneeling down and teaching us how to make straight lefts and follow up with a right cross. Marvellous tuition, so much so that we used to appear as a special exhibition over three (or four) rounds in the intervals of some of the big boxing matches at the Gaiety, the Coliseum and on the Pier. We were, no credit to us and all due to father, quite skillful—-straight lefts, a feint then a right, bobbing and weaving, ducking and side stepping, all that kind of thing. We used to wear white jerseys and pants and Frank had a blue sash and I had a red one. We had a big collecting box and after our bout we would go round with it and collect money for our service men that had been made prisoners of war.

"Father was so keen on developing our skills that when Jimmy Buck, the lightweight champion of the Navy, came to box exhibitions with Jimmy Wilde, the world flyweight champion, he invited him to the house to talk to us and give us hints. The two champs put on a very clever exhibition; they were both so light on their feet. Jimmy Wilde couldn't have been more than four and a half stone but he packed a wallop. He always put his weight behind it, bearing out what father used to say, 'Don't just hit, get your weight behind it'. (See note 12.) I know it embarrasses Frank to talk about it, these days, but we were quite a little turn; worth seeing, because father had so assiduously trained us, and we did raise quite a lot of money.

"But a very sad thing happened, only a short time after one of our bouts. We appeared in the interval during boxing matches put on for the Manchester Regiment, which was in barracks in Grimsby. At the end of our exhibition, the Colonel of the Regiment presented us both with a silver medal. Only a week or two later a zeppelin came over on a raid and dropped a bomb, which by most unlucky chance hit the church where a number of the men were billeted," (see note 13).

Childhood holidays: Father's memories of family holidays also go back to the time of the Great War:

"Father and mother had occasional holidays together when Nora was old enough to look after us. They went to Blackpool once and they used to go and stay with relations in Greenwich. Father also took mother to see the Derby. He always hired a car, and Johnny Horner took them there and back in a Daimler.

"During the War, when mother was expecting we all used to go and stay with some friends of theirs called the Waltons in Bourne, in the Wolds. Mr Walton was a guard on the railway and father had met him on the train and got talking, and invited him down to the docks, which had led to a friendship between the two families. The Waltons had a big orchard and used to send us fruit and vegetables, while father sent them, boxes of fish. They were always asking, 'Can the boys come again'? Mrs. Walton was wonderful cook; she put a dozen eggs in her fruitcake and six in the Yorkshire pudding so we had plenty to eat there. It was an unusual friendship between two very different men, a man who had never been to sea and a man who knew nothing about the country, yet found something in common.

"Another unusual friendship of my father was with a doctor and his family who had a cottage in Tealby. So there was father, who boasted that he had never wasted time reading a novel, very friendly with a cultivated medical man. Again it must have been the attraction of being able to share their quite different life experiences. Anyhow, one summer we spent a long holiday in the cottage with mother, when the Doctor and his family were away. We boys had a great time playing round the village but Jack (the eldest brother) got into trouble because he put goldfish in the village water well. Father had to pay a fiver to have it cleaned out!"

St. James School: By the time Father and his brother Frank were of school age, Grandfather was better off and when they were both about ten they were sent to St. James (photos 2-1 top right):

"Both Frank and I went to St. James School. I suppose, in those days quite a modest establishment. It was a Church school and I was a probationer in the church choir. This meant I didn't get to wear the full choir-boy's surplice but a sort of gray tunic. But I did get to sing hymns from the church tower on Ascension Day, which was memorable experience.

"Languages were taught by a funny old chap called Hoffman and we did Latin, French and German with him. We also did Pitman's Shorthand with a very efficient teacher called Mr. Rand. They say you should be young to learn languages and this also applies to shorthand. I very quickly mastered the basics and found it very useful later in life.

"We had a PT instructor in the school called Mr. Coalbrook. He was the proprietor of a hotel in the town and had a gymnasium on the top floor, which was used by a lot of young fellows. This led to him being asked to take charge of the boxing in St. James. He was very good and father gave us permission to join. We went to a number of places with the team and one big event was a fund raising gala for the orphans of fishermen and sailors at Hull. He also put us in for the Schoolboys Boxing Championship and I got through in my weight at Leeds and then three of us had to go up to London with Mr. Coalbrook and his wife to the finals. They gave us a lovely weekend. We stayed at the Charing Cross Hotel and while we were there they took us to see "Cinderella" in Drury Lane. It was quite an experience. (See note 14.) On one occasion, boxing at Hull, I was ahead on points but I had to retire because making a straight left to the other boy's head I put my thumb out. I tried to carry on just using my right but the ref. stopped the fight and made me go to the corner and take my glove off. He then made me withdraw from the contest. I was very upset about it but that same night I did see another boy from St. James, called Harry Smith, win his bout with a marvellous performance. He was about two years older than me. He was about 8 stones 6 lbs in weight and a wonderful English style boxer. You know—-, straight left and then right, very well taught. Harry was boxing a boy called O'Kelly. His father, Con O'Kelly was a promoter and had been a world-class wrestler—a huge fellow. His son was a tough looking customer too. I think everyone thought that O'Kelly would win easily, but he was a bit of a bar room brawler, swinging rights and lefts, and Smithy was able to keep him at a distance for the whole three rounds. He did a wonderful job on him and won the contest. When the

Police gave out the prizes, Smithy was presented with this solid gold medal, a really beautiful thing. Despite this setback O'Kelly went on to become a champion in America but then he gave it all up and went into the Church, becoming a typical, American Roman Catholic priest!

"By an amazing coincidence, one day many years later, after I had returned to Grimsby and, indeed, long after I had retired, I was passing Lloyds Bank and I heard a voice say, 'It is Rolly Haynes isn't it'? I thought it was Smithy but it turned out to be his brother who had just been looking at Harry's gold medal, which was being kept with his other personal effects in the Bank. He said, 'You are probably, the only person still living, who saw him win it' (sixty years before!). What is also amazing is that Smithy's brother should have recognized me after all those years but they say you never forget the faces of old schoolmates."

On his elder brother, Jack: Father's eldest brother Jack, was six years older than he was and left the Council School at the age of fourteen:

"After Jack left school he wanted to work on a pilot boat, like father at that time of the war, but the training is very tough and he didn't settle down to it, finally failing his examinations. What he really wanted to do was something mechanical, to do with engines, and he should have worked in a garage or gone into engineering. However, eventually, father got together with Uncle Jack (Vincent) to set up their two eldest sons in a wholesale fish business on the docks.

"I must tell you about the Vincent family. Uncle Jack was left as a baby on the steps of a Liverpool Foundling Home and he was an example of one of those boys brought out of the institutions and bound apprentice on a fishing smack. He did well and after becoming mate on father's boat, became a skipper in his own right. He became father's brother-in-law when he married Aunt Lillie, one of mother's younger sisters. They had nine children, three girls and six boys, of whom our cousin Jack (later called 'Fighting Jack') was the eldest.

"I don't know how much money father and Uncle Jack put up, probably about a hundred to two hundred pounds a-piece, you didn't need a tremendous lot to get started then, enough to buy the boxes, the labels and the tallies. It's incredible when I think of it now, because neither of them had any idea about selling, contacting buyers, the whole business of marketing as we know it today. But that is how lots of little businesses began on the docks—so they started off, 'Haynes and Vincent'.

"It was actually a very good partnership, our cousin, Jack Vincent, went to Clee Grammar School and had been quite a bright pupil. It turned out that he had a very astute business brain, although he was no salesman, he didn't have the right personality for it. My brother Jack had left the ordinary Council School when he was fourteen and he had little business sense. However, he was a man's man and very popular as a young man, people took to him and he had this flair which made him a success as a salesman.

"They got on quite well for a time but things became a bit tough when the post war boom in fishing was followed by a depression. Jack went everywhere on his motorbike, not only round Lincolnshire but as far as Leicester, Coventry and Birmingham. Years later, after World War II when I had joined the Ross Group, I met a buyer in Coventry who still remembered him with affection and was delighted to find out I was his brother. (See note 15.)

"One of the things that stood Jack in good stead was his very, very, good memory. He was a member of the 'Antediluvian Order of Buffaloes', a working man's organization equivalent to the Masons. He memorized all the ritual and in after years, when he had broken off his partnership with our cousin, and lived in Aylesbury, he became Grand Master for Buckinghamshire and he was noted for his wonderful grasp of the rules and all the details of the membership in the county."

The move to Aylesbury: During the war, fish stocks in the North Sea were given time to recover, and in the immediate post-war period fishermen did well. Unfortunately, Grandfather was not able to enjoy this boom time for more than three or four years:

"Father did very well after the war, for a while, but his health finally broke down and for a long period he was unable to go to sea. But the free spending continued at home. There was always money behind the clock in the living room and when it was gone, father would say, 'Jack, you will have to go down to the bank and draw some more money out'. I don't know how it was, but perhaps he was advised by his bank manager to invest in a business. It so-happened that Charles was working in a Wine and Spirits Shop to gain experience and this led father to look for a Wine and Spirits business. My goodness, very luckily, they came up with this plum, in Buckinghamshire, in the heart of England, lovely and warm for father: a wine store in the middle of Aylesbury, and a house at least two hundred years old.

"Charles and father went down to see it and when it was all decided, and we made the move, Frank and I went down in the furniture van. I was about twelve or thirteen years old at that time and Frank about fourteen, so we had a most exciting journey down through England."

These reminiscences of Father have required a little more editing and rearrangement than Mother's, as they were recorded over a longer period of time, towards the end of his life, and also include notes made after conversations. As a very successful salesman, he was a great storyteller and fond of embellishing his anecdotes with direct speech (as Mother said, "Your father always liked to dramatize everything"). I have edited this out if he was not actually present at the incident described, while at the same time trying to stay as close as possible to a verbatim account, so that his true voice comes over with all his characteristic energy and enthusiasm for life.

I am greatly in debt to my cousin, Ian Harper (the grandson of my Father's eldest brother, Jack) for the details of the Haynes/Cooper family trees.

1) The Lancet, 16/8/02. Item quoted by David Derbyshire in the Telegraph.

2) *The Toughest Job in the World,* Henry Morgan, 1954, E. T. Heron & Co. London.

Henry Morgan (an ex-miner) was president of the National Fish Fryers Association. He was a friend of my father (one of the Directors of the Ross Group) who invited him to take a trip on their trawler, *Laforey,* to experience life at sea. He made two trips and then after the tragic loss of the *Laforey* with all twenty of the crew, wrote an account of his voyages, with the proceeds of his book going to the Grimsby Fishermen's Dependent's Fund. Father's second wife, Edith, was responsible for the highly appropriate title. An excellent account of deep-sea fishing, it was republished in serial form, with a large number of extra photographs, by the Grimsby Evening Telegraph in May and June 1991.

3) *Grimsby, the World's Premier Fishing Port.* 1956. The Grimsby Fishing Vessel Owner's Association. E. D. J. Burrow & Co. Ltd. Cheltenham and London.

4) The resistance of the cod-liner men to trawling was not without good reason. A primitive trawl, the 'wondyrechoon' had been used in the Thames in mediaeval times but was banned in the time of Edward III, because it disturbed the spawning grounds. After William of Orange landed in Brixham at the time of the Glorious Revolution (1688), the Dutch trawl was introduced and its use gradually spread round the South Coast reaching the East Coast in the nineteenth century. It should be pointed out that bottom-fishing long-lining for cod is different from pelagic long-lining, where the hooks and bait are dragged along near surface and which is much more damaging environmentally because of the 'by-catch'.

5) Greenwich as an Ancient fishing port. Mrs. Thomas Norledge, 1915. *Transactions of the Greenwich and Lewisham Antiquarian Society.* Vol.1, pages 356-372.

6) *British Sea-Fishermen.* Peter F. Anson, 1944. William Collins, London.

7) *Sea Fishing Apprentices of Grimsby.* David Boswell, 1974.

8) *Grimsby Fish.* Charles Ekburg. 1984. Barracuda Books Ltd. Buckingham. (Jacket Printed by Cheney and Sons, Banbury.)

Charlie Ekberg, the son of the Finnish Consul and a Grimsby woman, was a journalist and a good friend of my father. His book is a very fine, balanced account of the history of fishing from Grimsby and the 'Cod Wars'. Grandfather, 'Lucky Jack' of the *Othello* is featured in the photograph of a postcard entitled 'The World's largest Fishing Port' on page 12, top left, second from left, mending a net; Father on a photograph on page 144, top right, and his cousin, 'Fighting Jack' Vincent, on page 104, top left, and 105, top right.

9) *The Sea Fisheries of Great Britain and Ireland*. George L. Alward, 1932. Albert Gate, Grimsby.

10) *Sailing Trawlers*. Edgar J. March.1953, Percival Marshall& Co.

11) Grandfather's Board of Trade 'Continuous Certificate of Discharge,' shows that he took command of the *Andlo* and then the *Kelso* in 1917, presumably after this period as a pilot. Two hundred and ninety eight Grimsby steam trawlers were lost during World War I, the majority through enemy action, that is, one every five days. The *Othello* survived these hostilities and Grandfather was able to take command of her again in February 1919, finally being discharged in July 1920, presumably being too ill to continue prior to the move to Aylesbury the following year. The last entry in the log-book shows that he was re-engaged on his old vessel in July 1928, but there are no further entries. The *Othello* was eventually sunk in the Second World War.

12) Grimsby in the early days was not only known for 'Fishing' but also for 'Fighting', somewhat in the manner of the Rhondda and Merthyr Tydfil, the nursery of fine boxers like Jimmy Wilde, 'the ghost with the hammer', and Tommy Farr (another hero of my father) who went the full distance with Joe Louis, the world champion heavyweight. Ramshackle industrial growth with inadequate policing, similarly led to a reliance on fists in settling disputes, and every self-respecting young man was expected to 'learn to look after himself'. Not only young men; my Aunt Irene, closest sister to Father, remembered being put up on a chair to be taught how to deliver a straight left and of sparring with the boys.

13) The medals were presented by Colonel Oram, of the 3rd Manchester Regiment, and the zeppelin raid occurred on the 16th of April, 1916. Thirty-one men were killed when the Baptist Church in Alexander Road, Grimsby took a direct hit.

14) It may have been at these Schoolboy Championships that Father was presented with two pairs of professional boxing gloves, as a runner up, by Jimmy Wilde. My brothers and I liked using these 'real' boxing gloves because they were less padded over the knuckles than our sparring gloves, although they were much too big for us. There were black labels on the wrists with gold letters, which indicated that the gloves were presented by the world, flyweight champion.

15) Father was reticent about the reasons for the breakup of 'Haynes and Vincent'. It may have been a quarrel or, more to do with his brother's personal difficulties. He 'got a girl into trouble' and had to get married, which scandalized his strict Baptist parents (a matter of much greater moment in those days than now). This may have been behind his sudden departure from Grimsby.

Fighting Jack Vincent went on to build up the wholesale firm and demonstrated his keen business sense when he amalgamated with J. Carl Ross, a pioneer builder of oil fired trawlers in the 1930's.They became partners in Trawlers Grimsby Ltd, which then integrated trawler construction, fishing and marketing. Interestingly, he appears to have been the only person to serve, both as Chairman of the Grimsby Fish Merchants Association and as President of the Trawler Owners Association. Father's cousin showed the same insight when in 1948, he tempted Father away from a small publishing firm he had established in partnership with a friend called Peter Hoy (Sentinel Press, Soho) to spearhead the marketing and sales side; Father therefore returned to Grimsby right at the beginning of the introduction of 'Quick Freezing" and began the sale of fish in plastic packs. In 1953, he was given a seat on the Board as Sales and Advertising Director. The firm became very successful in the fifties and sixties and was renamed the Ross Group in 1958, when it had a fleet of 45 trawlers almost equally split between near-water, mid- and distant-water fishing.

An encounter revealing of these new developments occurred when Father was asked to escort Lady Mortimer Wheeler round the docks. He picked her up from her hotel at 6am and found her well prepared with thick rubber boots and mackintosh:

"I took her down the docks to see the trawlers landing their catch, fish splashing about. Then she watched the boxes being put on lorries and dispatched from the pontoons in the old-fashioned way. I lamented that it was not very hygienic by modern standards and took her into our factory to see the fish packed in the modern way: the girls in their overalls and hats, hygiene, hygiene, hygiene. I carried on about this over our bacon and eggs later, and finally, exasperated, she burst out, 'Please don't talk any more about hygiene because I've spent a considerable time on digs outside the walls of Jericho. The muck and filth was indescribable, and what with the flies on our food you can imagine what it was like; but when you and I were brought up, we did get flies on our food and we did get sick and have diarrhea when we were young, and how fortunate, because we are quite immune to the things that young people get today. So I'm fed up with all this talk of hygiene!'".

Jack Vincent showed his ruthless business side during the 'Cod Wars', which broke out when Iceland extended its fishing limits to four miles in 1952. He then became, as Charlie Ekberg put it (8), the 'Implacable enemy of Iceland', and in response to their exclusion from near-shore, Icelandic waters, the Trawler Owners Association, in retaliation, banned Iceland trawlers from the market. When George Dawson tried to beat the ban, by bringing in the Icelanders' fish in his own vessel, Fighting Jack ('The White Haired Wizard of Fish', as a local newspaper called him) savagely undercut his prices and drove him out of business.

Iceland and Norway gradually extended their fishing limits further, to 200 miles in 1974. This meant the end for the Grimsby deep-sea fishing fleet, but not for Grimsby as a great fish distribution center. With nice symmetry, it has returned to the position it held in mediaeval times. There is, also, a certain symmetry in that the three generations of the Haynes family covered the entire history of the rise and fall of trawling from the port.

In fairness to Father, he told me privately that he sympathized with the desire of the Icelanders to protect their fish stocks, and thought that we should have done the same. He was greatly saddened by the final outcome. On a final note, when the Hanson Group took over the Ross Group, in 1968, Jack Vincent retired as a millionaire. The Haynes's as usual, contrived not to gather any moss. Indeed, not only did Father have very few shares in the company but when he was made redundant it appeared that there were no arrangements for him to receive a proper pension. Apparently, it was only through the friendly intervention of a fellow director (Mr. Alexander) that a halfway adequate pension was finally paid to him. This meant that he and Edith (his second wife) had to sell their property in Humberstone Avenue, with its extensive grounds and orchard, and move into a small two-bedroom bungalow. He then cut himself off from most of his former business friends and active social life. Inevitably there were times in later life that feelings of bitterness broke through his usual urbanity. (Fortunately, he did keep up his golf—-handicap 12, and contact with some of his golfing friends.)

CHAPTER 3

AYLESBURY IN THE 1920s

MY FATHER'S MEMORIES

The Wine Shop: My father's family moved to Aylesbury some time in the summer of 1921, before he was thirteen, and when his brother Frank had turned fourteen. The wine and spirits business and adjacent butchers' shop (Tilbury's) were at the top of Walton Street, nos. 4 and 6, opposite the White Swan Hotel, near the junction with the Market Square (see note 1—photo 65a). All the top, west side of Walton Street, including these properties, together with much of the west side of the Market Square, was demolished in the early 1960s to make way for new council offices, a new library and a shopping centre (unfortunately, in the then current, concrete and glass 'brutalist' style). My father's memories of his old home are therefore of some interest (see photos 3-1, top left).

"It was a lovely, double-fronted place, with the shop on the left and a store on the right in which there were pipes (large casks) of wine for doing the filling and bottling; and underneath was a big cellar for the expensive wines and spirits. Behind the shop was a large lounge leading into a conservatory and up stone steps into a lovely garden where Mr. Fowler, the previous owner, a rose lover, had laid out different beds, perhaps a dozen, for the different roses. In the far corner was a bit of a lawn and a rockery where you could sit and admire them. Upstairs, over the lounge, there was a big kitchen, a nice room looking over the garden. Then we were in rooms at the top, where there were four bedrooms. The trouble was that down below there was only this huge lounge, so mother didn't know what to do with all our furniture. She hadn't thought about it before coming and a lot of it had to go back in the vans to Grimsby to store and sell, which was distressing for her! But the business was a very good business. We used to bottle our own port and sherry at Christmas time, from huge casks—sealing them and putting a label on them—J.C. Haynes & Sons, you know. We were all expected to pitch in and help; and in those early days, as soon as I'd got home from school, I often had to go out on the bicycle we had, with a big basket on the front, to deliver an order, sometimes miles away."

'Six of the best': Aylesbury Grammar School, which began in a chapel of St. Mary's Church, later occupied buildings in St. Mary's Square and Church Street (now the County Museum). It was here that my uncle, 'Chub' Wheeler, was admitted in 1900. Then, in 1907, the school was removed to new premises in Walton Road (see note 1—Photo 53a). It seems that Father was given a place there in the autumn of 1921, a little before his thirteenth birthday. Father could easily walk to school, straight down Walton Street, past the canal basin to the junction with Walton Road and then down by Walton Pond with its Aylesbury ducks. More directly, he could go via the Market Square under the arch of the Corn Exchange and down through the cattle market to a lane that leads to a footbridge over the canal and then up Highbridge Road by Queen's Park Council School, a route I was to take myself many years later when I briefly attended both these schools. Father greatly enjoyed school, being good at all sports. The photo (photos 9-1) shows him when he was the youngest, and apparently, the smallest member of the cricket team. He went on to become captain of both the cricket team and the football team by the time he was fifteen. He didn't shine quite so brightly academically, although good at English, French and geography, and he boasted that he regularly got one or other of the girls to do his homework. When we were children, my sister, Ann, and I discovered a pile of his old exercise books in the corner of the parental wardrobe and were delighted to discover that he regularly scored nought for his chemistry homework. Presumably, he couldn't find a girlfriend prepared to do his homework for him in that subject.

The Headmaster, when Father attended the school, was Thomas Osborne, and the way he built up the teaching staff after his appointment to the new school in 1907 is described in the commemorative volume by Bill Mead (see note 2). To let my father speak:

"I did a lot of sport, got into the team and very much enjoyed it. We had a wonderful sports master, Harry Deeming (also English master). We had a very tough Headmaster, Osborne, and he was building the foundation of what became a damn good grammar school—-one of the best in the country. He didn't hesitate to give you six of the best, either, on the backside or on your hands, for any misdemeanors, and it didn't do anyone any harm. For instance—-one day I had one of those rubber catapults for firing bits of paper at my pals and the form master caught me at it and sent me out to wait by the Headmaster's office. Old Osborne came along, 'What have you been sent out for? Right, come into my office. Where will you have them?' I said, 'On the hands, Sir.' 'All on one?' he said, 'No, two on each, Sir.' Bang! Bang! Bang! Bang! 'Did you wince, Haynes?' 'No Sir.' 'Good, and let me tell you, Haynes, that if you had dipped those pellets in ink beforehand you would have got six and a detention. Go back to your class,' and swishing the cane at me, added, 'Don't let me see you again.' Back in the classroom: 'Did it hurt?': 'No it didn't', all this. One of my pals said 'Where did you have it, on the hands? I always think it's better to have it on the backside because he always gives you an extra one on the backside when you go out anyway!'"

Photos 3-1 Aylesbury during the 1920s

Top left-: The rose garden behind the wine shop in 1923, now occupied by the Civic Centre.
Top right-: Father's youngest brother Norman; an eye for girls and dogs.
Middle-: A rare photo of Grannie Haynes, on the right outside Clee Church on the occasion of the marriage of her second daughter Irene.
Bottom-: A.G.S. 1st Eleven in 1923. Father then fourteen years old, second left at the back, standing next to Harry Deeming, sports master as well as English master at the time.

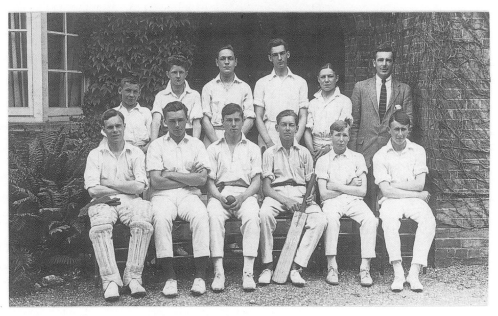

His brother Frank: Although Father quickly found a place in the Grammar School there were difficulties in the case of his older brother, Frank:

"Although I went straight into the Grammar School because there was a vacancy in my age group, unfortunately, there was no vacancy for Frank. He was then fourteen and a half, so he didn't actually have to go back to school, and it so happened that while he was waiting for a vacancy, someone came in and told father that a bright young man was wanted in the coroner's office, just down the street. So instead of going back to school, Frank found himself going down to be interviewed by Mr. Wilkins, who was a solicitor as well as the county coroner, and getting the job. This was in some ways a pity, and something he often regretted later, because he was very bright and in the top form in St. James and would have gone to University in another era. Anyhow, the junior solicitors took to him and, eventually, he was articled to Mr. Wilkins and got through all his exams; he was very good, disciplined about that," (see note 3 and photos 4-2).

Social life and the Congregational Church: Although Father had been a probationer in the choir of the Anglican Church in Grimsby, he eventually began going to the Sunday school of the Congregational Church in Aylesbury. I have given my mother's memories of Sunday school in Chapter 2 but it is worth recording my father's as well, not only because they confirm and amplify her account but because it was clearly a major element in their social life at an important phase of their early youth and led to his choice of career. It also illustrates very well that neither of their families were at all bigoted in matters of religion. As Father said:

"When we came down to Aylesbury, I had a note of recommendation from the vicar of St. James Church in Grimsby to give to the vicar and choirmaster at St. Mary's, so that I could join the choir. But before I got round to doing this I became friendly with a boy who attended the Congregational Church and one day he invited me to go with him that evening to their youth club in the High Street. They had a couple of big tables for table tennis, a billiard table and you could play darts and dominoes. It was held twice a week. I enjoyed my visit to the club and a week or two later, my friend invited me to go again. Afterwards, he said 'I won't be able to invite you again, Rolly, because I can only do it twice. But why don't you join our Sunday school class?' So I said, 'I'm supposed to go to church, but I'll talk to my mother.'

"I told mother that I was no longer bothered about getting into the choir. Also, that I hadn't really taken to the vicar who seemed so different in the pulpit compared with his attitude in the vestry, which made it seem artificial. So mother, who was a Baptist herself, said she would look into it for me. Apparently, the Congregational Church was founded in the time of Henry VIII, or one Henry's time. It was midway between high and low, something in the middle (see note 4). Anyhow, mother said I could go to the Sunday school, and there I occasionally had the pleasure of listening to the great J. Thompson Gerald (Jarrold?), who was an incredibly good speaker. What a difference compared with the Anglican Church. It was redbrick inside with brass candlesticks, I remember daffodils—-it must have been springtime—-but no ostentation, when I first heard him speak. I've never forgotten it—-he just came to the front and began quite naturally, 'When I was coming along today I couldn't help noticing,' and so he gradually worked into a sermon. He always made these everyday links. There might be a quotation but it was never taken from some verse in the Gospel, leading to a high faluting sermon unrelated to everyday things. That was the characteristic of his sermons they always did seem to relate to one's life.

"The most important Sunday school teacher was Mr. Yea. He took the senior boys' Bible class, while the senior girls went with Winnie Hunt. He used to say, 'If there is anything that bothers you about the Bible, then we'll discuss it.' I remember that I once told him that I didn't think prayer could be that important because my particular view of God, was that he would say, 'Get up and do something about it and don't come appealing to me'. On the one hand, prayers did seem sometimes to be answered miraculously, but on the other, in perhaps more deserving cases they were not, for instance, a widow praying to God to make her wayward son a good boy, with no sign that it worked. What bothered me was that prayer sometimes seemed to work, perhaps by coincidence, and sometimes it didn't. Mr. Yea found this difficult to answer, with all the other chaps throwing in their points of view. But he made it a discussion, which you looked forward to, you see. (Mr. Yea was employed by the County Council Health Department.)

"Mr. Yea also took charge of the club on the Tuesdays and Wednesdays and he was keen on table tennis himself. In those days we all played using the ordinary grip, with finger and thumb, but one year he invited the winning Hungarian team down from London, I don't know who paid the bills (presumably the Church). Our first team had to play them and I was in the team. Of course we were absolutely whitewashed, but one chap did win one game! It was then we realized, from their style of play, that the best grip was to hold the bat across your hand, for both forehand and backhand play. So I tried to adopt this style and naturally for a while I didn't win anything, but eventually I did win our little championship. The following year when I had perfected this grip with a flick, I became quite a good exponent—-entirely due to Mr. Yea inviting the Hungarian team down. It entirely altered the scene in table tennis for us and we began to win lots of interclub matches, until it became the general thing. Although, strangely enough, I think the Chinese still play in the old way today."
(Note-My cousin, James Robins, tells me that the Hungarian team was led by Victor Barna, the world champion, who was famous for the 'Barna flick' with the backhand.)

Going to work at Hunt Barnard's: Although Father greatly enjoyed school, he was to leave at fifteen before taking the School Certificate:

"The reason I've told you so much about the 'Cons' (Congregational Church) is because I met Winnie Hunt there. She was the daughter of George T. Hunt, the chairman of Hunt Barnard and Co. the printers in Aylesbury. There was an older daughter, Nellie, and a son Leonard. His wife was a lovely, charming, old-fashioned woman and they had a beautiful house in Church Street. One evening at the club, when Mr. Yea and Winnie Hunt were both there, Winnie said, 'what are you going to do when you leave school, Roland?' I was fifteen at the time and thinking about a job with the big brewers, Watney, Coombe and Reed, up in London. If I got my School Certificate I could join them as an apprentice. I explained this to Winnie Hunt and she said, 'I see, following your father's business. If you haven't made up your mind, you might be interested in a job with us in printing; we have a vacancy in the office. Perhaps you would like to come and see the works?' This was fatal of course, because, you see, once I saw the printing machines and all what was happening, I was so interested that I thought, 'I like this and it means I don't have to leave Aylesbury.' Anyhow, Mr. Hunt came to see father. Of course, he had to come through the Wine Shop and although the Hunts were not strictly teetotal, they were very much against the abuse of 'strong drink'! So mother and father made him welcome, 'cup of tea, Mr. Hunt' etc. Father was concerned that it might be a dead end job but Mr. Hunt reassured him, saying, 'You have my promise. He won't just be an office boy. I'll make sure he learns the business of printing. We are very fond of Roland and I am sure he will do well.' So Mum and Dad agreed and I started my training, getting ten shillings a week (50p).

"Hunt Barnard's were very good printers. They did a lot of work for publishers like Hodder and Stoughton, Marshall, Morgan and Scott, Galloways and Shaw's. They printed a host of these Sunday school prizes and those slips given out at Sunday school, which you stick in a book in order to be able to go on the Sunday school treat!

"When I started work the firm was in Granville Street on the corner into Buckingham Street, right in the middle of Aylesbury. George Hunt and his wife ran a mission in Lisson Grove, up in London, for deprived boys and he had brought some of these boys down to train as apprentices, and they lived in a hostel. The firm originally had a place in Blandford Street in West London, which they closed down, bringing all the work people and the machinery down to Aylesbury. But the move was a disaster, because the London families couldn't settle down and the rates of pay were lower and became a matter of great dissension with the men. So eventually the litho printing went back to London and the letterpress side was retained in Aylesbury.

"I had to be an early bird and get to the office by 8 o'clock. Our family tended to be late, because the Wine Shop never opened until 10 o'clock. At Walton Street then, I found myself the first one up, making the early morning tea and mother saying, like most mothers, 'That's the best cup of tea of the day, Roland, don't forget to have some breakfast.' So I would make tea for father and mother and Nora then make my own breakfast, as I was quite independent. 'Have some bacon and eggs, Roland.' Then Nora would chip in, 'Don't you have two eggs,' thinking of the housekeeping, because she was in charge. But mother would say, 'you have two eggs if you want them, Roland, going out on these cold mornings.' All this happened, because although the kitchen was away from the rest of the house, it was close to the bedrooms. In those days we used to get through three score eggs a week, with ten of us and plenty of cakes and puddings. We used to go out to Meadle for them, a little farm, to get these fresh eggs. Of course, Nora got worried because we always seemed hungry, and she had to keep control or she would come home and find we had eaten all the bread and used up the potatoes making chips.

"I enjoyed it very much in the Granville Street office. The manager was Sam Johnson, and he took me under his wing. I found myself helping him, making out work tickets, answering the phone and gradually learning about the business. One day, taking some directions down in longhand over the phone, for corrections in a galley proof, I suddenly remembered that it would be quicker in shorthand.

"We sent out long galley proofs for each book and there would be corrections and when there were only a few, we would take them over the phone: 'Galley number 5, ten lines down, in place of such-and-such, substitute so-and-so.' But it was more critical in page proofs, where if an alteration was made it had to be the same number of characters to fit in, otherwise, you had to push the type from page to page until you got to a chapter ending. This made me realize that it would be very beneficial if I brushed up my shorthand again.

"So that autumn, I joined evening classes and took shorthand and bookkeeping. After the first term I gave up bookkeeping but I kept up the shorthand and it all came back amazingly quickly. In the first examination I did 80 words a minute, and in the second, a year later, 120 words a minute. I was now able to take down messages from the phone with great ease. When asked, 'Am I going too quickly,' I could say, 'No, please continue.' I could then type out the correction, clip it to the galley and go straight up to the composing room with it. So this was much quicker, and had the advantage of cheapness over the phone. It came in useful in many ways later.

"Mr. Hunt kept his word about my training. In those days, the apprentices all trained over seven years, starting at fourteen, whether they were in the machine room, the composing room, the warehouse or the bindery. The biggest printers in the area were Hazell, Watson and Viney's and together with all the other master printers in Buckinghamshire made up the Bucks Alliance. Hazell's was big enough to put on extra courses for the apprentices, with very good instructors (see note 1—photo 52a). So once a week I went with each group in turn, the composing room apprentices, the machine room apprentices and the binders. When there were visits to see papermaking I joined the party, we went to the Apsley Mills, Nash Mills and Dickinson mills in Hemel Hempstead. In those days, Dickinsons were pure paper makers, making a variety of papers and envelopes. When we had been through the factories we had to write an essay on papermaking and I won first prize, three pounds worth of books, which of course, I spent on books about printing. Then we saw the ink making in Hazell's own plant over in Southcourt. We also went up to

London to see block making and engraving. Altogether, it gave me quite a good training and by the end I had acquired quite a good knowledge of printing.

"There was a wonderful variety of printing, including colour work. We printed several magazines: all the Liberty catalogues, and one for Laxtons, the nurserymen; religious booklets—-anti-Catholic propaganda, like the 'Red scourge of Rome', because they were strongly nonconformist and didn't see any good in the wonderful Catholic religion! The pamphlets used to roll off the press for bodies like 'The Evangelical Union of South America.' We also printed 'Living Waters' by a Miss A. M. Boyse of Bournemouth and a monthly with four sermons by P. I. Beeman Kirfield of Hook in Hampshire. One of the biggest projects was 'Spurgeon's Sermons', a huge publication for parsons who needed help in composing their own, which hadn't been reprinted for twenty years. 'John Ploughman's Pictures' was another.

"We also did travel books, 'Livingstone on the Zambezi and his adventures in Africa', as well as some marvelous instruction books by an Egyptian called Mapius, and language texts. It was quite incredible, the variety of work, from ready reckoners to Jemima Puddleduck, and the prosperity of the firm at that time.

"One profitable contract we had was with John F. Shaw, for big print runs of large books with large print to be given mainly as Sunday school prizes. Printed sections of 8 to 16 pages with different stories were kept in stock as separate 'sigs'. Different combinations of the sigs were bound in volumes, each with a different paste-on title, like, 'Summer Days', 'By the Sea' or 'Holiday Time.' Of course, if you won more than one or two you would find that you had read all the stories before! When we needed to print more sigs, it was not done from the valuable 'founder's type', but from plates made by pressing several sheets of paper, which had been rolled together wet, called a throng, over the original type. The throng, when it was dried, was put in another press and hot metal was poured over it. When it was pulled out you had a plate with the type in reverse and you could print a number of runs from it. (Note-In these days of photographic reproduction, this 'hot metal' process is less and less used, except for special purposes.)

"Something else we printed and I'll never forget it because we worked on them so many times, were Allison Bread wrappers. Unlike now when Allisons Bread comes fully wrapped, in those less hygienic days it was sold with a simple band round the middle, about 20 inches long by 3 inches wide. These were printed on huge sheets of 30 by 40 inch, Quad Crown Furnival, and cut up afterwards. Sam would say, 'check the stock of Allison Bread wrappers, Ro. we need to give them a bit more work in the machine room: alright, we'll print another 10,000.' So the old Furnival would begin to roll again. Sometimes we never seemed to do anything else but print these bread wrappers!"

In trouble with _Roman Studies_: Hunt Barnard's also printed certain journals and Father found this work particularly interesting:

"We also printed the *Archaeological Journal* and the *Journal of Roman Studies*. This work was very interesting because many of the contributors eventually became famous, Professors and people going round the world doing these digs, such as Mortimer Wheeler. I had to go up to London on the train once, to give him some late proofs that had to be ready for a council meeting the next morning. Normally, all the work connected with *Roman Studies* went to the Editor, who was a Miss N. V. Taylor, M.A., F.S.A., 45, Woodstock Road, Oxford, a very capable woman. Her ancestors were, I believe, connected with the Museum (Ashmolean?) in Oxford, that huge building in the Broad in Oxford, opposite the Randolph Hotel. She was an extremely efficient woman, and I had the pleasure of calling on her when some 'separates' (separate copies of short papers by the different authors) were late and I had to take some over by bus.

"We would print 200 to 400 copies of the separate papers as they came in and by the end of the year we would have from six to ten in the store. Each paper would then be folded and sown, uncut, with a wrap-round cover stuck to the back. Miss Taylor would send these out to the authors and to the members of the committee before the journal was put together, whereas we sent the bound volume of all the papers out ourselves.

"It so happened, that when Sam Johnson was away and I had to take responsibility and run the show, that we had a big problem with the bound volumes for the year. Joe Munday, the binder, came in and said, 'What about this then, Roland?' He showed me the spine of one of the volumes and I looked at it and said, 'Is there something wrong with the volume number?': 'No, read it again Ro.' So, I read it again, like a trained Reader, instead of reading what I thought was there—- JOURNAL OF ROMAN SUDIES . They had missed the T out. 'How did this happen, Joe?': 'Well, the type had worn and they took it out and forgot to reset it. The copies have all been printed and they have to go off this week!'

"I was shattered. I rang through to our paper department and found that we only had enough brown buckler, cover paper, a lovely brown colour, for another 50 copies. I then rang the paper makers, Smith's, and they were closed. At this point, the boss, Mr. Hunt came in to see how things were going, so I showed him the bound volume. 'Good,' he said 'Carry on.' Should I tell him, I thought; he'll hit the roof! No, I'll ring Sam at his home; but he was not available, so I decided we should just have to wait until the morning.

"As soon as Sam came in, I showed him the volume. 'Oh,' he said, 'Good,' but when I showed him the fault he went to the window with his hands over his ears, he was very religious, and appealed to God Almighty! He then made an incredible, rather brave, decision: he went straight to the machine room with those blank covers that were left and had them printed correctly; these went to the members of the committee. The bulk copies, with incorrect titles, were sent off, and they are in different universities and libraries round the world to this day. We waited for someone to write in to us about it, but no one ever did!

"A great joke was made about it in the office, because no one spotted it until it reached the bindery. The reason Joe Munday saw it was because in those days the binding was not done automatically, but by hand, the covers being gummed down by being pulled over a xylonite stick, like a straight shoehorn; doing that he suddenly saw the error. Mistakes will happen, because things can go wrong all the way through, especially in the comping (type setting). It always upset the House when we got these big spelling mistakes. On one occasion, we had printed a new edition of the 'Engineer', a well-known British trade magazine, with a big advert for 'British Timpkin' on the front page. Unfortunately, it read 'British Tigmen'! We had to print their next ad free. Today you would say, 'Any mistake is a good one, as long as the names are spelt right.' But printers do tend to get very upset and blow up over mistakes like that.

"The whole business of 'Reading' is very interesting. You either have the gift, or you haven't. Usually it's an ex-comp that graduates to 'Reading'. In Hunt Barnard's they were fortunate in having an extremely good 'Reader' and I had a few months with him. If you made a mistake you always had to look the word up, and if it was very difficult, he made you write it out six times straight away. Although he had never learnt Latin or any foreign language, he was so good, that he got a letter every year from the committee of the *Journal of Roman Studies*, complimenting him on the quality of the 'Reading'. Some of these Professors would send in hand-written additions on odd scraps of paper. We could set Latin and Greek from the type box, you see. Somehow, he could 'Read' it perfectly, without any knowledge of the language."

A voyage to South Africa: Despite the interest of the work in Hunt Barnard's and his full social life (he was already 'walking out' with Mother) Father began to feel the ancestral pull of the sea:

"When I was seventeen I had the desire to see the world. I thought, with my shorthand and typing, I could apply to one of the shipping lines for a job on one of their boats. So I wrote to Cunard, and Union Castle and other companies. I had a reply from the Union Castle Line and I had to go up and see them. They hadn't got a vacancy but they said, 'We will hire you to go as a saloon boy, to work with the chief and second steward and do their typing, the menus and the office work they have to do. If you like it, then we will transfer you to a clerical post later.' 'I don't want to do waiting,' I said. But they said, 'It will be good experience.' The Hunts were upset but I don't know if they knew what was going to happen, that I was going to come back with my tail between my legs. They didn't fill my vacant post and apparently, Winnie said; 'I'm certain Roland will be back. I don't think that's the life he wants, when he finds out what it is really like.' And my goodness, I did!

"I went up to London to make the final arrangements. I had the name of a firm where I could buy kit and a cabin box. The gear cost about twelve pounds and the pay was a pound or so a week for the duration of the voyage, which was of three and a half months' duration. We sailed from London in the July of 1926, which was the year of the General Strike. All the men were prepared to walk off the ship if they got the chance, but the Captain extracted a promise from them when we embarked that they wouldn't on this particular trip. As it turned out, they didn't keep their word.

"We set off from London in the *Glen Gorm Castle,* an intermediate vessel for passengers and cargo, about 40-50 passengers in the first class, and about the same number in the second class. Our route was Tenerife, Ascension, St. Helena to Cape Town. We dropped mainly cargo at Tenerife. At Ascension, where the Government ran a radio and signalling station, the operatives and their families came on as their replacements got off. At St. Helena it was mainly dropping off cargo again with one or two people getting on or off. But at Cape Town the whole crew walked off and stayed in a special camp, so we were in harbour for a few weeks. For me, and some of the others, it was a wonderful opportunity to go and look round ashore, to climb Table Mountain and to go up country on the train.

"I had one peculiar experience. I saw a cinema advertised and I went in but there was no pay box. The attendant said, 'You sit and see the film but you must take tea afterwards.' So I went in, saw the picture and then they brought me a tray with a pot of tea, a sandwich and a cake. You paid for it and then went out after eating it. I've never experienced anything like that before or since, but it was quite pleasant.

"In those days the blacks shuffled along the streets and it was quite obvious they were the depressed classes. This was brought home to me later in the trip. When the crew finally agreed to come back on board, the voyage continued round the coast to East London and Durban and then to Lourenco Marques and Beira (in Portuguese East Africa). We went ashore at some ports and not in others where in those days there were no docks and goods and passengers went ashore by tender. One day when we were unloading into a tender at Beira, one of the ship's officers who had put a bait of pork out, caught a shark. It was not particularly large, about 7 or 8 feet long, and he was able to pull it onto the deck. The men unloading the boat were all black and were sitting around waiting for operations to begin when the shark was pulled aboard. They all raced towards it with their knives to cut chunks off it, but the Portuguese master went amongst them whipping and beating them to make them back off. Then someone cut the teeth out before the rest of the carcass was thrown back overboard. It was quite an interesting side-glance at the lives of those poor devils.

"The work on the ship was interesting. I typed the menus and kept simple records, but of course, as a saloon boy I only helped with waiting to begin with. I saw how everything was very carefully done, laying the tables, even filling the mustard pots—-no spot had to touch the sides. Everything had to be done correctly and the flowers properly arranged, especially as it was the first class saloon. The steward would take me round the tables and say, 'What is wrong with this?' I was shown how the 'dumb waiter' worked and how to fold the table napkins into fantastic shapes, like swans or other things. Then I had to wait on the Chief Steward and

Second Steward. I had to do it from the correct side, and take away from the other, and listen to what they mumbled when I showed them the menu. They tried to show me what it was actually like, serving passengers.

"I must have done pretty well, because when we got to Beira, the Captain's servant or valet, they called him the Captain's 'Tiger', who used to wait on him as well, went on leave. So the Chief Steward told me I would have to take his place serving on the Captain's table. But he said, 'You won't hear what he says, so get hold of his 'Tiger' before he leaves the ship and find out what he usually has.' I suppose I didn't do too badly, but it was rather a nerve-racking experience.

"The trip home was uneventful. I suffered quite a lot with seasickness, every time we left port on another leg of the voyage, but I shall never forget going out on deck in the early dawn and at sunset. After we got back to Cape Town, instead of going to St. Helena and Ascension we sailed back directly to Tenerife, and then to London, arriving back on December 11th. I had already realized that although the food and conditions were very good, altogether it wasn't the kind of life I was going to like, because it would be the same trip all the time. You would have to change ships to get a change of environment otherwise it could become very boring. I'd also experienced the seamy side of shipboard life, because the saloon boys were considered fair game for the homosexuals in the crew. On the bigger ships the boys were in the charge of the head woman, but you were vulnerable if you weren't very careful on the smaller ships. There was one very persistent, aggressive homosexual on board, and in the end I had to give him a pasting. This solved the problem but didn't improve the atmosphere.

"I hadn't spent very much when on shore during the trip, which had eventually lasted five months, and I was able to pay my father back the outlay on my kit. So I hadn't been a great expense to him, and fortunately, shortly after I got home, I had a letter from Winnie Hunt, saying that she hoped I'd enjoyed the trip and got the idea of going to sea out of my system, and would I like my old job back?"

Mother's memories of this time: As Mother said, the first time she ever spoke to Father was when he came to walk his sister home on Boxing Day (? 1923) although they had both noticed each other at Sunday school, and Mother had seen Father on his bike with all the bottles in the basket, in the Market Square, riding along whistling. After they had met formally, they went out for long walks together, as boys and girls did in those days, and became sweethearts, although as Father said, "Sex never reared its ugly head: we just used to hold hands and kiss." I will let Mother describe what happened to her when he went away:

"Ro got the urge to join the Merchant Navy and he went as a trainee on one of those liners that sail between England and South Africa. I didn't know when I'd see him again, and some time after he had gone, I heard the girls in the office talking about a lovely young chap who had come to work in Janes the Chemists. So I made it my business to go there and ask for a box of Ponds face powder, which I used, girls didn't use much make-up then. I also thought he was nice.

"It so happened that there was a dance at the end of the week put on at the Church House. We started with the Paul Jones, a dance which got things going, where the boys went round in a ring on the outside and the girls held hands in a ring on the inside. When the music stopped the boys were supposed to dance with the girl opposite them. On this occasion, when the music stopped three boys jostled in front of me, including this nice boy from Janes the Chemists and the other two pushed him over on the slippery floor. True to the British instinct to help the underdog, I helped him up and when we danced I found out that his name was Don Pengelly, and that he was from Looe in Cornwall. He took me home from the dance that night and later to the fair in Kingsbury Square as well as for walks into the country. I discovered that he was studying pharmacy in Kings College, up in London, and that his father had a chemist's shop in the High Street in Looe. We were very attracted to each other, although he was about five years older than me, especially as we both played the piano and were fond of music. "After a few weeks Don had to go back to his digs in Clapham and continue his studies in London, but he wrote to me and he told me I was the first girl he had told his mother about. However, after some months, Ro came back to Aylesbury, having decided that he didn't like the life at sea, and one day we met by accident in the street and resumed our friendship. When Don wrote me another nice letter, I wrote back and said that I didn't want him to write to me anymore because my previous boy friend had returned from Africa. I afterwards regretted this.

"There was an interesting sequel, years later, when we had a holiday at Seaton in Cornwall, with you four children. As there was a nicer beach there we used to go over to Looe, which had fishing boats in the harbour as well as a sandy beach. One day, on the way through Looe, we stopped outside the Chemist's shop so that I could take in a film with snaps of the family on the beach. Over the shop it said, 'D. Pengelly & Son', so I naturally assumed it meant Don and his son. I hesitated about going in and Ro said, 'Go on, I know you want to go in,' and this gave me the courage to go in. There were a number of assistants and I waited until Don was free to serve me and asked for a box of Ponds peach coloured face powder. He gave me the box and then, as he put the change in my hand, to my amazement he said, 'Aylesbury, 16 years ago, so many months and so many days'. He wasn't married and I wondered if poor Don had been carrying a torch for me all those years! I rather regretted going into the shop, but I heard later that he did finally get married."

Father works at Hunt Barnard's again: After his experiences at sea, Father went back to his old life at Hunts with enthusiasm. As he said:

"I was very glad to be back at Hunt Barnard's, especially as it was the time of the move into the new factory, which was built on the outskirts of Aylesbury, at the end of Chiltern Street, and was designed by Hollis Hunt who was George Hunt's nephew (see note 1—photo 79a). Mr. Hunt's brother and sister-in-law had been missionaries in China and were killed in the massacre of foreigners that took place during the Boxer Risings. Hollis and his sister had been at the Choufou School, a public school where most of the missionaries' children were sent, so they escaped and eventually came back to England to be looked after by the Hunts.

"An amusing story is told of the time when Mr. Hunt went to meet his nephew and niece at the docks. Hollis grew up to be a huge fellow, six feet four inches and a barrel chest to match, a magnificent figure of a man, and he was very tall as a young boy. Apparently, Mr. Hunt spent a long time looking around for them until a ship's officer said, 'Yes Sir, they have arrived and there is young Mr. Hunt, Sir.' Mr. Hunt was only a little above five foot in height, and to his surprise he found that his 'little nephew' was bigger than he was!

"Hollis turned out to be a really first class fellow. He invented a number of mechanical things, including the first idea of an oil braking system for cars. He built his own car from separate parts and used to take his family down to Cornwall in it, to where he had converted a schooner into a holiday home, with berths taken from the old *Mauretania*. So he employed these talents in designing the new factory. In Granville Street we were split between several floors, which made it very inefficient, with paper and other things being carried up and down. The ideal for printing is the one floor factory, and this he was able to achieve on our magnificent new site, with the different units arranged logically. It meant, eventually, with quicker production, a lowering of costs. We also got new machinery, including a very fast American printing machine that we demonstrated when we had an exhibition in Aylesbury, opened by the Duke and Duchess of York (who later became George VI and Queen Elizabeth), printing a leaflet for the opening with their picture on it. By and large it became a very good and successful business."

Lucky Jack goes back to trawling: Shortly after Father came home from sea, his parents decided to sell the wine shop. As he said:

"It was about this time that father and mother decided to go back to Grimsby, despite the fact that they had a very good business in Aylesbury. We had a T- type Ford van and delivered orders over a wide area. I learnt to drive early in life, when I was seventeen or eighteen. There was no test in those days. If you could drive it you drove it. What Charles (his elder brother by four years) should have been doing, was canvassing for new business when we took orders out in to the country. For instance, we used to do a delivery to Loosely Road, near Princes Risborough, about twelve miles out. Well, later on when I was older, I would have called at places en-route and round about, telling them we could deliver wines and spirits, beer and lemonade and anything else they drank. But Charles, although he could now manage everything in the shop, didn't think to do any of that. So although we had a solid core of customers buying whisky and port, the business didn't develop as it should have done.

"The fact is, mother and father didn't have enough to do in the shop to keep themselves fully occupied and they found it hard to make new friends to replace close friends left behind in Grimsby. Father amused himself by studying the form of horses and betting over the phone and quite often went to the races. I remember one amusing incident when we went to Towcester Races with five of us in the back of the van. When we got out a policeman came over and asked Dad if he didn't think his van was overloaded. Dad pointed to the side of the van, where it was labelled, 'J.C. Haynes & Sons' and said, 'I'm J.C. Haynes, and these are my sons,' which sorted that problem out!

"Anyhow, father decided to go back to deep-sea trawling. The shop was sold to the Victoria Wine Company, with Charles staying on as manager, though they retained ownership of the butcher's shop next door. The younger children, Irene, Floss and Norman went back to Grimsby with them, while Frank and I stayed on with Charles in Aylesbury."

Although Father didn't mention how Grandfather's health was at this time, it seems that it had improved, and doubtless this was a factor in his decision to return to sea, where, of course, with luck, the returns were greater than in the rather static wine and spirits business. No doubt too, he was finding the shopkeeper's life increasingly boring, compared with the adventurous (gambling) life of a trawler skipper. He must certainly have missed catching the morning tide, and in the calm of a summer dawn, leaving the harbour behind and feeling the first, swelling lift of the open sea with its far horizons (see note 5).

AN UNTIMELY ARRIVAL

A personal 'tragedy': When Father came back from his voyage to South Africa he called at Mother's home in New Street but she was out. By a 'quirk of fate' as he said, he later met her out walking with a friend, who tactfully left them to have a talk, and from that time they began 'to walk out together again,' (see photos 3-2).

They were in many ways well suited. Although Father didn't play a musical instrument, he loved listening to Mother playing the piano and singing. Both of them loved books and poetry and were keen on sport. They both enjoyed tennis, Father being particularly good, being able to put a vicious spin on the ball and send it away from you on either side. He won a number of cups for it, at this time, as he did for swimming.

Although fairly small for his age in his early teens, Father rapidly made up for this and by his late teens was coming near to his eventual height of 5 foot 10 inches. He had black hair with gray eyes (his mother's were hazel) and something I was conscious of from earliest childhood, very smooth, clear, facial skin. Mother was eventually quite tall, reaching 5 foot 4 inches, with black, naturally curly hair and velvet brown eyes. She had quite broad shoulders, big hands and feet, the long straight nose of her mother and the Brooks line, as well as a characteristic gap between her front teeth.

They both shared in the religious and social life of the 'Cons'. However, by her late teens Mother had reacted strongly against a literal interpretation of the Bible. When she read through the Old Testament herself, she was 'appalled', to the point of thinking that it would be better banned, or at least completely detached from the New Testament. She took up an extreme position, going beyond Unitarianism, and considered Jesus to have been simply a very good man who had shown through his teaching that we create heaven and hell here on earth by our actions; and 'live on' through our effect on the lives of others. Father, at that stage of his life, still retained more traditional beliefs. In his early teens, under the influence of Winnie Hunt, he had for a while thought of being a missionary. Late in his life, he asked me if I believed in an 'afterlife' and hesitating momentarily, I said, 'not literally Dad.' He smiled, a little sadly, saying, 'But we don't really know do we, John?' To some extent these differences of outlook help to explain their differing reactions to what happened next.

Their relationship deepened over the next year or two, and in the summer of 1928, when they were both nineteen, they were regularly walking out into the country in the long evenings. Their favourite walk was down the Hartwell Road and round by Hartwell Church, lingering by the Egyptian Springs and 'spooning' (kissing and cuddling) in the long grass as they returned through Hartwell Park.

In the September, Grand-dad Watson took Grandmother with him when he went on a fishing holiday to Marlow, on the Thames. My mother's elder sister, Blanche, was left in charge of the household in New Street and she became increasingly concerned as her younger sister, Jess, fell ill and had trouble keeping her meals down. The family doctor, Dr. Dale, was called in and at first he ruled out pregnancy, because he found that Mother was still a virgin, and he asked Blanche if there was any TB in the family. However, it soon became clear that it was pregnancy and after questioning Mother further, he was able to explain to her what had happened: apparently, Mother and Father, like many young couples in those days (and still today) had been making love, 'safely,' that is, without penetration. Somehow, the far-travelling carrier of a Y chromosome had been able to make the epic journey to fertilize an egg, and so, to my Mother's consternation, she had conceived, although technically still a virgin.

Photos 3-2 Mother and Father at Eighteen

Top left-: Mother, Jess Watson (June 1927) dressed for a summer walk.
Top middle-: Mother with her friend Mary Porter and sister, Trix, on the right, out with Grannie Watson on a picnic down Dunsham lane.
Top right-: Mother (April 1927) looking for a way to cross the river Thame.
Bottom left-: Father, Ro Haynes, after returning from sea to work at Hunt Barnards.
Bottom right-: Mother reading in the garden at 89, New Street, Aylesbury.

73

My father was 'shattered,' and as he put it, "Tragedy had struck in my young life!" When Mother told him, he had burst into tears; at which, Mother said, "I felt my heart go cold."

In fairness to Mother, a high proportion of young couples got married in those days, where a prolonged courtship had led to a pregnancy, the marriage being expedited so that the dates weren't too awry. It had the advantage of showing that the couple, were at the very least fertile and sexually compatible. Her mother and father had taken to Roland, so she had assumed they would be married, eventually, and when she got over the shock she looked forward to my arrival.

In fairness to Father, he knew only too well what his parents' reaction would be to a repeat performance of his elder brother Jack's misadventures, and they were, indeed, initially outraged. It will also be clear from the foregoing that Father was highly ambitious and determined to 'get on.' Quite apart from the thought of being saddled with a young child, when only just out of his teens, he feared for his job with the Hunts, considering that they were strict Nonconformists and pillars of respectability in the town. However, his fears were groundless, the Hunts were very kind about it and showed that they were indeed fond of him, by curtailing his last year or so of training and bringing forward the plan for him to go out and represent them on the road, as a salesman.

My parents' marriage: The couple got married in the October, in the local Registry Office, just after Mother reached twenty and while Father was still nineteen. The reception was held in Mother's home in New Street. Apparently, it was at this party, that Grand-dad Watson advised Father, he should remember, during the marriage, 'To hold a forest horse by the head'. (See note 6.)

They had their honeymoon with Mother's sister Nan and her husband Harold (Hurst). Harold had taken the tenancy of New Inn Farm on the Stowe estate north of Buckingham. This farm is a few hundred yards from the Corinthian Arch, at the end of Stowe Avenue, with its commanding view of the neoclassical façade of Stowe House across the lakes. The New Inn was actually built to accommodate visitors to the house and landscape gardens, which were open to the public from the earliest days. Stowe House had become a public school only a few years before, in 1923. Mother had already stayed on holiday at the New Inn on a number of occasions, sometimes helping Nan prepare high teas, including egg and chips, for the Stowe boys out for walks on their half-days off, and it was ideal for a hurriedly arranged honeymoon. She was able to introduce Father to the delights of wandering through Stowe Grounds, which in those days of the great headmaster, J.F. Roxburgh, were freely open to the locals, as they still remained in my boyhood.

The remaining months of Mother's pregnancy were untroubled. Grannie Watson lent them the money to put down on 39, Chiltern Street, a small terrace house along the west side of the railway line, off the Old Stoke Road in Walton, on the outskirts of Aylesbury (see note 1—photo 79a). It was very convenient for Father, being just a step from Hunt Barnard's new works, erected in fields at the end of the street. I was born a few months after the move into Chiltern Street, at 6 o'clock on a fine Sunday evening (the 21st of April, 1929) when, as Mother remembers, the bells were ringing from Walton Parish Church and a blackbird was singing in the railway cutting. My birth was trouble free but had taken a little longer than expected, so that both the midwife and Doctor Dale (and Mother's sister Blanche) were present. I weighed in at 9lbs 8ozs, a weight considered good then, but would, no doubt, now be thought too heavy. I proved to belong to blood group, O rhesus positive. My hair, initially golden soon turned black, like that of both my parents, and my eyes to green hazel, a mixture of my father's blue-gray and my mother's deep, velvet brown.

SOURCES/NOTES—-CHAPTER 3

1) Viney, E. & Nightingale, P. 1976, *Old Aylesbury.* White Crescent Press Ltd., London. A view of the Wine Shop from the Market Square is given in their Photo 65a.

The old Grammar School in Church Street, is shown in Photo 25a, and its replacement, occupied in 1907, in Photo 53a.

The printing works of Hazell, Watson and Viney are shown in Photo 52a, taken in 1913, at the time my uncle Chub Wheeler would have been working there. His eldest son, Lionel, also worked there, as did Grandmother's brother, Walter, and apparently, her sisters Maud and Minnie, and possibly three cousins, as noted in chapter 1.

The end of Chiltern Street, when it ended in fields, is shown in Photo 79a, an aerial photo taken in 1921, after the construction of the Rivet Works but before the erection of the printing works for Hunt Barnard's.

2) Mead, W. R. 1998, *Aylesbury Grammar School—-a commemorative volume.* The Peterhouse Press, Brill, Aylesbury.
A comprehensive historical account by Professor Bill Mead, a former pupil and later a geographer at UCL, who was the son of Mead's the Grocers at 37, Buckingham Street. Their garden ran down close to where Grandmother was born at no.11, Buckingham Arms Yard. Coincidentally, although unknown to me at the time, he was external examiner for the old Geography Department at University of Wales Aberystwyth.

3) Frank served as a 'writer' in the Navy during the Second World War, when he was a lieutenant on the battleship *Renown* in the Mediterranean theatre. Afterwards, he worked as a lawyer in the Admiralty in London. One of his less happy assignments was dealing with the Mountbatten estate after the assassination. Frank's marriage to Kath, one of the 'Leggett Girls' (in 1939) is interesting in that she had been married before. Her husband went out to Australia and expected her to follow him when he was established, but she kept dillydallying, finding various excuses, and eventually he filed for a divorce. Frank handled Kath's side of the case and when the divorce went through they found they had fallen in love and so they got married. Sadly, Kath became seriously ill later in life and finally had to go to a nursing home. This led to Frank's early retirement. Mother always said that it was Frank, who was quieter, less out-going and more 'academic' than Father, that she was first attracted to, in the Haynes household.

According to Father, Harry Deeming (English and Sports Master at the Grammar School) also courted one of the 'Leggett Girls'. However, he apparently remained single until the end of his life. According to my cousin, James Robins, this may have been Muriel Leggett, who was secretary to the headmaster, G.P. Furneaux, in the thirties. By the time James was at the Grammar School in 1931, Harry Deeming was no longer Sports Master, but James remembers him playing with three other adults, in the school team when they played a match against Merton College, Oxford, in 1936, when he scored 16 runs. James was opening bat in this match together with H. P. Crabtree, an amateur who regularly opened for Essex. Crabtree made 31 before he was out, and James made 23, but stayed in longer. The Merton team included A V. Hurst, an old boy, and Halliday, a cricket blue, who later married Mr. Furneaux's daughter, Loveday.

4) The origins of the Congregational Church do go back to the Reformation, but the first recognizable congregation was formed in London in 1571, in Elizabethan times. Essentially, the basis of the church is that authority lies within the whole congregation, rather than with a hierarchy of vicars, bishops and archbishops, or, on the other hand with the individual conscience of the Presbyterian or Quaker; so it is true, as my father said, that this Church lies, 'somewhere in between.'

5) The one surviving logbook from Grandfather's 'Continuous Certificate of Discharge,' shows that he was re-engaged as Skipper of the *Othello* in July 1928. There are no more entries and presumably he continued in command until some time before his death in 1936, when, according to Father, he was surviving on 'half a lung', (which raises the possibility that he went back to sea thinking it might improve his health).

6) In chapter 1 I refer to my recent discovery that my maternal Grandparents 'had to get married', this explains why their attitude to the hasty marriage of my parents was apparently quite relaxed, in contrast to the initial hostility of my Grandparents in Grimsby.

CHAPTER 4

EARLY CHILDHOOD

AYLESBURY 1929-31

My first months: I have no memories stretching back to the first two years of my life. According to my father, I was called John Roland, rather than John Charles, after Grandfather, because of my Grandparents' initial, hostile reaction to my unauthorized advent. However, they thawed out after I was born. I was after all, their first grandson, and they proudly weighed me on some scales when I was taken up to Grimsby for them to see me, when I was about eight months old.

Mother said that she breast fed me for the first six months, according to the strict regime popularized by Truby King, a New Zealand doctor, who at that time wielded an influence as great as that of Dr. Spock later in the century. Apparently, I was a hungry baby, and took some time to submit to this arbitrary arrangement, not before giving my parents some sleepless nights. No doubt a useful first lesson in life, that being a "beller'ead" (bellow head) as my mother put it, would get me nowhere. Later on when I learnt to crawl, Mother had to watch out that I didn't raid the coal bucket, or similarly, lick pebbles in the garden. This general propensity, which appears to have been more highly developed in me than in my later siblings, would eventually prove useful in the geological appraisal of pieces of rock.

Photos taken of me when my hair was still golden show me at one year old (photos 4-1 top left) and in the back garden of 39, Chiltern Street in the summer of 1930 (top middle and right). I was by then quite steady on my feet and clutching (suspiciously) a new toy duck (additional to an Aylesbury duck given to me by Uncle Frank when I was born that was finally passed on to my youngest daughter). The back garden ran down to the railway cutting and I would be lifted up to watch the 'Sheffield Cutler' pounding through on its way north. I also used to be taken out regularly in the pram by my Mother's youngest sister, Kit, then fourteen, who would show me off to her friends.

'Sell something simple': My father took the opportunity to go out 'on the road' as a salesman for Hunt Barnard's, with enthusiasm. He had been earning little more than a pound a week in the office prior to my arrival but now he had to earn enough to support a wife and family. Years later, when he described his experiences to me, he explained how he gradually learned to put his case across to customers, simply and clearly. For a long while he nursed the ambition to write a book about this period of his life, entitled, 'Sell something simple' but he always preferred to talk about it instead. To begin with, it seems, George Hunt had to curb his impetuosity. As Father put it:

"I always talked very quickly, and one day Mr. Hunt said, 'It's no good, Roland, you will have to learn to speak slowly and quietly. You know all about the works and what we do but if you are going to interest the customers you must slow down and talk clearly. Now go outside with my brief case and knock on the door and I'll act as a customer.' So I went outside and knocked. 'Come in. Ah! Mr. Haynes, from Hunt Barnard's; take a seat Mr. Haynes. What have you got to tell me? Yes, I do buy printing. What have you got that's different?' In reply I said, 'Thank you for seeing me, Sir, we have a fine new factory at Aylesbury in which we have reduced costs considerably. We have some extremely modern and fast machinery and we can do extremely good colour work, and a whole range of letterpress and litho work.' 'Very good,' said Mr. Hunt, 'but take it a little slower and don't open your bag yet. I'll tell you if I want to see some samples, or a bit later on you could ask me if I want to see some samples of your work.'

"This was how Mr. Hunt advised me and when I first began making calls and I felt a bit embarrassed, I would think, 'What was it that Mr. Hunt said'; then I found I wasn't rushing it so much. It had a braking effect on my impetuosity.

"Hunt Barnard's didn't give me any specific instructions to do this or that. To begin with I said to Mr. Hunt, 'What shall I do today?' and he replied, 'That's up to you, Roland, go where you like. You have to find work that you know will suit our factory. Don't waste your time, or that of the clients, by taking enquires about work that we don't do, like beer labels'. I did know the kind of work we did and tried to use my imagination in going out to find new firms that would take our print. I checked for names of likely firms in catalogues and if I passed a big factory I would find out what they did there in case we could print for them.

"This led to incidents that are amusing in retrospect. On one occasion I passed this huge place, Clarke and Sherwell Ltd. Wondering what they did I went in and asked one of the girls in the office if I could see the print buyer. So she showed me in. 'Ah! Mr. Haynes of Hunt Barnard's, what can I do for you?' So I went into my act. 'That's interesting he said, you know we are Clarke and Sherwell.' This was a famous name in the printing trade and the best-known name for photogravure in the country, but unknown to me then. 'We do photogravure, he said.' 'Oh! I see Sir, but you don't do letterpress or litho?' 'No,' he said. So thinking quickly, I said, 'perhaps we could help you there.' I then confessed that I made it my practice to call on any new factory that looked as if it might require printing services. 'Well, I admire your keenness,' he said, with a laugh. I then told him I would pass on any enquires about photogravure I had to them and also that if he was in Aylesbury, I would be pleased to show him over our new factory. So I left on a friendly note but I felt very embarrassed and foolish.

"My inexperience also led to embarrassment over the matter of expenses. After the first occasion that I had to put in a claim for overnight expenses, I was surprised to be asked to go to Mr. Hunt's office to discuss them, because I had stayed in the cheapest bed and breakfast accommodation I could find. When I explained this to

Mr. Hunt, he smiled and said, 'In future, Roland, when you represent the firm you stay in one of the best hotels available.'

Wider horizons and the furniture trade: Learning from his mistakes, Father grew in confidence and Mr. Hunt decided the time had come to expand the business into new areas in the Home Counties; as he said to Father, 'This is all new territory, because we have always worked mainly for firms in the London area. Go away and find out what you can. We shall pay all your expenses but initially you won't have a car because I think that salesmen are made on their feet. So for a year you will do it by bus and train.' Father described his experiences as follows:

"I used to go to Luton on the bus, as well as Rugby and Banbury via Brackley on the train and I started to get a lot of new business. Where I did particularly well was in High Wycombe, where we already had six accounts, including Gomm and Bartletts, well-known names in the furniture trade. I soon found myself going to High Wycombe once a week and eventually I managed to get more than forty firms on our account.

"The furniture industry started in this part of Bucks because of the beech woods on the Chilterns. It was here in the old days that they learnt to bend the wood by heating and pinning it without breaking it to make the chairs. Firms like Gomm became famous for their furniture, such as bedroom suites, that were exported to foreign countries including America. Other big firms came along, like Ercolani, Bartletts and Birch, which did tremendous business in the boom period for building after World War 1. High Wycombe concentrated particularly on wooden furniture while most of the upholstery was made in London.

"The big firms like Gomm issued catalogues but most of the small firms still had a very old fashioned way of selling their furniture. They would make new designs, photograph them and have the new furniture ready for the autumn on the idea that it sold better in the winter. A traveller working on commission, then took the photographs round with the price and details on the back to show the retailers. I knew that there must be a better way of doing it. So I discussed a better method when I called on J. C. Lane, one of the new firms on our account. John Christopher Lane was a funny little fellow, a bit like Mr. Hunt, only about 5ft 2ins tall. He was reputed to have invented the first commercial adjustable chair, with a movable back, but he never patented it."

"Mr. Lane's partner or co-director was Mr. Bexon, who had sold his brewery for a very large sum and invested it in J. C. Lane. I put my ideas to him: 'Why wait until the end of the year to get your new designs publicized? Why don't you get the details out early, not only to the trade but also to the public? At the moment, it's the Buyer for the shop who decides whether one of your new designs is accepted, and if he is old-fashioned, he might say of a new design, 'Oh! That won't sell here.' 'What I would suggest is that you get out a leaflet that describes the new furniture, with a strip-off, price-slip on the side. The leaflet can then be shown to prospective

customers, while the Buyer keeps the price-list for his own use. The leaflets can also be posted out to customers.' Both Mr. Bexon and Mr. Lane thought this would be a good idea, but I found they didn't even have a list of the retailers. So I went up to London and got together a list of all the main retailers, from the big stores right down to the small furniture shops.

"The leaflet I had printed was a simple three-fold brochure, illustrating the furniture. It led to a marked increase in orders, especially for individual pieces. Instead of the one sales drive at the end of the year, J. C. Lane now had sales going more evenly through the year. Mr. Lane was appreciative of my help and he offered me a job as representative for his firm but I turned it down, out of loyalty to Mr. Hunt, possibly a big mistake."

Father on his youngest brother, Norman: Although Father didn't take up the offer of a job with J. C. Lane, as a result of his good work for them he was able, sometime later, to get a job there for Norman, his younger brother. Norman was born in 1915, and a schoolboy when the family returned to Grimsby. Father relates what followed:

" Norman was quite good in school and when he left at fifteen, mother (Grandma Haynes) got him a job as a trainee with David Smith's, a big multiple store in Grimsby. A trainee would work for a time in each department and then be assigned to the one thought most suitable for him. If he did well he would become assistant manager, then manager and finally the Buyer responsible for that Department, if he was bright enough.

"Norman was bright and also very attractive to women. He was that aggressive type that many women like. He was a very good boxer and indeed, fighter. If anyone insulted him or issued a challenge he would take it up immediately on the basis of 'the bigger they come, the harder they fall.' He would hit them in no time! (See photos 3-1 top right.)

"All went well for sometime but then the manager found Norman on a bed in the bedding department with an attractive young girl. Fortunately, no one had any clothes off, so Norman simply got a warning. But some months later, after another attractive young girl had joined the firm, Norman was found in a large wardrobe with her, actually in the act. So he was sacked.

Photographs 4-1, the golden (hair) time 1930-31
Top left-: Mother with John, aged one.
Top middle and right-: John examining the strange birthday duck, in the garden of 39, Chiltern Street.
Middle right-: John aged two, out for a walk with Mother's friend Mary Porter.
Middle left and bottom right-: John helping Father in the garden of Towyn. The house, where Ann was born, was similar to the one attached to it and shown behind us.
Bottom left-: Aunt Trix reading to John in the garden of 89, New Street.

"Mother didn't know the full story, only that Norman had been found unsuitable and wanted to get away from Grimsby. She asked me if I thought there were any good prospects for him around Aylesbury. I told her I would think about it and the next time I visited J. C. Lane's I spoke to Mr. Bexon about the possibility of Norman joining them as a junior salesman and they took him on, although he had to provide his own car. So Norman bought this Morris Cowley. He didn't know how to drive, so I took him out in my car on three successive evenings, round Aylesbury and out down some of the main roads, until he got used to the gears. The next day, he collected his car from the garage and drove all the way to Grimsby without incident!

"When he returned he started with J. C. Lane's and they took to him, not only for my sake but because he had an attractive personality, as well as the gift of the gab. He soon made money bringing in business but he did too well, too soon. He didn't drink but he did like the girls, which led to wild behaviour. On one occasion, he went to Exeter because he had met a girl there, when he should have been in Brighton. The next day he scooted over to Brighton to make his calls. He then popped over to France to have a bit of a do in Boulogne. When he arrived back he said, 'I'm worn out, Ro, I think I'll go up to Grimsby and stay with mother'. When I saw mother later, she said, 'Poor Norman, he works too hard, Roland, he came home last time absolutely worn out. I do wish he would find a girl friend and settle down.' Poor mother, little did she know how many girl friends he actually had!

"This was how he carried on. When he should have been in Bournemouth showing clients new designs he would be somewhere else. He also had a very bad car crash on one of his trips, and was only saved by holding on to this huge great dog he always took everywhere with him. That's the kind of chap he was, absolutely incredible!"

Another address in Aylesbury: We continued to live at 39, Chiltern Street until I was about eighteen months old. Then, apparently in order to be able to pay back the loan to Grandma Watson, my parents sold this house and we moved into a rented, semi-detached house, only a few hundred yards away, off the Old Stoke Road, called 'Towyn', (see photos 4-1).It was here that my sister, Ann, was born on September 16th, 1931.

Ann arrived a little overdue and Dr. Dale was somewhat concerned when he detected a slight heart murmur. However, all went well afterwards and she proved to be a contented, placid baby, though as Mother said, stubborn, with a mind of her own. She had blue-hazel eyes and after a slow start, nut-brown hair, which in childhood was worn in long plaits, until she insisted on having it cut off, much to the distress of Father. Ann and I got on well with each other from the earliest days. Later on, when I was left in charge of my siblings, which was quite often, I had to take care that she was not disadvantaged, as the only girl. However, there is no doubt that in later years when we lived in the country, which suited us boys very well, it was a disadvantage and she became bored, being a town girl at heart.

Difficulties at Hunt Barnard's: About the time Ann was born there were changes at Hunt Barnard's. My father's mentor, George T. Hunt, died, and his son Leonard, and his nephew,

Hollis, took over. Despite his great admiration for Hollis Hunt, this led to difficulties for Father. As he said:

"Leonard was a bit wayward and never really took to the business. He was a sportsman and a very good tennis player, up to Wimbledon standard. To the dismay of his parents, he also took to 'strong drink' and he spent a lot of time in the Literary Club playing cards and snooker. He and a man called John Monk ran the London office and instead of emphasizing service and quality, they sold entirely on price, on the theory that this would lead to sufficient volume to bring in profits. This led to embarrassing losses.

"There had always been jealousy on Leonard's part about his cousin, Hollis, who was older than he was. George Hunt had tended to lean towards the more mature, evenly balanced personality of his nephew, rather than towards his own, more mercurial son. So there was friction. Hollis had been a careful man and bought shares in the company. When George Hunt died, it turned out, to Leonard's surprise, that Hollis had the majority holding. Things then became a little sticky in the boardroom.

"The reason things became difficult for me was because Leonard brought in a man called Bowers, who knew nothing about printing but was a well known personality. His people were the Bowers of Bowers and Simonette, ivory dealers in Old Bond Street, and he had been in the 'Blues' or one of the top regiments. He was even more of a playboy than Leonard and bad at taking responsibility. On two occasions I found that he had misled our customers. As I was responsible for these accounts this reflected on my honesty and integrity."

KENTON, MIDDLESEX 1931-32

A false move: The difficulties he experienced in Hunt Barnard's led my father to consider finding another job and when through his contacts in London he found what appeared to be a suitable post with a printing firm there, he decided to take it. This necessitated another move. My parents found a new, three bed-roomed, semi-detached house in Kenton, Middlesex. This was in a new suburb, typical of developments being put up by speculative builders to the northwest of London at this time, within reach of the Metropolitan Line. (Mother's brother, Alec and his wife moved to 20, Burwell Avenue, Kenton about this time, which may be connected with this decision to live there.)

Kenton was a short bus ride from both Harrow-on-the-Hill and Pinner. The house, at a price of about six or seven hundred pounds, was bought on a mortgage and we moved into 28, Alveston Avenue (named 'Ridley' after Father's house in Aylesbury Grammar School) sometime in the autumn or winter of 1931/32, while Ann was still a babe in arms. As Mother said, "This was the period when such houses were known as 'Jerry built'. This proved to be the case, because we hadn't been there long when the fireplace fell out!"

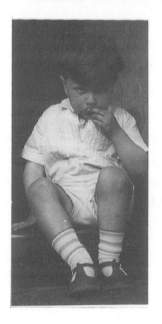

The photo (4-2 top left) shows the family standing on the concrete patio at the back of the house in the early spring of 1932. Behind is the turned over soil of the new garden, surrounded by a high wooden fence, with an identical pair of semis to our own beyond. My father is in his plus-fours, Mother in a frock fashionable at the time. Ann is looking very aware and I am standing legs astride, looking watchfully (for the Dicky bird) straight at the camera. When I showed my brother this photo, on his return from Australia, after more than twenty years' absence, he exclaimed, "Nineteen thirties Yuppies!" That is to say, young and upwardly striving, but this was only partly true. Certainly, Father had every intention of 'getting on' in the new world of light industry and services that was opening up as the country moved out of the Great Slump (that had coincided with my birth). Mother, on the other hand, liked Kenton no better than she had Streatham. In particular, she was censorious of the pretensions of many of her neighbours, who although only possessing semis that had small kitchens and just two reception rooms, actually employed maids dressed up in full uniform.

Another reason for Mother's dislike of the new house was probably the accident that I had while she was out one day. Father had stoked up a small 'Ascot' boiler that heated the water in the kitchen and in childish innocence I took it for a stool and sat on it. Although badly burnt, I have no memory of this incident but I still have the white scar, about two inches long on my thigh.

The only memory I have of Kenton, the first memory of my life, is of being lost. I had found my way out of the front gate and went off to explore. Eventually, I came back to what I thought was our house but although it was in the right position it was in the wrong street. As I ran up to the front door a strange woman came out. Realizing I was lost she took me by the hand and we went down the road to meet Mother running towards us, quite distraught. No doubt this memory (together with the influence of seafaring ancestors) plays its part in my tendency to feel distinctly unhappy unless I know exactly where I am geographically and where I am going (and when), not always appreciated by others.

We stayed in Kenton until the summer of 1932, when Mother found herself pregnant again. She had not become reconciled to living there, greatly missing her sisters and friends in Aylesbury and when she realized she was going to have another baby, it made it worse, because, as she said, "It was the sort of place where they either had one child or none!" Unfortunately/fortunately, Father had come to regret leaving Hunt Barnard's, finding the policies and ethical standards of his new firm quite unacceptable. (Interestingly, he never mentioned the name of this firm later.) It says a great deal for the esteem in which the Hunts held him, that after enquiry, he was invited to come back to his old job once again.

Photographs 4-2 Kenton 1932
Top left-: "Nineteen- thirties Yuppies"—-Father and Mother, Ann and John, in the back-garden of Ridley, the houses beyond, in the next street, identical to ours.
Top right-: John (third birthday) proudly trying out his new car on the patio.
Middle left-: John, as Father said, "Looking for those seeds Daddy planted".
Middle right-: Mother and her in-laws, Charles left with his wife Mabel; Frank right, with the youngest sister Flossie.
Bottom left-: John, 'Looking for the birdie', hair now almost black.
Bottom right-: Mother caught reading, as usual.

Father had now bought a car, and as it was now unnecessary to live right next to the Works in Aylesbury, Mother wrote to her two sisters at Stowe, Nan at the New Inn Farm and Lill ('Chubbie') at Blackpit Farm to ask them to look out for a nearby house for rent. Almost immediately, they found the empty Lodge of the Manor House at Lillingstone Lovell, available for a few shillings a week rent. (Recently, seventy years later, the Lodge was advertised for rent at £900 a month, a multiple of many hundreds!)

LILLINGSTONE LOVELL 1932-33

Country child: We moved to Lillingstone Lovell a few months after my third birthday, for me, the first of many lucky breaks (apart from my luck in being born in the first place). It meant that just as I was becoming aware of the external world, I was exposed to the sights and sounds of remote, deep country. The village, really just a hamlet with a few cottages strung along the brook, with the end one then a shop, is well off the main road between Buckingham and Towcester. The Lodge is half a mile from the village in the lane to the Manor, placed at the corner of a field, up against a wood (part of Whittlewood Forest) which hides the Manor House, making it a place of mystery to me as a child. The photo (4-3 bottom) shows that the Lodge was then smothered with ivy and quite picturesque. It also had a large garden with a strip of copse and fruit trees.

My first memory of Lovell (and the second memory of my life) is not of the Lodge but of a long walk with Mother to see her sister Nan, not long after we arrived. It was a very hot, late summer day. Mother pushed Ann in the pram while I ran alongside, as we took the back lanes that make a circuit of Stowe Park to the village of Chackmore, and thence up to the Corinthian Arch and the New Inn. In those days there were many tall, luxuriant English elms along the lanes and every so often we stopped in their shade to sip water from a bottle Mother had wrapped in a damp cloth for the journey.

When we reached the farm we went in under a lofty, golden-yellow archway (that led to an interior courtyard) with the entrance to the kitchen in its right side. Here, my aunt welcomed us effusively and I was given a large brown egg with bread fingers for my tea.

On the way home, in the late evening, I was delighted to find, running ahead, that it was now warmer under the trees than in the open. Eventually, exhausted, I had to join Ann in the pram. It was quite dark before we got home but I retained the impression of the white lanes glimmering in the dusk.

The Lodge was ideal for Mother. She could have the windows open in all weathers and play the piano and sing without any care about what neighbours might think. Another advantage for her was the close proximity of her sisters (see photos 4-4). Father also took to country life, acquiring a .410 shotgun and a small dog called Sam, a cross between a terrier and a Sealyham. One morning when he had been out shooting early, I ran down the field opposite the Lodge to meet him, with his gun under his arm carrying a rabbit he had shot, and he took me to see a tree that had been struck by lightning during a thunderstorm in the night (which I must have slept through).

I played great games with Sam in the garden and one afternoon when Mother sent me out to play while she had a nap, we played a sort of tag round the lavender bushes that edged the vegetable plot. When we had both tired of it and Sam had gone off about his own affairs, on impulse I crawled under the hedge into the adjacent wood. I wandered in a far as I dared, half frightened and half in awe of the deep, slumbrous hush of the late summer woods.

Father's car at the time was a two-seater, with a dickie seat at the rear where I was allowed to sit in the open when it was fine. One day, by chance, the car broke down in a water-splash near the village and Father had to take off his shoes and wade out to go and get help. While he was gone a herd of cows came to drink and one leaned over me, dripping water as she examined me with her big, mild eyes.

Father worked hard in the garden and in the autumn he built up a very large bonfire, ready for a party on the Fifth of November to which our relations from Blackpit and the New Inn were invited. For some reason, a misdemeanour I have forgotten, possibly defiance, which neither Mother nor Father would countenance for a moment, I was sent to bed as punishment. However, I was able to watch the fireworks through my bedroom window.

As her pregnancy progressed, Mother engaged a girl from the village to take Ann (in the pram) and me for a walk in the afternoon while she rested. On the first occasion, I refused to go with this strange girl and was locked out in the garden to occupy myself until they came back. It so happened that the Grafton Hunt drew the local woods that day and after a while I heard the distant sounds of a horn and hounds giving tongue. Gradually the noise grew louder as the hunt came down the side of the wood in the field opposite the Lodge. Trying to see what was happening I got down on the gravel path to look under the high wooden gates at the side of the cottage and was just in time to see a fox cross the front lawn, followed soon after by hounds. The fox went through into the field at the back of the house leaving the hounds milling about in the front garden until they were whipped-off by the huntsman. Of course, I was too young to know what was going on, but the scene was impressed vividly upon my memory.

The winter of 1932/33 was quite hard and during bitter, February weather, Mother, who persisted in hanging out the washing in a deep frost, developed pleurisy. As she remained poorly for some weeks it was decided, that when the time came, she would have the baby in Aylesbury, in the care of her older sister, Blanche. It was for this reason that my brother David was born at No.7, Willow Road, Aylesbury (on the 28th of April, 1933) while we were actually living at Lovell. He was a healthy baby, at 9lbs 10ozs rather heavier at birth than the rest of us were, but as Mother said, always a finicky feeder. Despite this he grew up to be taller and heavier boned than me and with bigger hands and feet, suitable for a future champion swimmer. His hair was stiffly straight and black from birth, together with green-hazel eyes and Mother's long Brooks' nose.

From the recollections of my cousin James, it seems that his mother, Blanche, was in great demand as honorary midwife by the family, and was concerned with the births of

Hurst and Wheeler children as well as my own arrival. During these times James was sent to stay with other relations. He thinks there may have been a tradition at that time, of one of the older girls in big families taking on this duty. I have no memory of these events. Only of my mother, on my fourth birthday, taking me by the hand into the front garden and showing me the flowering current, in full bloom and to me, seemingly full of bees. This was just before she went to Willow Road to have David.

A family christening: After David's birth, Mother and Father appear to have felt somewhat remiss in that none of their children were christened and it was decided that there should be a joint ceremony, which was in Lovell parish church on the 19th of June, 1933. Uncles Frank and Harold were godfathers for David and me, with Aunt Nan godmother. Ann had Aunt 'Chubbie' as additional godmother, together with Frank. The solemnity of the proceedings was somewhat marred, when becoming worried by the turn events were taking when David was lifted to the font, I broke away from Mother and made a run for it down the aisle. I was quickly collared and to general amusement was carried back to have the cool, calming cross inscribed on my forehead.

Afterwards, at the christening party, we were presented with our silver mugs and spoons as the bottles of champagne were opened. The thoughts of the adults then soon turned to other matters and I found my way outside and went to play in Father's car. I went over the controls, mimicking Father, and eventually released the handbrake. The car was backed up on a slope, so it ran off, not stopping until it ran up the opposite bank some distance down the lane. I scrambled out and in guilty fear, ran in to tell Father. At first, glass in hand and in full flow of an anecdote, he took no notice of me nervously trying to attract his attention, but finally, in response to my 'Dad, Dad, the car'. He dashed out and finding no harm done spent some time going over the controls with me. He realized I had learnt my lesson regarding the handbrake!

First visit to Grimsby: Grandfather and Grandma Haynes appear to have stayed at the Lodge to attend the christening (photo 4-3 top left) and when the time came for them to leave I was taken with them to Grimsby. I was shown off to various great aunts and taken to a green painted, wooden grocery shop, which I think was being run by Aunt Nora) where Grandfather proudly weighed me (again) on some scales. On a visit to the docks with Grandfather, which we reached by tram, I was greatly impressed with the multitude of black trawlers and the fish laid out on the fish pontoon, where I saw a cat make off with a cod's head. Afterwards we went out to Cleethorpes on the top of an open decked trolley bus and for the first time I was exposed to the glittering immensity of the sea and saw a line-up of trawlers waiting for the tide. For some time afterwards, I found it difficult to believe that a seaside place was the 'real' sea unless there was shipping, or at least a scroll of smoke indicating a vessel hull down over the horizon.

Photographs 4-3, the Lodge Lillingstone Lovell 1933
Top left -: Grandfather Jack Haynes (at 57) with his eldest grandson. Note that my index finger is intact.
Top right -: John tells Ann to 'watch for the birdie'.
Middle -: John keeps a straight bat while Mother and Ann keep wicket.
Bottom -: The Lodge, showing how the garden contrasted with that of Ridley in Kenton.

An aborted summer holiday: Shortly after my return from Grimsby, my parents made preparations for a holiday in Cornwall. In those days there were no paid holidays, so it meant Father taking a week off work without pay. On the afternoon before the journey I watched him strapping our cases onto the open luggage 'grid' at the back of the car. The grid was of three ironwork sections that were laid out flat for loading. Curious, I poked my index finger through an interesting oval slot, just as he brought the two free sections up smartly to clamp down over the cases, smashing though the second joint.

He had to thread the mangled top joints of my finger back through the slot, before I could be roughly bandaged up and taken (still in shock and not really conscious of the pain) to a doctor in Buckingham. It was then decided that in order to try and save the top joints, to transfer me to a specialist in Northampton, where I spent a few days in a nursing home. My only memory of pain during these proceedings was when the surgeon was probing my finger with a sharp instrument. In the end it was decided that I would be better off without the damaged joints and they were neatly amputated.

My parents were very concerned at the possible future consequences for me but in later life I have never been conscious of the loss except when others have mentioned it. My middle finger took over as 'index' finger and the main effect of this was to tilt my hand over to the left, tending to give my handwriting a backward slope. Although it has made writing more laborious, this has probably accentuated my natural tendency to summarize rather than to report at length; (some time later, Mother was careful to see that I had piano lessons. This also helped to obviate any difficulty the loss might have caused me).

The prize 'bullet': There was no fully comprehensive health service in my childhood, so money saved for the holiday must have gone to pay the doctor's bills (unless Father was in an insurance scheme that helped). Father also appears to have had to borrow money at this time. It must have been welcome relief when he won a prize of fifty pounds (a lot of money then) in the 'Bullets' competition, run by the magazine 'John Bull'. This involved adding three or four words to a given phrase to make a snappy, epigrammatic sentence; (the magazine was still running this competition in the 1950s and I tried my hand at it several times but without my father's success, or the success of Uncle Alec, Mother's brother, who was very good at it and won several prizes).

Photographs 4-4 Blackpit and the Wheeler cousins

The move to Lillingstone Lovell put us in close proximity to our Wheeler cousins. The top left and bottom right photos record a visit sometime in the late summer of 1932.
Top left -: Jose (the Maria of T.H. White's *Mistress Masham's Repose),* looking concerned as Ann pinches her father's cheek.
Bottom right -: Mother and Ann near Blackpit Lake with Aunt Chubbie and Jose.
Top right and bottom left-: Our cousins Graham and Robert as boys, both actually older than Jose.
Middle right -: Chub with his collie Jip, in the long riding, out side 'The Cottage'.

An unwelcome consequence was that during the party celebrating his win, Mother noticed a man lurking in the garden. Father went out with his shotgun and crept up behind the intruder and poked it into his back, saying 'What are you doing?' Meanwhile Mother had telephoned the police, so Father held the man in the kitchen until they arrived. It turned out that the intruder was a local man, deemed 'a bit simple', no doubt his envy excited by news of the win. As he had been frightened to death by my father poking a gun into his back, it was thought sufficient that he be allowed to go with a caution. Although this incident ended smoothly, it upset Mother who now began to feel vulnerable, alone with three young children in the isolated cottage, with Father away all day, often until late in the evening and sometimes overnight. By chance, it so happened that a house became vacant in Aylesbury, in Havelock Street, very near to where Grandma and Grandpa Watson now lived at no 62, Fleet Street, and my parents decided to make another move.

AYLESBURY AGAIN, 1933-35

No. 3, Havelock Street, 1933-34: We moved to the house in Havelock Street sometime in the late autumn of 1933. The main advantage of the new house, for Mother, was that the back garden adjoined the back garden of her parents. I was able to visit them by climbing over some boxes arranged as steps over the fence, and when we first arrived, helped Grandfather when he was digging out potatoes between his rows of apple trees.

At Christmas, my parents took me to the Hunt's Christmas party at which Henry Hall and his orchestra had been engaged to play for the dancing. During an interval, Father introduced me to the members of the band and one of them, to amuse me, blew one of those unrolling 'bazookers' into my face. Unfortunately, it startled me and I began to howl inconsolably (more out of shyness and embarrassment than fear, I think) and I was taken home in disgrace, where I was left while my parents went back to the party.

In the New Year (1934) I began to attend the infant class in St. John's Church School, just round the corner from New Street on the Bierton Road; the same school attended by Mother twenty years before. My only memories of this period are of writing letters on a slate and the wonderful satisfaction of obtaining a pristine shine by wiping them off with a wet rag, and also the solicitous care of some older girls when we were out in the playground.

A brush with the 'White Death': These recollections of St. John's School are brief because my education was soon interrupted. During the spring of 1934, it became apparent that I had a swollen gland on the right side of my neck and it proved to be infected with the tuberculosis bacillus. For many years I was quite confused about the course of events at this time, partly because of the reticence of my parents about the actual nature of my affliction (in those days even a hint of TB was a social and employment disaster). According to Mother, our family doctor decided that the gland could be drained and that when this was found to be ineffective after several attempts, it was removed (leading to considerable scarring on my neck). However, what may also have happened was that the doctor, suspecting TB, drained off the fluid so that it could be cultured and analyzed, and that this procedure was repeated. I certainly remember the doctor coming more than once (see note 1). One afternoon, by then well acquainted with the implications of the doctor's visit, I ran into the garden to hide. Dad soon found me and took me up to the bedroom where I wriggled free and took refuge under the bed; but I was dragged out by the heels and laid on the bed to have the chloroform mask pushed down over my face, soon falling into purple/black oblivion. Afterwards, I remember running round a flowerbed in the back garden, the colours seeming all the brighter for my deliverance.

I was eventually taken to the Royal Bucks Hospital, presumably to have the gland removed. If so, I have no memory of this event, only of its aftermath when I was recuperating in the infants' ward. It was visiting time one afternoon; my parents hadn't come but the ward was full of people giving their children presents. When the bell went for the visitors to leave and the parents began to go, a child started howling and almost immediately general pandemonium broke out. The children all began crying and throwing their presents out of their cots. The little boy next to me had been given one of those chunky picture books with thick cardboard pages and he hurled it straight out of the open window between our cots. I watched all this with growing amazement. Eventually, the uproar died down, apart from the occasional snuffle, the evening breeze lifting the curtains in the open windows. It was my first, salutary, experience of mass hysteria.

One day, when back at home after the operation, I went into the field at the bottom of Fleet Street and Havelock Street (today occupied by a very large mosque). Two chestnut mares (shire horses) were grazing there and as I edged as close to them as I dared, the buttercups coming up to my chest, one of them lifted its tail and produced a flashing, amber stream. The memory occupied my thoughts before I fell asleep that night, and for many nights afterwards when I imagined being curled up securely in the great mare's belly.

The sanatorium at Peppard Common:

"The sanatorium buildings are not planned for the feeble, chronic case—- (yet) a tuberculous colony, wind-swept, sun-washed, and effectively managed is a remarkably healthy spot in which to live". Dr. Esther Carling, chief medical officer for the Berks and Bucks Joint Sanatorium. (See note 2.)

Out-patient treatment after my operation included a number of sessions under the sunlamp in the Royal Bucks (it was thought this might be generally effective against TB, see note 3). Unfortunately, the nurse was called away during one session and I was badly burned in her absence, so they were called off. A general review of my case then took place and it was discovered I had an infected patch on the left lung. A place was then found for me in the TB sanatorium at Peppard Common, on the westward continuation of the Chilterns, north of Reading (and then in Berkshire).

Although Robert Koch, the great German microbiologist, had discovered and described the rod-like bacterium responsible for TB in 1882, no adequate vaccine or other means of cure had ever been found (and were not until the advent of the anti-biotic Streptomycin in 1944). All that could be suggested (because some victims did recover) was that patients should be removed to a hospice or sanatorium where the body's natural defenses could be assisted by fresh air, rest and a good, milk-based diet supplemented with cod-liver oil; an idea that goes back to the ancient Roman world and the teaching of Areteus the Cappodocian, who recommended that those weak in the lungs should have prolonged rest in the cypress groves of the Temple of Apollo at Aquinum (in Turkey) in the care of the Sun God.

The nineteenth century sanatorium movement began in Germany to combat the huge rise in the incidence of TB that accompanied the Industrial Revolution. It was combined with the idea that the patients should live as high above sea-level as possible, which appealed to the romantic identification of mountains with spiritual and physical renewal and led to the building of sanatoria in the Bavarian and Swiss Alps. The movement spread worldwide and by the early twentieth century there were almost a hundred in Great Britain. (See note 4.)

This will explain how in the summer of 1934, I found myself in a jumble of buildings, including a large number of wooden huts, many on stilts for free circulation of air underneath, high up on the Chilterns, with a large number of other boys and girls. Many of the huts had balconies where the beds could be drawn out into the open air, unless the weather was impossibly bad. Windows were kept open most of the time and open neck shirts and shorts with plimsolls (rubber soled canvas shoes) were standard for the boys. This was no particular hardship for me, as Mother preferred cold weather and a Spartan way of life, never lighting the living room fire, the only source of heat in the house, until 4pm (except on Sundays and holidays). She kept the windows open, and believed that if it was cold you simply put more clothes on, or worked harder. There was never any heat in our bedrooms; (most of the children in the sanatorium had, probably, experienced similar regimes at home).

I have no memory of my first arrival at Peppard, but I do remember being put at first into a big dormitory with younger children, all of us still in cots (the children's section of the sanatorium was called the 'Kindercot'). This may have been while my condition was being closely monitored. For a while, an older girl tucked me in at night, her dark hair falling round my face as she kissed my forehead. When she stopped coming (perhaps her condition worsened) the memory lingered. As in all sanatoria, there were strict rules, with lights out early and nurses on patrol. Parents were only allowed one visit a month, for two hours, without other children (to guard against them catching the disease, though it seems in retrospect that TB was not, in general, particularly contagious). In any case there were difficulties for my parents. Mother was expecting her fourth child and Father was often on business on the Saturday, so they couldn't make it very often.

On one occasion when my father came on his own, it was possibly in the August, he gave me a toy aeroplane with green cellophane wings and a wind-up propellor attached to elastic, capable of quite a long flight. When he had gone I took it out on the playing field to fly it, soon attracting a crowd of boys, some of the older ones soon taking it over. When they were getting bored, one boy suggested scrumping some apples (still green) from the neighbouring orchard and in the subsequent rush the plane was dropped and trodden on. I was left with the broken-winged plane in my hand, staring ruefully after them; (this could only have strengthened my aversion to mob activities of any kind).

Despite experiences of this sort, I settled down with the other boys and girls. There was a strong emphasis on outdoor activities and games and there were regular sessions of 'Swedish drill'. We were also allowed fairly long, unsupervised, play periods when we played various running and ball games, taking shelter under the huts on stilts when it rained. One day that summer one of the girls showed me how to fire off the head of a plantain, by looping the stem and drawing the flower head quickly through it. In later years, showing this trick to my own children always brought back a keen memory of this time.

Other sharp memories are of long walks, in a 'crocodile' over the common and along the Downs, on one occasion, that autumn, past a long row of trees dropping scarlet and vermillion leaves (probably wild cherry) and an enormous pile of logs on the common with a very life-like Guy on top, ready for Bonfire Night. Around Christmas time, we also walked to a nearby church, after a heavy snowfall, a day of sparkling sunshine with blue shadows in the drifts.

The sanatorium also ran normal school classes for the children and this is where I learnt to do simple sums and read simple sentences for the first time. We also 'played shop', weighing out dried peas and beans on scales, learning to use the brass weights, and filling up those blue sugar bags of different sizes that used to be standard in grocery shops. We then had to act as buyers and sellers, trying to get the prices and change right, using token money.

However, my education was again interrupted, some time into the New Year, when I caught chicken pox. I was removed to a large wooden hut that had about six beds in it that acted as an isolation hospital within the sanatorium, and was there for several weeks, until fully recovered. In those days rather a rather longer period was allowed for recuperation than is usual now.

I was certainly recovered by the time of the Oxford and Cambridge Boat Race. One day, I was approached in the playground by an older girl carrying a tray of light and dark blue ribbons and she said, "Are you Oxford or Cambridge?" "I don't know" I replied. Then she said, "Where are you from?" "Aylesbury" I replied. "Alright" she said, "You're Oxford", and pinned a dark blue ribbon to my shirt. Needless to say, I have been "Oxford" ever since; (this is the first conversation in my life I can remember).

On the occasion of my sixth birthday in April, both my parents came and I was allowed to go with them for a picnic on the common. We sat down near a patch of gorse in full bloom and afterwards I found my way into a clearing in the middle of the thicket. I sat there for a few moments, hugging my knees with joy because I was with my parents again. Since then I have always been ready to believe the story of the great Swedish botanist Linnaeus, falling on his knees and thanking God for the glory of the gorse in bloom. (The photo, 4-5 middle, taken of Mother and me in front of one of the huts, apparently at this

time, appears, from the expression on my face, to be when I was told I would soon be allowed to go home.)

On the day, a few weeks later, when I was finally allowed to leave, three or four of us were gathered in a big cloakroom in the afternoon to wait for our parents. One by one, the other children were picked up until I was the only one left; and eventually, it began to get dark. At the side of the cloakroom there were big divided shelves, for storage of large suitcases, behind curtains. Feeling tired, I climbed onto an empty shelf and went to sleep. When my father finally came, the nurses, who thought I had already gone, were most surprised to find me there. Father carried me to the car and put me on the back seat to carry on sleeping while he drove home.

Postscript: It was not until much later in life, that I realized that I was "One of the lucky few, who after half a century are still alive, returned cured. The majority went on to years of ill health and a host of complications in distant organs and usually died within ten to fifteen years," (see note 1). This majority numbered millions though the nineteenth century and into the early twentieth century, including such luminaries as the Brontes, Keats, Chopin, Chekhov, Richard Jefferies, D.H. Lawrence and Orwell. However, although it was many years before I realized the full extent of my illness, I have always been sustained by a subconscious, well-spring of optimism that is, perhaps, connected to this deliverance. (See note 5.)

It is not surprising, that considering the carnage it caused and the vagaries and uncertainties of its course, families tended to react to any manifestations of TB with denial. All I was told, by my parents, was that I had had an 'infected' gland removed and that I recovered after convalescence in Peppard. In my case, there is no doubt they were right. I didn't then go on through boyhood thinking I was some sort of invalid. My parents remained worried of course, and Father would sometimes exclaim, "Why is that boy so thin and pale?" I had no inkling that I'd had an infected lung until, when twenty-five years old, I went for a medical, preparatory to emigrating to Canada; it was then revealed by the doctor, as he made a routine examination of my chest by tapping and stethoscope.

Photographs 4-5, Aylesbury again 1934-35

Top left -: David and Ann (still not used to my reappearance, back from Peppard TB Sanatorium) May 1935.

Top right -: Father, aged 26, in the back garden at 24, Havelock Street.

Middle photo -: Mother with me at Peppard Sanatorium; probably on my birthday, when I was told that I would shortly be allowed home.

Bottom left -: David, now a toddler, in the back garden at 24, Havelock Street.

Bottom right -: Father and Mother wearing stylish bathing suits, somewhere on the South Coast at this time

My father always blamed unpasteurized milk and bovine TB for my condition but this is highly unlikely. Bovine TB causes intestinal TB and attacks the bones and joints, whereas pulmonary TB is 'almost always' caused by the human strain of the bacillus.   While reading about the history of TB in order to get a better idea of my own brush with the disease, I thought of Father's comments on Grandfather's lifelong battle with asthma and bronchitis and the doctor's description of him surviving on only half a lung towards the end. Although TB was never mentioned, this leads to the surmise that he may have had TB from quite early on in his life. It may be more than coincidence that my Grandparents visited us when I was four at Lillingstone Lovell and I went back with them to Grimsby that summer, developing a tubercular gland the following spring; (the family doctor thought the shock of the accident, when I lost the top of my index finger, could have precipitated the disease). If there is any truth in this surmise, Grandfather lived up to his nickname of 'Lucky Jack' in forging a successful career at sea and living until sixty in spite of it, dying in 1936, two years after their visit. I probably have him to thank for a constitution that enabled me to fight off the attack. (See note 6.)

No. 26, Havelock Street: The first morning after I came back from Peppard Common Sanatorium, my sister Ann led me out into the back garden to see the new baby, Max, in his pram (born on the 1st of January, 1935) and named after the American world heavyweight boxing champion, Max Baer). So as well as finding that Mother had moved further up the street to a three bed-roomed, semi-detached house about half way up on the left side, I found that I had a new brother. Apparently, David, while learning to walk, had fallen from the steep steps into the back garden at No. 3, and injured himself. This was one of the reasons prompting the move, but Mother may also have wanted to get away from the house where I had become ill. (One also has to say that Mother couldn't resist an empty house if it promised to be more pleasant to live in than the one she was in.)

The only memory I have of this new house, apart from that first morning in the back garden, is of my bedroom one evening when I had been left in charge of the other children, all peacefully sleeping, while our parents went out; (this was quite normal in those relaxed days). The sunset light flooded the room, illuminating two Indian scenes printed at Hunt Barnard's, which Father had had framed. One was of an avenue leading to a temple, the other of a high prowed boat drawn up on the sands, somewhere south of Madras, with turbaned figures crowding round. I imagined I was in these pictures as I drifted off to sleep. The impression they made no doubt accounts for the sense of familiarity I felt, years later, when I encountered similar scenes in India.

I arrived home just in time to enjoy the celebrations for the jubilee of George V and Queen Mary in the May of 1935. On Jubilee Day there were stalls and roundabouts in the Market Square and I was given sixpence to make a 'lucky dip' into a bran tub. I fished out an interesting looking package and was most disappointed to find that it contained a tea strainer. This is my only memory of that historic day. Fortunately, it turned out that Mother happened to be in need of a tea strainer and she was still using it well into my adulthood (along with the yellow and green tin plate that I had first used as a child).

As well as having a new home I now went to a new school, going on to Queens Park, Council Junior School, instead of returning to St. John's—thus following in Mother's footsteps, down through the Market Square and under the arch by the Corn Exchange, across the Old Rec. (recreation ground) and down Highbridge Walk to the footbridge over the canal to the school (twice a day, as I ran home for lunch).

I have little recollection of the lessons given in the school, but I do remember a temporary teacher coming to teach us English through phonetics (an enthusiasm that seems to recur with every generation). As English is not a phonetic language, and it was some years since I had wiped preliminary exercises like, 'the c-a-t s-a-t on the m-a-t' off my slate, I felt quite baffled, and was glad that after a fortnight or so, the teacher moved on to another school and we returned to the usual mixture of phonetics with 'look and say', more appropriate by then.

A lesson I did learn, was not to be led into trouble by older boys. One day I went to school the proud possessor of a whistle I'd been given by a relation, similar to a scout's whistle. At playtime, I showed it off to another boy when we were both in the bicycle shed, and he dared me to blow it. When I did, it was quite a blast and all the children in the playground lined up to go back into school. A teacher then came out and angrily demanded to know who had blown the whistle. The boy and I stayed as quiet as mice at the back of the bicycle shed and no one gave us away. I didn't take the whistle to school again.

Little toy handguns that fired explosive caps were common at this time, as well as lead 'bombs' made of two halves held together on a string. A number of caps could be put between the halves and would go off with a most satisfying bang when the 'bomb' was dropped. One day, on the way home from school, I was playing with these 'bombs' with another boy. Running out of caps we went into Woolworths at the top of the High Street to buy some more. On the way out this boy showed me how easy it was to swipe a handful of sweets from the open display chests. I was horrified and immediately made myself scarce, having nothing more to do with him again (stealing and indeed, lying, being more or less capital offences as far as my parents were concerned).

Another important lesson learned, also came about through incidents on the way home from school. Sometimes, instead of going straight home over the canal footbridge, I went along the canal towpath to the road bridge in the High Street, to look at water birds or perhaps sail a reed boat, the sort made by turning over the end of the leaf and tucking it through a slit to make a sail to catch the breeze. One day, a pretty fair-haired girl in my class, who lived in a house immediately adjacent to the bridge came out and asked me to play with her. But I shook my head, saying that I had to go home. The next day the same thing happened and being too shy (although I was attracted to her) I just ran on. The following day, the headmistress lined up all the boys in our class in the playground and brought the little girl along to pick out the boy she claimed had molested her. Of course, she immediately picked me out. The headmistress then spoke to us separately in her office and afterwards she (wisely) simply told us to run along home, realizing it was just a case of female chagrin. (I don't know what she said to the little girl!)

The peculiar horror of being falsely accused has stayed with me, together with the greatest sympathy for those finding themselves in the same position. It also made me wary of arousing false expectations, even at the cost of being considered 'painfully' shy and 'slow'. In any case, it is the woman who decides in these matters.

Father finally leaves Hunt Barnard's: It seems that the difficulties that had led Father to leave Hunt Barnard's to go to London had not been entirely resolved on his return to the company and in the summer of 1935 he took a job as representative for the printing firm, 'Cheneys of Banbury'. This was a very old, family printing firm established by John Cheney the first, in 1767 and with a name for taste, quality and service that appealed to Father; (it printed an early edition of Dr. Johnson's *Rasselas).* Early in the 1930s the firm had expanded its premises and installed new, automatic equipment; and by the time Father joined, the fifth generation of the family, John and his brother Walter were fully in control. Father greatly admired his new employers and always spoke most highly of them. (Sadly, this firm recently went out of business, having just survived into the 21st century.)

Father's new job prompted another house move, so I left Queens Park School at the end of the summer term. My last memory of that time in Aylesbury is of being taken by Father to the new, open air swimming baths, shortly after they had been opened in the Vale recreation grounds (see note 7). At first I clung to the rail at the shallow end in some bewilderment, but soon gained confidence, splashing about, after he lifted me into the pool surrounding the fountain, with its spectacular waterfall. When Max was old enough to come with us, swimming became a feature of most of our outings and family life. Mother always said Max should be a good swimmer, because Father taught her to swim in the reservoir near Tring, when she was carrying him. He did turn out to be the best, most balanced diver in the family. (Earlier that summer, before the Vale baths opened, when we were out at the reservoir one evening, a man got caught in a patch of weeds and drowned. Father helped to bring the man out but all efforts to revive him failed. No doubt my parents thought the Vale a much safer place to take us to swim, after that.)

SOURCES/NOTES—CHAPTER 4

I am greatly indebted to Laura Robinson, archivist at the Centre for Buckinghamshire Studies, who directed me to the article on Peppard Common Sanatorium by Esther Carling (see below); also to Lisa Spurling, archivist at the Berks Record Office, who researched the minutes of the Berks and Bucks Joint Sanatorium Committee minutes for 1934-1936 on my behalf.

1) Dormandy T. 1999. *The White Death—a history of Tuberculosis* . The Hambledon Press, London.
According to Thomas Dormandy, it was thought that the TB bacillus (*Myobacterium tuberculosa*) gained access to the lymph glands in the neck by being carried there after gaining entry through the tonsils. Diagnosis involved both culturing and analysis of the fluid as well as injecting it into guinea pigs, where, if active, it caused abdominal TB. This took six to eight weeks. The scar caused by drainage took time to heal, multiple scars in my case, the disfigurement much upsetting my mother.

2) Carling, Esther M.D. *Thirty Years of Sanatorium Life.* The Lancet, June 22, 1929, pp. 1321-1322.

3) It was known that the UV in sunlight destroyed the TB bacillus and the Dane, Niels Finsen, found, as had apparently been known earlier to Arab physicians, that it cured lesions caused by skin TB, which led him to invent the 'Sun-ray Lamp' and to the Nobel Prize in 1902.

4) Hermann Bremer was responsible for the first sanatorium in the Bavarian Alps in 1854, at Gobersdorf, following up his idea that TB was associated with a weak heart and that this could be relieved by moving to a higher altitude. Patients were housed in wooden chalets with open balconies and this became the standard pattern when the idea was copied. The most famous was established in Nordrack, at 1500 ft in the Black Forest and it was after a visit by the Duke of Cambridge, the Commander in Chief of the British Army in 1889, who was very keen on medical welfare, that they were copied in Britain, the first one in Edinburgh. Particular interest was aroused by the publication of an account by a chemist called Gibson, of his cure in the Black Forest in 1898. Following this, several private sanatoria were set up in 1899, including the one at Peppard. As Esther Carling put it, "Thus a very small experiment, started here in 1899, grew steadily by ones and twos. Patients were housed in huts and shelters with a minimum of capital expenditure, and year by year more and more pressure was made to extend the accommodation. There were certain dramatic moments when interested callers left cheques for £500, or when a deputation from a county council urged on us to 'sell our boots but provide beds'." The Sanatorium also had a herd of cows to ensure good quality milk, and there were also pigs and horses as well as the big orchard, mentioned above. More secure financial arrangements were put in place after the National Health Insurance Act of 1911, when the sanatorium became part of the public medical service and the Berks and Bucks Councils took it over. At the time Dr. Carling wrote her article, in 1929, the sanatorium, with 180 beds, cost £20,000 a year to run. The accounts for the Committee for 1934/35, note that a total of £5206 was paid by the two County Councils for their own patients, and £4449 by other local authorities and private patients. The farm contributed £77 and the remaining £12,000 was covered by the two Councils. Seventy five of the beds were for children, 39 for girls and 28 for boys, only 14 of these being free places (20 were 'let' to the West Riding of Yorkshire and when these were released in January 1935 they became available at a rate reduced to about £2 a week). Unless my stay was covered by the Bucks Council, it would have cost my parents about £100, and may explain some of Father's monetary difficulties at that time.

5) Peppard was unusual in having large numbers of children as patients, not all of them actually ill. This was because of the policy of removing vulnerable children from 'tuberculous homes' and building up their strength over a few weeks or months before sending them back home with the hope that they would then be resistant to the disease. The 1934/35 Report of the Berks and Bucks Joint Committee, shows that the average stay of these children was 41 weeks 3 days (not far off the length of mine). Dr. Carling also believed that the presence of children was helpful to the adult patients. As she put it "Experience here shows that there is everything to be gained. The life of the children is quite separate, but they give brightness and vigour—-they can be seen at play and heard shouting, and they make the place more homely."

6) Ironically, considering my remarks about my grandfather, 'Lucky Jack', possibly the first prototype of a sanatorium was set up by John Lettsom, a Quaker physician, in Margate, in 1791, because he had been told that fishermen didn't catch scrofula, the form of TB causing neck tumours, and that it could be cured by sea bathing. (It was also called the 'King's Evil' because it used to be thought that it could be cured by the royal touch.) An infirmary with eighty-six beds was established, with open balconies and access for gentle exercise on the beach. However, swimming was not compulsory and as there was a lack of strict medical supervision, the idea didn't find favour with physicians.

7) The 1930s were the great age of the open-air swimming bath, or Lido. A large number were opened around the country. Unfortunately they went into decline with the Second World War and there are now only one or two still open. This is a pity because swimming in an open-air pool is much more pleasurable than in an overheated, steamy, covered-in pool, even in the rain (or especially in the rain).

CHAPTER 5

VILLAGE BOYHOOD

BODICOTE 1935-36

A question of schooling: In the late summer of 1935 we moved to the village of Bodicote, which is about two miles from Banbury, down the main road to Oxford, and in those days, still separated from the town by countryside. (Since then the suburbs have advanced to the village boundary). One of the reasons Mother elected to live in the village, apart from not wanting to live in Banbury, was because when I was discharged from Peppard Sanatorium, she was advised to see that I lived an open air life as far as possible and wear an open necked shirt with no tie.

The house was a modern, three bed-roomed 'semi' with a garage (photos 5-1). It had some good features, including quite a large kitchen with a red quarry-tiled floor and outside storage and coalhouse reached under cover from the back door, where swallows regularly nested. There were two large reception rooms and the rear sitting room had French windows onto the lawn and a view of the rose bed. However, there were disadvantages: it was not really in the village but out on the main road to Oxford, right on the turn down to the village and therefore on a busy corner. Our front gate opened onto the main road, which was of some concern to Mother with her young children, especially David who from the time he could walk was an inveterate wanderer. One of David's first memories is of hiding in the culvert that ran beneath our gateway and jumping out to surprise passers-by. My only memory of being in the front garden is of playing there one evening and hearing through the open window a radio announcement that Italian planes had dropped bombs in Abyssinia, lodging in the mind as a permanent source of disquiet.

There was another difficulty: Father, worried by my fragmentary schooling, decided that I should go to a 'good' school, rather than the one in the village and arrangements were made for me to attend one in Banbury, which had been recommended to him. I started at the beginning of the autumn term (I don't know what the fees were). All went well for a week or two and I remember that we were given coloured merit badges that, I think, denoted our position in weekly tests. The problem was that although Father could take me to the school by car in the morning, there were no facilities for dinner at the school and packed lunches were not allowed, which meant I had to go home by service bus in the dinner hour, when I could just manage to snatch a quick meal and then return. In the evening, I was allowed to travel home on a bus that brought older children back from the Council Senior School to the village. One evening the school bus took another route and when we had reached an outlying suburb of Banbury and all the other children had got off, the driver told me that this was as far as he went. Perhaps the schedules had been changed and as I was the odd child out, Mother had not been informed. Anyhow, the bus driver told me how to get to the Banbury/Oxford road and drove off. Somewhat bewildered, I was soon lost and had to ask someone the way. Eventually, I got onto the main road but it was now getting dark and I had to keep well over on the grass verge as the traffic went by. Fortunately, when I was about half way home, Father came along in the car looking for me, and picked me out in the beam of the headlights. After this scare, my parents decided that this was all too much for a boy of six and it would be just as well (and Mother probably thought, a lot cheaper) if I went to the village school, where I could go with other village children and easily run home for my lunch. After this, it is perhaps not surprising that I became apprehensive whenever Father bought up the subject of a 'good' school again!

I enjoyed going to Bodicote village school, with its large pictures of children from around the world, in national dress, on the walls. One lesson I particularly remember, was when the local doctor came in and gave us a talk on illness and disease, likening the white blood cells to soldiers being mustered to fight the disease germs. The following summer this same doctor gave me and another boy sixpence each for collecting poppies for him, mostly gathered from the big wheat field across the road from our house, when the corn was still green in the ear. He didn't tell us why he wanted them. In the spring there were lengthy preparations for May Day. The boys in my class were dressed up as elves with cellophane wings and the mistress became most upset at the extensive repair jobs that had to be carried out after we raced round the playground pretending we were aeroplanes. My memory of the actual event is hazy. Not so, however, of the sports day held sometime later. I was well ahead in the fifty yards dash but stopped just short of the tape, thinking I had won. Of course, all the other boys swept past me and I was judged last, to Father's great disgust.

When my brother David was three, he became very curious about me attending school and one afternoon insisted on following me as I went back after dinner, despite my efforts to dissuade him. However, the mistress let him sit by me and he remained very attentive until it was time to go home. His highly developed curiosity was causing problems for Mother and Father. As the days lengthened in the spring, he would climb out of his cot to explore, emptying everything out of drawers and cupboards. Father bought a pig-net to tie over the cot to keep him in, but more often than not David worked away at the knots until he could get out. This culminated in a grand demonstration when he went down into the kitchen very early and emptied out all the bags of flour, currants, sugar and cereals, together with packets of tea and cocoa, in a heap on the floor and mixed them up with water. He wasn't severely punished, apart from a light smacking. Father realized that he was, at least in part, seeking attention, as the third child, with little more than eighteen months between him and Ann and also between him and Max, then only a toddler. (Dad was more amused than annoyed, bringing me and Ann down to view the scene, and to help him clear up.)

Photographs 5-1 Bodicote 1935-6

Top -: Father and his brood outside the French windows of the new 'semi'. As he wrote on the back of the photo, "Mummy forgot to tell everyone to smile"; (Mother was the one interested in photography and took most of the family photos.)
Middle left -: Max showing an early propensity for ball games.
Bottom left -: Father and Mother reading together in the well-lit 1930s dining room.
Bottom right -: John (at seven) happy to be in Bodicote village school, where this was taken.

Ann was still only about four and a half, when an incident occurred that revealed her self-possessed, forthright character. On the other side of the road to the village, opposite our house, there were some large wooden gates leading to a house hidden in trees. We were playing in the garden and we could see some children climbing up and dropping a kitten over the gates, then doing it again when it crept back underneath. We went over to remonstrate with them and Ann marched forward boldly and roundly told them off for being so cruel. Surprised and abashed the children, shamefaced, jumped down and disappeared, taking the kitten with them.

When I started in the village school, I began piano lessons with a lady in a house a short distance down the road. I took to the lessons quite readily, especially as she had a fair-haired, blue-eyed daughter, the same age as me. The music teacher encouraged our friendship and one day she came over to our house to play with me and (at her instigation) we innocently played 'Doctor and patient' in front of the kitchen window. Mother didn't interfere but later told me off, saying, "What would her mother think?" Sometime later, a pretty, dark haired girl came to live next-door to us, also my age, or a little older. She was more circumspect. She invited me into their garage and hugged and kissed me soundly, to my surprise but satisfaction.

Seventh birthday: Not long before my seventh birthday, a door-to-door salesman called one evening, selling an encyclopaedia called *The Book of Knowledge.* Father was home and perhaps to compensate for the failure to get me into a 'good' school, decided he would buy it for me. The evening before my birthday, my parents went out leaving me in charge. I had no idea what I was to get for my birthday but I had noticed an interesting looking package in the sitting room. As soon as they had gone out, I slipped downstairs to look at it. Mother had fully carpeted the room in royal blue and there were also full-length blue curtains covering the French windows, making it dark except for a gold bar of sunset light, which illuminated this big, brown cardboard box. It had been opened and not yet packed up again, so I was able to pull out the top volume. It was the index to the set of volumes and the frontispiece was an excellent illustration of various birds' eggs with very good colour rendition. Fearful of disturbing the package more, I put the volume back and went happily back to bed.

In the morning, the set proved to be of eight volumes, including the index. It became the constant background to all my other reading up to my early teens. Eventually, I knew some of the articles almost by heart. As a bonus, another book called *The Book of the Sea* was included with the set. This covered the whole of our naval history from Alfred's sea battles with the Danes to the Battle of Jutland and highlights such as Sir Richard Grenville's exploits on the *Revenge* and the races between the tea clippers, stirring to the blood of any boy.

An incident took place a few weeks later, always connected in my mind with the arrival of these books on my birthday and the picture of the birds' eggs. Father got us up very early one morning, to watch the young swallows under the porch being coaxed from the nest and encouraged to fly, first fluttering tentatively to the top of the garden trellis before taking off in earnest. For many evenings afterwards, before falling asleep, I imagined I was a swallow, from breaking out of the egg, to learning to fly, and eventually, at the end of the summer, circling the village before setting off with the rest of the flock to Africa. Many years later, on my thirtieth birthday, when I was working in the Sahara, I returned at sunset to find several swallows perched on my tent and two that had flown in through the open tent flap to sit, exhausted, on my camp bed. I lifted these two out to join the others on the roof. I woke at first light but they had already all flown on. It was a hundred miles to the Gulf of Sirte and the sea, many more to Italy and the far away Alps, which they were probably going to cross, in the epic flight I had imagined as a boy. By strange chance, it seems, they had chosen my tent from six others in our small encampment, as somewhere to rest, on a day that just happened to be my birthday.

We move again: In those days, tramps were a common sight on the roads, particularly on the main road past our house, as they travelled between the work- houses at Banbury and Oxford. Many called at our kitchen door, because they soon discovered that Mother was soft hearted and would make them tea and give them a bite to eat; and David and I spent some time looking for the signs which we had been told they left for each other to indicate a kindly household. One day we had a grizzled old chap, in a battered old hat and an old black overcoat tied up with string, sitting in our kitchen; and while Mother made him tea in his blue billy-can, he told David and me about his life on the road and how he sometimes slept in barns or in a shelter of branches in the woods. When he left he gave us some nuts, in return for the hospitality.

At some point in the early summer (1936) we had a break-in during the night. It may have been a professional burglar, or possibly a tramp that had seen the possibilities, because some food was taken as well as money and some jewelry. Naturally, it greatly upset Mother, who was already unhappy with the exposed position of the house on the outskirts of the village, on the main road; and it strengthened her inclination to move, as she was also worried about the expense of renting and running it.

Mother was always most meticulous with the household accounts, kept with every item noted to the farthing and took pride in more than living within her income, where-as father, with his expansive view of life, was generous to a fault and, as Mother said "Always hand in pocket". As small children we were never short of toys, games and sports equipment, as well as books and comics. Of course, there were times when Mother appreciated his generosity, as when, early in their marriage, she found it hard to choose between two different frocks in a shop in Oxford and then, when they got home, found that Father had bought both of them. However, on one occasion at Bodicote, he arrived home with a present of cutlery for her, but not just one complete canteen, but two, and poor Mother was so upset, she burst into tears.

So for a number of reasons, Mother became anxious to move. Luckily, Aunt Nan (her sister) and Uncle Harold (Hurst) had by this time moved from the 'New Inn Farm' at Stowe to another farm, called 'The Boxes', in Slapton, a village near Towcester. This was only four or five miles away, just over the Northamptonshire border from our Wheeler relations at 'Black Pit Farm' in Stowe Ridings in Bucks; so when Nan discovered that the Lodge Cottage of a country house in Slapton was empty, Mother jumped at the chance of renting it and living near her two sisters again. It also meant that we children would be near our Hurst cousins, who were close to us in age: Tony, a year older than me, Richard, a year younger, and Jill, three years younger and quite close in age to my sister Ann. Tony and Jill were fair and blue eyed like their father and Richard dark like his mother.

HALCYON DAYS—-SLAPTON AND ABTHORPE 1936-1939

A 'typical' village: As there was no school in Slapton, after we moved we children attended the school in neighbouring Abthorpe. In the year after our arrival, I was pleased to find that, despite the lack of a school and being more of a hamlet when compared with the bigger village of Abthorpe, Slapton did have many of the features of the typical English village, shown on a map in one of the pamphlets the school received to accompany BBC radio broadcasts (I think, to illustrate a series on 'Town and Country'). We had a small church, on a green of sorts, with a former vicarage nearby, a chapel, several big country houses and a scatter of small cottages, some still thatched, as well as a pub, the 'Royal Oak', which included a village shop and post office. Best of all, there was a brook lined with pollard willows and a 'lasher' (a sluice-gate with a weir pool and leat to a water-wheel at a mill), which was to figure large in our childhood; what features our village lacked, were more than made up for those of the more populous village of Abthorpe. (See notes 1, 2 and map inside front cover.)

The Lodge Cottage: The Lodge Cottage consists of two small, stone cottages knocked into one, with a brick facade, on the left side of the drive, with its ornamental gates (always open) leading down to 'The Lodge' (a country house then occupied by Major Lamb, and out of sight behind a copse). It's the first house in Slapton as you come in from Abthorpe, though there used to be a cottage a little before it on the left, but that has gone now. However, Slapton is not greatly changed over the sixty years since our time, apart from the catastrophic loss of the elms and the final disappearance of a number of dilapidated cottages; there are also fewer children.

Although knocked into one, the cottage still had two staircases (ideal for children's games). The entrance nearest the drive gates had been retained as the front door, with a former kitchen as a lobby leading to one flight of stairs and the drawing room which looked over the back garden. A door had been put through the wall into the former left hand cottage, leading to the dining room, overlooking the road, and the second staircase. The kitchen was a lean-to addition at the back, converting the former kitchen into an internal larder and cool-room with cold slabs (where, in summer, Mother could keep the milk, or hang the sour milk to drip in a muslin bag to make cottage cheese, and get our favourite summer treat, green jelly with mandarin oranges and cornflower blanc-mange to set). It was the sort of house where Mother could see the 'possibilities' and much preferred to a stereotypical semi. This was despite the fact, that although there was a phone, there was no sanitation and water was from a pump outside the back door.

To the left of the cottage was a large, lean-to outhouse, open to a brick paved yard that led up to the kitchen door. This allowed entrance to the swallows that always nested there. There was a copper in the corner of the outhouse for washing clothes (fired from underneath by sticks and coal) and in the yard, in addition to the pump, a water-butt for rainwater (that Mother used for washing her hair) and an outside loo with bucket, (see note 3). The yard was separated from the copse by a high brick wall and the rest of the garden, mostly lawn, from the drive to the Lodge, by chestnut palings. There were three large yews by the kitchen, another in the left hand corner of the garden and a small, red flowering chestnut at the other end; (the yews are still there, but cut back, while the chestnut is now well grown).

We didn't move immediately into the cottage because Father spent some time going over at weekends, painting and decorating, sometimes taking me for company. He painted the woodwork in the sitting room blue, to go with Mother's carpet and curtains, and that in the dining room marigold, including the big floor cupboards either side of the fireplace, which rather took Mother aback when she first saw it. It must have been some time before midsummer that we finally moved in, because Ann remembers running down the village street to the 'Boxes' to give our cousin Jill a birthday card, which would have been on June 28th 1936.

Friends in Slapton: My first memory of life in the village is of collecting the eggs with my Hurst cousins at the Boxes. The hens ranged freely throughout the farm buildings and it was exciting to explore the cowsheds and hay loft to find where they had chosen to lay. Jill boldly drove the hens off the nests and she and Ann began collecting the eggs in their aprons. When Aunt Nan came to check how we were getting on, she was terrified they would drop them, fearing the financial loss which was an important part of her weekly income, and was only mollified when they were all transferred safely to a basket.

To the right side of the drive into the farmyard there was a clump of tall trees. Here Uncle Harold had roped up a very high swing, made more vertiginous by a down-slope in front. There was also a seesaw made from an enormous beam. It was very heavy and actually quite dangerous, because when one end hit the ground you were bounced up in the air if you were at the other end. However, no one got badly hurt there, but one day my cousin Jill and I were doing a 'pigeon toed' tight-rope walk along the iron railings at the side of the house, when she slipped and was caught on one of the spikes, Fortunately, the spike only penetrated the soft skin on her stomach and although she was frightened to death, as was her mother (Nan) who rushed out of the kitchen to lift her off, she was not seriously injured.

In the front garden at the Boxes the paths were lined with large conch shells that acted as a haven for snails and one day my cousin Richard showed me how we could have an interesting game racing several of them against each other, on a sheet of glass; a game we often played later and that I played with other village boys. Once, when I was invited to have tea at the Boxes, Richard said we would be having something good called biznins. It was like junket, which Aunt Nan explained was made from the first milk a cow produced after it had a calf; (I've never had it since).

My first memory of Abthorpe also involved Richard. His father (Harold) allowed the two of us to ride on the back of his carthorse when he took it to the Blacksmith's, that then still operated in School Lane, to have it re-shod. So my first memory of Abthorpe is combined with the shower of sparks from the anvil, the sizzling of the quenched horseshoe and my feeling of 'surely it must hurt' as the hoof was pared down and the nails hammered home.

My cousin Tony (Hurst), a tall, thin boy only a year or two older than me, quickly became a great friend. He was 'technically minded' from an early age and had a very good, quite large-scale, model of a traction engine that worked with real steam, as well as a very comprehensive model farm. There was also a full sized bagatelle board at the Boxes, the first I had played on. However, we also got into some scrapes. We got hold of some matches and made little fires in old hay that had been left in front of a barn, about two fields away from the farmhouse. We stamped them out (we thought) but in the night the wind got up and fanned the smouldering remains into a conflagration that threatened to burn down the barn and finally involved the local fire brigade. Tony got most of the blame, being the eldest, but I had a good dressing down first thing in the morning from Dad, who wisely decided to accompany his strictures with teaching me how to lay and light the fire in the living room, which I then did regularly for him. To help make amends, Tony and I had to clean out a chicken house on wheels that stood in the middle of a field on the other side of the road from the farmhouse. The droppings were up to the perches and we had to hold our breath as we dug each shovel full. It was calculated to make sure we didn't forget!

Father was always very fair in matters of discipline when we were small (taking pride in distancing himself from the over-bearing Victorian patriarch) but he wouldn't countenance dissent or defiance for a moment, or any over-reaction to punishment such as 'dog howling'. Sulking, which was also quite out of the question, earned you another dose; you took your medicine and got on with it. Mother was very good in this too, she had a fiery temper and if pushed beyond patience would deliver slaps all round but immediately afterwards when order was restored she would be smiling and laughing with us as usual. Mother amused us all one day when she lost her temper chasing a mouse out of the kitchen. It darted out over the bricks of the yard, twisting and turning as she tried to hit it with the back of a coal shovel, finally escaping under the stones of the rockery, which made her laugh too. This style of upbringing meant that after I returned from the sanatorium Father never had to resort to physical punishment.

An example of my father's fairness and forbearance is an episode one day when he was giving me a boxing lesson. We had the gloves on and he was on his knees in the sitting room, on the royal blue carpet, teaching me how to keep my guard up and how to follow a straight left with a right cross. However much I tried, I couldn't get a blow in, until, momentarily, his attention was distracted by the phone ringing in the living room and as he looked away I dotted him with one, right on the nose. He blinked, and the force of the blow brought the tears to his eyes. I expected immediate, severe retribution, but after a slight pause, he said quietly, "that shows how you have to keep your guard up, John", and the lesson went on.

I almost never got into a fight with any of my contemporaries in those days (Father taught us to box fairly and fight only in self defense) except with my friend and classmate, Harry

Hayward, who also lived in Slapton; there always seemed to be an underlying bone of contention between us. We were of about the same physique, but he was fair and blue eyed with rosy cheeks (the archetypal son of the 'hay ward' who was in charge of field boundaries under the old manorial system) and full of mischievous pranks. Harry, who also had a pretty, fair haired younger sister, Cicely and a little brother called Johnny, lived in a row of thatched cottages on the left of the lane going up to the church (I think in the only one then still habitable at that time); the ones further up had the thatch tumbling in with grass and poppies growing on it.

We generally got on quite well out at play but minor disagreements sometimes led to a scrap. If I stayed on my feet, remembering what I'd been taught, I could more than hold my own, but usually we ended up on the ground, half wrestling and giving as good as we got, becoming dishevelled and sometimes getting a bleeding nose. Of course, this had to be explained away when one got home, as the result of 'falling out of a tree' or 'off my bike'; (adults were considered to have no jurisdiction over these matters).

Despite these occasional clashes, Harry and I enjoyed expeditions over the fields and, particularly, birds nesting; once finding the beautifully, lichen-finished nest of 'bumbarrels' (Long tailed Tits) not many yards from the mossy cup of a 'pink' (chaffinch) in the hedge down the field opposite the Lodge Cottage. Father had taught me how to pierce an egg with a pin and 'blow it' along with the admonition, 'never take more than one' and this rule was adhered to; (however, I gave up egg collecting by the time I was ten and had learnt more about birds).

We also went fishing together, most successfully, one day, in the brook where it runs by Wappenham Station. It takes some skill, using a stick with a bent pin on a string, especially as the worm usually wriggles off. Harry stuck immediately he had a bite and luckily, as he hauled the fish straight out it fell off the hook into the grass. It was a roach and to us it seemed enormous, certainly the biggest fish any of us boys ever caught in Slapton Brook (and the only roach). Harry grabbed it and raced off home to show his father, and I think, had it for his tea.

I did see a school of roach some time later. On a hot summer day, I was walking along the bank of the brook below Lodge Cottage, where there is a quiet, wide stretch running through a copse, and I came on them hanging almost stationary in the amber water, their fins hardly moving, lit by a bar of sunlight through the trees. For a few moments, I was transfixed by this visionary apparition, then crept away and ran home to get my rod. When I got back to the brook, I used my best Red Indian hunter skills to approach the spot, but when I reached it they had gone, although they remained bright in the memory.

Other friends were my classmate, Christine Smith, from Manor Farm near the church, a jolly, friendly girl (a real farmer's daughter who used to invite us to splendid birthday parties) and Jill Burridge, who had a younger brother, Peter. They lived in a cottage in the middle of the village, almost opposite the big house of Major Lewis, where their father worked. The lane through the village was relatively flat past their cottage and acted as a central meeting place for children. Traffic through the village was at that time light, and we could play ball games there, play marbles, spin tops and bowl our hoops with impunity; also, as we got older, learn to ride our bikes with no hands or standing up on the saddle. The Burridge's cottage had a large garden as it had taken over the gardens of a row of tumbledown thatched cottages on the right hand side, by a rivulet that came down from the Glebe. Although they were dangerously dilapidated, we used to play hide and seek round them. One day Jill and I went a bit further away and hid in a haystack in the neighbouring field. As it was some time before we were found, we fell, naturally, to kissing.

A variant on hide and seek that we played, was highracky (or highacky) the pole. A telephone pole or equivalent, such as the kissing gate at the church entrance, would be home base, where the child 'on' would wait with eyes closed while the other children hid. This child would then go to look for the others, and on seeing one would cry out, for instance, ' 'ighracky, 'arry 'ayward' and race back to base to touch it, crying ' 'ighracky the pole, you're out'. Harry would then have to be the one 'on'. However, if Harry could get back and touch the pole first, he could run off and hide again. As can be imagined, this game could go on for a long time on summer evenings. (The pole may have been the maypole, originally.)

My best friend of all, in those days was Peter Lawrence. He was a year younger with dark hair and eyes, as pale in complexion as me but with freckles. We got on very well with each other and I can't remember us ever having a quarrel. The Lawrence's lived in the second house on the right up Church Lane and Peter had two older brothers, who assisted their father in an agricultural contracting business.

My introduction to the family came when Peter took me to see his rabbit, which we fed with 'keck' (cow parsley) from the lane; (later he showed me how you could make a whistle from the hollow stems, as you could, similarly, from elder stems with the pith removed). There was a Reverend Wilkes apple tree in the middle of their cottage garden, which grew the biggest apples I'd ever seen, and a tall, Blenheim Orange by the gate with its apples of old-gold in the autumn. One of our first games was damming the rivulet that runs down from the Glebe on the east side of the field, the 'Green', by the church, using the plastic clay from the banks. We also used the clay to make marbles and little cups, which we baked in his mother's oven. Peter's mother was very kind (as this will indicate) and hospitable and I usually ended up having tea there, as Peter did with us in return.

It was great fun when we were allowed to go with Peter's father and brothers on a job threshing out a corn stack on a farm near Wappenham; to see the giant, steam engine with its shining brass, which powered the belt to the threshing box, and watch as the sheaves were pitched into the open trap on top and with dusty, grinding clangour, came out separately as straw and chaff, the grain being caught in sacks at the back.

At that time there were regular train services from Northampton via Towcester, through Wappenham station and on through Helmdon to Banbury. Peter's brothers regularly met the evening train to collect newspapers to distribute round the village and we sometimes went with them to see the train come in. Anther attraction was a dispensing machine where we could get ha'penny bars of Nestle's milk chocolate.

We were also allowed to go with them when they were coppicing the hazel bushes in a wood near Wappenham (this may have been the west side of Bucknell's Wood), watching as they used their sharp billhooks to cut the hazel poles and trim off the small branches for faggots; leaning back in the sweet smelling piles of branches to eat our lunch with them and thinking it would be good to work in the woods when we were grown up. (Coppicing of oak woods took place at intervals of from five to ten years, the poles being used for bean sticks or hurdles and the faggots for pea sticks or firewood; and as more light was let into the woods in early spring, it meant that there was a rather better display of windflowers, primroses and bluebells in those days than now.) This expert demonstration of the use of the billhook led us into trouble later. We were out looking for bow sticks and unable to find the right size of the preferred ash or hazel poles near the village we decided to go down to the brook and cut off some willow branches. As we were also finding our penknives inadequate for the job, Peter decided to borrow (on the quiet) one of his father's billhooks. We climbed up into a pollard willow, the first on the left down the path from the lasher (the sluice that used to divert the brook along the leat to the millwheel). At first all went well and we cut and trimmed one branch but starting on the other, Peter struck a glancing blow and cut through a vein in his foot. We did everything we could to staunch the flow of blood, without success, and eventually he had to limp home to face the music.

There were happier days by the lasher in high summer. It was the main bathing place for the village lads. One could stand on the mossy spillway, in the cool glissade of water, and dive off into the deep pool excavated by the winter floods in front. It was also a good place for fishing. Peter and I waded and swam as far as we could in either direction along the brook and fished with our nets. One day finding a large school of 'soldiers' (minnows and sticklebacks in mating colours) near the bridge where the brook goes under the railway line to the Abthorpe side, catching some for my aquarium (a large square, glass tank that, I think, my parents gave me for my eighth birthday).A particularly good place to fish was where the brook narrowed below the lasher. Here, we caught stone loach and bullheads, the occasional, freshwater crayfish, and one year, there was a tremendous run of elvers, about six to nine inches long. There were also newts in the millpond and I was very nonplussed, at first, to find that when I put one into the aquarium in the evening it had gone by the morning. When we were fishing we often saw water voles, as well as moorhens and the occasional heron.

It was not often that Abthorpe children came over to play in Slapton, maybe the railway line made a psychological barrier; but one day, on Abthorpe Green in the company of some older boys (from the Senior school) I blurted out that there were a lot of apples up the Glebe, in the orchard of an empty farmhouse called Slapton Hill Farm, lost in the fields above Manor Farm. Two of them cajoled me into showing them the way there one evening and I went reluctantly, not wanting to be called a 'fritbab' (frightened baby). These two lads climbed up into one of the apple trees and threw apples down to me, which I began stacking into a little pile at the foot of the tree. Suddenly, I saw the farmer's dog coming under the gate by the farmhouse and next, Mr. Smith himself climbing over it. With a warning cry, I went straight out of the orchard under the hawthorn hedge, getting badly scratched, into the field and away down the other side of the hedge like a hare, hearing shouts and the dog barking, having got the boys well treed. I had the full story a day or two later: Mr. Smith had shut them into one of the empty rooms of the farmhouse and told them he was going to get the police, then after a while, he went back and let them out, with a stern warning not to come back. The boys were annoyed with me for clearing off, but I'd seen no good reason for delay.

Going to school: As we moved to Slapton around midsummer 1936, I spent the last part of the summer term in Abthorpe School, up to the summer holidays, which in those days started about August 1st (holidays were shorter and terms longer in those days). Although we were sometimes taken to school by car in the winter (although never by Father) we always walked home and often ran home for dinner, and back, pell-mell:

Down the village street, past the copse and the 'Royal Oak' and through a gate beyond the Lodge; across a field with scattered chestnut trees (where I once climbed up in evening sunshine after rain, a memory always linked with the line, 'When showers be-tumble the chestnut spikes'); through a further field at the back of Major Lewis's (where there were crowds of wild daffodils in spring); diagonally down through the orchards behind the Roberts'; round the mill with its big wheel and sinister mill pond (where we were afraid to venture, even onto the thickest ice); over the brook by the plank bridge to the railway embankment (where Peter and I would put pins on the rail in the shape of our initials and hide behind the hedge to see if the passing train would press them in); through the big 'Meadow' that runs up to Abthorpe Manor; over the stile into the 'Old Orchard'; through the hedge into 'Tinkers Close'; over the final stile into Abthorpe village (next to the Redfords' cottage where my classmate, 'Kate'=Kath, lived); up the lane to Abthorpe Green; down past Barfords' farm and farm buildings (where my classmate Joyce and her brother David always went for dinner with their grandparents) opposite the house and walled garden of the Richardsons' farmhouse (where my classmate Margaret lived); and so to school.

Photographs 5-2 Abthorpe School

Top left -: Abthorpe Green. The former post office was behind the post box.

Top right -: John (sixty-five years on) in front of the infants' classroom. Note the Great Oolite, ashlar stonework with courses of dark red ironstone. (See note 1a)

Bottom -: Abthorpe School, founded in 1642; the old school, which became the infants' classroom to the left of the figures, and the big additional classroom beyond.

Abthorpe Church School: The school is at the east end of the village green, near the entrance to what was then the vicarage, 'Leeson house' (see photos 5-2). It was founded and built by Mrs Jane Leeson in the reign of Charles I, and completed in 1642 (the year of the inconclusive battle of Edgehill, at the start of the Civil War) for the education of poor children of the parish, 'for ever' as it says on the plaque set in the front wall, together with the proud inscription, 'Fear God and honour the King'.

The building, as completed in 1642, was 30 feet long by 15 feet wide, of two stories, comprising two equal sized rooms about 7 or 8 feet high, in the warm buff, local limestone (Great Oolite) with decorative courses of dark red, Northampton ironstone, (see note 1a). As can be seen from the photo, where the old school is shown left of the standing figures, there were three downstairs windows, with stone mullions and diamond panes, and a single, dormer window in the roof upstairs. (The school bell, now crowning the roof of the big schoolroom, may have been in the dormer originally.)

By the terms of Jane Leeson's will in 1648, the first schoolmaster, Henry Bendbow, was paid eight pounds a year, with four pounds set aside for repairs, and he was allowed to occupy the upstairs room as a living room and study bedroom (but he was not allowed to accommodate a wife or children in it). The school existed in this form for over two hundred years and the master's salary stayed the same, supplemented by fifteen pounds from the poor rate (called the school pence) until the Local Authority began to assist, with a grant of about thirty pounds, from 1850.

In 1863, after a visit from H.M. Inspector of Schools, it was decided that the rooms were too low and the continuance of the grant was made conditional on enlargement. This took place over the winter of 1864/65 and the school was rebuilt into its present L shape by the addition of a large schoolroom, 37 feet long by 21 feet wide (seen to the right of the figures). The ceiling of the old schoolroom was removed to give the necessary height but the sockets for the joists of the upper floor remain and the closed fireplace in the end-wall of the former bedroom, evocative of the generations of dedicated teachers that rested and warmed their tired feet there (see note 4).

The photo shows the large, west window of the new 'big schoolroom', which brings back an abiding memory of the Lord's Prayer at the end of the school day, with the evening sun gilding the diamond panes; and the joyous sense of relief as we raced out onto the village green on the way home.

In our time the school was in the capable hands of Hilma Abberley, the head mistress, a stout, formidable woman, who kept good discipline (only rarely finding it necessary to enforce it with a rap on the knuckles) and Kathleen Henson, a tall, fair girl who taught the infants, children up to age seven, in the small schoolroom. All the children from their eighth year up to eleven were taught in the big schoolroom, and the two oldest year groups, nine rising to eleven, were taught together in one block under the west window, helping to reinforce the teaching that led to the 'scholarship' exam. (The School Log Book shows that total pupil numbers ranged from about 35 when we arrived to about 45 by the time I was in the top class—see note 4a).

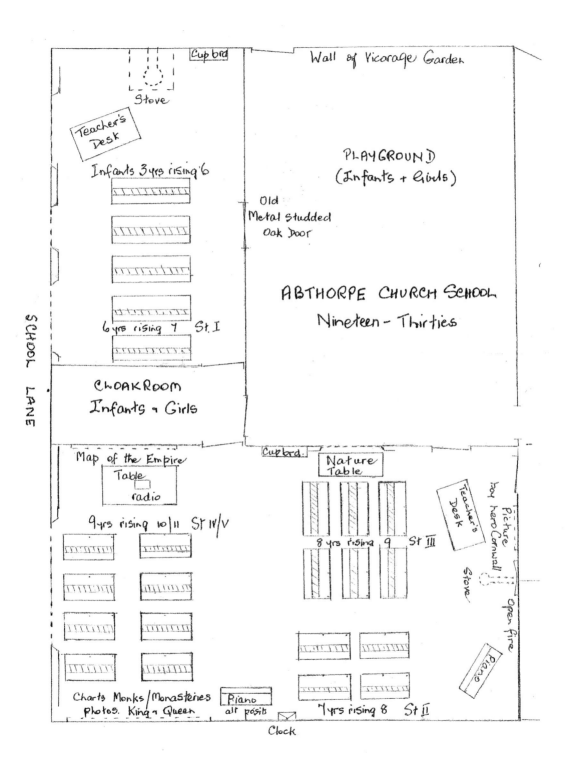

Cup brd

Stove

Teacher's Desk

Infants 3 yrs rising 6

Wall of Vicarage Garden

PLAYGROUND
(Infants + Girls)

Old
Metal studded
Oak Door

ABTHORPE CHURCH SCHOOL
Nineteen - Thirties

6 yrs rising 7   St. I

CLOAKROOM
Infants + Girls

SCHOOL LANE

Map of the Empire
Table
radio

9 yrs rising 10/11   St IV/V

Charts Monks/Monasteries
Photos. King + Queen

Cup brd.

Nature Table

8 yrs rising 9   St III

Teacher's Desk

Picture boy hero Cornwall

Stove

Open fire

Piano

Piano
alt positn

7 yrs rising 8   St II

Clock

117

The photos (5-3) show my year group when we had reached our final year in the combined class, Standards IV/V, two photos with the boys below being necessary to show everyone: Christine Smith, Margaret Richardson, 'Kate' (Kath) Redford, Betty Cann and Joyce Barford, Harry Hayward and me. Charlie Slack, with Peter Lawrence, holding the blackboard and David Barford were in the first year of the combined class, so Harry and I were in the pleasant position of being in a year group of seven, with five, attractive, good-natured girls in it. It may be noticed that apart from David, Peter and me, all the children are fair. (Some sixty years after this photo was taken, in 2002, I was lucky enough to meet three of my old class mates, Kate, Joyce and Margaret at Abthorpe Fete, and because my four years with my class were to prove the longest and most settled period of my boyhood, I have widened my account of this time with some of their reminiscences, to give a fuller picture of our school life.)

Life in the Small (Infants) Schoolroom: As we arrived in Slapton in the summer of 1936, not very long after my seventh birthday and before the end of the school year, I spent the last part of the summer term in the final year group of Miss Henson's infant class in the small schoolroom. I have no memory of my first day, perhaps because I had already attended five different schools, but my classmates, who had entered earlier at four to five years old (in 1934), have vivid recollections of their introduction to the vicar and to the teachers. The vicar asked Kath what her name was and she replied indignantly, " Well, I used to be called Kath, but now they call me Kate," (Kate, was, indeed, what all the village children called her and what I always believed her name to be until our reunion sixty years later!). Joyce had just turned five and her brother, David was not quite four and tiny for his age. When the vicar asked him, "What is your name little man?" He drew himself up, puffed out his chest out and answered in a flash, "David Thomas Barford after Grandad," to delighted, general laughter.

Miss Henson had to be quite skillful in teaching reading and writing, together with simple arithmetic, to children ranging from four to seven and keeping the different year groups occupied. Tables were chanted in unison in the traditional way, with the happy result that one can remember automatically the sum of awkward multiples like 7x8, 8x9, or 12x11. This laid the basis for mental arithmetic, encouraged from an early age. We also went on nature walks, into the fields or up Brackley Lane, bringing back flowers to draw or crayon. Kath remembers getting a boy called Arthur Zucher (a Barnado boy) to pick poppies for her from a cottage garden on one of these walks. Much use was made of modelling clay by the youngest, while we older children made things like raffia mats, winding different coloured lengths of raffia through strings on a cardboard disc; (Mother used one of mine for many years).

We also did recitations and one day, Charlie Slack had to do his turn out in front with 'Jack and Jill'. He had a gray pullover on and as he started the poem, he rolled the hem up to his chin as Jack and Jill climbed the hill and rolled it down again as they came down. (Joyce thinks this was because he was so nervous but it could be taken as a piece of inspired play-acting!)

Miss Henson was an excellent teacher and was always very kind to me, but she could be cruel to be kind. My cousin Richard (Hurst) was a great sucker of his thumb when in a reflective or dreamy mood. Miss Henson finally lost patience with him and tied his hands behind his back with a yellow blackboard duster. She kept him like that for quite a long while and the girls, especially, were very sorry for him. (See note 5.)

An event that caused trepidation amongst the girls was the arrival of the 'nit-nurse'. As Kath puts it, "Standing in line awaiting your turn, praying you wouldn't be sent home and mum producing the nit comb". Joyce remembers that a couple of gypsy children at the school temporarily were blamed, probably quite unfairly, for the outbreak. These children were called Chip and Bella Swinford, and they shared the desk in front of hers. She recalls that, "Bella had long, dark wavy hair. Chip was fair and looked under-nourished. He was smaller and younger than Bella". Also that one day, "Suddenly, I had an urge to pull Bella's long hair. She must have made a noise because her little brother swung round defiantly and threatened me just like an adult, saying, 'Don't you dare 'urt ar Bella!' It did the trick, because I never touched her again, and I never forgot what I thought was his great courage in sticking up for his sister, bless him".

Joyce came top of the class (of her year group) at the end of the school year, in the summer of 1934. She still has the prize book, with the sticker on the back, saying "Joyce Barford, Top of 1st Group of infants, Abthorpe 1934". This was to continue as our year group progressed through the school. Joyce and Kath were always at the top of the class. I was second sometimes but I don't think I ever got a prize book. I wasn't in the least envious, especially as I had taken to Joyce at sight and always admired her. Kath, a tall, friendly girl, crucially remembers, "Running to be first in the line-up to go back in to school" (after the play period). Not something I remember we boys ever did!

We moved on that autumn into the big schoolroom, but at lunchtime, I went with the other children who came from a distance, to eat my sandwiches (taken in bad weather) by the hot stove ('Tortoise Stove') in the small schoolroom, where our bottles of milk, often frozen, were put round the stove to warm up. One winter day, when it was too wet to play outside, I rummaged amongst some books stored in a big cupboard by the stove and found an old battered tome, which I think, was about the people of the world. I found a chapter on the evolution of man and one of the illustrations was of an ape in a tree, sheltering itself from the worst of a rainstorm by holding its hands over its head. The book explained that this was why the hairs on our forearms run downwards. The idea of the evolution of man chimed with the articles in my 'Books of Knowledge' and a picture in one of them, entitled, 'Before the Seas were Salt', which sparked my interest in geological time, but it was this curious suggestion, that struck me as odd, even then, that makes this memory of the small schoolroom one of my sharpest.

Life in the Big Schoolroom: In the big schoolroom we were divided into age groups sitting in three, separate blocks of double desks, as is shown in the sketch (page 117) in which the details benefit from the memory of our classmate, Margaret, who went on to become a teacher herself. On entry, seven rising eight years old (Standard II), we were in the block at the east end, opposite the teacher's desk and near the fire, which was still open and coal burning then, before being replaced by an enclosed 'tortoise' stove. One of my early memories of this time is of doing a pastel picture of a dwarf with a red cap (which was commended by Miss Abberley) on a gloomy, late autumn afternoon made bright and cozy by this fire. Left of the fire, before the door to the boys' cloakroom, was a large picture of the seaman-boy hero of the Battle of Jutland, called Cornwall. The piano was to the right of the fire, or was sometimes brought up to the middle of the room, as shown in the sketch. Miss Henson played for our singing and the hymns for the assembly of the whole school in the morning, when the vicar (Alistair Daniell Kenworthy Clowes, in tenure from 1936-1939, a gifted musician himself) came in for a short service.

Some of my classmates had mixed feelings about the singing, because the teachers were quite forthright in their criticism. As Joyce says, "I was scared of her (Miss Abberley's) wrath" and she well recalls the day when she sang an odd note. Miss Abberley asked, "Who made that horrible noise?" and she had to own up, very shame- faced. Margaret fared no better, standing by the piano and given a note and asked to sing it, she was told, "That's how not to sing!" She was also told not to sing on May Day, because she 'growled' and had to take round the collecting tin instead. I don't remember being criticized, but Mother was not impressed with my singing at that age, although she thought my brother David could become a singer with the right training. I was rather aggrieved about this, as I liked singing (but later on Mother always said she loved to hear me 'chanting' and that I should be a monk). However, both Joyce and I had lessons on the piano with Miss Henson, on some evenings after school ended for the day, and here, my efforts were rewarded with Mother's approval. Joyce and I were allowed to sit and listen to each other play while we were waiting our turn. Pieces from my primer that I particularly liked were a simple tune called 'Simplicity' and another of chords called 'Violincello', both illustrated on the page with woodcuts in antique style.

We now used printed sum books and copybooks for our spellings and 'compositions,' which allowed Miss Abberley to work efficiently around the three groups. Joyce remembers, in particular, that we also had colouring books from Oxo, and said she adored hers because the captions were so clever, but that the only page she remembered clearly was a picture of a teacher wearing a mortar board, and the caption, 'Y. Knott B.A. regular drinker of Oxo'.

An event took place after Christmas 1936, important for the future teaching. This was a pantomime with the proceeds going towards the purchase of a school 'wireless' (radio), which would greatly help Miss Abberley manage all the three age groups. I wasn't in the pantomime, possibly because of the difficulty of getting to rehearsals from Slapton, but some of my classmates were prominent. Margaret remembers, "Being dressed as Little Miss Muffet in mob cap and long white dress with daisies on it" but making "a mess of it" when she sat on her tuffet and it collapsed! Kath played Bo-peep, with borrowed crook, also a fairy with green stockings and made Miss Abberley annoyed by going round the stage the wrong way in rehearsal, although it was alright on the night. Joyce was Fairy Queen, "Totally miscast because I was too well nourished and couldn't sing. The song was such a disaster and imprinted so much on my memory that I can still remember snatches of the words but not the tune." Despite these disclaimers, we in the audience were highly amused by the pantomime, especially by the performance of Joyce's brother David (still only six) as Red Riding Hood's grandmother!

The pantomime was given at the school on the evening of 29th of January (1937) and again at the Towcester Conservative Club on February 2nd, and successfully raised eleven pounds and sixpence for a school radio, which was installed later that month. The importance of this development was marked by a visit from Mr. Francis, the Education Officer, from the BBC in Birmingham, later in the year on the 24th of September, for advice and to check on its use. The school broadcasts, with the excellent booklets that accompanied them by authors such as Rhoda Power and C.C. Gadam, were greatly to widen the scope of our lessons in history and geography, and included 'Music and Movement' with Ann Driver. We were fortunate that the advent of the radio coincided with our entry into the big schoolroom.

In the autumn, when we were in Standard III, to encourage our interest in growing plants, we were asked to bring money to school to buy a bowl and some bulbs to put in compost and take back home. I chose grape hyacinths and what I thought was easily the best bowl, with a magnificent red and gold pattern. I took this home over the fields, carefully wrapped. Mother was disappointed with the bulbs and horrified by the bowl. I had to take them back next day and I changed the bulbs for 'real' hyacinths and the bowl for a plain green one, much to Miss Abberley's irritation. No doubt this was a lesson in good taste.

At the end of the autumn term (December 1937) we decorated the Big Schoolroom with looped lengths of coloured paper, crimped at the edges ready for a Christmas Party. There was a very large Christmas tree and we were each given an orange from a basket underneath. The food, provided by the parents, was highly enticing, with lemonade provided for the children, but I made the mistake of choosing to have tea, provided in tin mugs for the adults, which scalded the roof of my mouth, so I couldn't enjoy any of it. However, I still managed to enjoy the games: 'A hunting we will go,' 'Oranges and Lemons,' 'Pass the Parcel' and 'Musical Chairs.'

We were in the second block of desks for the 8 rising to 9 year olds = Standard III, (next to the 'nature table', as shown on the fig.), when I first remember a visit from a vicar who came to test our religious knowledge, with simple questions about the New Testament and Bible stories and the catechism. I think I did quite well, already being interested in history (and I may already have had at home the illustrated book of stories taken from the Bible by Arthur Mee—-or was it a prize received at this time?). Margaret remembers one scripture examiner talking about 'God's plan' and that we had to repeat after Miss Abberley, the 'Alphabet of Texts' beginning with A—A soft answer turneth away wrath.

School Log Book, Report of the inspection of religious instruction 25th of March, 1938:
"The school was taken in one group, with opening prayers taken by the Head Teacher, and an appropriate hymn sung by the children. The work done by the teachers is most commendable and I noticed that not only facts and stories were well taught, but that detail had been given a prominent place, so that the instruction

was made to have a personal application to the children. The instruction is given in a happy as well as in an interesting manner."

The 'nature table,' as well as catkins and flowers in season, had glass jars with beans or peas behind blotting paper so we could study (and draw) the stages of growth and also, in the spring, frog spawn, so we could see the gradual development of the tadpoles (I brought some in from the pond near Slapton Church).

What really brings this time in school back to mind, was learning 'Drake's Drum' and reciting it in class with some aplomb. This led Miss Abberley to ask me to perform for a visitor a few weeks later. However, though I remember facts and figures, my rote memory is very short term (unlike that of my parents) and I soon stumbled to a halt, going back to my desk in chagrin, fighting back tears. I did somewhat better at home with recitations of the comic piece 'One Fish Ball', repeated often enough to keep it in mind. When my Wheeler cousins (Bob and Graham, then in their teens) came over from Blackpit in Stowe Ridings, I would be hauled out of bed and stood up on the dining-room table to deliver it; my cousins waiting with broad grins for me to reach the punch line, 'We don't sell bread with one fish ball', amid general laughter. They used to give me sixpence for this performance. (Joyce remembers writing a poem for a competition but I don't remember writing one at any time in childhood.)

I think it was the early summer of the year I was in Standard III, that Peter and I got into trouble with Miss Abberley, after picking dandelions for his mother and for the lady in Hillside Cottage at the bottom of Slapton Hill, near the Boxes, so they could make dandelion wine. We went up into the field where my cousin Tony and I had cleaned out my Aunt Nan's henhouse, which had induced a good growth of dandelions. We spent a Saturday morning picking off heads and eventually our hands were stained brown with the juice. We couldn't wash it off so we had to go to school on the Monday with hands like gypsies. Miss Abberley was horrified, 'How could your mothers send you to school like this?' And we were sent home to get them clean. Mother tried hard with a pummy (pumice) stone until my hands were sore, to no avail, so it just had to be left to wear off, much to Miss Abberley's annoyance.

As well as 'Swedish drill' in the playground, we played competitive line games, such as the one where a beanbag is passed back overhead, the child at the back then running to the front. The girls played a number of skipping games, and sometimes we boys joined in as well, if the rope was long enough for several children to skip at a time; (we were a bit too shy to join in on our own). As well as ball games there were different forms of touch or 'tig', including chain tig, in which the child touched joins the chain (Kath remembers this was called 'slag slag aroney'). As the chain lengthened, those on the end were whirled round the playground at frightening speed. There were some hard winters at that period; girls as well as boys enjoyed sliding on patches of ice in the playground and on one occasion, Kath, to her mortification, was told by Miss Abberley to sprinkle salt on them, bringing this activity to an end. A favourite game was five stones or dab stones, which has a large number of more and more difficult combinations after the first simple sequence of throwing up one pebble and catching it on the back of the hand and then in the palm, through to five. Outside the school entrance, along the base of the wall of old Mr. Barford's farm buildings, there were some flat stones jutting out, perfect for sitting on to play this game in the lunch hour; (they are still there). We also played 'statues' against the end wall of the school. Other games at lunchtime were football on the Green in the winter and rounders, wrestling matches and cricket in the summer (usually watched by Reg Chapman's big Airedale).

It was when we were in the combined top class (Standards IV/V) of nine rising to eleven year olds, that the BBC pamphlets came into their own. We now faced the teachers' table with the wireless on it, and the big map of the world on the wall behind with the vast territories of the British Empire shown in red. There was an illustrated book for history and we did a project with Miss Abberley on 'Monks and Monasteries'. We also made drawings and illustrative wall charts. I was particularly fond of a drawing I did of villeins clod breaking (that was put on the wall behind me when I was in the right rear desk). This always made me think of Slapton church and a party of villeins swinging their mattocks, just visible in the mist. This idea was, perhaps not far from reality. At Domesday, when the Lucy family held Slapton Manor, the land was divided into 31 virgates of 14 acres each. The family held 11 of them, and there were twenty villeins, that is, peasants, each having one as a bond of service to the Lord of the Manor.

Sums were copied from the blackboard and worked from textbooks and sometimes there was individual teaching, but Margaret remembers being so scared of being told off, that on those occasions she couldn't take anything in, and she had to get Joyce to teach her how to do long division. Compositions were written in rough, checked then copied into 'best books' as tidily as we could manage. We also had to write from dictation and put a given passage of prose into our own words (paraphrase), or, alternatively, write a summary (something which I found I liked to do). We also had spelling tests and Spelling Bees (then popular on the wireless). Margaret remembers spelling biscuit correctly and Miss Abberley saying, 'Is that all?' probably wanting her to say the word. But Margaret thought she was trying to help and added an E, and got it wrong!

School Log Book, Report of H.M.I. Mr. H.N. Parker (21st of July 1938):
"This worthy little school continues to merit the good opinion expressed in previous reports. Characteristic steadfastness of purpose and honest endeavour are supported by a friendly, cheerful spirit. The written work of the juniors is commendably neat whilst their response to oral questions on History, Geography and Literature reveals a lively interest and good general knowledge of the ground covered. The teaching of these subjects is enlivened by an intelligent use of illustrative material. Written tests in Arithmetic produced satisfactory results. Recitation, a matter for care in all classes is marked by pleasing spirited delivery in Standards 1V and V (Top class). Handwork, though not yet of a fully progressive nature, is more educational than formerly. The older girls take great interest in needlework. The neat stitching and fresh appearance of the work seen during the inspection reflect credit on the teaching."
Comment from report of H.M.I. on the school buildings (21st of September 1938):
"It is a cause for much regret that the premises, which house this pleasant little community are in such urgent need of repair and redecoration."
School Log Book (9th of January 1939): Miss Abberley writes:

"On Jan 2nd I wrote to the Secretary (of the School Board) informing him of the broken windows and stating how cold this makes our school." (Previous notes had been ignored but the windows were mended on the last day of the month. Meanwhile the boiler broke down and the open fire had to be reinstalled. On March 15th one of the doorposts in the boys' lavatories fell down, but, "Luckily the post fell clear of the children". It was not until the 1950s that flush sanitation was installed.)

Amongst Mother's effects, I found one surviving report on my personal progress during these early years (Fig. page 125). These reports were hand written by the Head Teacher and apparently, normally returned after the parents had read them and signed them. For some reason Mother had been able to keep the very first one that I was given after the third term exams for Standard II, when I was eight. It shows that my highest marks were in Arithmetic and Reading, lowest in Handwriting with less than half marks, but also that my handwriting still shows Miss Abberley's strong influence! When I was in the top class, Miss Abberley made me 'monitor' and I helped her in the lunch hour or after school with simple tasks, helping her tidy up, and sometimes washing the inkwells and filling them with fresh ink, mixed from bags of ink powder, and fitting new nibs to the pens where they were needed.

As we were a church school the even tenor of our daily round of lessons was punctuated by religious festivals and there were days off for the Slapton and the Abthorpe feasts (fêtes) in July. We went as a school group to Abthorpe church on occasions like Ascension Day and also to file past and salute the War Memorial on Remembrance Day, after a short service. Kath dreaded the moment when it came to her turn to salute because she was left handed and was afraid of getting it wrong. May Day (1939) for which we had a special songbook, was a happier occasion; Kath remembers that she, Margaret and Joyce were the May Queen's attendants, kneeling on the Richardson's lawn for their photograph, 'Looking like angels' with John Foster, a boy in the year ahead of us, wearing a jester's outfit; but embarrassment, indeed, consternation, was caused on Empire Day (later in May 1939). The Union Jack was raised in the school playground and we were mustered to file round and salute it in turn. Margaret remembers wearing a white dress and a circlet of daisies representing the different countries under the Crown. When it came to Harry's turn, he refused to salute and had to be hustled away and sent home in disgrace (no doubt his father, sometimes out of work, had said something derogatory about the Empire).

Harry also caused some excitement later on in the winter, when the threshing box was brought to Mr. Richardson's rick-yard, adjacent to the school (a stone built cottage is there now). It so happened that the men got down to the lowest layers of the corn rick in the school lunch-hour. All the village boys gathered round with sticks, waiting for the last sheaves to be lifted and hammering the rats and mice as they leapt out in all directions. Harry quietly secreted several mice in his pocket ready to release them in school at the right moment. Unfortunately, they escaped as soon as we got back in, before all the children had returned, but a most satisfactory pandemonium was created with girls screaming and jumping up onto the desks as the mice ran hither and thither. However, Miss Abberley was equal to the occasion: we were crossly told to chase them out into the playground, which we did with great glee.

Third Term Examination

John Haynes.   Std II

Arithmetic. Accuracy $\frac{48}{60}$
Arithmetic. Reasoning Power. $\frac{35}{40}$
Reading. $\frac{18}{20}$
Writing. $\frac{9}{20}$
Spellings $\frac{15}{20}$ A most promising
Composition $\frac{15}{20}$ boy.
English. $\frac{15}{20}$

Total Marks. $\frac{155}{200}$

Position in class 2nd   Number in class 5.

Head Teacher.

Parent's Signature.

John Haynes - My handwriting, still shows
    Miss Abberley's influence!

125

My brother, David, started school in the summer term just after he had turned four. Sometime in the following winter, during a lunch break, we both went up the lane towards Bucknells Wood, to follow a foxhunt. After a while, I reluctantly decided it was time to go back to school but David flatly refused to go with me, so I had to go without him. Miss Abberley told me to go straight back to look for him and bring him to school without fail. I ran along Brackley Lane and up towards the woods, and on the way opened a gate for a huntsman, so he didn't have to get off his horse. He was very smartly dressed, I think possibly in forest green, the traditional colour of the Grafton, and unexpectedly, he gave me a new sixpence. I studied this coin in some surprise, as it was equal to my Saturday's sixpence, earned by doing jobs for my parents and including tuppence ha'penny I got for feeding the chickens and collecting the eggs, daily, for Mr. Draper at the 'Royal Oak'. I found David eventually, but it was almost time to go home when we finally arrived back at school. Joyce, Margaret and Kath still remember this quite clearly, and their relief when we returned; (I wasn't quite so concerned, because I was used to David's wanderings, which usually seemed to turn out alright in the end).

However, there was a more serious incident the following summer. One day, a policeman called at the school to see Miss Abberley, and after he had spoken a few words to her, she addressed us all in the big schoolroom, saying that a number of windows had been broken at the Glebe (Slapton Hill) farmhouse and asked if anyone knew about it. No one did, and the policeman went away. That evening, to my surprise, the policeman called at the Lodge Cottage. It seemed that Harry's mother, Mrs. Hayward, had seen two boys returning over the field behind their house on a previous evening, so suspicion had fallen on me and David. The policeman questioned me, with Father present, and it soon became clear that I knew nothing about it; but while they were talking to me, David took the opportunity to slip, furtively, out of the room and into the garden. Dad saw him go and went after him and found him hiding in one of the big yew trees. He was collared and brought back in and the story came out. He had gone up to the Glebe with Max (still only three at that time) and they had thrown stones and knocked some of the panes out with sticks. David had a tanning, and I was sorry about that, but mightily relieved that I was no longer the chief suspect. It was another uncomfortable experience of being falsely accused. (Interestingly, David now has no recollection of this imbroglio at all.) He wasn't always being a nuisance. One day I was looking for him around Abthorpe Green, to bring him home after school. Finally, I found him coming out of the shop that used to be on the corner opposite the church entrance. He came out onto the top step, hand in hand with a little girl called Janet Slack (Charlie's younger sister) and they both had sherbet dabs, triangular, yellow packets with a licorice tube. This has stayed in my mind like an old print of village life (see note 6).

Going home from school: As most children walked home from school, some of them considerable distances, there were often 'alarms and excursions' along the way. Joyce and her brother David, lived at Mile Oak Farm at the eastern extremity of Abthorpe Parish, not far from Towcester itself, and their father brought them to school in the morning by horse and trap. Two children called Phyllis and John Barnard used to come with them. These two were about the same age as Joyce and her brother. They lived in a remote cottage on a track between Handley Park Farm and Silverstone and their mother brought them along every morning to ride in with Mr. Barford, "Little John wrapped in so many coats that he looked like a little ball".

One evening, when Joyce and Phyllis were still only five or six years old, and the younger ones only three or four, they were walking home, and as Joyce says, "We had all stopped to look at the water flowing into a pipe that went under the road just before you get to Mr. Coles' wood yard. Without warning, little John ran across the road to see where the water flowed out into the stream and was knocked down by a car coming from the Towcester direction. Inside were two gentlemen dressed in dark overcoats and wearing those black, moulded, hard felt hats that were fashionable at the time. Thinking about it, they were probably solicitors, but whatever they were, they were the first city gents that I had seen. They were devastated by what had happened, and rushed to pick little John up. To my relief, he was not dead but had a nasty bump on his temple. Meanwhile, David, who was always very sensitive, had run on towards home crying."

The men turned the car round to take them home, picking up her brother, still crying, as he was running up the steep hill at Foscote, Joyce having to pluck up her courage to say, "Please Sir, this is my brother, could you stop for him?" Joyce and David were put down at the farm gate at Mile Oak while the car sped on to take the other children home. The two of them then decided to say nothing about it to their mother; but as Joyce said, "Unfortunately, as we were sitting on the rug in front of the fire after tea, David suddenly gave a quiet sob, or a series of indrawn breaths, like you find happens after you have cried for a long time. Mother immediately pounced, and wanted to know why he had been crying, so, of course, the story all came out. Mother hit the roof, saying, 'What will Mrs. Barnard think of me that I haven't been to enquire how that boy is?' We were sent straight to bed (but we didn't sleep) while she tore up the fields in the dark. Eventually she came home with the news that he would be alright, and we then fell asleep with relief, but not before Mother had chalked me off for being the eldest and not looking after the others. I think I was only six at the time so I did feel she was being unfair. After that, Phyllis and John used to walk back (with us) to Foscote and then take a footpath to Silverstone, which started back of the horse pond at the bottom of Foscote hill. What a trek for those poor kids!"

In the winter, the frequent flooding of the water meadows by the brook often enlivened the return walk for us children from Slapton. We always loved it when the cry went up, 'The floods are out!', and we would go down and wade out as far as we could, an exciting (and hazardous) game, trying to get to one of the pollard willows by the brook and climb up in the middle of the floodwater, without it topping our Wellingtons. One evening, on the way home from school, a party of us lingered by the plank bridge because the water level was up to the floorboards. My brothers, David and Max (who had not long started school, aged four) began playing about on the handrails of the bridge. Before any of us could do anything, David gave Max a nudge and he went over into the brown rush of waters and was swept down stream. Fortunately, he was carried down near the bank at the first bend and we raced round and were able to pull him out. It was quite difficult explaining to Mother, while being sparing with the facts, just how Max had got completely soaked. I was, of course, roundly condemned for not looking after him properly.

As well as the floods and winter snow drifts, both Joyce and I remember going home along the white lanes of summer: Joyce, especially the heaps of gravel along the verge with "lovely pink convolvulus growing over them," and "stones in our shoes, plus a cheery

Mr. Redford (the roadman) as he waved us on our weary way"; and me, the gleaming traction engine rolling down the new gravel and the smell of tar, and hearing the bells of the uniformed, ice-cream men on their tricycles, pink ice-cream from the Eldorado man, but best of all, the three-cornered, green water-ices, from the Walls man.

Home life in Slapton: As Slapton is some fifteen miles from Banbury, Father now had a longer drive when he needed to report to the office of Cheneys' printing firm. However, as at that time there was still a railway line from Northampton to Banbury, and a station about half a mile from the cottage on the Abthorpe to Wappenham road, in an emergency and when the car wouldn't start, there were trains that could get him to Banbury in the morning and home at night. In any case, he was now well established with the firm and it usually wasn't necessary for him to call in, except to report on his activities and give details of his new contracts, and he always did this regularly on Saturdays.

He usually had a lie-in when he was home and had his breakfast in peace when we had gone to school; and he was often late coming back in the evening, sometimes being away all night when making distant calls, which he did regularly as far away as Southampton. This meant that there was extra pleasure when he came home at midday on Saturdays from Banbury, where he shopped for Mother after making his report. There was always a row of oranges in the rear window of the car and he'd bring us comics, which by the time I was nine or ten, included the Children's Newspaper and perhaps a new Rupert Bear book in its yellow binding (Ann eventually had thirty-six of these).

Every two or three weeks he took me, together with David, with him on Saturday morning for our regulation 'short back and sides' haircut. Afterwards, we would have lemonade and Banbury cakes in a café near Banbury Cross. Sometimes, if we were lucky, we were allowed to go into the printing works with him and see the printing machines and once, memorably, to see the extensive collection of butterflies built up by John Cheney, one of the two brothers that ran the firm.

On Saturday afternoons he enjoyed teaching us the finer points of cricket, the correct grip of the bat and particularly the art of defending the wicket, arguing that properly conducted it should be almost impossible for the bowler to get you out. I was a poor student in this regard, being incapable of resisting my impulse to lash out at a tempting ball! He was also keen for us to learn to kick the football with both feet and made us practise shooting at goal from different angles. (Father always retained an interest in the position of Grimsby Town in the Football League, and was also an Arsenal supporter—possibly related to the Greenwich connection, close to Woolwich Arsenal.)

As well as a great capacity for telling us stories, Father also had an immense fund of indoor games, especially those you could play with cigarette cards and with playing cards, ranging from 'Beat your Neighbour' to Brag and Crib. My cousin Jose says that they always looked forward to the fun and games when 'Uncle Ro and Aunt Jess' went over to Blackpit.

Father was quite helpful to Mother in the house when he was home (teaching us the right way to wash-up, and how to peel an apple or potato in one go) and we always knew that if he was making the dinner when Mother was out or away it would either be bangers and mash, or his favourite, corn beef hash, with cream and about 4ozs of butter mixed into the potatoes. His recipe for porridge used similar amounts of cream and sugar, plus a few handfuls of sultanas. Needless to say, Mother, who ran a tight household account, was not too appreciative of this extravagance.

Mother, as was general in those days, followed a weekly menu designed to make the most of a limited budget: usually, roast leg of lamb on Sunday, with Yorkshire pudding; cold lamb on Monday (after washing the clothes in the copper, which she always wrung out by hand); shepherd's pie on Tuesday (my favourite meal, for which I would run home across the fields at my fastest speed); a broth made from the bone with vegetables on Wednesday; sausages on Thursday; fish on Friday. Travelling vans delivered bread, meat, fish and vegetables and it was one of my jobs to get the milk daily from the Boxes. Mother also baked a fruitcake every week, a large custard tart for Father and a batch of rock cakes (also my favourite).

Mother didn't mind how long we stayed out to play on long, summer evenings —-it meant 'we were out of her hair'. However, in the winter we were generally sent to bed after the 'Children's Hour' on the radio, and favourite programs like 'Toy Town' with Dennis and Larry the lamb, and 'Worzel Gummidge'. As I got older, I was allowed to stay up longer and I would try to stretch it out by sitting on the floor by Father, in his armchair listening to the radio, with my back to the wall; thinking he wouldn't notice if I just went on quietly reading. He would enter into the spirit of the thing and eventually say with pretended surprise, "Good Lord, John, are you still there, it's eight o'clock, off you go to bed." (I could also string it out a bit by practising the piano.)

If Father wanted to speak to me seriously, he would suggest a walk. Swinging his walking stick as we went across the fields, he would poke at the centers of the rosettes of young thistles, saying, "You see, John, if every one did this, we could soon get rid of them." In this way he would introduce some subject such as 'The birds and the bees', which as a country child I was hardly in need of, being familiar with mating animals and, indeed, having seen my cat 'Tibbles' unexpectedly have her kittens on the carpet in front of the living room fire.

More seriously, one evening he returned to the difficulty of not being able to afford to send me to a 'good' school. I think he had called to see Miss Abberley at a time when Harry and I were not at the top of her list of pupils likely to do well. I wasn't at all unhappy to be told that the 'good' school was still out of the question. Only a short while previously, I'd been out with Peter, late one evening, in the field opposite his house. We lay on our backs in the long grass looking up at a flock of swifts, very high up, catching the last glint of the setting sun, and congratulating each other that we didn't have to go away to school, like poor Fred Messenger from the farm up the lane past the Boxes. (Fred went to a prep school and could only play with us in the holidays.) To my mind, such a school was little different to the 'Borstal', a grim, red brick building on the road between Towcester and Northampton, that Dad would point out, with some relish, as the place where very badly behaved boys were sent to be reformed. David and I always went rather quiet when we passed it.

I think this was, probably, the only time Father did call on Miss Abberley at the school. Mother came more often, of course, as when David and Max first started, and also to the school events, which Dad could rarely manage. We were always very proud of Mother, thinking (as kids do) that she was prettier and better dressed than any of the other mothers; with some justification in our case though, because in her dress and colour sense she was the true grand-daughter of Richard Watson, who was a tailor as well as a publican. She bought high quality clothes, being especially fond of smart, tweed suits, ('costumes') with the object of making them last (some a lifetime) in her colours of russet, green and brown.

On Saturday evenings, Father and Mother often went out, being quite happy to leave me in charge, now I was eight or nine years old (though they did have to dampen my ardour when I used to bank up the fire in the living room to make things cozy against their return). They enjoyed visits to our Hurst and Wheeler relations, which usually ended with singing round the piano. On return visits Mother used to leave the door on the stairs open so we could hear. Mother was in great demand for her arias from 'La Bohème' and 'Madam Butterfly', especially *One Fine Day*. Father often asked Mother to play for him when he got back in the evening from his travels, generally Chopin waltzes and nocturnes, Mendelssohn's 'Songs without Words' or his particular favourite, the 'Moonlight Sonata'. She also used to play as an accompanist for one of the Roberts sisters who lived near the Boxes, up the village. When this lady, a handsome woman with an Eton crop, came to practise her songs, we little philistines upstairs had to stuff the sheets in our mouths to hide our paroxysms of laughter, because she had such a surprisingly rich, deep contralto (sadly, long gone out of fashion).

It was during these years that Father and Mother became friendly with Tim White who was then living in the cottage in Stowe Ridings, rented from our Wheeler relations at Blackpit during the time he wrote, *England have my Bones* and *The Sword in the Stone*. One day he called at Lodge Cottage when we were out and hit his head on the lintel of the side entrance, commemorated by a note he pinned to the door, 'This cottage was built for the bloody dwarves!" (It was about this time that we were taken to see 'Snow White and the Seven Dwarves' in the Tivoli Cinema, Northampton.) One Saturday evening, he invited Father and Mother to join him with another guest for dinner at his cottage. This lady friend, a nurse from the hospital in Buckingham, didn't turn up. Mother admitted later, that she was not at all put out to get Tim's full attention in this girl's absence and remembered what a marvellous game soup he had concocted.

Tim was in the process of training his hawk, 'Gos' when he gathered from Father that John Cheney, as well as being a keen entomologist, was also an enthusiastic photographer and arrangements were made for 'Gos' to have his portrait taken. Father drove them over to Banbury after a suitable perch had been put in the back of his car. By the time they got back, 'Gos' had managed to make a considerable mess. This quite annoyed Father, especially as Tim was quite unconcerned. My cousin Graham, who had been drafted in to help with 'Gos' and found himself blamed for his eventual loss (by turning up at the wrong moment and frightening him off the top of an oak tree when Tim was trying to entice him down) said later, "Yes, Tim was like that". Tim clearly got away with being somewhat 'seigneurial' by personal charm. He was, however, very kind to young people, and was particularly fond of my cousin Jose (a pretty, dark girl with big brown eyes and long plaits, four years older than me) who called on him regularly to see his animals and birds. He made her the heroine of *Mistress Masham's Repose* and always said he wanted to marry her when she grew up.

My parents also became friendly at this time with the Barfords at Mile Oak farm, the parents of Joyce and her brother David. On our first visit as a family, Mrs. Barford made us stewed pears from their orchard; and I can still remember distinctly the smell of paraffin mixed with that of rubber boots in the passage as we went out into the garden where a tennis court had been marked out, and we had our first lesson in the game (which I grew to like very much). These visits were returned, of course, and on one occasion when we children were playing hide-and-seek, Joyce and I hid under the eiderdown on the parental bed, kissing for the first time. However, the next day in school, I was as shy as before, admiring from afar.

Most Sunday mornings, Father drove us the fourteen miles to the new swimming baths in Northampton, very early, in order to arrive sometime just after eight o'clock. He was keen that we all learned to swim as soon as possible, and we all could by seven years old, Max being very proficient by six. We were then taught to dive in off the side without doing belly flops. An incident that illustrates David's contrary nature occurred when Dad tried to take him down the water chute when he was about five. Howling loudly, he resisted and Dad gave up, but was then quite disgusted when David went down happily with someone else! We were all impressed though, when Max (aged about three) slipped out of his rubber belt down in the deep-end and Dad did a champion's crawl down the full length of the baths to his rescue.

On Saturdays, Father and Mother often went in to the Tivoli Cinema in Northampton, and as Mother said many years later, sometimes on the way back on warm summer evenings, they would stop the car and make love in the fields, recapturing, no doubt, something of their courtship days. Both of them always said that this was the happiest period of their married lives: the years before "Hitler's War ruined everything". Nothing brings back the memory of my parents at this time, together with the gathering rumours of war, more clearly to me, than the bittersweet melody of the song 'Vilja' from the 'Merry Widow', which I must have heard sometime then (from the Lehar operetta, that Hitler is reputed to have gone to see seven times).

Slapton Church and Sunday school: Our Sunday morning swimming precluded family attendance at the church and when Dad, rather guiltily, explained matters to the vicar, the Reverend Clowes dryly answered, "Well, cleanliness is next to Godliness". However, we were sent to Sunday school, not only because our parents valued their lie-in on Sunday afternoon, but because although they had no wish to indoctrinate us with a particular viewpoint, they considered it part of our education. We were fortunate that Mother, in particular, made it clear that the Bible was not to be taken literally. This means that there was no 'crisis of conscience', only exasperation later, when in classes given before confirmation (at thirteen) well-meaning but misguided adults tried to insist that it should. After all, as children we were soon familiar with the major collections of fairy tales and gradually, I came to take Bible stories, such as that of Jesus walking on the water and multiplying the loaves and fishes, in the same spirit as the moral fables of Aesop. In this way, I was eventually to appreciate the Bible as a revelation of the Christian message through poetry and myth.

Although it is described as a 'low, mean edifice' in Baker's history (see note 1a) I have fond memories of the ancient, mediaeval church, which dates back to Norman times. It is, indeed, small, with a nave only some five or six yards long, and only one aisle (the south), with a pointed arch into the chancel and a porch, where swallows usually nested. While we lived in Slapton, wall paintings that had been white-washed over in the Reformation, were being restored, and these greeted us when we went in: the ones I particularly remember, being St. Christopher, the patron saint of travellers, carrying the infant Jesus across a river, and a mermaid, combing her golden hair and looking at herself in a mirror, symbolizing the dangers of vanity (see note 1b). We were, of course, sent to Sunday school in our best clothes and with well-polished shoes. However, this did not deter us from hunting, hopefully, for walnuts under the fallen leaves of the big walnut tree, which used to be on the left, at the beginning of the track up to the church, while waiting to go in (they could still be found well into the New Year). Or I would have a quick look to see if the moorhens were present and correct in the little pond on the east side of the church; (there was an overhanging branch that came down to the water, which allowed you to see into the nest in the spring).

There were two pleasant, good-hearted girls (I think, called Dora and Edna Gimson) who helped with the Sunday school. They gave us illustrated texts each week to paste into little books, with a prize for full attendance. We didn't achieve this because of our parents' fondness for Sunday trips out in the car, but we enjoyed how the texts marked the major church festivals of the year; particularly, Palm Sunday, when we took branches of 'Pussy Palm' (Pussy or Goat Willow) and were given in return little crosses of palm to take home. Despite imperfect attendance, we were taken on the Sunday school outings by charabanc—-more than once to Wicksteed Park, near Kettering, a show place for various children's swings and roundabouts, with a miniature train; and also to Clacton, where I remember we were pleased and gratified to be given sixpence each for ice creams. These two girls organized the carol singing at Christmas time, teaching us carefully before taking us round the village, with a lantern, to perform. At the bigger houses, like Major Lamb's, we were invited inside and in return for several carols would be rewarded with mince pies and lemonade. Christmas parties were arranged for us in the old vicarage—-beyond the rivulet on the east side of the 'Green'; then lived in by Mrs. Thompson and her three daughters. At one of these parties, after the usual games of 'musical chairs' and 'pass the parcel', I played 'postman's knock' for the first time and when I answered the knock, going out into the dark passageway I was quite surprised to get a big smacking kiss from one of them (but not displeased!).

Unless it was raining heavily we were not allowed to go back home after Sunday school until teatime (when there would be bread and jam, fruit salad, plus the single contentious cherry, and fruit cake) but were expected to go for a walk, and unless it was very dry to stay on the road or lanes. This was difficult in spring when there was some competition to find the first examples of spring flowers, the first violets by the railway bridge, the first primroses and cowslips near the old sand pit in a field near the station; but we hoped that Mother would be pleased enough with them to overlook muddy shoes.

Early reading: As an alternative to Sunday school, Mother once or twice took us to a service in the little stone chapel (just beyond the Haywards') where Peter's father was a lay preacher (see note 1c). What I chiefly remember about the chapel is that there was a side room from which library books could be borrowed once a week. Mother sometimes sent me to exchange ones that she had borrowed. I used to read them as well (when she was out) everything being grist to the mental mill in those days. However, the most memorable borrowing was when I was in bed (aged about nine) recovering from mumps. Mother, no doubt pleased for us all to be getting childhood diseases like German measles and mumps out of the way, brought me *Tarka the Otter* to read. It appealed directly to my sense of identification with the natural world. I'd already read books by 'Grey Owl' (Archie Belaney), who had become a great hero, and I was following *Out with Romany* (Bramwell Evens) on the wireless, and this book by Henry Williamson became my favourite (or perhaps equal favourite with *The Sword in the Stone*). I was to read it many times into my early teens; usually stopping before reaching the end, which I knew by heart: when that last bubble shakes up through the sea-going waters, marking the final, fatal conflict between Tarka and Deadlock.

Although Mother and Father had been quite impoverished at the beginning of their hasty marriage, they had a small bookcase with books from their childhood and youth. Mother had the *The Cloister and the Hearth*, *Ben Hur* and a copy of *A Girl of the Limberlost* with a green cover and an appealing inset picture of a girl in a white dress against a golden-yellow background. Father had preserved his copies of *Westward Ho*, *Treasure Island*, *The Swiss family Robinson* and *Robinson Crusoe* and also had Stevenson's *The Black Arrow* with its sympathetic portrait of Richard Crookback. He also had some of the novels of Walter Scott, including *Rob Roy*, *Old Mortality* and *Kenilworth* as well as *The Lady of the Lake*. There was also his school copy of *Hiawatha*, the complete poems of Byron and more recently acquired copies of *The Good Companions*, *The Silver Land* which described the explorations of Gino Watkins in Greenland and *Lorenzo the Magnificent* with its exotic picture of renaissance Italy. (See note 7.)

I was impressed from the earliest days with our parents' capacity for recall of well-loved passages from Shakespeare. Mother would quote 'Over hill and over dale' and 'I know a bank' from *Midsummer Nights Dream;* Father from *Hamlet* and *The Merchant of Venice*, especially Portia's famous speech. Lines that have, in particular, haunted me since that time, are those beginning, 'Come unto these yellow sands', from *The Tempest*, at once mysterious and yearning.

The wider world: What I find remarkable now, is that although Father averaged about 500 miles a week in the car doing business, he was still ready to take us out on long trips on Sundays and bank holidays in the summer, for a day at the seaside: to Clacton on the east coast, Burnham-on-Sea in Somerset and to Hunstanton on the Wash, where we walked out for miles across the mud but never did reach the distant blue line of the sea. Country roads were relatively quiet, but main roads could be very busy at holiday times (then as now road building failed to keep up with the number of cars coming out of the factories). On the way back from Hunstanton we were brought to a halt by a traffic-jam alongside a dyke somewhere in the Fens. Dad allowed David and me to stand up through the open sunroof and we were able to look back at a long string of beetle-black cars shining in the sun as far as we could see.

Although I don't remember Father ever singing a solo at the piano, we would often get him to sing for us on long journeys in the car, when we were tired of the usual competitive games, collecting passing car makes, colours and county number plates or roadside adverts for Robin Starch, Reckitts Blue and Bisto. He had a repertoire of Victorian songs such as the one about the well-set-up and handsome 'Captain John McPherson', of the schooner *Ben Macrae* who was pursued by all the ladies; and little, cautionary ditties such as those concerning, 'Joe Briggs', who 'used to feed the pigs, and kick them with his hobnail boots', with predictably gruesome consequences; and the one about, 'Little Billie Bates' who 'fastened on his skates, but the ice was thin', leading to the wonderful punch line, 'Heaven's gates'. What we also particularly liked to hear was his rendition of 'The Wreck of the *Hesperus*' that 'sailed the wintry seas', and the sad fate of the skipper's 'blue eyed daughter', lashed to the mast, 'The salt sea frozen on her breast'.

Early in our time at Slapton, Mother and Father had a holiday on their own, while Grannie Haynes looked after us; camping near the Gannel at Newquay in Cornwall. Mother thought this the best holiday of her life (swimming before having a big breakfast in a neighbouring boarding house) and in following years we had annual holidays in Cornwall, renting a small wooden bungalow in the wooded gorge of the river at Seaton, a small village east of Looe. We always went in June, taking a week off school, as our parents were keen to avoid crowds and preferred isolated beaches. It did mean that Father, who didn't like cold water (and it is cold off the Cornish coast, especially in June) would only make a quick dash in and out of the sea each day, to our great amusement. It was on these holidays that I became aware of the beauty of the colours and textures of the rocks in the cliffs and the interest of the marine life in the rock pools.

A revealing incident took place during one holiday when Father was driving us up to Grimsby, where Ann and I were to be left for a while to stay with Granny Haynes (now a widow). We stopped in Stamford after he had spotted a likely restaurant for a late breakfast, but Mother refused to get out of the car and go in, it was 'too posh' (no doubt she thought, for us children). Things were very quiet in the car for many miles after that. However, things were lively on the holiday; no one enjoyed the fun of the fair more than Father, and you had to do everything from the coconut shies and shooting galleries to the dodgems, so before we were left on our own, he introduced us to all the 'beach attractions' in Cleethorpes, especially the water-chute and the helter–skelter. When we were left with

Grandma, I became friendly with a girl I met in the recreation grounds and we went far out over the sands to dig cockles, which her parents (who lived in a backstreet of Cleethorpes) showed us how to prepare for cooking. With this girl, I bought some candy-floss in the sea-front arcade, for the first and last time (not worth the effort in trying to eat it!).

During the school holidays, Father would often take me with him for company when making his business trips: to Coventry, past the radio masts at Daventry, returning by Warwick, my first tour of a castle, and Stratford, where he pointed out Shakespeare's birthplace and the new theatre; to Bedford, where he took me to the cinema for the first time, to see 'Little Lord Fauntleroy', which left me somewhat baffled but I always remembered the broad and shining River Ouse; to Slough, where he took me to Windsor Castle and down the Thames to Runnymede, where I waded out to a coot's nest with eggs; to the Miles aircraft factory at Woodley in Berkshire, where, while he went in, he left me in the car to watch the little yellow planes taking off and landing on the green airfield (Miles Magisters and Miles Masters that would be so important in the training of fighter pilots a year or two later). On these trips he would point out, with satisfaction, the progress the country was making in building new roads and replacing tumbledown cottages with new council houses.

Father didn't believe in allowing these trips to become boring. One summer day on a very quiet country road with wide verges and no other traffic about, he decided to demonstrate to me that the car could practically drive its-self. Slowing right down, he took his hands off the wheel to show how the car would continue straight on following the camber. Then giving the car extra choke he opened the sunroof and sat on the roof steering with his feet. Finally getting out of the car and running along-side for a few yards. This knowledge of the car's behaviour did come in useful one day when the whole family was in it. We were on a sweeping downhill bend leading to a humpbacked bridge, when he realized that the steering had gone; so braking very gently he gradually slowed the car, which ran off into the grass verge just before we got to the bridge (all this to our great surprise, because he didn't say a word until we stopped).

WAR AND RUMOURS OF WAR

Rumours of war: During the years we lived in Slapton the countries of Europe gradually moved onto a collision course. The Nazi dictatorship was fully established by 1934 and in 1935 Hitler repudiated the Treaty of Versailles and began to re-arm. In the same year Mussolini invaded Abyssinia (Ethiopia) in defiance of the League of Nations, which proved to have neither the unity nor the will to stand up to these new dictatorships. Thus encouraged, in the following year, Germany occupied the Rhineland and Italy annexed Ethiopia. Some far-sighted politicians like Churchill were aware of the danger to the democracies from the beginning and the need to re-arm, but it was less than twenty years since the carnage of World War I and to most people another war was unthinkable and because it shouldn't happen, wouldn't happen; and as always, they found it easier to project their fears onto the 'messengers' and label them the warmongers. (I can remember this actually being said about Churchill, when our parents had some friends in for the evening.)

Neville Chamberlain became Prime Minister in 1937, at the same time as Hitler began sabre rattling about the German-speaking population of western Czechoslovakia; and in 1938 both Austria and the Sudetenland were absorbed into the German Reich. At first it seemed that this ruthless redrawing of the map of Europe would trigger a war and emergency measures were pushed through Parliament in Britain, but Chamberlain was convinced he could negotiate a settlement and in September flew to Munich to meet Hitler.

School Log September 29th 1938: Miss Abberley writes:
"Leaving the school, for a time in the charge of Mrs. Varney the infants' teacher, as I am acting as Billeting Officer in one part of the village." (This was to find billets for the expected evacuees from London and other major cities if war broke out.)

School Log September 30th: "God Bless Mr. Chamberlain."
This poignant entry, the only one for that day, indicates the general sense of relief that almost everyone felt when Mr. Chamberlain returned, waving his paper agreement of "Peace with honour". To us, with the advantage of hindsight it doesn't look honourable and is seen as 'appeasement'. Churchill was quite right, it didn't mark the end of Hitler's 'territorial claims in Europe' and was immediately followed by the infamous 'Crystal Night', when Jewish property was destroyed and windows smashed, and early in the next year, by the occupation of Bohemia and Moravia. However, it did give us a year's breathing space and time to gird up the sinews of war.

In the summer of the Munich crisis we had a week's holiday in a rented house on Hayling Island. One morning we children were walking with Father across a patch of common with brambles in flower and he pointed out the great Cunard liner *Queen Mary* steaming down the Solent to Spithead; and one evening my sister Ann and I went up onto the flat roof of the house to watch our parents playing tennis in the square: in all directions but particularly towards the docks at Portsmouth and Southampton there were barrage balloons, deployed to prevent enemy aircraft flying below the defensive curtain of radar and ack-ack gunfire. (Combined with these memories is one of an earlier holiday on Hayling, when the waves crashing on the beach seemed immense, and I was fascinated by the colours of the sea-wet pebbles.)

By this time, Father had already joined the Territorials (252-City of Oxford Battery R.A.) being numbered amongst those who could 'see it coming'. There was the beginning of a rift here between our parents. Mother, with her quick sympathy for the underdog was much more susceptible to the socialist/pacifist viewpoint. She also suspected that Father joined so he could get away and enjoy himself with his men friends. To some extent this was true. He did, indeed, enjoy the training with its order, discipline and cameraderie, and joined together with his best friend, Peter 'Granville' (actually Rose) an artist and at the time in charge of the window dressing in the big dress shop 'Elliston and Cavell' in Oxford. No doubt he was glad to get away from family responsibility occasionally. After all, he had been 'saddled' with one when barely out of his teens and with three more children in short order. However, to put the emphasis on this is unfair. Always conservative in politics and highly patriotic, he had a clear-sighted appreciation of the menace to our way of life presented by both the far right and the far left, and seeing the war coming, knew where his duty lay.

My own reaction at that time, built up from fragments of conversation overheard and also announcements on the radio, was heavily influenced, if not dominated by the graphic accounts of World War I in my encyclopaedias; particularly by a picture of Tommies in the trenches, waiting to go over the top into a hail of machine gun bullets, the gas horns wailing. I would sometimes lie awake at night, thinking of Father floundering in the Flanders mud. It was to be a year or two into the war before this nightmare vision faded and I realized it was not, in general, that kind of static conflict this time round.

The international scene darkened further in the spring of 1939, after the dismemberment of Czechoslovakia. Hitler demanded the German acquisition of the Polish port of Danzig, and in the April, Mussolini invaded Albania. This led to the introduction of conscription in Britain for men aged 20-22.

In that last summer of the interwar peace, we went down once more to Seaton in Cornwall for our annual holiday, this time usually going round to Looe to swim from the sandy beach there. It was to be some years before we saw the sea again.

The Granvilles also had four children, and one of them, Georgina, stayed with us that summer. She was between Ann and me in age with a blond, pageboy bob, which led me to call her 'The Willful Princess' as depicted in Ann's latest Rupert book. One day we went up the Glebe to pick moon daisies and quaking grass, and a herd of gadding cattle made us take refuge in a thicket of gorse. When I realized they were only bullocks, I was able to demonstrate my 'bravery' to the 'princess' (which would have quickly evaporated if there had been a real bull amongst them!).

Later that summer, I was playing rounders with some boys on Abthorpe Green and eventually we flopped 'puffed out' on to the grass by the churchyard wall. We watched as a small, single-engine aeroplane flew over, high up in the pale, peaceful evening sky. One boy said, "My Dad says, 'there ain't gunna be no war'."

In the August of 1939, the Nazi-Soviet Pact was signed, secretly and cynically dividing up Poland between the communist and fascist powers. Despite an ultimatum from Britain, Hitler invaded Poland on the 1st of September and seized Danzig. This led, inevitably, to the declaration of war on September the 3rd.

The first year of the war, 1939-40: Father had gone to the Territorials' summer training camp in August 1939, and was still there when war broke out. This meant that he was immediately conscripted into the army and was not to return as a civilian for six years.

School Log September 22nd 1939: Miss Abberley writes:
   "Received roll of film paper for re-enforcing windows." (This was to help minimize
   damage caused by bomb blast.)

One evening, on his first home leave that autumn, Father went out with me for a walk down through the village in the dark, for a 'serious' talk. It happened to be a moonless, starry night made more brilliant by the blackout, which was now compulsory. He explained as far as he could about the war and also that he thought it was going to be a long one. While he was away, he emphasized that I was to be "Mother's right hand man" and do all I could to help her; also that I must work hard in school for the scholarship exam that would be held in the spring. Years later, when Dad was in his eighties, he remembered this talk and something I had entirely forgotten. He had been impressed with my knowledge of the names of the major constellations; when he had asked how I knew them, I had apparently said, "Because of the star maps in my 'Books of Knowledge'," which no doubt convinced him they had been a good investment.

I did take Father's injunction about the scholarship seriously. I asked Miss Abberley if we could have homework and she gave those of us prepared to do it, exercises from old scholarship papers. I enjoyed the homework, especially the sums, because I found I could usually manage to listen to the Children's Hour, the news of the war and other programs, while doing them.

At this early stage of the war everyone was being exhorted to 'do their bit' towards the war effort. In school Miss Abberley decided that the older children, boys as well as girls, should learn to knit 'comforters' for the troops. This included everything from simple scarves and mittens to socks, gloves, woolly hats and balaclavas. So we had to learn the different stitches, and the intricacies of casting on and off with four needles. The photo 5-3 shows us having made a good start that autumn. I think the parents donated the wool, in the colours of the three services. I made gloves and a balaclava for my father, which he said, came in very useful on his ack-ack gunsite in the cold winter of 1940. A parcel of the woollens was sent to the Militia Camp at Brigstock in our home county of Northamptonshire. Margaret has carefully preserved the letter of thanks from a George Randall of 403 Company, who received the "beautifully made" mittens that she had made. After clothing was rationed, every effort had to be made to save material to 'make and mend'; and Mother bought each of us one of those wooden 'mushrooms' for darning our socks (which we could do while listening to the Children's Hour on the wireless).

At the beginning of the war it was also feared that there would be aerial gas attacks, so everyone was given a gas mask. School children were issued with theirs in school and instructed in how to use them. We boys soon drove Miss Abberley to distraction running round with them on, pretending to be monsters, after we discovered you could make parping noises by blowing air out between the mask and your cheeks. The masks came in rectangular cardboard boxes and Mother made shoulder bags to fit ours into. As time went on it became apparent that gas was not likely to be used after all and the shoulder bags and boxes came in very handy for carrying our lunch to school.

At Christmas time 1939, Father gave me a little, five-year diary. (I had completely forgotten the existence of this little diary until I discovered it in my mother's effects. Unfortunately, an earlier one that he gave me for 1939 has disappeared.) As is the way of things it started brightly but faded away. However, the first year's entries are almost complete to begin with because I made them regularly after doing my homework on sums and composition (and listening to the news on the wireless). I will give selected examples, with my spelling uncorrected, to show how I assiduously followed the progress of the war at the same time as enjoying my normal village life:

> January 1st 1940: "Max's birthday, he had a shilling, the snow has nearly gone, went sliding on Messenger's pond.

> January 8th: "Rashioning started. Italy and Hungary made an alliance. Fin(n)s destroyed a Russian division."

Shortly after the first Christmas of the war, with the Battle of the Atlantic now fully under way, rationing was made necessary by the tremendous losses of our shipping. Mother now had to use her ingenuity to keep us well fed, as basic commodities like sugar, and butter, cheese, bacon and meat were reduced to a few ounces a week, plus one egg. Fortunately, supplies of potatoes and bread were kept up and we had plenty of milk. Equally serious was the fall in living standards when Father was drafted into the Forces. Before being called up, Father was on a salary of £500 a year, plus expenses and use of a car, a good income in those days. He was now on soldiers' pay and Mother received about twenty-five shillings (£1.25) a week as a dependent, with ten shillings for me and progressively lesser amounts for the others. Fortunately, Mother always preferred to have the challenge of having to make do, rather than having to deal with excess (see note 9).

In this light, Mother's feelings can be imagined when she made a cake for Father, using up all the eggs. She put it out on the wall of the yard to cool and Draper's smooth-haired terrier somehow scrambled up and took a big bite out of it. However, she patched it up and posted it to him and was somewhat mollified when he said that he and the rest of his gun crew had polished it straight off, voting it one of the best they had tasted!

> January 12th 1940: "Enemy plane sighted over Thames Estary. Grimsby trawler bombed (but) got home safely.

> January 19th: "The brook froze so hard that it bore us. Russian aircraft bombed Helsinki. Swedish volanteers brought down six aircraft."

Under the terms of the Nazi-Soviet Pact, Russia occupied Bessarabia and part of Finland. However, the Finns put up an unexpectedly fierce resistance, supported by many Swedes (as well as Old Man Winter, as Hitler failed to note!).

> January 20th: "27° of frost (below freezing Fahrenheit, in England) coldest day in Finland for ¾ of a century.

> January 23rd: "A destroyer was sunk by enemy mine. Its name was Exmouth—-getting colder.

> January 25th: "32° F. on school (room) Th (thermometer)—what heat! Three

German bombers droped (sic) 6 bombs on mainland Shetland isles on no military object."(We were allowed to wear our overcoats and crowd round the stoves.)

January 27th: "23° of frost. Serious floods in Greece to considerable depth—-snowed in the night. FOUND FROZEN RABBIT.

January 28th: "21° of frost—-Thames froze for ten miles—-SNOW 6 inches deep—-Got 6 inches deeper in afternoon." (The school was now closed for three days.)

January 30th: "Hitler made a speech—-more air raids on Helsinki—-seven attacks on ships.

February 3rd: "Our planes brought down 3 enemy planes and disabled a fourth over Yorkshire.

February 8th; "Feb. 1 2 3 4 5 6 7 8—-the snow which was a foot deep melted in three days—-flooded all over Lamb's field (below Lodge Cottage).

February 15th: "HMS Exeter came home to Plymouth. WINSTON CHURCHILL met the crew. We sunk another U-boat—-snow fall on WESTON FRONT.

February 17th: "A Brittish destroyer boarded the German prison ship Altmark and rescued the prison(er)s.

February 21st: "Russians bombed a Swedish town—-burnt three houses—-damaged a church. Our fishermen shot back at German planes.

February 23rd: "The king decorated men of the Exeter and HMS Ajax when they marched through London streets."

Photographs 5-3 'Doing Our Bit' 1939

Top -: The top class showing off their knitting at the beginning of the War. From the left at the back are, Christine Smith, Margaret Richardson, Kate Redford, Harry Hayward, Betty Cann, Joyce Barford; in front are David Barford (picking up his needles) John Haynes, Peter Lawrence, with the blackboard.

Bottom -: Showing all the boys with their knitting, from the left are, David Barford, John Haynes, Harry Hayward, Charlie Slack (left out of the top photo, as was David!). Peter in front again with the blackboard.

Note that we are quite well-dressed to go to school, despite 'relative poverty' then, compared with today, also that I am wearing wellingtons, to cross the muddy fields from Slapton.

These were sailors from the cruisers that had successfully driven the German battleship *Admiral Graf Spee* to seek refuge in the estuary of the River Plate, where the crew scuttled it. This dramatic action took place in December 1939, and we were allowed to listen to a commentary about the battle on the school wireless. Ann was only eight at the time and had just moved up from the Infants, making this one of her strongest memories of life in the big classroom.

February 26th: "I found my first snowdrop and primroses. Mr. Sumner Welles (American Secretary of State) met Mussolini."

In early March my father wrote an entry in the diary, entering into the spirit of mine—-

March 8th: "Finns refuse Russian peace terms. Dad started seven days leave". Then I added, "AIR FORCE (ours) FLEW OVER POLAND—-700 MILES."

At this stage of the war, Father was still in intensive training with his ack-ack battery and in his spare time he composed stories for Ann, some of them rhymed in the manner of the Rupert column in the *Daily Express*, beautifully illustrated by his friend Peter Granville. When he came home on leave he would recite them to us. Ann still has three examples of these stories, and in particular, a longer story called *Twinkletoes* that she has sometimes contemplated getting published.

March 13th: "I went to Silverstone to have my scholarship (exam). Fin (n) s accepted peace terms."

School Log Book for the day, Miss Abberley writes:
"Annual Schools Exam. Joyce Barford, Margaret Richardson, Kate Redford, Betty Cann, Christine Smith, John Haynes and Harry Hayward are attending Silverstone Council School as the entrants."

We were all taken to the neighbouring village of Silverstone by car. With my experience of other schools, I must have found a strange schoolroom less disorientating than the other children, especially Joyce, who had been ill and was not fully recovered. I got straight down to the papers and worked steadily through the sums but couldn't quite finish the last one (always a tester). The English paper might have been a disaster if I hadn't liked any of the topics for the composition, but there was one on a 'Day Out', which enabled me to describe a trip we had once done by car for a picnic in Burnham Beeches, so I worked away very happily on that. I remember that one question in the English usage section asked us to distinguish between transparent and opaque. The Intelligence Test was quite good fun, picking the odd geometric shape, number or word out and so on, and I managed to finish it.

After the exam, despite having no homework, I continued to listen regularly to the evening news and my laconic entries continued:

March 14th: "I found my first daisy and frog spawn—-had a shepherd's pie. It snowed in the morning.

March 15th: "Dad went back to camp—to Botley Hill House to have his arm pricked for typhus.

March 16th: "Went to Wappenham on bicycle—-Peter Lawrence lost a 2/6d bit—- a nice day." (Hardly a 'nice day' for Peter, to lose half a crown was a disaster in our childhood!)

March 17th: "Palm Sunday—-Mr. Brody (Brodie) gave us a cross at church made from a palm leaf. It rained. (See photos 5-4, middle right.)

March 19th: "Had exams in school—-sums and composition. Our planes bombed the island of Silt (Sylt, a German island off Denmark) set munition works on fire.

March 21st: "I was second in exam (end of term in school). Queen Mary left New York for Halifax, to be a troop ship.

March 25th: "Easter Monday. I had a shilling instead of an egg. I made a catapult. Found my first celandine. I got a bunch of blue and white violets from up the bridge—-me and Ann.

March 26th: "Went with Peter Lawrence (to play) in the engine yard (his father's) and made a lot of junks and ships.

April 1st: "A new train on the Wappenham line. Harry and I saw it over Oxbridge.

April 6th: "Still in bed. Uncle Chub brought Mum a bike from Blackpit tied on his car with a rope." (I'd been in bed for a week with a sore throat and chest pains. A bicycle was now necessary for Mother with Father in the Army, and no car.)

April 8th: "Germany invaded Norway and Denmark. The Prime Minister reviewed the situation.

April 9th: "HMS. HUNTER SUNK—- HMS. HARDY GONE AGROUND in Norway.

April 11th: "Denmark completely took (sic) over by Germans. A shell went straight through the HMS RENOWN."

Unknown to me at that time, my father's elder brother Frank was serving as a lieutenant and 'writer' on HMS *Renown*. Fortunately, the shell went through without exploding.

April 12th: "Me and Mum went over to Uncle Chub's at Blackpit (on our bikes). I went shepherding with him. Mum went to Shalstone to look at a house. It was a hovel (!)"

This entry is an indication of the changes that were taking place in our life in Slapton at this time. Our relations at the Boxes, the Hursts, had already left a year or so earlier, forced out by the depression in farming and Harold had taken a job with Jack Davies at the Home farm at Dadford, near Stowe. Mother had now been given notice to leave the Lodge Cottage by Major Lamb and was looking for somewhere else for us to live. However, it was to be some months before we moved and meanwhile our life in the village continued:

April 13th: "Found two birds nests in the hedge one just building and one with eggs.

April 15th: "My blackbird has now got four eggs in nest.

April 16th: "Saw my first swallow flying over school. Mum went to Auntie Chub's on bike.

April 21st: "My (eleventh) Birthday, had a Carpenter's set. Mother gave me a shilling & Aunt Nan gave sixpence." (I also had a shilling from Grannie Watson the day before and two shillings from Grannie Haynes the next day.)

April 23rd: "British troops recaptured Hamer and Elverum (in Norway). We danced round maypole (practising for May Day).

Photographs 5-4 Abthorpe and Slapton 1939-40

Top left -: John bird -watching with Mother's opera glasses in the garden of the Lodge Cottage (they weren't much help!).

Top right -: John and Max after a swim in the Lasher. Note muddy knees.

Middle left -: The top class, and some others, dancing round the maypole on the vicarage lawn (May 1940). Fronting the maypole from the left are, Kate Redford, Harry Hayward, Ann (with plaits) Charlie Slack, Margaret Richardson. Behind the maypole are one or two indeterminate figures, David Barford, Peter Lawrence, one of the Smith girls, and me.

Middle right -: Vicar Brodie with some of his flock, in the front row are, from the left, Johnny Hayward, Cicely Hayward and Max (looking up at the Vicar); kneeling are, Ann and Janet Slack; standing are David Haynes, Harry Hayward, John Haynes and Charlie Slack.

Bottom left -: Mother's three boys in blue (showing off her knitting) on Holman's Bridge (then) just outside Aylesbury on the Buckingham Road.

Bottom right -: Max asleep over his book in the garden of the Lodge Cottage.

April 26th: "Ribbentrop made a speech—-said we (Britain) intended to invade Norway in first place." (This was correct: Hitler, who initially respected Norwegian neutrality, invaded after Churchill decided to mine Norwegian waters to cut off his supply of Swedish iron ore.)

April 27th: 'Went fishing—-caught an eel, a crawfish, a rockling and eight soldiers (minnows) - DAD CAME HOME.

April 29th: "Went fishing in the evening. Found two of Mr. Messenger's ducks write (right) up by the Station.

April 30th: "Went to Northampton Baths. Brought (bought) a glider—-we went on train. David and Max got a cap-gun each.

May 1st: "We had a May Queen and went round the Village singing. We danced round the Maypole—-I won 10d in the sports at night."

This deserves amplification. On this occasion, Joyce was Queen, Margaret and Kath were attendants and I was dressed as attendant 'Green Man' (more a green page, with leaves on my head; probably the idea of the new vicar, Mr. Brodie) and in charge of the crown for the ceremony. Afterwards, we perambulated round the two villages in Joyce's father's horse and cart, and as it often is on May Day, it was very cold (modern May Day being eleven days earlier than it was in mediaeval times). Kath remembers how we were entertained with lemonade on the Roberts's lawn in Slapton and enjoying it despite being chilled to the bone. (The Roberts's also used to give us Slapton village children regular Magic Lantern shows on their lawn.)

Our tour of the villages was followed by tea in the 'Leeson Room' at the vicarage (with cakes and salmon paste sandwiches laid out on a big table, according to Kath). There was then dancing round the maypole on the vicarage lawn and we greatly enjoyed winding then unwinding the intricate patterns made by our ribbons on the pole as we danced in and out (see photos 5-4, middle left).

May 3rd: "Opened the May Day collecting boxes and found £3. 5. 9d. We collect(ed) some cowslips."

As the vicar wrote later in the Parish Magazine, the three pounds, five shillings and nine pence collected, paid for the tea and prizes, leaving enough over for the tea on Empire Day.

May 5th: "Biked to Dadford and went to Church (Stowe) with Tony. Aunt Nan made a frock for Ann."

Dadford, where the Hursts were now living, is three miles down the byroad from Silverstone to Buckingham. Incidentally, petrol rationing, with its restriction to essential travel, made the roads much quieter and safer for children.

May 7th: "Went to school with no socks. Went fishing in the evening—-caught a frog." (We always looked forward to that time in spring when we could go to school in our plimsolls without socks, see photos 5-4 bottom left.)

May 8th: "Mr. Chamberlain nearly had to resign—-had 280 (votes) against (his) 100.

May 10th: "Germany invaded Holland and Belgium—-landed parachutists at 3.0 o'clock.

May 11th: "Mr. Chamberlain resigned. Mr. Churchill elected Prime Minister.

May 14th: "Had to practise folk dances in school, big attack developing in Belgium.

The success of the May Day celebrations led the vicar, (Alistair George Brodie, incumbent 1939-1943) who was very kind man and fond of children, to encourage us in country dancing on the vicarage lawn. This led to an incident, amusing in retrospect. We were taught our first steps in the big classroom. Harry, who as always was wearing his boots, was not very happy and decided it was beneath his dignity dancing with the girls and began to kick out rather dangerously. (I must explain, that many of the village boys wore boots winter and summer, heavily studded with metal 'blakies' to save the soles. Peter and I wore plimsolls (canvas shoes) in the summer, without socks, which had the great advantage of allowing us to wade in the brook and then let them dry on our feet. In the winter though, we would be rather envious of those boys able to make sparks when sliding on the frozen puddles, and would try and get our parents to put 'blakies' on our shoes!) Miss Abberley finally became exasperated with Harry making a nuisance of himself in his heavy boots and told him that he must make up his mind whether he wanted to do join in the dancing or not.

Before the next dancing session, Harry talked it over with me, saying he wasn't going to do it because it was 'sissy'. In a misguided show of male solidarity and because I didn't want to be thought a sissy, I opted out too. We soon realized our mistake. The next session was on a hot afternoon and the class was taken out onto the vicarage lawn, while we sat inside doing some extra work. As soon as I could catch Miss Abberley alone at her desk during playtime the next day, and with shamed-face, I said we were sorry for behaving as we did and could we be allowed to rejoin the dancing class. No more was said about it and we thoroughly enjoyed learning the steps of dances such as 'Milkmaids' and 'Shepherds Hay', performing them one evening in front of our parents.

May 20th: "David and Ann stopped having music (piano lessons). I kept on having mine." (David and Ann weren't practising and Mother presented them with an ultimatum: practise or give it up.)

May 30th: "A large body of the B.E.F. (British Expeditionary Force) has been evacuated by an armada of ships of all shapes and sizes."

Two of our cousins were amongst those taken off the beach at Dunkirk: Lionel, the oldest of the Wheeler boys, who went on to win the MBE and the DFC in the Italian campaign and eventually retired from the regular army as a major; and James (Robins) who went on to win the MC in Burma and also attained the rank of major.

June 3rd: "Went swimming in the brook. (See photos 5-4 top right) German planes bombed Paris—-200 cas (ualties)."

Lacking the discipline of evening homework, my entries in the diary now become increasingly scattered. In part this was also because of the increasing gravity of the Allied position with the collapse of Holland, Belgium and Norway. Air raids were increasing and there was fear of imminent invasion. Our parents, like many others, looked into the possibility of evacuating us to Canada, such was their concern, even though this would have meant splitting us up.

June 10th: "Italy came in on Germany's side.

June 18th: "France gave in. I went swimming down station, got bit(t)en by a gadfly.

June 19th: "A (n) air raid over Lincoln—6 private houses wiped out.

June 20th: "7 school children killed in a (n) air raid—-a Hurricane squadron machine gunned an aerodrome (in France).

June 22nd: "We went to the pictures (Northampton) to see the Wizard of Oz.

June 24th: "Mother sent a letter about us going to Canada in a (n) evacuation sc(h)eme.

June 25th: "A German plane went over Wappenham——they bombed Peterbourgh.

June 27th: "We had a form sent back for Mother to fill up about Canada.

June 30th: "The German occupation of France now extends to the Spanish border.

July 1st: "Enemy landings have been made in Jersey and Guernsey.

July 2nd: "The beach has been closed at Brighton.

July 3rd: "Six German planes shot down over England.

July 4th: "At Oran 4 (French) battleships and (many) destroyers were sunk to prevent them from falling into enemy hands." (The French North African territories had refused to join the Free French under De Gaulle.)

July 5th: "Some of the southern coast has been declared a defence area."

This is the last entry for two months. In the event, we didn't go to Canada. This was because the scheduled liner, *City of Benares,* was sunk in mid Atlantic by a U-boat and 74 of the 90 children on board were lost.

The results of the Scholarship Exam were announced sometime during the late spring. One morning, Miss Abberley, at the big table under the map of the Empire, opened an important looking envelope and told the class, to our great surprise, that I had passed. Not least to mine, because like everyone else, I thought that if any one should pass it should be Joyce (I think there was an enquiry). I had ridden in on my bike that morning and I was allowed to go home on it to tell my mother. I raced off, speeding down Abthorpe Hill towards the railway bridge, excited by my success but upset about Joyce and convinced there must have been a mistake. When I got home, Mother was busy in the kitchen, and delighted by the news, immediately phoned up Father's Ack-Ack battery to pass it on to him. No doubt he was pleased that his encouragement had borne fruit. Significantly, there is no mention of all this in my diary, probably because of my uncertainty about whether I had really got it! Fortunately, Joyce was able to go to Towcester Grammar School in the September as a fee-paying pupil (as a result of the upturn in farm incomes with the war) together with her brother David, and Margaret went there as well. Unfortunately, the paths of the top class in our 'pleasant little community' now diverged, as the other children moved on to the Council Senior School in Silverstone, and my scholarship was transferred to the Royal Latin School in Buckingham.

The reason for the abrupt cessation of the diary entries in July is that we moved to Dadford, and I didn't make any more until I was already in the Latin School in the autumn. Aunt Nan had once again come to Mother's rescue. She discovered that one of the new council houses in the village was still vacant and Mother (with the high priority of having four children and a husband in the army) was able to rent it.

SOURCES/NOTES—-CHAPTER FIVE

I am indebted to John Riches, the local correspondent for the *Brackley and Towcester Advertiser* (contacted through the good offices of the vicar, the Rev. Bridget Smith) who put me in touch with three former classmates in Abthorpe School: Joyce Law (née Barford), Kath Salmons (née Redford) and Margaret Pitchford (née Richardson) whose reminiscences I have included here; and also for letting me see his copy of the Abthorpe Millennium Disc. I also must thank, Sarah Bridges, County Archivist, Northamptonshire Record Office, for kindly making the Abthorpe School Log Book available to me (relevant pages photographed by Peter Moyse of Helpstone). Mary Hulbert kindly helped me with details of the map and school buildings, and my old school friend, Peter Lawrence with information about Slapton and the chapel.

1a) Baker, G. 1831. *The history and antiquities of the county of Northampton*, Vol. 2, John Bowyer Nicols & Son and John Rodwell, London.
According to Baker, the stone used for the building of Towcester church was obtained from

quarries at Handley Park, only a mile or two from Abthorpe, so these may well be the source for the limestone used to build the school. Joyce Law also tells me that stone for Abthorpe church was obtained from two pits at the Delph, on the Abthorpe side of Mile Oak farm. Diane Sutherland in her book *Northamptonshire Stone* (Dovecote Press, 2003) notes that the limestone is the Blisworth Limestone formation of the Great Oolite Series. As well as being characteristic of the underlying Northampton Sands (Inferior Oolite) there is also an ironstone facies (ferruginous lithological variant) at the base of the overlying Blisworth Clay. Towcester Church is almost entirely of the ironstone.

1b) Slapton Church is described in the following works:

Pevsner, N. 1973, *Northamptonshire,* 2nd ed. revised by Bridget Cherry. Newhaven and London: Yale University Press, 2002.

Mee, Arthur, 1975, *Northamptonshire,* revised and edited by F. R. Banks. London: Hodder and Stoughton (The King's England).

Chapman, R. 1976, *Saint Botolph's Church, Slapton & its wall-paintings,* published by R. Chapman, Abthorpe, printed by Percy Gilkes, Banbury.

1c) According to T. D. Martin, the pastor since 2002, Slapton Chapel, 'quaint and cozy in its early Victorian Gothic', dates from 1844. In 1995 the Methodist societies of Wappenham and Slapton formed a new, independent church with a Reformed Confession of Faith. Chapel Corner 212, Pages 26 and 27, in *Cheering Words,* February 2004.

2) Chapman, R.J. 1992. *These I have loved—-the story of a Northamptonshire village*. R.J. Chapman, Abthorpe. Percy Gilkes, Printers, Banbury.

According to the late Reg Chapman, the local historian (of Chapman's shop and post office on the green), Abthorpe began in Saxon times as a hamlet (Torp) within the parish of Towcester, with an outlying Chapel of Ease that was taken over by the Abbot of Fontonelle after the Conquest. However, it should be noted that another Abthorpe historian, Mary Hulbert, pers. comm., points out that the village is not mentioned in Domesday Book and the first historical reference to it is in the Luffield Abbey Charter in 1290. This also confirms that the village was not a Danish 'thorpe', it being in any case, outside the Danelaw, which after the Treaty of Wedmore lay north of the line Bedford to Stoney Stratford and from thence east of the Watling Street. The Danes were briefly in occupation of North Bucks after the death of Alfred but quickly dispossessed by his son Edward the Elder. At the Conquest, the parishes of Towcester and Greens Norton (which included Slapton) were consolidated into the royal forest of Whittlewood and Silverstone (Silvas town or Wood town) became the site of a favourite hunting lodge, particularly of King John later, rumoured to be Handley Park Farm. The major landowner in Towcester before the Conquest was Tostig, the infamous brother of Harold Godwin; succeeded later in late mediaeval times by the Greys of Ruthin, North Wales, who settled some of their Welsh retainers in the district.

By the end of the nineteenth century there were about ninety houses and over five hundred inhabitants in Abthorpe; with eleven farms and three small- holdings, a butcher, a baker, a general store, a blacksmith and two pubs (the landlord of 'The Stockingframe' was also a carpenter and undertaker). Only the 'New Inn', actually the oldest, still survives. There were also a number of lace makers and a small shoe factory, which prepared soles, heels and uppers for some twenty cobblers working in cottages in the village. However, by the end of the twentieth century these shops and village industries had, as Reg Chapman put it 'melted into the past, into thin air'. The largest employer is now the computer industry, according to John Riches, the local newspaper correspondent, and it is a 'switched-on' place, with 'astronomical' house prices.

3) Colin and June Webster, the present owners of the Lodge, have now modernized the Lodge Cottage as a holiday home and in the summer of 2002 allowed me, and my sister, Ann, to see the skillful transformation that has taken place, with the removal of the former lean-to kitchen. When I explained to June that my mother used to wash her hair in water from the water butt, where I used to catch mosquito larvae for observation in a jam pot, and that my father used to bury the contents of the loo bucket under the turf of the lawn, she threw her hands in the air and exclaimed, 'tell me no more!'

4) Reg Chapman gives a very interesting account of the fourteen masters who presided in the school from Henry Bendbow, up to the time of its rebuilding in 1864, and it is worth repeating details of some of the more noteworthy here. For instance, Humphrey Nicoll, appointed in 1662, with twenty-two years' experience, was master for a further eighteen years in Abthorpe and as he put it, 'My success, my pupils regularly entered both universities, is manifest'. One of these was his son John, who went to Oxford and whose own son John (the grandson) became headmaster of Westminster School. Humphrey's third son, Thomas, left money in his will for a Sunday school on the premises, from 1720, a very early date for such schools, and a bequest to the church that was instrumental in Abthorpe becoming a full parish in 1737.

Robert Porter, who was appointed to the school in 1690, was master for 49 years and became the first vicar of Abthorpe in 1747. From this time, until well into the nineteenth century, the classes were either taught by the vicar (living in the Leeson House, that had become the rectory) or more often by their assistant curate (living over the schoolroom). These included a number of Welshmen. Remarkable amongst these were the Rev. Pryce-Jones of Caersws in Montgomery (1793-1831) whose salary was withheld from 1819-29, because he had taken to the bottle, a Georgian scandal commemorated in the ditty:

> "Abthorpe is a village of peculiar people
> A drunken parson and a wooden steeple."

And, probably, most remarkable of all, John Price, a yeoman's son from Llandeilo in Carmarthenshire, an enthusiastic Greek scholar, who graduated in classics from Cambridge and was appointed curate in Abthorpe in 1834. He taught for six years here before taking other posts and finally being made vicar of Llanbedr-Painscastle, a neglected parish without a vicarage, in the Welsh borders. Here, he became known as the 'Solitary' of Painscastle (described in Kilvert's Diary) living very frugally in three converted bathing huts and famous for preaching to a congregation of tramps and homeless people on Sunday mornings. He provided them with breakfast and gave them sixpence for attendance, and five shillings to unmarried couples if they were willing to regularize their unions.

The schoolmaster in post at the time the big classroom was built was Alfred Goodall, (1863 to 1905) bringing him into the time of the grandparents of many of the children I went to school with. Initially, he was criticized by H.M. Inspector for not keeping good discipline but he soon made up for this, becoming known as stern but just, and praised and respected, even by those he had flogged for serious misdemeanors. A number of scholarships were obtained and on the lighter side, maypole dancing was reintroduced. After the 1870 Elementary Education Act, girls were admitted for the first time, together with a number of older girls, employed as lace-makers in the village and who were taught part-time from 1869 (under the Factory Acts). Children from Slapton and Bradden were now also admitted. As older boys working in agriculture were also taught part-time from 1874, the numbers grew to over eighty pupils and peaked at a hundred and two in 1895, requiring new desks and the employment of 'pupil teachers' and girls as monitors. However, it must be pointed out that the numbers were often well down because many children were absent doing agricultural work, or through measles or whooping cough, and those from Slapton and Bradden cut off by floods or snow drifts; though in the fourth week of May 1888, it is recorded in the Log Book that attendance 'was very thin, because many were away gathering cowslips'.

By the end of the nineteenth century, additional mistresses had been appointed, to teach sewing (Mrs. Christian) and Miss B. Maude Barrett to teach the infants, her task being made easier by the erection, over the Easter holidays in 1900, of wooden and glass partitions (recycled from the gallery of Abthorpe Church) between the two classrooms, with the girls' cloakroom between. During the Great War (1916) Miss Hilma A. Abberley was made an assistant teacher, becoming head mistress in 1922. After Miss Kathleen Henson came to teach the infants in 1925, and when the older children were transferred to the Senior School in Silverstone in 1931, the school became the intimate, little Church Junior School it was in our time. The school finally closed down in 1959. At this time, by coincidence, it was in the charge of a supply teacher called Miss Haynes who had studied geology in Aberystwyth! Happily, it is presently a nursery school. (Some of these facts are from the Abthorpe Millennium Disc.)

5) Miss Henson was not well during the later part of 1936 and through 1937 into 1938. As is shown by the School Log Book, she had a suspected stomach ulcer, which may well have contributed to her sharpness. Miss Leslie from Whittlebury deputized for her during most of these absences, and Mrs. Varney in 1938.

6) This shop is shown in a photo taken in 1935, in Chapman's history, page 294.

7) Most of these books, including my encyclopaedias, were sold when Mother auctioned off all the household goods and chattels in 1944.

8) Standard I (six years old rising seven) was variously taught in either schoolroom according to the numbers in the different year groups. For instance the Log Book shows that in January 1939, when recourse had to be made to the open fire again, this class, which was then in the big schoolroom, was transferred back to the small one.

9) House of Commons Research Paper 99/20, Feb. 1998 indicates that by that date, £1 in 1938 was equivalent to £35.81. By today the multiple would be about 40. Of course, this does not take into account relative price movements. Our rent at the Lodge was (I think) about nine shillings (45p) a week, which would require a multiple of 200+! Also, although my father's pay was very good compared with that of farm-labourers, on £1.50 to £2 a week, these workers usually occupied tied cottages and earned more in the summer with overtime and when doing piece work.

NB. Two books in particular, have helped me to amplify the remarks quoted from my schoolboy diary on the progress of the Second World War:

Bayly, C. and Harper, T. 2004, *Forgotten Armies.* Allen Lane, Penguin, England.
Waller, P. and Rowett, J. 1995, *Chronology of the Twentieth Century.* Helicon Publication Ltd., Oxford.

CHAPTER SIX

EARLY DAYS, ROYAL LATIN SCHOOL

DADFORD 1940-42

The move back to Bucks: Our new house in Dadford was no.13, at the southeast corner of the new Council Estate, which consisted of houses grouped round a concrete turning area and pan-handle access road, on the hill to the north of the village, (now partly privatized and called Northhill—see map). Mother had to get used to having neighbours again, as we had a childless couple called Nash in the other half of our semi, to our right, and the Dormer family in the nearest house to our left. However, the views were open at the back, directly east towards the obelisk of the Wolfe Monument (which was erected to commemorate the capture of Quebec); northeast over the fields up towards Stowe Woods on the horizon; southeast to the north front of Stowe House on the ridge, and south over the vicarage towards Home Farm where our Hurst relations now lived and Harold was working for Jack Davies.

Dadford is a peculiar village in that it has a vicarage but no church. Indeed, there were few facilities even in our time. The village school had already been shut down and the one shop, and post office, sold little more than sweets and cigarettes, little enough now rationing was imposed. The shop was run by two elderly ladies (Miss Gregory and her daughter Ann, who had a leg iron) reputed to be the last traditional Buckinghamshire lace makers, and when you went in you would often see them throwing the bobbins over their cushions. The lack of shops was made up for by the regular calls of tradesmen bringing groceries and other goods in their vans, and there was a cobbler called Seamus who mended our boots and shoes in a shed in the back garden of his cottage.

The reason for the lack of a true village structure was that when Stowe landscape gardens were created in the Eighteenth Century, the inhabitants of Stowe village were moved to Dadford, together with their vicar, but the Church authorities would not allow the removal of Stowe church. The church therefore remains in the Gardens, restored in Eighteenth Century style but well screened with trees so that it is out of sight of the nearby Stowe House—-and actually quite hard to find. It's also a stiff climb up the ridge past Home Farm for the people from Dadford!

Our new house had three bedrooms and a bathroom and all the pipe-work for sanitation and the kitchen was in place, but the water hadn't been laid on, which necessitated going out for it to the pump on the access road. Fortunately, we children were quite used to going

154

out, in turn, with buckets to a hand-pump in Slapton. The garden, in front of No. 13, was quite restricted, narrowing to the turning area, but the back garden was a large corner plot and simply the rough grass of the fenced off former field when we arrived. Through the late summer and early autumn, Mother and I began digging this over. I came to enjoy and get great satisfaction in double digging, chopping the sod square, turning it over in the trench and covering it with the next spit. Our labours were well rewarded the following year when we took seven large sacks of potatoes off this plot—-no small thing in a time of food shortages.

Another early memory of that autumn is of running across to join Uncle Harold (Hurst) on the footplate of the new, yellow/orange Fordson tractor, when he was ploughing the field up towards the Wolfe Monument—-watching the turned earth rolling away from the gleaming ploughshares and the rooks jostling for the worms; staying with him until he decided it was too dark to continue. (There was now a vigorous drive to increase the acreage of arable land and especially wheat production; and fortunately, the emphasis on dairying in the Thirties meant that there was considerable stored up fertility in the old permanent pastures. Incidentally, children are not allowed on the footplate for safety reasons nowadays, and the driver has to have a protective metal cage, usually covered in so that he works in a glass box.)

The Hursts now lived in a modernized corner of the farm buildings at Home farm and we were able to renew our friendship with our cousins Tony, Richard and Jill. Harold was a skillful gardener, and when I went to view his fine vegetable garden he passed on tips to me about autumn planting of broad beans and potatoes for early crops. He also showed me the secrets of his greenhouse and his method of treating tomatoes with the night-time contents of the chamber pot.

I now had to go and get the milk from Home farm, usually in the evening but also in the morning at weekends and when I paid the bill. The lane down to the farm was then bordered by very tall English elms, and in the winter, a stormcock (Mistle Thrush) would regularly sing from the topmost branches of one of them, flinging his notes defiantly into the gales. On the north side of the lane near to the farm was a lake with a dense growth of reeds on the opposite side, a roosting site for immense flocks of starlings and, in the autumn, flights of migrating swallows. My cousin Tony and I fished for pike here, but we never caught any as big as some of those that used to get caught in the fish trap (together with eels) when Jack Davies diverted the overflow from the lake through his hydro-electric generating plant—-I used to regularly check the trap when I passed on my way to get the milk. It was at Aunt Nan's that I first tasted stuffed pike, eel, squab (pigeon) pie and also rook pie made from young rooks shot in the annual cull of young birds in the elm tree rookery.

Two new schools: We arrived in Dadford early in the July. As I was not to take up my scholarship place until the autumn term started, I had to spend the two or three weeks before the school holidays in the Council Junior School in Buckingham, going in with Ann and David, and the other village children on Payne's school bus. The Junior School was then in Well Street, backing on the River Ouse. (Since then the school has taken over the buildings of the former Latin School in Chandos Road and the old premises have become a day center.) Not surprisingly, I don't remember much about my brief time in yet another school but I do remember we had weekly tests and that you were moved round the class according to your position. I began by being placed at the bottom right but spent the last two weeks in the back row, which spoke well of the teaching in Abthorpe School. I also remember being attracted by a girl called Margaret Pateman, who lived near the entrance gates to Stowe Avenue and would also be in Standard I at the Latin School.

My little 'five-year-diary' is silent on this period in my life—-too much was going on. This is a pity in that our move coincided with the beginning of the Battle of Britain that was desperately fought out in the summer skies over the harvest fields of southern England, as Hitler attempted to knock out our air force. This was in order to gain command of the Channel, preparatory to invasion by means of barges already massed on the Channel coast. We were north of the main action that summer but the sound of aircraft always brought us village boys out and we could soon distinguish the flights of Hurricanes from Spitfires and the particular features of the Messerschmitt fighter plane.

During this time, David and I sometimes biked over to see our friends in Slapton and Abthorpe. On one occasion, we biked over to the Barfords at Mile Oak for the day, to see Joyce and her brother David, and left our bikes propped up against the trunk of the big oak tree in the field leading up to the farm. When we came back to get them to ride home, we found that two cart horses, while spending the afternoon in the shade of the tree, had stamped on them and badly buckled the wheels. Mr Barford had to drive us back to Dadford in his car. Fortunately, especially as I would need my bike to go to school, he came back a day or two later with the bikes roped on top of his car, perfectly mended!

My diary began again when I started at the Latin School:
9/9/40: "Mum's Birthday—-started at Latin School. We did not do no work, we just put our names on books."

As the lovely (Northamptonshire) double negative indicates, we spent the first day after we had met our form teacher and been allotted a desk, putting the names of the different subjects on our exercise books and text books. We were fortunate in those days in that we had a form room and each of us had a desk to keep our books and papers in, only having to take the necessary items into the science laboratory, or home to do our homework. Since then it has become the rule for secondary school children to keep their books and papers at home, taking in what is necessary for the day; which would have been a problem for me on my bike. (See note 1.)

I had to go on my bike to school because I was not allowed on the school bus, which was for the children going in to the Council Junior and Council Senior schools, only. The council took no responsibility for the fee-paying children at the Latin School, or the scholarship children. So I had a four-mile journey in the morning and back in the evening whatever the weather. I often got soaked through, taking an hour or two to dry off in class, which led Mother to write quite a few letters to the Council, but it was some years before the policy was changed. Of course, it was very enjoyable in fine weather.

It was fortunate that I had a good bike, otherwise Mother might have found it difficult having to buy one at the same time as kitting me out for the school: with the necessary gray suit with short trousers, white shirts with black and red striped tie, knee socks with red circle round the top, black school cap, also with a red circle, and dark navy gabardine raincoat, as well as sports gear, football boots, shorts and shirts and white flannels for cricket. Girls wore black gymslips in the winter, with white blouses or red jerseys, and pink dresses in the summer. Betty Jones, the eldest daughter of Cecil Jones, who worked for Tommy Osborne at Parkfields Farm, which is on the opposite side of the Silverstone road to our Wheeler relations in Stowe Ridings, passed the scholarship exam a year or two before me but, sadly, her parents decided the outlay would be too great for them to let her to take it up.

Father had bought the bike for my tenth birthday while we still lived in Slapton, for a pound, from 'Mick Lewis' (not his real name, which no one seemed to know), the Irish groom who worked for Major Lewis. It was built up from spare parts and was much too big for me, so that to begin with I could only just ride tiptoe with the saddle right down. However, it had a particularly good feature in that the rear brake was in the hub (a coaster-brake hub) activated by pedalling backwards, a boon going down long hills. This bike stood me in good stead down through the years, to the extent that I was still using it for geological fieldwork more than ten years later.

On the evening of that first day in the Latin School, as I rode home through the village, my new satchel on my back, anticipating Mother's birthday tea, I got off my bike to push it up Dadford Hill towards the council houses, and several of my erstwhile schoolmates from the Buckingham Junior school (taken home by bus and already out to play) gathered on the verge, shouting, "Bulldog, Bulldog from the Snob School, he won't talk to us now", and such like. I ignored it and went home and had tea. Afterwards, I went out in my ordinary clothes to play with the village lads and the incident was quickly forgotten. It was not repeated, and I never did find out why Latin School boys were called bulldogs!

I soon settled down in the Latin School and enjoyed the lessons. Our form mistress was Miss Hough, tall and fair, who taught geography, and liking that subject I took to her, as I did to Miss Cox, the history teacher. She was quite short in stature, with black hair tied in a v-shaped roll and very bright blue eyes, and she generally commended my efforts, especially when I illustrated one exam answer with a quick sketch of a goose-girl with a line of geese. My cousin Jose remembers how attractive she was (with a 'fantastic range of colourful high-heeled shoes') and that she was part Irish, teaching her class about 'The Troubles' for School Cert. English was taught by Miss Merry, a tall, angular, elderly lady, with high colour in her cheeks and gray hair that was also tied in a roll (a fashion set by women increasingly being employed in factories on war work where long hair was a danger). She was known unkindly as the 'Old Hen', but was a good teacher, and that first term I was in the school we did *The Christmas Carol* which I enjoyed very much.

My relations with some of the masters were a little more equivocal, not to say edgy in the case of 'Taffy' Williams who taught us French. Jose remembers that he was habitually dressed in a black jacket with striped trousers, and always addressed her in an exaggerated

French accent, as Josephine. I was enthusiastic in both Latin and French subjects to begin with but my interest fell away later as I became more engrossed with history, geography, and maths. Again, he was a good teacher but a strict disciplinarian as I found out to my cost. One of my best friends in those years was 'Tom' (Lionel) Brazier. He was the son of a farmer and well-known cattle dealer from Granborough, near Winslow on the Aylesbury Road. A very clever boy, usually near, if not top of the class, he was also a boy soprano who amazed us all with his beautifully clear rendition of *Oh for the wings of a Dove* in Buckingham church on an occasion when the school attended a service. Later in life he went on to become a tea planter in East Africa and later a director of Brook Bonds. The two of us were sharing a textbook during a French lesson one day and had been set to work on an exercise. We were whispering together, not realizing that Taffy was quietly coming down the aisle behind us, and he smartly clapped our heads together. We both saw stars for quite a while afterwards and had sore heads for longer. Mind you, neither of us ever forgot it!

Despite this manifestation of the iron rule of the old school, Taffy was a good influence on me in a number of ways, as the following examples will show. Sometime later, he had to set us to work while he was engaged elsewhere. He had told us previously about his upbringing in a South Wales valley and he asked us to write a short account (in English) to show what it was like. I imagined a walk over the mountain to a neighbouring village and then a difficult walk back, in mist and the gathering dusk, over boggy ground down to the lights of the home village. He was pleased with my efforts and had me read it out in the next lesson, which was, of course, very encouraging. On a later occasion again, I think after the exams before the Christmas of the second year I was there, he decided we should use the lesson time in a debate on the pros and cons of fox hunting. After a few of the children had made their points, mostly against, he managed to get me to overcome my habitual shyness and diffidence, to make, 'off the cuff', quite a lively defense of hunting, on the grounds that all the other suggested methods of control involved more cruelty and that if I were the fox I would choose to make a run for it. I've forgotten how the voting went (probably against) but this experience was good for me.

Our Headmaster at the time was H.B. Toft, a well-known figure on the rugby field, renowned for his prowess as a hooker and one time captain of the England team. (One of the former students at the University of Wales, Aberystwyth, recalling student days in the Thirties, notes that he was very pleased to hook one against the head when playing opposite 'the great H.B. Toft' in an intervarsity match—-meaning that he was able to heel the ball back although Toft had the advantage of being fed by his own scrum half when the ball was put into the scrum.) Although Headmaster, Mr. Toft liked to keep his hand in by teaching at the chalk face and took us for maths in the first form. He would come in and immediately fire off questions to different pupils at random, to keep us on our toes in mental arithmetic. This was great fun, and even better was that on other occasions he would come in with his recorder and jump up onto the long desk in front of the blackboard, sit on it with his legs dangling down and play us some tunes. He was very keen to interest as many children as possible in learning to play the recorder, thinking it an excellent way of bringing children to music. However, Mother decided she was in no position to buy me a recorder, and in any case, although I was no longer having lessons, I was still playing the piano for pleasure.

His wife had been a journalist, and one day when she was invited to tea, Jose, who fancied being one herself, raised the idea and was told, quite firmly, to put the idea out of her head because she was too soft-hearted!

Mr. Toft was also a firm disciplinarian and despite (indeed, because of) this was well liked and respected. Very serious misdemeanours and offences against the school rules were, in the case of boys, punished with three strokes on the backside with the gym shoe, quite effective when wielded by Toft's brawny arm, to the extent that I only remember a few occasions when he had to resort to it. One was after two older boys grabbed two of us first formers and hauled us into a brick air raid shelter that had been erected by the school. My assailant started on me with the usual knee in the back, skin 'burning' and arm-twisting. I just remained silent, determined not to make a murmur, but my classmate made the mistake of crying out for his mother and my attacker immediately left me alone and homed in on him as well, so I escaped. The upshot was that my classmate complained to his parents and the two bullies were punished and summarily expelled.

The Influence of Stowe, 'a work to wonder at':

"Nature shall join you; time shall make it grow
A work to wonder at—-perhaps a Stowe."
Pope, The Dynasty, 1731.

"Oh! Lead me to the wide extended walks,
The fair majestic paradise of Stowe."
Thompson, The Seasons, added 1744.

"Every boy who goes out of Stowe will know beauty when he sees it."
J.F. Roxburgh, 'Headmaster of genius'.

"Stowe—-where it seems so natural to be at peace with oneself."
G. Wilson Knight, The Dynasty of Stowe.

Although Headmaster Roxborough may not have realized it, boys (and girls) other than his pupils would come under the influence of Stowe, and thus know beauty when they saw it.

On my way to the Latin School in the morning, I usually went the longer, easier way, along the Dadford to Buckingham road, round by the Oxford Lodges, skirting the Landscape Gardens to join Stowe Avenue at Chackmore crossroads. Sometimes I had the company of my cousin, Jose Wheeler, from Blackpit, who was three or four years ahead of me at the Latin School, or perhaps that of another pretty, dark girl called Dora Stokes, two years ahead of me, whose parents worked at Boycott Manor, just down the road towards the Lodges. (Dora, an only child, was later, tragically, knocked off her bicycle and killed by a post-office van on the corner by the vicarage.)

On my way home I was usually alone, and after biking a mile or so up Stowe Avenue from Buckingham, with its very wide grass verges and stately elms with 'their murmuring leaves', I would take the track from Chackmore crossroads, that leads up to the Corinthian Arch. On one occasion, a girl in my class, whose family lived in the left side of the Arch, invited me to tea and took me up to see the spectacular view from the top—-south down the Avenue to Buckingham, and north over the lakes to the south front of Stowe House (see end-map).

From the Corinthian Arch, I would take the track down to the Octagon Lake; turn left by the Lake Pavilions (Roman Doric follies, designed by Vanbrugh); cross the bridge at the cascade, which connects the Octagon Lake with the lower, Eleven Acre Lake (where I once heard a starling perfectly imitate a peewit); ride up past the Rotunda (a dome raised on pillars, designed by Vanbrugh as a focus for the gardens); take the track round the west end of Stowe School; ride out of the gardens through the north entrance and down the steep hill to Home Farm and Dadford (usually checking out the sand martin colony in Jack Davies's big sand pit as I went by).

It was when biking back from school that first autumn as the leaves coloured, that I first became familiar with the beauties of these great landscape gardens. I was to experience them at all seasons, and although I was unaware then of the art and philosophical ideas that had gone into their construction, they provided, as it were, a subconscious education, supporting my gradual realization that freedom depends on order and continuity; also, as shown by the final, financial collapse under the last dukes, that nemesis inevitably follows hubris.

After two hundred years, the gardens had become overgrown with large mature trees and rampant growth of bushes, tending to hide many of the follies and grottos. This became a positive advantage during the War, when the Army found that it was a good place to hide large stores of supplies and ordinance in well-camouflaged, Nissen huts and tin sheds, difficult to spot from the air. There was even a long line of open-ended tin sheds all the way down Stowe Avenue under the trees. These were not kept locked, because the shells and other ammunition weren't primed, so you could easily get in and have a look in the boxes. Looking back, it seems quite apposite that Stowe Gardens, which celebrated the Seven Years War and other victories in the Eighteenth Century, should have played its part in the Twentieth Century struggle for Europe against 'the slavish systems of usurped authority'—-as one of the inscriptions says in the Temple of British Worthies (see map and note 2).

The Blitz begins: In the Autumn, after the RAF had successfully fought off the daytime attack of the German air force, Hitler switched to night-time bombing of major cities and industrial areas—'The Blitz'.

The second entry in my diary at the new address reads:
14/9/40: "We are now living in Dadford, Bucks—-could not write before because we moved (from Slapton). We have had many great air raids on London.

15/9/40: "Went conkering—-some evacs (evacuees) came to Dadford—-went to play down in (Jack) Davies's barns.

16/9/40: "Ann's birthday (9th), brought (sic) her a torch (now very useful in the blackout) Helped Mr. Davies get ready for threshing." (As I was now going daily to get the milk from Home Farm, I sometimes helped with odd jobs.)

17/9/40: "RAF brought down 165 planes."

The change in enemy tactics towards night bombing of London accelerated the evacuation of children to safer parts of the country, which included the evacuation of the Marylebone Central School to Buckingham, and a number of the children were farmed out into nearby villages. The billeting officer called at our house but decided that as Mother already had four kids to look after she could hardly be expected to take any, especially as we boys were already sleeping three in a bed. However, a number of children were found lodging in the Council Houses and two boys of my age called Stan Bunting and Fred (Charles Frederick) Teague came to stay next door with Mr. and Mrs. Nash, quickly becoming part of our village 'gang'. Fred (later in life, Brigadier Charles Teague) had a younger sister, Joyce, who was billeted in one of the older Council Houses below our new development, and who soon became friendly with Ann. Their father had been captured at Dunkirk and was a prisoner-of-war, and rather than stay on in London on her own, their mother came down after a few months and rented one of the old, thatched cottages near the post office so that they could be reunited.

There were problems as the authorities struggled to find teaching space for the Marylebone classes, which led to halftime teaching in the Latin School for a while. It was also decided to reopen the village school in Dadford for the juniors, which Ann and David, together with Joyce, now attended. There was now considerable difficulty in finding qualified teachers, as so many had joined the Forces.

Amongst David's friends at Dadford School were the Bower boys, who first came to live with their mother, their older sister June and an aunt in the cottage next to the Teagues, but then moved out to Gorrell farm. One winter day, Max and I were up there with David, rough-housing with the two Bower boys on the hay in the Dutch barn. The hay was piled up just to the shuttering coming down from the roof of the barn at the sides, and in the melee, Max slipped out through the gap. We heard this squelching thud and then there was silence. Racing down we found that he had fallen a good fifteen feet straight onto his back, in the thick mud of the lane leading to the farmyard. All the breath was knocked out of him but he was quite unharmed, thanks to the cattle that had poached up the mud in the wet weather until it was about a foot deep! We had some explaining to do to Mother about the state of his clothes. She was also not very amused one day when David came home and asked why he couldn't take paste sandwiches for his school lunch like the Bower boys. Meat paste and meat pies were not on her shopping list as a matter of principle, or 'bought cake'; all considered signs of poor housekeeping.

However, Mother was quite enthusiastic when we were invited to a birthday party up at Gorrel, and the aunt who was an artistic lady (who taught dancing at the village school) decided we should come in fancy dress. Some of the village mothers thought it was asking too much 'in wartime', but Mother and Mrs Teague responded, showing what could be done with very simple props, to the effect that Fred won the prize dressed as a girl, and Ann came second dressed as a squaw. I went as a highwayman, with my army cape, a trilby squashed into a tricorn hat, an old opera mask and a toy gun; and David went as a pirate.

As the enemy night-bombing raids increased, the air battle intensified and large numbers of German planes were destroyed. However, it now appears that some of the very high figures claimed for the RAF were exaggerated (in order to raise morale). My father always felt that the part played by the Ack-Ack was down played and was particularly annoyed when they had carefully plotted the course of an enemy bomber by Radar, only to be told to stand down and let the RAF deal with it. (This also happened later in the War in the case of the 'doodle bugs' i.e. flying bombs.)

> Diary 24/9/40: "Began having the Wizard comic—-its a good one. London had a lot of alerts.

> 25/9/40: "I ('ve) caught a dose of measles—-have to stay in bed—-it is a go because Dad is coming home tomorrow."
> At least I could read my new comic. The serial in it that I liked best was about a spaceship with anti-gravity panels, which enabled the spacemen to visit inhabited planets in distant stellar systems.

> 29/9/40: "Dad and Mum went to church (Stowe), it was the Harvest Festival. David has also got measles."
> We were both off school for a fortnight, together with Ann who it was thought might be a carrier.

> 2/10/40: "Dad went back to camp. He got a lift to Brackley in the vicar's car."

The vicar was Mr. Fernihough. His housekeeper, Mrs. Eavis, had a son called Marcus, of my brother David's age, being educated at a prep school. David got friendly with this boy in the summer holidays and one day, when I went to the vicarage with him, the vicar asked me about myself, which led to us attending Sunday school in the old village school and that autumn, I began going to choir practice with my cousin Tony. When Mr. Fernihough found that I was borrowing books from the village lending library, he said I would do much better reading some of the books in his library; and one I particularly remember is *The White Company* by Conan Doyle.

Prior to the War, Tim White (the novelist) lived in 'the Cottage in the Ridings' in Stowe Woods and Aunt Chubbie was his landlady. From an early age Jose had visited him there, and one of the things he had told her, was not to take any notice of the vicar because he was a fraud, who didn't actually believe in God. After Tim had gone to live in Ireland, just before the beginning of the War, leaving all his furniture and effects at the cottage, the vicar asked Aunt Chubbie if he could borrow some of the books. She wrote to Tim, but he was very loath to allow it. He wrote back saying that Jose was to go with her to the cottage (because after many visits she knew where every book was) and make sure she removed a mediaeval *Bestiary* and also a book called the *Intermediate Sex*, given to him by some 'disgusting old clergyman in Cambridge'. Jose was also to keep a list of the books that the vicar borrowed. In the event, the vicar never got round to visiting the cottage, and Jose (who now lives in the cottage) still has the *Intermediate Sex* in a bookcase in her bedroom, which used to be Tim's study, but like him has never got round to actually reading it!

3/10/40: "I have got up and have been wooding. I got a good lot."
This was mainly for kindling to start our open fire but also for small logs to eke out our coal, which was now rationed to aid the war effort.

12/10/40: "Went acorning—-got 12 and a 1/2 lbs. Ann heard the siren at Wolverton (In northeast Bucks)".
We had been asked as part of the war effort to collect acorns, perhaps for pig food, and it happened to be a good year for them.

16/10/40: "Had Art in school—-got top marks (the Art master left at the end of the year and I was never taught to paint). Had an air raid warning and we slept downstairs."
Mother had fitted up the cupboard under the stairs with a mattress and bedding so that we could take cover and sleep there if there was an air raid warning.

In October, Hitler postponed his planned invasion of Britain and extended his bombing campaign to attack, not only London, but also our industrial heartland in the Midlands and the North. It was particularly intense during the third week of the month. Ironically, although we were some sixty to seventy miles away from London and in a place considered safe for evacuated children, we were actually on the flight path of enemy bombers skirting London and coming in from the southeast towards the Midlands. We got used to the play of searchlights southeast towards the London area and also away to the northwest towards Coventry. We village boys also learnt to recognize the particular engine sounds of the two main enemy bombers: the steady drone of the Dornier and the peculiar, lurching throb of the Heinkel.

By the end of October I was pretty well recovered from the measles, and enjoying my usual round of activities, and as well as following the course of the bombing, I was playing close attention to the war in the Mediterranean theatre, especially Mussolini's ill-judged attack on Greece.

28/10/40:"Italy declared war on Greece, 6am. Workmen are finishing the laying of pipes and we expect to have the water in soon.

29/10/40: "Greece claimed two (Italian) bombers shot down—-water is on in some of the houses but there is a flood because of leaks in the pipes."
The pipes hadn't been checked since the houses were built. When this was sorted out

we had the first piped water since leaving Bodicote five years before.

30/10/40: "I have just set seeds in a flower pot for next spring.

1/11/40: "Set some more seeds in the garden.

6/11/40: "British (have) taken Gallabat, Sudan.

12/11/40: "Fleet Air Arm cripple Duce's fleet at Taranto.

17/11/40: "Last (Italian) invader driven from Greece." (However, the German army soon replaced the Italians.)

Some of the heaviest raids of the war took place on the night of the 14/15th November, and the centre of Coventry, including the cathedral, was destroyed and over 500 people were killed (this led to our retaliatory attack on Hamburg). Despite being only on the flight path, Dadford did not entirely escape the bombing. One bright moonlit night a lone raider dropped a stick (cluster) of bombs about half a mile away from us, close to Parkfields, Tommy Osborne's farm, on the other side of the road to Silverstone from the Wheelers in Stowe Ridings; possibly aiming at Stowe School, starkly visible on the ridge in the light of a 'bomber's moon'. As soon as we got home from school the next day, we village boys went over to gape at the craters and pick up bits of shrapnel for souvenirs. Luckily there was no real damage to the farm. During one of these raids a German plane was brought down close to Handley Park, on the Abthorpe side of Mile Oak farm where our old school friends, Joyce and David Barford lived. My brother David and I biked over to see it (I think it was a Dornier). The bodies of the crew had been removed but there was a lot of debris and a crowd of people collecting souvenirs. Particularly prized by young men in those days were pieces of Perspex from the cockpit windows, from which they could fashion rings for their girl friends! (Note that on occasions like this the Diary was forgotten!)

18/11/40: "Mechanized Italian division surrendered to Jugo-Slav internment.

21/11/40: "Italians lose five tanks (and) 119 men in desert battle."
The battles to prevent the Axis powers seizing Egypt had begun as British forces under General Wavell advanced into Libya. I followed the see-saw fluctuation of this conflict keenly on the wireless over the next year.

28/11/40: "We had a science test at school—-science mistress said it was simply shocking! 1250 Italians captured in Albania.

30/11/40 (Sat.): "Went threshing down Davies's farm—-jolly cold—-got a wet foot trying to slide on thin ice.

1/12/40(Sun.): "Cold. I made mother a cup of tea in bed and lit the fire. Got some logs of wood in and chopped them up this afternoon.

3/12/40: "Attempt to kill Quisling in Norway.

5/12/40: "A German pilot gave his iron cross to the spitfire pilot that shot him down.

12/12/40: "We captured Sidi Barani (Libya) and captured two Italian Generals. The figure for captured soldiers has risen to 20,000.

27/12/40: "Had a party at the school in the village. It was rotten."
One of the heaviest air-raids of the War took place over the Xmas holidays with the fire-bombing of the square mile round St Paul's Cathedral on the 29th.

School progress: Despite the excitement of the War and being absent on 28 occasions that first term in the Royal Latin School, I managed to do reasonably well. The spell at home with measles accounts for a large part of the absences but I must have been unwell at other times, marked by the blanks in my diary. I also lost a day or two when my bike was stolen, just when I had recovered from the measles. It was returned by the police, after being found abandoned, and in the meantime I had tried to get a lift in the school car, which had replaced the school bus when the village school was reopened for the juniors (including David and Ann), but the driver refused to let me get on and go in to Buckingham with the seniors from the Council School. (As I have explained, this was Council policy.)

My first term's report shows a pattern that tended to be repeated in later years, though with some interesting differences. There were 46 pupils in the first year class (amalgamated because of teacher shortages) and I came tenth in exam position and twelfth on term assessment. Overall I came in the top half of the class in all subjects, except in term assessment of Latin (just below). I was near the top in history, geography and French, middling in English, maths and science. I was to keep up this performance in history and geography, but I was never to do so well in French again, but I was top in maths in the following Easter term, and usually near the top, or top in it, thereafter.

I achieved high marks in my favoured subjects, history and geography as well as maths, in the Easter term, although I was absent even more often, on 32 occasions. The New Year (1941) began with snow and hard weather, which continued into the spring with the roads icy.

6/1/41: "We went over Uncle Jub's (Chub's) Lake (Blackpit) all day—-it was frozen 3in-6ins thick. We captured Bardia in Libya. Dad came home 9.30pm."

The capture of Bardia was followed quite quickly by the capture of Bengazi; this led Hitler to put Rommel in command of the Axis troops and we were forced back into Egypt by the end of April (with Tobruk surrounded) but the British regained Cyrenaica by the end of the year. It was sometime during this snowy spell, that Ann fell on the ice and cut her leg open so badly that she had to be taken in the vicar's car to the Cottage Hospital in Buckingham to have it sewn up.

I had a series of colds that term, and at the end of January (something I had entirely forgotten but revealed by the diary) I had an infected finger, followed by a boil, that Mother treated with hot poultices. I was put to bed because I became feverish and I was confined to it for a fortnight before beginning to get up for brief periods and then spent time outdoors recuperating. Although in bed, as soon as I felt better, I made entries in my diary about the War; (we had a portable wireless with a big dry battery that lasted several months).

11/2/41: "I am still in bed. Streams of German troops are massing on the borders of Bulgaria.

13/2/41: "Franco met Musso and had secret talks."

From about the 14th I was allowed to get up:
16/2/41: "Stayed in doors because of the rain.

17/2/41: "Mum went to Uncle Bob's funeral at Aylesbury (Bob Robins, the father of my cousin James). Mum ment (meant) to get us marbles but didn't. Saw first snowdrop." (There was a marble craze in the village.)

18/2/41: "Went to bed again. Turkey and Bulgaria signed a pact and Turkey will not fight if Germany takes Bulgaria."

I was in bed again for two days but then finally began to get well:
20/2/41: "Tony said he would get me some marbles. He tried but the shops were shut. Saw a violet.

22/2/41: "I did a lot of digging. I think I've now done a ¼ of the garden.

23/2/41: "Went with Max over to the Woods (Stowe Woods) and I dug up some wild primroses.

24/2/41: "I went back to school, to find they had packed up for half holiday. What a sell. I had to walk home (because of a problem with my bike).

27/2/41: "An overwhelming victory for us in Somaliland—-most of it is in our hands. A wet day - a NAZI bomber dived over Buckingham—-dropped two bombs on Bicester." (It was during alerts like this that we were ushered into the air-raid shelters at school.)

The hard weather continued into March, that second term, as my diary shows:
6/3/41: "It is pretty cold going to school on my bike.

7/3/41: "It snowed all day—- very cold. There was a whistling wind.

15/3/41: "David (not yet eight years old) walked to Slapton (a round trip of more than ten miles).

16/3/41: "Me and Tony went on our bikes to Silverstone, Towcester and Slapton.

22/3/41: "Dad came home—-loud cheers."

There was a further slight mishap just before the end of the term:

24/3/41: "I caught my finger in a door—-made a great cut down my finger."
The door was the main entrance of the Latin School, and was slammed on my hand by a boy who ran through ahead of me. It should have been stitched up but was left to Mother Nature, and as it healed, stiffened.

25/3/41: "I still could not move my finger. I don't expect I shall be able to write for a few weeks."

In the event it took about ten days to heal; probably there was a slight fracture. As it was the middle finger of my right hand, which now acted as my 'index finger' following the earlier accident to my forefinger, it was lucky we did not have end of term exams, as well as the usual assessment based on the term's marked exercises.

I have detailed the course of the forgotten episode of illness revealed by the diary, not only because it helps to explain the very high total of absences from the Latin School in my second term, but because I was to suffer two further dangerous bouts of 'blood poisoning' (septicemia) in my life. It certainly explains the remarks of my form mistress, Miss Hough, on my report: (4/4/41) "A pupil of ability but his frequent absences are a handicap to his French and Latin."

Our overlarge class was now split into two, as a teacher had been found to alleviate the war-time shortage of staff, and I was now in IB, with my friend 'Tom' Brazier, and another friend, Barry Payne, the son of Mr. Payne of Payne's Buses and Garage. Barry, known as 'Agger'= Agony, was keen on natural history like me and Tom, once causing a sensation, and screams from some of the girls, by coming into class with two big snails symmetrically climbing both cheeks. My nickname was 'Tre' (as in Trex) because in French lessons I always pronounced très (very) incorrectly, as for instance, saying 'tray' bon—-which naturally exasperated Taffy Williams! No doubt it was thought that the nickname would help me. This fault was similar to the way in which I tended to mix up bought and brought (and still do sometimes). Later on my nickname became 'Hairy', because when it was allowed to grow, my hair was thick and curly.

Some of the attractive girls in the class included Margaret 'Bunny' Bunyan, Beryl Lambourne, and Wendy Chivers, a clever girl with long ringlets of red hair, who was usually top of the class and who, I think, liked me. I was particularly attracted by Gwen Biddlecombe, a farmer's daughter from Steeple Claydon, a girl with brown hair and hazel eyes, but as is the way of things, she too was sweet on someone else.

I soon recovered from the bout of illness I had that February, and my subsequent reports show a gradual fall in the number of times I was absent from school over the next year or so. My diary shows that in the improved spring weather, towards my twelfth birthday, in the Easter holidays, I was certainly enjoying my usual activities of birds' nesting and fishing, as well as following the war news.

2/4/41: "A great battle was fought in the medit (e) rranean—-8 Italian ships sunk (the battle of Cape Matapan, which took place on the 28th of March).

6/4/41: "Germany declared war on Jugoslavia and Greece in pretence of fighting us—-Addis Ababa captured (Ethiopia).

8/4/41: "Jugo-Slavia made a thrust to meet the Greeks in Albania. I found my first birds nest of this year—-a blackbirds with one egg.

9/4/41: "Germans made a thrust and captured Salonika. A bad raid on Coventry—-a lot of bombs dropped. I found two more nests.

10/4/41: "Nazis reached Albania thus cutting Jugo-Slavia in two. I found a mistle thrushes nest with four eggs.

13/4/41: "I saw two swallows as I was going for the milk—-first ones this year. I found a robins nest in a bank—-three eggs.

14/4/41: "An attack was made on Tobruk (Libya) but repulsed with los(s)es.

16/4/41: "I went fishing at Uncle Chubbs and I caught eleven—-9 perch and two mud carp (in Blackpit Lake in Stowe Woods).

17/4/41: "I went fishing. I caught nine—-mum packed up my dinner—-a great raid on London—-many casualties.

18/4/41: "Max and David came with me fishing and we had dinner in the wood."

These entries reveal an almost fanatical devotion to fishing at this time. I had bought myself a good cane fishing rod and tackle at the wonderful (to a boy) old, country sports-gear shop, Herrings that once stood on the square in Buckingham, near the Old Gaol. I used to go up to Blackpit Lake with my rod lashed to the crossbar of my bike. However, I followed this spell of fishing with spring planting in the garden.

A cousin comes to stay: My cousin Tony, who was about eighteen months older than me, had already acquired a good deal of gardening lore from his father (Harold) and he helped me planting the potatoes and other vegetables. He came to stay just before my twelfth birthday:

20/4/41: "British line still holds in Greece (we now had 60,000 troops there). Tony came over on his bike from Dinton."

Earlier that spring the Hursts had moved once more; this time to Dinton, about four miles from Aylesbury, where Harold had found a job on another farm. (Aunt Nan was therefore returning to the ancestral mid-Bucks area of the Watsons, and specifically to the home villages, Dinton and Westlington of Eliza Gutteridge—- her, and Mother's, paternal grandmother.) At this time, Tony was in his last year at the Council Senior School in

Buckingham, and Nan arranged with Mother for him to stay with us so that he could complete his last term there. It was hoped he would then get a place in the Wolverton Technical College, as he had already shown himself 'mechanically minded'. Meanwhile, Ann went over to Dinton to stay with her cousins Jill and Richard and go to school with them for the summer term. Tony was a keen cyclist and as the diary shows cycled over from Dinton, a distance of thirty miles, towards the end of the Easter holidays, carrying his gear in the saddlebag and panniers.

21/4/41: "I had three cards and 1/s from Grandma Watson and 2/s from Grandma Haynes. Tripoli was bombarded by units of the British Navy.

22/4/41: "Plymouth was bombed but all fires were put out before morning. Our troops changed positions in Greece.

23/4/41: "Tony and I planted some potatoes. A part of the Greek army has made a sep (e) rate armistice.

24/4/41: "Started school again——more evacuees in Dadford—-5 in all. Tony and I rode home on bicycles."
Tony and I now went together into school and back on our bikes (although he could have gone in the school car). The arrival of more evacuees was connected with the latest severe bombing of London.

After the hard weather of the winter and early spring that year, the late spring and early summer were warm and dry. In these more benign conditions, as the diary shows, Tony and I got on with the gardening, as well as going on bike rides; and at school, I enjoyed the cricket and the athletics. There were also walks up to Stowe Woods, to have picnics by the lake, especially enjoyable when Father managed to get home on leave. There were no May Day celebrations in our small, isolated hamlet but we village boys organized a cricket match.

1/5/41: "We had a game (of) criket (sic). I got sixteen runs. Max had a sock from the ball, which made his nose bleed." (Max was fielding at 'silly mid-on' and the ball hit him at very close range on the bridge of the nose and in the center of the forehead with considerable force and he was out for a minute or two.)

3/5/41: "Tony and I went to the pictures and saw Laurel and Hardy in SAPS AT SEA."
Films were shown on certain nights at Stowe School for families and friends of the ancillary staff, and villagers were also allowed to attend.

4/5/41: "I found my first cowslip and bluebell and heard first cuckoo.

5/5/41: "We played criket at School. I put a row of peas in and five rows of potatoes. Night fighters brought down 167 (planes, indicated by a swastika).

6/5/41: "Tony and I put another five lines of potatoes in and Tony put some pea sticks in.

7/5/41: "I found a pink's (chaffinches) nest with four eggs."

8/5/41: "I planted some Dwarf beans and some scarlet runners.

9/5/41: "We at school had criket with mister Toft.

11/5/41: "We had criket at school. Rudolph Hess landed in England in a meshasmit (Messerschmitt)."

This curious incident, which was not properly explained at the time, actually occurred in Scotland on the tenth. Apparently, Hess brought peace proposals, which were however, rejected. Coincidentally, or by design, the heaviest air raid of the war took place on the same day with the destruction of the House of Commons.

15/5/41: "Tony has got a place in the Wolverton technical. Auntie Nan had her new grate put in.

17/5/41: "Dad came home. Tony and I went to The Great Dictator (Chaplin). Bucks War Weapons Week started." (A county wide appeal for money for armaments.)

18/5/41: "We went for a picnic and Tony and I swam in the lake (at Blackpit) for first time this year (see photo 6-1, top).

One day about this time, Tony and I were fishing from the jetty at Blackpit, and in attempting to cast far out I managed to catch him in the lip with my hook. We tried vainly to get it out but in the end we had to walk up to the farm with me holding the rod and Tony on the end of the line! Aunt Chubbie was able to get it out by pushing it right through and snipping it off. It made me doubly careful afterwards, and wary of other fishermen.

20/5/41: "Tony and I rode (on our bikes) to Slapton—-they've had a lot of bombs. We had a play in school. Dad went back."

Photographs 6-1 Dadford 1941-42

Top -: A walk through Stowe Woods in the ride that runs diagonally down to Blackpit Lake when Father was on leave; from left, Max, David in front of Father, John and Tony.

Bottom -: Taken when Father, second from left, and the fellow officer cadets in his 'serial' were on short-leave in Oxford (while training at Shrivenham).

Over the Whitsun half term holiday, Tony and I went over to Dinton, where Ann was already staying with her cousin Jill:

23/5/41: "Tony and I caught the bus to Aylesbury (leaving our bikes in Buckingham) and then the bus to Dinton and Aunt Nan's. We found a nest with young in the garden (while studying Uncle Harold's new vegetable plot)."

This was the first time I had been to Dinton. I was greatly intrigued by the well-preserved stocks on the village green below the church, almost opposite the cottage where Nan and Harold now lived. Another abiding memory is of the view from upstairs in their cottage, on a pearly May morning, of the nearby Chilterns, rolling away westwards (the first time I became conscious of a 'view').

24/5/41: "Ann, Jill, Tony and I went into Aylesbury and saw Grandma and Grandad (Watson) and brought (bought) some model planes.

25/5/41: "We flew our aeroplanes. Went back home and found our bikes had gone from the WEST END GARAGE (What a to-do) but the vicar gave us a lift home. Somebody must have a cheek to steal bikes from a garage." (My original brackets in this case.)

26/5/41: "Tony and I informed the police that our bikes had been stolen and they were found abandoned (and returned) by a man called Dealy." (The second time my bike had been stolen and returned.)

While we were having this excitement a great naval battle was being fought in the Atlantic:

27/5/41: "The battleship Hood has been sunk by the Bismark off Greenland—-the battle is still going on." (A shell hit the magazine of the Hood, which went down with the loss of all except three of the men.)

28/5/41: "The Bismark has been sunk by planes and the Royal Navy. We went swimming and found a moorhens nest in a clump (of reeds).

2/6/41: "Tony and I went (on our bikes) to Slapton. There is a white sparrow at Roberts." (The only sparrow I've seen with an appreciable number of white feathers.)

The good weather continued into June. Mother went up to Blackpit to help out Uncle Chubb with hoeing the mangolds and I got through the heats into the finals for the Junior championships (Forms I to III), in the Long Jump, the Hundred Yards and Throwing the Cricket Ball:

12/6/41: "We had our sports. I was second in the Long Jump and third in the Hundred Yards (I was unplaced in Throwing the Cricket Ball).

13/6/41: "I had bad pains in my ribs so I stayed at home."

This entry is interesting in that it illustrates that there was no thought of training for the sports at our level in those days and certainly no 'warming up'. You just went out and did it. As we were generally pretty fit with all our biking and running around this usually did no harm, but it was easy to strain hitherto unused muscles. I may have hurt myself falling awkwardly in the Long Jump, but succeeding entries in the Diary are in Tony's larger more rounded hand, which seems to indicate I had strained my arm (and ribs) striving to get a place in the Cricket Ball. Although I had presumably recovered by the following day, because we went round the village collecting salvage (for the war effort) Tony went on doing the writing up of the Diary, mostly at my dictation, but some of the entries are his own:

16/6/41: "We went swimming again (at Blackpit)—-Stan and George, and Auntie Jess came with us."(Stan Bunting and George Dormer were the boys living each side of us.)

17/6/41: "John had a bad ear and could not go swimming with the others."

I had probably got water trapped in my ear. The lake is a muddy brown, carp pond (dating back to the time of Luffield Abbey) with cattle, standing hock deep, in the shallow end in hot weather. We also swallowed quite a lot of water without it doing us much harm. My ear was better by the next weekend, because Tony and I went over to Dinton again, and found a good place to swim in the river Thame near Nether Winchendon, and we also swam in the open-air pool in Aylesbury the following day.

22/6/41: Tony wrote at my dictation, "Tony and I left Auntie Nans, we had to walk from Buckingham." Then I added in my own hand, "Germany declared war on Russia at 5am."
Thus began Hitler's ill-fated Napoleonic adventure in Russia—-code named 'Barbarossa', a month after his attempt to put Britain on the sidelines with his peace plan.

The fine hot weather, and our swimming and fishing excursions, continued through late June and into July, when Tony finally ended his long stay with us and I took some days off school to go with Mother up to Blackpit to help with the haymaking.

29/6/41: "Went fishing and brought some home to eat."
I did this when I had caught a reasonably sized perch, which although bony are quite good eating.

3/7/41: "I did not go to school but went haymaking. Mum drove a horse for the first time in her life."

Mother had ridden on the back of a horse, but had never driven a horse-drawn vehicle or machine and she enjoyed managing the swathe turner drawn by a quiet gelding. I think this was, probably, also the first time I used a hayfork and a hay rake.

5/7/41: "I killed a fish with a stone. It was a mud carp."

This makes somewhat uncomfortable reading in this more sensitive age. It was a hot day and there was a large mud carp sunning itself near the surface, well out of reach of my rod, and chancing my arm I threw a stone and scored a hit. In mitigation, it must be said, after I'd swum out to retrieve it, I took it home to eat. Mother did her best, but as she said, it needed more herbs to make it tasty!

11/7/41: "Mum and I went hay making and a thunder storm came on. We got soaked—-the first rain for a long time. I finished (varnishing) my pencil box.

12/7/41: It thundered and rained again—-the ground needed it. My beans are getting all dryed (dried) up. I painted my pencil box.

13/7/41: "I had a few of my broad beans for dinner and we had a new potato each. I am going to give my pencil box to Ann (for her birthday)."

The rains came in the nick of time for my crops. I had made the pencil box in woodwork classes, which were taught in a well-equipped workshop by Mr. Gooch, at the Senior School, a short walk from the Latin School. We boys enjoyed this and one day we were whistling while we worked and Mr. Gooch, suddenly said, "Who is that whistling descant?" It turned out to be me, quite unknowingly!

Embarkation leave: It was at this time that we had the disturbing news that Father was going to be sent abroad.

14/7/41: "We played criket at school. I took two wickets. Dad came home on Embarkation leave before going out East.

20/7/41: "We had a picnic in Woody Park (while) Mum and Dad went to the Edriches to tea."

Woody Park adjoins Stowe Woods, and is also part of the Tile House Estate, which in those days included Blackpit Farm as well as Tile House Farm run by the Edriches, 'Bill Senior' and Edith, the parents of the cricketing Edrich brothers (Eric, Geoffrey, Bill and Brian and their sister Ena).

21/7/41: "Dad went back to Southend to wait until some (other) men have gone on leave before going east.

22/7/41: "Mum and I went hoeing in Uncle Chub's mangle (mangold) field.

23/7/41: "Finished our exams in school—-good job. I had a headache in the evening and went to bed.

24/7/41: "Stayed in bed all day with headache." (I was also sick.)

I was upset about Father's imminent departure overseas and this was probably combined with the pressure of the exams. The results of the exams speak for themselves. My final position was eighteenth in a class of 24, and although in term assessment I was top in geography and second in maths, all I managed in the exam was ninth in each case. In history my position fell from seventh to fifteenth in the class.

3/8/41: "Mum went to Southend for a week to see Dad before he embarks.

4/8/41: "Jose came at 9.30pm (and) stayed for breakfast. I had to get dinner."

It had been arranged that our cousin Jose should come over from Blackpit after tea, and stay overnight with us while Mother was away. As it happened she had met a young soldier, a sergeant in the King's Royal Rifle Corps, stationed up at Silverstone and they were courting in the evenings, walking in the fields or up at Stowe. This pre-occupation was why Jose hadn't come to our house until very late. Unfortunately, her mother, Aunt Chubbie, decided to call on us the next evening to see how things were going and of course Jose was nowhere to be seen. She waited and waited and we didn't know what to say or whether one of us should slip out to warn Jose as she biked through the village. Finally, in high dudgeon, Aunt Chubbie went out and sat in her car, looking grim, until Jose finally turned up and had to face the music. This was Jose's last year in school and because she didn't want to stay on in the Sixth Form she joined the WAAFS, the Womens' Auxiliary Air-force, while still under sixteen because she found out that unlike the WRNS, the Womens' Royal Naval Service, they didn't demand a birth certificate. When her true age was discovered, she was discharged but later did join the WRNS, more happily, going overseas to Ceylon, finally serving at Bletchley Park.

After this upset, Aunt Chubbie decided that I was obviously quite competent to carry on looking after things on my own. My diary shows that this confidence was not entirely misplaced; Mother had left good supplies of tinned food and I now had plenty of vegetables coming in from the garden:

5/8/41: "We had soup for dinner and blancmange and jelly. I went mushrooming."

6/8/41: "Mum sent a card. We had salmon for dinner."

7/8/41: "We had Irish stew for dinner. I went mushrooming—-I got a lot."

8/8/41: "We had chops and treacle sponge and custard for dinner." (I made the sponge pudding from stale sponge cake.)

9/8/41: "We went to the pictures (film show up at Stowe) and mum came home while we were there."

When Mother returned we learned that Father's battalion had still not embarked. It seems that the Higher Command was waiting for good intelligence that the sea routes were safe enough for the troop ships to set sail. There was another anxious wait and then, on the 21st of August, Father was able to come home on forty–eight hours leave. Mother then went back with him to Southend and I looked after things for another week. This time I didn't write anything in my diary while she was away: no doubt I was too busy.

When Mother got back again she told us the welcome news that Father's battalion had been stood down indefinitely. Later, Father revealed what had happened. By this time he had risen through the ranks to sergeant, and prior to being mustered for embarkation at Southend had been sent to Manorbier, in Pembrokeshire, for a course of instruction on the use of Ack-Ack 37 guns in a mobile role (to provide cover for forward units of the Army against air attack):

> "The instructors really pushed and shoved you around. It was bloody hard work. Not quite like those chaps in the Royal Tournament, but similar. The guns were mounted on the back of a big army lorry. Your team had to detach it, uncover it and prepare it for action, by numbers: one side—-2, 4, 6, 8, the other side—-1, 3, 5, 7, in action, Fire! Then you had to push through the barrel to clean it ready for another firing, take it all down again, cover it up and attach it to the lorry out of action.

> "At the end of the course, my team reached the final of the team competition, against the team of instructing sergeants. They had never been beaten, because they were doing it all day long. Nothing could have made us jump into action quicker, even a gun up the backside, than being against these sergeants, who we managed to beat! We were then extremely unpopular with them and it was a good job it was the end of the course, or they would really have put us through it. All my team had worked on Ack-Ack 37 guns, as I had as a sergeant. I could take it all to bits and put it together myself, almost, in those days."

When he was mustered at Southend, Father found that they were to be sent out to take over Madagascar (a former French colony held by the Vichy government) and hold it until the end of the War. They were issued with tropical kit and he stock-piled as many razor blades as he could (93 three-hole blades) in the hope that they would see him out. On the final occasion that Mother stayed with him, the Colonel of the regiment had already gone on ahead with an advance party and had embarked at Liverpool. The battalion was scheduled to leave Southend at 5.30am one morning, and they were all ready to go on board their vessel with the guns greased up and packed, when at 2am the message came through cancelling embarkation until further notice. It appears that Intelligence had received information about 'wolf packs' of U-boats, lying in wait off Gibralter and West Africa to pick off any convoy going out east by the southern Cape route. This information came in the nick of time, Father saying "The cancellation came at the very last moment, otherwise we should have been on our way; we would have gone!" (See note 3.)

As a present for looking after things, Mother bought me a book in Southend, called *Whirlaway—-a story of the ages* by H.C.F. Morant. A big squarish book with a purple cover, illustrated with colour pictures and numerous line drawings, it told the story of the young daughter of a geologist who falls asleep by the fire over one of her father's books and dreams that a spark flies out to materialize as a sprite in a rainbow cloak. The sprite tells her he is called Whirlaway and that he is going to take her on a tour through geological time and show her all the different kinds of life that have formerly existed. They have various adventures, and, most memorably, in the late Cretaceous, when pursued by the dinosaur called *Tyrannosaurus rex,* they manage to escape into a cave. When they come out on the other side of the hills, the hot, fetid atmosphere of the Cretaceous has been replaced by a fresh breeze and there are singing birds and flowers in the grass. Whirlaway explains that they are now at the dawn of recent life (the Eocene) when living things began to become increasingly like they are today. After reading this book, I never forgot the names and order of the three main eras of life and main periods of geological time. It also so happened that I was to spend a good proportion of my professional life researching the beginning of the era of recent life in different parts of the world.

Stowe in the summer holidays: Some time before the start of our school holidays on the 1st of August, 1941, I went up to Stowe School to get myself a permit to fish in the lakes, and also a permit for all the family to go swimming there when it was closed for the vacation. I went in through the great, classical, south entrance with some trepidation, as I had not been there before, soon getting lost before being directed down a long passage to headmaster Roxborough's office, which was on the north front. He was most kind to me and soon set me at ease, asking me about myself, and where I went to school. When I had explained my connection with the Wheelers and how I fished in Blackpit Lake, he enquired about Chubb, whom he would have known since the time Tim White lived in the Cottage in Stowe Ridings. So there wasn't much difficulty in getting the permits.

I greatly enjoyed going up Stowe fishing, often setting off in the first light of a summer dawn and casting out while there was still a light mist on the water, sitting quietly in the reeds watching the water birds, which usually included a family of crested grebes on the Eleven Acre lake. Later on, in wintertime, I went fishing there with a skilled pike fisherman from the village, but I was never very happy about the necessary use of live-bait, like gudgeon or dace, and in any case preferred being on my own.

The swimming pools at Stowe School were at the south side of the Eleven Acre Lake. They were quite simple structures consisting of wooden walkways built out on timber piling driven into the bed of the lake, to make a beginners pool about twenty yards long with a wooden floor, and a bigger, deeper pool with a mud bottom, about fifty yards long that had diving boards. There was also an open wooden pavilion that served as a changing room and shelter. It was in the beginners' pool that Max, aged six, first began to swim without his water wings and shortly afterwards, with our encouragement, managed to swim up and down eighteen times, doing 360 yards. We had many pleasant summer afternoons and evenings here, and Mother particularly liked swimming there in the late evening when the moon was rising. Stowe School now has an indoor swimming pool and the last time I walked round the Eleven Acre Lake, I could find no trace of the old outdoor pools, so the enjoyment of swimming in the limpid lake water, the fish darting away, now exists only in the memory.

As well as fishing and swimming up at Stowe, I sometimes enjoyed other activities in Stowe grounds with our village gang, during the quiet periods of the school holidays when there were very few staff about.

3/8/41: "We all went up Stowe Redoubt again——-its good and its got dungeons and you can see for miles from the top."

The 'redoubt', actually the Bourbon Tower, is on the east side of the grounds well away from the school (see map). It's a double round tower with a base of three stories plus the dungeons and an octagonal, upper observation tower about thirty feet high that rises from an open courtyard with a low wall. The upper tower tops the surrounding trees and you can indeed, 'see for miles' from it (see note 4). It was a favourite place for our war games, for sword fights, quarter-staves and sieges with bows and arrows, especially as it had dungeons for 'prisoners'. The tower was made more exciting (and hazardous) because the floors and stairs were dilapidated. In particular, the stairway to the courtyard from the third story was hanging loose over a big hole in the floor and it was a test of nerve to climb it. We were in action one day, when a lad called Peter Stanton (a younger boy from a family that lived two doors from us) scrambled up onto the narrow parapet of the upper tower. It was about a foot wide and he began to march slowly round saluting. We all froze, not daring to make a movement until he got right round and jumped down inside safely. This earned him considerable prestige (though it wouldn't have pleased his mother if she had found out!).

On another occasion, coming back from the 'Redoubt' past the Cobham monument, we came by the Queen's Temple and on impulse one of us tried the door (I think Stan Bunting and Fred Teague were with me). It wasn't locked so we went inside and found that it was the place where the Stowe boys practised fencing. The foils and masks were up on racks on the walls, so we took some down and while one of us kept watch we had a great time with 'on guard' and 'touché', imagining we were one or other of the Three Musketeers, preferably D'Artagnon, of course. When we had had enough, we carefully put the gear back where we had found it and stole quietly away.

A Grandmother's influence: Towards the end of the summer holidays that year, I had an invitation to go and stay in Aylesbury for a few days.

4/9/41: "I was enochulated (inoculated) for diphtheria——-had a letter from Grandma to stay 4 days.

6/9/41: "Tony and I went to the museum (in Church Street, Aylesbury) in the afternoon and he stayed with me at Grandma's at night."
This was my first visit to a museum, and a sight of displays of fossils, especially ammonites, and of Roman artifacts.

This was also the first of many short holidays with Grandmother. She was, of course, very aware of Mother's difficulties with Father away in the Forces and the problems that summer when he was on standby for embarkation overseas, and had probably decided to help. She also seemed to like having me and often arranged for one of my cousins to stay at the same time, usually Tony, or Bert Watson, 'Young Bert' the son of Mother's brother Bert ('Bert's Bert' the son of 'Old Bert' our Grandfather) who was about the same age as me. On these visits, I used to go on my bike to Buckingham and leave it at the West End Garage before catching the bus to Aylesbury, as I did when going over to Dinton.

My regular appearance at 62, Fleet Street, used to lead Grand-dad, with his sense of fun, to make joking remarks at my expense when he came in and found me there, such as, "Do you live 'ere?" or, at mealtimes, "Isn't it time you got your feet under somebody else's table?" At which, Grandmother would say, "Don't listen to his silly nonsense". He would then respond by singing, "You're my Lilly of Laguna" which he knew she hated. In fact, he enjoyed my visits too, letting me help him in the garden and passing on tips, such as how he struck cuttings of his favourite carnations (which he always wore in his lapel when he went up to open the wine-shop, 'Old Bert's' in Cambridge Street, taking me with him to help in serving the customers). He also took me with him went he went to fish in Hartwell Pits, flooded clay pits a mile or two down the Oxford road, on the opposite side to Hartwell Park, or I would take his lunch out with tea in a blue billy-can, and we would watch the float while listening to the birds in the pussy willows.

I think it was when I was staying in Fleet Street shortly after Christmas 1941, that Grandmother, discovering that we had done *Christmas Carol* in school with the 'Old Hen' (Miss Merry) got me to read aloud selected bits from *Pickwick Papers* including Christmas at Dingley Dell and the episode involving the Fat Boy at the picnic. What she particularly liked was to have me read to her while she curled her hair, heating the curling irons by the open coal fire and tying up the curls with paper or rag strips. She still boiled water and potatoes on this open fire (which had an oven alongside producing marvellous rice puddings) and shelves to the right of it held many of her books.

Grandma seemed to find humorous writing all the more amusing when listening to me reading, and during successive holidays I read from *We Three and Troddles* and from *Three Men in a Boat* as well as from several Surtees novels. This often led to tremendous outbursts of hilarity, as in the case of Cowpers' *John Gilpin* where I ended up rolling on the floor breathless with laughter while tears ran down her face. McGonagall's poems produced a similar result, especially the one about the 'Silvery Tay' and needless to say, there had to be a few repeats. (Inevitably, I have always suspected that the sardonic Scot, master of bathos, knew exactly what he was doing!)

I think it was during the first year of my visits that she gave me the Fennimore-Cooper novels, *The Deer Slayer* and *The Last of the Mohicans,* and Lord Lytton's *Last days of Pompeii* to read. Later on, she lent me Borrow's *The Bible in Spain, Lavengro* and *The Romany Rye* from which she had me read aloud the episode of the *Fight with the Flaming Tinman*. Grandmother kept her classic novels, which included a number of Trollope's, in a bookcase in her front room (the 'sitting room,' rarely sat in because kept for special occasions). One day she took me in to see them and said that Trollope was very good but I should read him when I was older; funnily enough, I still haven't!

I have a clear memory of the hall in Grandmother's house because it was decorated with brass ornaments and other mementoes her eldest son Val had brought back from Egypt after his service in the Middle East and Gallipoli. She was very fond of history and would talk to me about the different administrations of Gladstone and Disraeli and the events leading up to the Great War. Although brought up a Wesleyan, she was a Conservative and much admired Disraeli (unlike her mother, a Liberal, who harangued passers-by on the corner of Kingsbury Square about the merits of Home Rule for Ireland).

It was during these visits that I discovered Weatherhead's famous bookshop, just round the corner from Kingsbury Square, in Buckingham Road. To go there I would sometimes cut up through the big walled garden that backed on New Street behind Wally Cartwright's house and dairy on Buckingham Road. He still delivered milk by horse and milk-float down Fleet Street, dipping it straight from the churn into the jug for you: the horse walking a few paces automatically between each stop. There were also regular visits by the knife grinder, working his wheel by treadle.

Autumn pursuits and an enthusiasm for football: During the autumn of the second year of the War, our school work was often interrupted by the needs of local farmers short of labour.

12/9/41: "Instead of woodwork, our form went potato picking at Sanfords farm outside Buckingham. I bought my kitten home (a ginger tabby I christened Koko).

13/9/41: "David, Max and I picked 6lb of blackberries in Woody Park. Dad went back this morning (after 48 hours leave) to Northampton with Mum."

When rationing started, Mother quickly got us used to doing without sugar in our tea and other drinks, or on cereals or porridge, and saved up as much as she could for jam making. There was also a special allowance of sugar, specifically for that purpose. So every autumn we children spent many afternoons picking blackberries as well as crab apples for crab jelly.

The entries made in the diary in my second year in the Latin School also reveal that I played a lot of football, and somewhat to my surprise, that amongst my other interests, including the work in the garden, I was prepared at this time to bike into Buckingham on a Saturday to take part in a game:

15/9/41: "Played football at school against Form 1—-it was a draw.

18/9/41: "Dug up some more potatoes—-we have dug up ½ of them up and got 5 sacks (eventually filling seven big wheat sacks).

22/9/41: "Played football—-won by 6-1. I scored 1—-listened to Higher Command on the wireless. Two Italian liners—-25,000 tons sunk.

Photographs 6-2 Wartime Portraits

Top -: Taken in November 1941, from left, John (12), Max (6), David (8) and Ann (10).

Bottom left -: Taken at the same time as the above when Mother was thirty-three.

Bottom right -: Taken in 1942 when Father passed out of O.C.T.U. as an officer (also 33).

24/9/41: "Mr. Williams (Taffy) put up the team for Saturdays match. I am centre forward."

I liked playing in the forward line, and particularly at inside left, because I could shoot with both feet. However, I was not all that good at dribbling the ball or of reading the game, although I scored a few goals by being in the right place at the right time. Sports masters and various team captains usually preferred to put me at left back, knowing I was very quick and capable of clearing and booting the ball back up field with either foot. On the rough pastures we played on in those days this suited the 'long ball game'. (We played football in a field up the hill on the road to Maid's Moreton.)

26/9/41: "We are doing a dovetail joint in woodwork.

30/9/41: "I went threshing (at Blackpit Farm) and so did Mum—-we had dinner at Auntie Chubb's."

Usually, when I helped with the threshing at that age as odd-job boy, I was put on chaff carrying. This meant collecting the chaff as it came out of the threshing box, separately from the grain, on an opened-out sack and taking it to wherever it was to be stored (for mixing with horse feed). It was a simple enough job, but hot and dusty and often uncomfortable if the crop had been full of thistles, as the spines inevitably got into your hands and down the neck of your shirt.

6/10/41: "Played football—-they won 1-0, a good game.

13/10/41: "Instead of going to football, five other boys and I went potato picking." (The war effort came before football.)

21/10/41: "Moscow front is toured by Stalin in armoured train. Russians turn German pincer technique against claws of German pincer movement. I ordered the Observers book of birds at Smiths (in Buckingham)."

This is the first book that I remember buying with my own money, it cost a shilling. The second, bought the following spring at Weatherheads in Aylesbury, was *British Birds' nests and their Eggs* by C.J. Hall. On that occasion I also looked longingly at Witherby's magisterial, five volume *Handbook of British Birds* but knew I could never afford the five pounds required!

22/10/41: "Mum made an appoint(ment) for us to have our photo taken. I let one of my canaries out for a fly and then put it back in its cage."

The photo (6-2 top) was taken in Chapman's studio, which is still in operation at the corner of Well Street in Buckingham, and is a rare picture of all of us together, looking unnaturally angelic. Those of our parents were taken at the same time. I had bought a pair of canaries from my friend Tom (Lionel Brazier) who had a large aviary.

Problems getting the milk: As I have explained earlier, when we moved to Dadford, I started getting the milk from Jack Davies down at Home Farm. This went well while our Hurst relations were there, but after Harold moved to another job in Dinton, Jack Davies seemed less pleased to see me, probably sore at losing a good ploughman. I think this was aggravated by a quarrel he had with my Uncle Chubb Wheeler about an heifer, which he claimed was his, that had somehow got into Chubb's fields and then been taken over. Of course, Chub dismissed this as a fantasy but Jack Davies refused to listen and the case eventually came to Court at Buckingham; where it was thrown out because of lack of any evidence. Apparently, afterwards outside the Court, Chub offered to shake hands and let bygones be bygones but Jack was too angry. Whether or not this affected matters, he certainly became peculiar with me, and one Saturday, when I went to pay the bill, he was so off hand that I decided not to go back for milk there again. This will help to explain the following diary entry:

14/10/41: "Dad came with me for the milk. We walked (over to Blackpit by the footpath shown on the end-map)."

After I fell out with Jack Davies, I went over to see my Aunt Chubbie Wheeler, to see if I could get our milk from Blackpit. She was a bit dubious because of the long walk for me, but I explained that it would now be much the same if I went to other farms. So that autumn I began my evening tramps over the fields and up the long riding through Stowe woods, to the track down to the farm to get the milk. This may explain why my diary entries become a little thin, later that autumn into the winter. I had my home-work to attend to as well so I was pretty busy in the evenings, after biking home from school. However, I enjoyed the walks, especially later in the year, when as the evenings got darker it was pleasant go into the lamp-lit cowshed, warm with the breath of cattle munching their hay, to find my cousins Bob and Graham, each with their heads tucked into the flanks of a cow, milking by hand into a pail. Usually, I would hear them singing as I came down the track before I got there: perhaps a current popular song such as *Begin the Beguine* by Hutch. Apparently, the cows liked the singing and let their milk down more easily. However, both our cousins had fine voices, particularly Graham, who was in great demand in pubs and clubs for miles around. As his younger brother, Jeremy, puts it appreciatively in an extract from one of his poems about the family (see note 5):

> For Graham by God a gift was given
> A voice that was pure as the sun in heaven
> He learned in Watford how to really sing
> Like an operatic tenor to bring
>
> Tears or laughter to those who heard his voice
> Shivers down their spines wanting to rejoice
> With songs like this 'Old House' He'd make us cry
> Be lovesick with a song like 'Passing-by'
>
> In pubs he'd just have to sing 'Bless This House'
> Every time he went there to carouse
> "Dan Cupid hath a Garden where women are the flowers
> And lovers' laughs and lovers' tears the sunshine and the showers"

When in his prime there was no one who could sing
That song at party or wedding like him
And 'I Sing of a Maiden' once at Stowe
I heard him sing many years long ago
And so if that song, paraphrase I may
His voice was the dew that falls on hay

An opera singer he could have been
But he still preferred the old country scene
Stayed on at the farm, performed in the parlour
For the cows instead of La Scala
'Ah Moon of my Delight that know'st no wane'
How often did the cows hear this refrain
They say in music, animals delight
His cows were serenaded every night

I also enjoyed walking home through the woods on moonlight nights, sparkling with frost, but there were times when the nights were black and moonless and I would have to go round the hedges in the fields to find the gate, watching I didn't stumble over sleeping cattle.

In the first months of 1942 the weather was hard and cold with long periods of heavy snow and deep frost, when the lakes froze down to four or five inches' depth, and we spent a good deal of time sliding on the ice as well as tobogganing. In late January, Father had 48 hours' leave, and the morning he went back it was too slippery for me to bike into school, so I walked with him to Oxford Lodges, and then continued on to school while he went down Oxford Avenue to go to Finmere to catch his train. The sun was brilliant on the snow and emphasized the colours of a Greater Spotted Woodpecker, that we saw low down on the trunk of a tree, just before we got to the Lodges. This was the first one that I had seen, because, although Green Woodpeckers were quite common, this species was rare round the village at that time. One good effect of the prolonged hard weather was that towards the end I was allowed to go in the school car with the children from the Senior School, which set a useful precedent.

One evening in early February, I was walking up through the snow towards the woods on my way for the milk, when I came on a wild (Brent) goose that had been shot and wounded, with a broken wing. I tried to catch it but it evaded me and took refuge under a thick hedge. I went on up to Blackpit and told my cousins about it when I collected the milk. On the way back it was too dark to look for it, so I went out at first light the next morning. When I found it still hiding under the hedge, it was too weak to put up much resistance. After I had carried it for a while under my arm, I put it down and found I could walk it all the way home guided by a stick, causing some amusement when I arrived outside the Council Houses.

At first I was determined to keep it, and put it in the coal-house, where I got it to gobble down some bread and milk. A little later on that morning I decided I'd better go up and let my cousins know what had happened. When I got to the scene of the action in the corner of the field up by the woods, I found my cousins and their friend, Brian (the youngest of the Edrich brothers) spread out in a half circle recumbent in the snow, their shot-guns at the ready. Brian had just sent in his Labrador to flush out the goose from the hedge, and there was, of course, no result. When I appeared, Brian asked me if they were in the right place and if I knew where it was. I had to tell them that it was now in our coal-house. At this, Brian threw his head back in a loud guffaw and after a moment, Bob and Graham, initially rather miffed at their wasted efforts, joined in. So we all had a good laugh, Bob clapping me on the back for being the 'early bird'. Of course, my cousins had to do the milking before they could go out on the wild goose chase. (See note 6.)

The goose soon made a mess of the coal-house and Mother decided that the kindest thing, considering its broken wing, after a gunshot wound, was to kill it. With considerable reluctance, and some difficulty (because it escaped and had to be rounded up with the help of the neighbours) I did this, and Mother drew and plucked it and cooked it for us to eat, but I didn't enjoy it much.

SOURCES/NOTES   CHAPTER SIX

1) The Royal Latin School is an ancient foundation and its history has been recently very well told in the following book: Poornan, Paul. 2001, *The Royal Latin School Buckingham.* Dusty Old Books Ltd. 7, Pear Tree Farm, Marsh Gibbon, Bicester.
The old school is the oldest building in Buckingham. It began in the late twelfth century, as a hospice of the Knight Hospitallers of the military Order of St. John of Jerusalem (set up by Richard the Lionheart). By the middle of the thirteenth century it had fallen into disuse and it was restored by Matthew Stratton, Archdeacon of Buckingham, who donated it before his death in 1268, to the Master of St. Thomas of Acon, in London, with an endowment of land, so that a chantry priest could be appointed to pray for his soul. This arrangement continued until the Reformation. Amongst others, another important endowment was the forty acre Hermit Grove of Brother Robert 'the hermit' of Wappenham. In mediaeval times most teachers were chantry priests. The first, written reference to one at the Chapel of St. Thomas of Acon is in 1423. So it can be said that the school originated sometime between 1289 and 1423.
The school escaped closure under the Chantry Acts of 1545 and 1548, at the Reformation, because it was run as a hospital, and a priest's pension of £5/6/8d per annum, was awarded to the incumbent, Thomas Hawkins, the first named teacher of the Grammar School. Towards the end of the century, monetary difficulties led to the amalgamation of the Thornton Church chantry (its foundation supported by the Barton family) with that of the Grammar School, for one year in 1592 and permanently in 1597; Thornton's Royal designation (from Edward VI) then passed to the Grammar School, which is how it became St. John's Royal Latin School.

During the nineteenth century the numbers in the school increased markedly, especially after the Education Acts of 1876, which made schooling obligatory for 50 percent of the time for 10-14 year-olds, and forbade employment of those under ten, and of 1880, which made full-time education compulsory for those under ten. The 1902 Education Act replaced the old School Boards with Local Education Authorities, and the new authority quickly decided a new school was necessary. The old school on Market Hill, off the Town square, was vacated and a new red brick building of 'Jacobean style' was occupied on Chandos Road. This was the school building at the time my brother, sister and I attended the school. There was a House system in operation, and we were in Stratton House. This name will now need no explanation. The other Houses were Denton and Newton. The Denton family held the manor of Hillesden, and they provided a number of the MPs for Buckingham in the seventeenth and early eighteenth centuries. It was a member of this family, Alexander Denton, who had the schoolmaster's house adjacent to the old school rebuilt in the late seventeenth century. Gabriel Newton, one time mayor of Leicester (1726) left a considerable sum in his will for the religious education of children. This supported the foundation of the 'Green Coat School' in Buckingham in 1760. After the 1902 Education Act, this bequest was amalgamated with those supporting the Royal Latin School.

Since we were pupils at the school, it has moved again, and occupies a new building, opened by the Queen Mother in 1963, at a site on Brookfield Lane. It also now has a Headmistress, Cecilia Galloway, the first in its long history. The school on Chandos Road is now the 'Grenville Combined School'.

2) Robinson, J.M. 1990, *Temples of Delight—-Stowe Landscape gardens.* George Philip Ltd, London, in association with The National Trust, 36, Queen Anne's Gate, London. (A beautifully illustrated work which figures the temples and follies mentioned.)

3) A successful attack was eventually made on Madagascar in April, 1942, after Father had gone for Officer training. By coincidence, my cousin James (Robins) narrowly missed being involved in this. He was commissioned in 1941 and his regiment was mustered to go out East, and some men were detailed to join in this attack. As he says, "My regiment, also in the convoy, was ordered to provide 6 teams of one officer and twelve other ranks to man AA guns on other ships on the convoy. I was selected to lead one of these teams. Originally, I was ordered to board the SS *Orontsay* at Liverpool. Then for reasons unknown to me this was countermanded, and I and my team were transferred to the RMS *Dominion Monarch*. The *Orontsay* carried one of the Brigades of 5 Division that landed at Diego Suarez. Had I stayed on it I would not have met Audrey in India later in August of that year!" James and Audrey were to be married in Bangalore, S. India, in 1944.

4) The Bourbon Tower was constructed in 1808 to commemorate the visit to Stowe of Louis XVIII, who at that time was in exile and living at Hartwell House near Aylesbury, the refuge found for him by the first Duke of Buckingham.

5) Wheeler, Jeremy 2000, *Tales of Stowe Ridings—-The Story of Three Generations of Wheelers.* Jeremy Wheeler, Byfield, Northants.

6) Brian was then nineteen, and a month later was on his way to train as a pilot in Canada. He served in India, flying Vultee Vengeance transport planes from Dum-Dum to Burma and later he was involved in air-sea rescue operations in Ceylon, finally being demobbed in 1946. Shortly afterwards he married our cousin Jose and recommenced his cricketing career with Kent, playing with the First Eleven from 1947.

CHAPTER SEVEN

STOWE RIDINGS 1942-44

THE COTTAGE IN THE RIDINGS

We move again: As a consequence of going daily up to Blackpit Farm to fetch the milk, in early March I discovered that the 'Cottage in the Ridings' had become vacant. This cottage is at the side of the long, broad ride that runs north through Stowe Woods and is opposite the Round Wood (see map and photos 7-1). A family called Hawkings had rented it for about eighteen months after moving out of London to escape the bombing and had now moved on. We assumed that they must have had a lot of dogs and had been used to servants as the following remarks will show. It was beautifully situated, and moreover where Tim White had lived immediately before the War and written *The Sword in the Stone*, so I suggested to my mother that we should ask if we could live there. She was enthusiastic too, especially because living close to her elder sister would help to alleviate the loneliness of Father's absence and the gnawing anxiety about the War; so, on my next walk for the milk I spoke to Aunt Chubbie Wheeler and it was soon all arranged.

23/3/42: "Did some digging over the cottage—-the primroses are all out and one little bush with golden bells on it.

24/3/42: "Did some digging over the cottage. We cleared up a bit round the garden which looks like a rubbish dump.

25/3/42: "Whitewashed (distempered, after stripping the wallpaper) the living room and painted (the) cupboard and fireplace over cottage—-even straw in the living room."

Photographs 7-1 Stowe Woods

Top left -: Father with his mother, Grannie Haynes on a visit to The Cottage in 1943 (photographs of grandmother are remarkably few, perhaps because in them she looks more formidable and severe than she was in life). The fruit tree on the wall is a nectarine planted by Tim White, alongside a fig tree out of view in the foreground.
Top right -: David in the wheat field east of Blackpit Lake, Blackpit farm buildings far left with the lake out of view below.
Middle right -: The Cottage in the Ridings and the well, with bucket and chain, in the foreground out towards the middle of the ride, as it was in our time (now covered in). It was in this cottage that T. H. White wrote *The Sword in the Stone*.
Bottom left -: The Cottage in the Ridings today with the garden skilfully developed by Jose.
Bottom right -: Woodlands as it is today. A 'Gentleman's Sporting Residence' restored by Robert's sons Steven and Paul.

According to my cousin Jose, Mrs Hawkings was very 'grand-dame', a member of the Byass sherry people with interests in Spain and would certainly have been used to servants. There were four children, one boy in Stowe School, and they did, indeed, have lots of dogs and ponies.

We had a particular problem clearing up the kitchen. The Hawkings' had cooked with a paraffin stove, which had been allowed to smoke until the walls and ceiling were completely blackened. This took some hours of backbreaking (and neck aching) washing down to get back to the fine, peach/apricot-coloured paint that had been applied by Tim White.

26/3/42: "We moved over cottage. Only two men came from Viles (Vyles the removal firm) but we soon finished." (After all her moves Mother didn't have much excess baggage.)

The cottage is actually one of a pair, both empty at the time we moved in to the one on the south side, of gray stone (Great Oolite) with large gardens that extend between the long riding and a woodland pasture, then with well-grown oak trees, and the cross riding running down to Blackpit Farm and the lake. The accommodation in the cottage was quite simple: a kitchen with a copper in the corner and sitting room downstairs, with a small entrance hall from the front door and three bedrooms upstairs. As well as indulging his taste for colour in the kitchen, Tim had painted the main bedroom deep carmine, with white woodwork; the second bedroom, where we boys slept, in gold, and the third small bedroom white.

At the beginning of the War, Tim had been in Ireland, and he chose to stay there for the duration working on his famous novel sequence, *The Once and Future King,* leaving all his furniture and books behind. When the cottage was rented out again the furniture and books were stored in the rustic barn, just outside the garden in the pasture, but the carpets and curtains were left in place (to our benefit when we had given them a good spring clean). I also benefited from the books, climbing in through the window of the barn, consulting in particular, the three-volume account, *The Birds of the British Isles and their eggs,* by T. A. Coward.

There were other signs of Tim's former occupation of the cottage: a huge, ornate, gold framed mirror that hung on the opposite wall to the window, reflecting the light in the back (boys') bedroom; a semi-circular metal plate, like a half-light, above the kitchen door, on which he had painted the naked Diana (Artemis) and her maidens, viewing the hounds mauling the impious Actaeon after he was changed into a stag (Tim claimed it would keep unwanted visitors away); also, a full impression of one of his visits to the outside lavatory, because when he put in concrete paths in the garden and before the concrete was fully set, he walked round to it in his hobnail boots with his dog, to sit on the wooden seat. (It now became my job to empty the lavatory bucket, taking it out through a trap door in the wall at the back. A pair of redstarts habitually nested in a hole just above this trap door, regularly producing a clutch of beautiful sky-blue eggs—-Jose says they continued to do so until about ten years ago.)

Tim had done a lot of work in the garden, creating lawns and a shrubbery, with a central path leading to a rockery, which included goldfish pools and was surmounted by a dovecote; all neglected and overgrown since he left, the goldfish pools cracked and empty. The garden has since been transformed by the present occupant, my cousin Jose, see photos 7-1 bottom left, although the rustic barn and the great oaks in the pasture have gone now. However, the stone outhouses, down the garden in front of the kitchen, where Tim mewed his hawk, Goss, and I kept various animal and birds, are still there; but I'm saddened by the loss of the oaks, because we boys in the back-bedroom, where the window was usually left open, were often lulled to sleep by the wind in these trees:

> Half woken by the wind
> The tap of branches
> And the casements rattle,
> I remember the oaks,
> The great oaks of Home pasture
> That filled our youthful dreams;
> That caught the west gales
> In their rigging,
> A far off murmur,
> Then the full ocean-swell
> Gradually ebbing.

There was no electricity of course, so it was paraffin lamps, which included an Aladdin Lamp with glowing mantle, in the living room and candles to bed. Mother cooked in a small oven (on a frame she made herself) over a paraffin stove. Water was boiled for tea on a Primus stove (requiring a meths starter and Primus prickers to keep the nozzle clear). The paraffin was delivered weekly by a van that called down the Riding with various items of hardware, as were bread, vegetables, groceries and meat. There was even a fish and chip van that came one evening every fortnight (this is now calling again at midday on Friday, sixty years later). Rationing simplified things, in one way for the suppliers, who had our ration books, and who took next week's order when they delivered. There was now a 'national loaf' with a lower extraction of wheat germ and bran, and Mother bought six large loaves a week. It got fairly dry and so by the end of the week we were eating quite a lot of toast with tinned beans or sardines, and it was often bread and milk for supper! (Bread and flour were never rationed during the War, only immediately afterwards when grain supplies from America were diverted to feed the starving in Europe.) Bread and butter pudding was also a favourite desert, replaced by apple batter when the cooking apples came on our two trees.

It was now just a short walk down through the pasture to fetch the milk. We now had four pints a day, and one dark night when Max went to fetch it, he tripped over a log and spilt it all: no light matter on Mother's budget. Our milk can had a clear mark to indicate the four pint level (five pints later) and I always preferred it when our cousin Jose came to the dairy to fill it up for me, because, unlike our other cousins, she would always pour in at least an extra half pint, but eventually she was told off by her father, he hadn't worked up from a smallholding to a successful farm during the depression years without watching every

191

penny. Our cousins carried the pails of milk from the cowshed to the dairy, suspended from a wooden yoke across their shoulders, where it was poured through a metal water-cooler into the churns. One evening, Chub caught David dipping himself a drink of milk from the churn and gave him a good hiding with his thumb-stick (something David remembers only too well!).

A peculiar feature of the cottage was that the water supply was a well, with bucket and chain, about twenty yards out from the front gate towards the middle of the Riding (photos 7-1, middle right, probably sited by a 'water diviner' on the supposition that water occurs in discrete pools, although the water table probably runs at much the same level under the cottage and the well might just as successfully been dug in the garden!). We children used to take turns to winch up two buckets first thing in the morning and we all had to pitch in to fill the copper for washday and to heat up water for bath night on Saturday (greatly enjoyed in the zinc bath before the fire in winter). We also had to keep up the supply of small sticks (faggots) for the copper.

We didn't find these chores particularly onerous; in general we enjoyed them, and the shopping trips, to Buckingham by bike, or to Towcester and Northampton, which necessitated either a walk over the fields to Lillingstone Dayrell, or a cycle ride up to Silverstone, to catch a bus. Often, when we walked over to Dayrell, Mother got us to buy vegetables and fruit from Mr. Bowyer, who ran a big walled garden for Tile House. I greatly enjoyed going round the garden with him when he picked fresh produce for us, giving me the chance to look at his fruit trees and the nectarines trained up the brick walls.

One Saturday, when I had just returned on my bike after shopping in Buckingham that morning, I found that we needed a new dry battery for the wireless, which meant that I did another ten mile round trip so we could listen in over the weekend. I don't remember being greatly put out, although these batteries were quite heavy and awkward to carry on a bike.

As we had no newspaper (or telephone, of course), we depended on the wireless for news of the War, and emergency announcements. Also, in the winter, it was our main source of entertainment apart from reading and the piano. As well as allowing us all to listen regularly to programs like *Monday Night at Seven* with Dicky Murdoch and Arthur Askey, *In Town Tonight* and *ITMA,* Mother also let the younger children stay up with us to hear complete performances of operas such as Gounod's *Faust* and, of course, *La Bohème,* and concerts with favourite pianists or singers like Heddle Nash, Tauber, Bjorling and Gigli. One program we used to listen to in bed was *Appointment with Fear,* a favourite of my brother David, who used to imitate the sepulchral voice of Valentine Dyall when we told each other stories in bed. (Making up stories was something Ann was very good at, like Father.)

Mother was very happy to be living in an isolated cottage again, despite the complete lack of mod cons, which were more than made up for by the freedom to play the piano and sing with the doors and windows open and only the birds for audience. We were also very pleased when she had a musical evening, especially when Graham came up to practise his songs, or Jose, also a fine pianist, who would play 'boogie-woogie' as well as her trademark *Warsaw Concerto.*

One evening, in the dusk, I went over the Riding to a high beech tree at the corner of the wood, to climb up to the top to enjoy the moonlight. Later, as I walked back across the Riding I could hear Mother playing the *Fantasy Impromptu:* an abiding memory of those days. By this time I had taught myself a number of Chopin pieces but that was too difficult for me and Mother played it really well.

It was on an occasion when I was at the top of this same beech tree that I was suddenly surprised by a voice from below, saying, "Hurumph! You there boy, what! What are you up to, what, what!" When I got down it was this tweedy looking gentleman, who turned out to be Squire Robarts and who asked where I was from, "What, what!" When I explained that I was from across the Riding and that I was Chub's nephew, we parted on good terms; and I was delighted to realize that I had met the living counterpart of King Pellinore in *The Sword in the Stone*!

Nature boy: It will be appreciated that for a thirteen to fourteen year old boy, to be living in Stowe Woods, in the actual cottage where Tim White had written his books, and kept his snakes (in the living room) and his hawks in the out-house, came close to an earthly paradise, especially as we saw many animals and birds close to the cottage: once a pheasant dusting in the flower bed and sometimes a fox or roe deer crossing the ride in the early dawn. Unsurprisingly, school work tended to be pushed into the background over the next year or two, and after we moved into the cottage my diary entries became very scattered. Part of the reason the diary languished was because I started a separate nature diary, but unfortunately, that has not survived. However, I did record my confirmation by the Bishop of Buckingham, in Stowe Church, on the 29th of March, three days after moving into the cottage. Also, a bird-count on the lake:

9/4/42: "Beat the carpet from my (boys) bedroom—-found 3 coots nests. There were 11 coots, 2 moorhens, 1 swan (a black swan) on the lake today."

That first spring and summer in the cottage, I spent most of my spare time when not working in the garden or doing odd jobs at the farm, wandering in the woods or fishing in the lake. We were allowed to use an old metal punt to fish from, and you could use it to travel out to a little island where wild ducks sometimes nested. It was my ambition to catch a tench, that beautiful bronze, fine-scaled, ruby-eyed fish, described in *The Sword in the Stone* as the 'Doctor Fish' able to cure the ailments of other fish with its healing slime; but I never did succeed in catching one, either at Blackpit or up at Stowe Lakes. One afternoon, I was fishing by the stone jetty at Blackpit, where the lake over-flows into a little brook, when a grass snake swam straight across the lake towards me its head held high, going up the bank within a yard or two without noticing me.

It was about this time that I became very interested in bird song as a means of identification, and I listened very attentively to the broadcasts of Ludwig Koch, the great pioneer of birdsong recording, with his famous catch phrase, "And zis is zer zound zat I heard". This led me to build a couple of simple bivouacs of branches, in different parts of the woods, where I could spend the night, in order to log which birds went on singing late and which were the first to start in the morning. I had a gray army blanket that Father had given me, which I could fasten up with blanket pins, together with a groundsheet to sleep on. Mother soon got used to these activities and she didn't worry about me.

One night in April or early May, I bivouacked up at the north end of Point Copse (not far from what later became Stowe Corner on the Silverstone race track). After the last, late blackbird, I was surprised how long a grasshopper warbler, in a low thicket, quite close to me, kept on singing. He was still reeling away at 2am. I was then unable to stay awake any longer, and I slept until I was woken up, in the gray of the early dawn, by the most tremendous burst of song. Without moving my head, I could see, through the loose branches of the bivouac, that it was a nightingale, about two feet away, perched with its head slightly down, on an inclined hazel bough, its throat pulsing with the power of its delivery. I lay motionless, while it went through its full repertoire of fluting cadences and measured silences, until I thought it had finished, but it then continued with another flourish; until it finally stopped and flew off to another part of its territory. (In those days nightingales were quite common in the woods, and my Uncle Chub knew the whereabouts of the territories of a number of pairs and the best places to hear them sing. However, my cousin Jose told me recently, that she hasn't heard a nightingale for some years, see note 1.)

My youthful absorption in nature was assisted by books I was reading at this time, which included *Rolf in the Woods* by Thompson Seton; the country books of the Northamptonshire writer BB, (Denys Watkins Pitchford) and the stories of Charles Roberts about the backwoods of New Brunswick.

When we moved up to the cottage, I transferred my canaries to a big outside cage made from an old linen chest; however, they escaped. My friend Tom was annoyed by my carelessness and only reluctantly replaced them, with a pair looking suspiciously like yellow hammers. Mysteriously, these also 'escaped', although the door was firmly shut. Although she now claims to have no memory whatsoever of this event, I think a certain cousin, older and wiser than me at the time had decided unilaterally on the right course of action! If so, I now applaud it. As Jeremy puts it in his poem about his sister Jose:

> Animals all love her, like she is the great God Pan
> They seem to love her much more than they do any man
> A kestrel once decided to live outside her house
> She fed him day old chicks and an occasional mouse

> Now Jose likes odd things in life-—both spiders and toads
> She used to take some food out for tramps along the roads
> And when she dies, so she says, that she would much prefer
> If in a hole in Round Wood we should bury her

During this time, Tom and I often spent weekends in each others homes and I greatly enjoyed staying with him at the farmhouse in Granborough and seeing his aviary. This led on one occasion to the following entry in my diary, one of the few for the rest of that year:

8/6/42: "Had a holiday—-went over Braziers—-had to walk home from Winslow because of bus—-13 miles (whew). Anthem-Footsore and weary the conquering hero marched home"

I got on the late bus at Granborough and, unexpectedly, it terminated at Winslow. It was a beautiful, fine evening so I just set off to walk home. A few cars passed but no one offered me a lift. I remember partridges calling from the green wheat fields as I trudged along. It was quite dark when I passed through Buckingham and a policeman on his bike stopped me and asked me what I was doing. I explained what had happened and he gave me a lift on his crossbar down Stowe Avenue as far as Chackmore crossroads. He put me off there as I assured him I knew my way home across Stowe grounds and through the woods and fields so well that it didn't matter it was dark. In fact it was one of those glimmering, white June nights; so there was no trouble finding my way, and I finally got home around 2am. Mother was most surprised as she thought I must have stayed over.

Evidence that schoolwork had been pushed to the back of my priorities, is shown by the contrast between my results for the first term of the second form, when I was placed third overall (I was top in maths and even second in Latin!), and the Easter term, when my position fell to tenth. Unfortunately, in the final results for the year we were not placed in order but simply given percentage marks in our reports. This was because after Easter there was a sharp change in regime. Mr. Toft went into the Forces and he was replaced by Dr. Charles Foster who had a doctorate in education from King's College London and was imbued with the latest 'progressive' ideas. Not only was rank order abandoned, but so was homework (and significantly, the number of times absent or late were no longer recorded). I have to admit I was delighted with that, having more interesting things to do than homework on summer evenings. However, I managed to score high percentages for class-work that summer, despite my other interests, eighty percent or over for English, geography and maths; but my exam results were dire, all subjects less than sixty percent, apart from maths. However, the change in educational regime was to have other, rather more serious effects.

A breakdown of discipline: The first intimation I had of the change in the way the school was run happened one day when another boy and I had been peeling potatoes (which we did in turns) outside the big hut where we had our school dinners. On the way back into school, we looked through the windows of our classroom where our classmates were getting ready for the next lesson. We still had our peeling knives and we jumped up and down in front of the windows with them in our mouths, grimacing and waving our hands. Dr. Foster happened to come out at that very moment and caught us fooling about. We were just told quietly to go to our class and both of us were surprised at getting away with it without the mildest rebuke.

A little later, during a lesson when the mistress was writing something up on the blackboard, a boy wound the cord of a window blind round the neck of the boy sitting in front of him. Unfortunately, it proved rather difficult to get off and the victim began to choke. The teacher managed to get it off but a doctor was called to check that he was alright. The culprit was sent to the head but he was not punished.

On another occasion, again when the mistress (a newly appointed young woman) was writing something up on the board, a boy began flicking paper pellets. Told to stop, he started doing it again, and, exasperated, the teacher told him to go and report to the

Headmaster. When he came back he was smirking because the Head had simply told him to go back to class and behave. The following day he began again, and was again sent to the head with the same result.

The teacher worked at a large, wooden desk, and the next time she took us for a lesson, this boy crept up and sat with his back to the desk, where she couldn't see him, pulling faces and waving his hands at us while she was trying to teach. It took her some time to understand why there was so much laughter and commotion, and when she did she just fled the room in tears. When she came back there was dead silence, and when this incorrigible boy started his antics again, the majority of us, amused to begin with but now as fed up with him as the teacher was, hissed him to silence. This young teacher then left, or was transferred, though I can't imagine her career could have recovered from this experience.

During this same period of time, another young teacher, a red haired young man who for some reason came to be called 'Felix', was appointed also straight from college, to teach maths. He was writing an equation up on the blackboard, when one of the congenital miscreants (there are always one or two in every class of thirteen to fourteen year olds) threw a piece of chalk at the board and it almost hit him. Felix whirled round, 'Who threw that!' But, of course, no one answered. As soon as Felix turned back to the board again, another boy chanced his arm. Felix turned quickly enough to catch him and sent him to the Head. This boy too, came back smiling, simply being told to go back to his class and behave. The chalk throwing soon began again, and Felix began shouting and finally rushed out of the room. This did have some effect and when he came back the lesson proceeded quietly.

Felix was on dinner duty in the big wooden dining hut, a day or so after this, and there happened to be potatoes baked in their jackets put out on the tables in wicker baskets. Even before Grace was finished, these same lads began trundling some of them under the trestle tables, to general confusion, as there were only enough to go round. Felix managed to sort this out and see that everyone got a dinner but then worse followed. The desert turned out to be blancmange and these boys began flicking it at each other with their spoons, an example that proved irresistible to a number of others, and it was soon on their faces and on the walls of the hut. Shouts from Felix only added to the din and the hysterical merriment, which only ended when he managed to get everyone to leave. Now it might be thought that this would have marked the end for poor Felix, but there was one more act to play in this tragicomedy.

One morning Felix took our class for gardening. As part of the War effort (the 'Dig for Victory' campaign) we were turning over some of the flower beds to vegetables (not that this was very effective but in any case this kind of activity was thought 'good for morale'). When Felix's back was turned, one of the troublemakers began picking up small lumps of soil and throwing them at him, finally hitting him at the back of the head. Felix spotted who it was; losing control and shouting with rage, he chased this boy round the shrubberies, while we all looked on in amazement. At this point the Headmaster appeared and quietly asked Felix to accompany him to his office. We never saw poor Felix again.

It's impossible to believe that Felix's career in teaching survived this debacle. However, as he was a mathematician, he would have had little difficulty in finding an alternative career to dealing with recalcitrant schoolboys, especially as part of the war effort. No doubt the Head put the blame on the teachers for their failure to keep order; but here we had two, young, inexperienced teachers, thrown in at the deep end with the most difficult age group, given no real back-up of authority by the Head and denied the simplest sanctions for enforcing discipline, not even the mildest aversion therapy of 'lines' or detention, let alone Toft's gym shoe, which those lads most surely deserved! (See note 2.)

Wartime propaganda: Another curious episode took place at the school during this time. After Hitler's invasion, Russia became one of the Allies and strenuous efforts were made by various Communist front organizations to make this palatable to the British public. One of these was the Anglo-Soviet Friendship Society, which made arrangements to hold a conference in the school hall and we were all told to attend. This was made memorable to me by the reactions of an agitated elderly man, who on a number of occasions got to his feet to complain bitterly about the crimes committed by the Communists in Russia. The chairman kept ruling him out of order and finally when he stood up again to try to speak, someone began hissing and it was taken up by the majority of the audience, until in obvious distress he left the hall. As I was already very suspicious of 'Our great Russian Allies' because of the dismemberment of Poland and the attack on Finland this made a deep impression on me (to the extent that I eventually became allergic to mass demonstrations of any kind, unless against dictatorship). The memory of this event was also a corrective, when as a student I tended to be swept along by the post-war tide of pro-Soviet, left-wing propaganda.

Possibly the slowest junior quarter mile on record: The school sports day in the summer of that year (1942) is memorable because of the very slow time in which the quarter mile race was run. I was second in the 100 yards, edged out by a tall, dark boy called Bastable, who also came first in the 220 yards, but I remember very little more about those races.

The quarter mile started off very slowly, and we all bunched together on the first bend, almost coming to a halt, no one sure of just how the race should be run, and we went down the back-straight at a jog trot (more suitable for the cross country run!) until, finally, exasperated by this slow progress I took off at my fastest speed. Before the other competitors woke up to it, I was away and out of reach and came in first. The captain of Stratton House came up to me afterwards and said he was very pleased because, he 'Didn't know we had anyone in this race' and it meant six more points. However, my time was 82 seconds; really, we could have walked round the track in that time!

SOME OF FATHER'S ARMY REMINISCENCES

Dark days of the war: Our move to the cottage in the Ridings coincided with a low point in the fortunes of the country. After the fall of France, and until the entry of the United States into the War, following the attack on Pearl Harbour on the 7th of December, 1941,

Britain and the Empire stood alone against Hitler; our spirits sustained by the robust rhetoric and defiance of Churchill. Shortly after the New Year, in February, there was a further sickening blow when the Japanese army overran Singapore, described by Churchill as "The worst disaster and largest capitulation in British history", and occupied Burma in the April and May. Then in June, Rommel retook Tobruk in Libya and our troops were forced to retreat to El Alamein in Egypt. The Japanese were now poised to mount a seaborne invasion of India and there was the distinct possibility that the Axis powers would break through into the Middle East (taking over the oil fields) and effectively encircle the USSR; but although it wasn't clear at the time, this was the high water mark for the Fascist Dictatorships.

Further disaster for the Allies was prevented by four famous victories. In June, 1942, United States forces won the great, naval Battle of Midway, in which four Japanese aircraft carriers were sunk, ending their hopes of a seaborne invasion of India, and in the August, American troops seized Henderson Airfield at Gaudalcanal, in the Solomon Islands, and held it against ferocious counter attacks. This was followed in the September by the repulse of the Japanese invasion of Papua New Guinea via the Kokoda Trail by a scratch force of Australian militia. This stemmed the Japanese tide. At the end of October, Monty and the Eighth Army defeated Rommel at El Alamein, who was forced to retreat west as US troops landed in Morocco (a crucial factor here being the relief of the siege of Malta in the previous August). Then in January, 1943, the Russians encircled the German army besieging Stalingrad and forced Von Paulus to surrender. As Churchill put it, El Alamein was preceded by a long catalogue of defeats but despite three more years of bitter struggle and many reverses there were only victories thereafter. (This was very true in the Far East, where some of the most bitter fighting of the War took place, much of it hand to hand, the campaign in which my cousin James won his M.C., see note 3.)

It was against this background that Father opted to accept an offer to go for Officer Training.

Officer Cadet Training Unit (OCTU): Prior to being mustered at Southend for embarkation to Madagascar (in July 1941), Father and a fellow sergeant (Tommy) had been offered the chance of officer training, but they had turned it down as they didn't want to be separated from their friends and team mates in their battalion when it was despatched abroad. However, after their experience of being on standby, as Father said:

"The thought of another period of waiting, cleaning our kit, being messed about, convinced us it would be better to take it up. We saw the major and told him we would accept training for a commission. He couldn't refuse us, once we had been selected. The only other way you could avoid embarkation and despatch abroad, by the way, was by standing for Parliament. One chap did this when he had got as far as Singapore and was sent back on the next ship. He stood for Mablethorpe, I think!

"Very soon (spring 1942) I found myself at Shrivenham, (in the Vale of the White Horse). We had hoped to go together, but my friend Tommy was sent to Llandrindod Wells, where he had a wonderful time. But the courses in Shrivenham were under the most strict discipline. They had just introduced—-after the dreadful defeat in Singapore—-tough jungle training. We were the second squad of cadets to undergo it. During the first course, they had killed one man and injured two others. The cadet was killed when the instructors started using real mustard gas in the mock exercises."

My cousin James, who, like Lionel, the eldest of the Wheeler boys, trained at Llandrindod Wells, confirms that, 'It was a fairly gentlemanly establishment. It was much more difficult, there, to enforce strict discipline as existed in Shrivenham as we were accommodated in hotels and vacant boarding houses around the town'. As Father explained it was rather different at Shrivenham:

"You had to jump different obstacles, climb trees, and swing across water on ropes; you just had to have confidence. We were sent across country and there were certain culverts we had to wriggle through, half full of water. In this particular one they had put barbed wire and thrown in vials of mustard gas, so you had to wear your gas mask. This poor chap got caught up in the wire and panicked, pulled his mask off, and died. Of course the instructors realised what bloody idiots they were after this and that they should have put brambles or other bushes in the culvert instead.

"I knew the officer concerned because he was in charge of our group on our serial (course). He was an officious little man, not very tall, but always trying to be bigger. He knew I'd been a sergeant and was always trying to take me down a peg. All your stripes were taken off and as cadets we had to take orders from anyone down through bombardier to lance-bombardier.

"By strange coincidence, this officer was himself involved in an unfortunate accident. He went one night to inspect the guard. He always loved doing that, turning out people at 2am. It so happened that the guard was just coming off duty, having been relieved, and he came in muttering, "I'm bloody glad that's over", when he suddenly saw the officer and in surprise dropped his gun. He must have had a round up the spout because it went off and a bullet hit the officer and he was killed. When charged with this offence, the poor chap got off because he had just come off duty, very cold, wanting his cup of cocoa and it was a pure accident. Shot him dead with his 303—-well he died in the course of duty—-nice letter from the CO to the relatives!

"I wasn't the oldest on our serial, but next to the oldest who was an insurance agent for Scottish Widows. I was still 30 when the war started and 33 when I was at OCTU in 1942, and the oldest chap was 35. We were up against the youngsters, fit schoolmasters, or should have been, but by this time I was very, very fit. I'd already been on one battle course and I'd been through all the ranks, getting used to pulling guns about, running round the parade ground in full kit. I was down to 10½ stone. Of course, most of the other poor buggers were call-ups (conscripts) and the instructors were always trying to break us down. However, the insurance agent had been a keen cyclist and he was pretty fit too. So they had you running in full kit, with your rifle, gas mask and steel helmet, plus a couple of bricks in your knapsack.

"We gradually built up to more strenuous exercises: marching five miles, then running half a mile, with every so often the shout of "Planes!" as an order to flop down, usually the muddiest field or ditch the instructors could find; and when you got back you had to clean and polish your kit. We had this officer running along side us in shorts, shouting "Pick 'em up, pick 'em up, the enemy are all around you!" When we got back, having a smoke, we began to grumble to the officer, "There you were in your running kit. How long is it since you were in full kit?" "What do you mean?" And because I was older than he was, I said, "You should do it like us, then you'd get more respect." So out he came next time in full kit, though I doubt if he put the two bricks in his knapsack. He put a good face on it, but we could see that he was straining a bit; and not to our surprise it was quite a short exercise that day! We knew he had too much beer in his belly. After that he was never quite so severe. Then we did a twenty-four hour march in full kit with rifle and ground sheet—- hard tack only because no lights or cooking were allowed, though if you were clever you could put an apple or orange in your knapsack. OCTU was a punishing experience but you can't dish out orders and keep discipline unless you can take it yourself.

"The instructors were generally very good chaps, they had been in the army all their lives and they knew their stuff. I learned to have a great respect for the way in which they dealt with the dreadful army training technique of repeat, repeat, repeat; necessary because they were used to fairly dumb recruits. They knew that over a period of weeks, months or years, if you kept pushing it in, however dumb the recruit he would do the right thing when he got the order, whatever it was, it was automatic."

Father illustrated this principle by referring to an incident that had occurred earlier in the War, in 1940, when the first conscripts arrived assigned to the Ack-Ack batteries and the trained members of the Territorial Army were dispersed amongst them to pass on their knowledge of the guns and ammunition and the use of RADAR and the Predictor in finding the height and range of the oncoming enemy aircraft:

"I had a squad on the Vickers Predictor with three weeks to teach them to operate it. So I had to take short cuts, as long as they knew what they were doing and could do it efficiently they didn't need to understand all the details. There were plenty of planes sent over to practise on. I would explain what information was given on the fascia panel of the machine, the layout and operation, and if, for example, they asked a question, such as how a displacement dial for altitude on the top of the instrument worked, although previously, my own sergeant instructor had told us it was 'One of the most important things on the machine' I would say 'Don't worry about that. You don't need to know how it works, only how to operate it, and for now don't touch it'. I didn't want the men fiddling with it. I thought the best method was to tell them to forget it, and not to waste time going into the whys and wherefores unnecessarily, it had nothing to do with getting the guns on target."

As well as the strenuous outdoor training at Shrivenham, Father had to attend a series of lectures and here he found his knowledge of shorthand a distinct advantage:

"I was able to take the lecture notes down even when the lecturer said, 'Don't try and take this down because there isn't time to do it at dictation speed'. This was very useful for a series of tests later in the course. These tests were in the form of a series of about twenty lecturettes that covered a range of topics. What they did, very cleverly, to make sure you revised every thing, was to put all the topics in one hat and the names of the cadets into another. On one occasion, the Brigadier came in when there were just three topics left and I was one of the three cadets left to give a talk. The topics were: the care and maintenance of the guns and ammunition, the duties of the officer in charge of the gun in action (GPO Ack-Ack) and one on ballistics. I thought 'I hope to God I don't get the one on ballistics!' Fortunately for the instructors, considering the Brigadier was there, the ex-insurance agent got the care and maintenance of guns and ammunition, the ex-schoolmaster the one on ballistics, and I got the duties of the GPO Ack-Ack, which I had done as a sergeant. It sounded as though we had been brilliantly taught and the Brigadier was most pleased!"

As Father admitted, although he was alright on the practical side operating guns and predictors, the theory was another matter, and he would probably have made the most lamentable effort on ballistics. He had left Aylesbury Grammar School to join Hunt Barnards before taking his School Certificate, and to some extent had, I think, bluffed his way through the Officer Selection Committee. At OCTU he worked hard to brush up his maths, and he benefited greatly from the kind help of the Welsh ex-schoolmaster, but he had to more or less 'parrot it off' in the tests.

An advantage of being at Shrivenham, for Father, was that he could fairly easily get home for a short leave, or Mother could meet him in Oxford. On one of these occasions when he had a twelve-hour leave, I went with her. We were supposed to meet at the central Bus Station but somehow we missed him, and after waiting a considerable time we went back, disconsolately, by bus to Buckingham and took a taxi home. We were put down at the top gate to our gated track, and as we set off to walk down to the cottage, Dad stepped out from behind a tree. Thinking we may have mistaken the day, he had decided to chance making it home and had arrived just before us. Of course, he only had an hour or two with Mother before he had to start back, an episode typical of the snatched meetings of many couples in those days. (The photo 6-1, bottom, shows Father and fellow cadets enjoying a few hours off in Oxford.)

Father also had battle training and extended field exercises, both at Tonfanau, on the coast in Merioneth, where they had to march in full kit from the camp to the top of Cader Idris and back, and in the Northwest Highlands at the Kyle of Loch Alsh. As Father always pushed himself to the limit this had an unfortunate (perhaps fortunate) effect in that the arches of his feet collapsed. He had to undergo two medical examinations in Glasgow and he was downgraded from A1 to B, which meant static service. He knew then that he was, "In Ack-Ack for good" and couldn't move on to join a field battery or rejoin his old battery (in a mobile role) in North Africa. This battery was involved in the landings in Southern Italy in the summer of 1943, and their vessel was badly shot up by German planes on the way over, with the loss of some officers and men. They arrived in some disarray and came under the command of Colonel Mortimer Wheeler, who commented that they were poorly organised and needed to be licked into shape. Father always smarted under, what he felt to be, this unfair criticism of his friends. However, when Peter (Granville) Dad's best friend, did a sketch of the landings, Colonel Wheeler liked it so much he had it hung in his quarters, which to some extent restored good feelings.

Another reason Father regretted not being able to rejoin his old battery in the Mediterranean theatre, was that his brother Frank was involved in the landings as a lieutenant on HMS *Renown,* and he was sorry that they weren't both in action there at the same time.

After Father parted company with Peter and his old friends, he carried on writing stories, some of them in rhyme, for Ann, and also poetry to Mother. Some of the poems were written when he was stationed near the Kyle of Loch Alsh, like this example, a poem called *Balmacara 1942,* quoted in part:

> There is peace in this lovely place
> Amongst the age-old hills,
> So quiet and so still.
> Are you weary?
> Then come with me up the mountain side.
> Give me your hand and we will climb together
> Though this beautiful land.
> You are close to heaven here.
> The clouds greet you tenderly with a kiss,
> White arms reach out to lead you on and on
> Up to the highest peak.
> Look down at all around you.
> Look up into the blue tent of heaven.
> So near for your prayers
> Of joy and thanksgiving.
> No sound here,
> Not since that time long ago
> When earth itself broke from the flying orb.
> Hold high your lovely head
> This is the world of eagles and nobler things.
> Here in the sunset's glory
> You can forget the world
> So far below, war weary, tired and gory.

After Father became an officer, we loved it when he came on leave, striding across the riding in his uniform, Sam Browne belt polished to shining perfection. On walks he would drill us in various marching manoeuvres, "Come on boys, heads up, chests out, Left! Left!

Left! However, in some ways it was a benefit for us boys that Father was never oppressively, omnipresent at home. Before the war he was away most of the time travelling, and we were always delighted when he found time to spend with us, and in the war, when we were at our most rumbustious (though Max and David undoubtedly missed his early influence). Father also had occasion to spruce himself up in his new uniform in the September of that year (1942). Both Ann and David were attending the village school in Dadford and in the spring, Ann, together with some other children, had sat a scholarship exam for entrance to the Latin School. No one passed. This is not too surprising given the difficulties there had been in finding teachers at this point in the War. As Ann says, an art master was appointed who, when not teaching them art, took them on nature walks. When he left, he was succeeded by a rather exotic mistress, who, habitually wearing a green turban, spent most of the time reading novels at her desk with her feet up. She would dish out sweets if the children were good and threaten them with maths if they weren't!

When Father came home on leave in the summer he was incensed: he always wanted Ann to become a teacher and she would have made a good one. He went to the County Offices in full dress uniform and informed them, in no uncertain terms, of the deficiencies of the village school, and Ann was allowed to take a place in the Latin School as a fee paying pupil. She retook the scholarship exam the following spring and passed (eventually getting a good School Cert. with London matriculation).

I should add that things greatly improved at Dadford School with the appointment of a mistress with old-fashioned values. As my cousin Jeremy, who attended the school a few years later, puts it, in an extract from one of his poems on the family:

> Two forms there were only in Dadford School
> Misbehave and you were hit with a rule
> Across the knuckles and it really hurt
> Our playground was just dug out of the dirt
>
> With the teaching good, the Headmistress no fool
> Quite a few went on to the Latin School
> Young Ivy Jones and Jimmy Faulkner too
> Were some of the bright ones to name but two

Jeremy left the village school to go to the prep school in Akeley. The reason for this was partly because he accidentally set fire to a straw rick, which almost set the nearby wood alight as well (after asking his mother for a box of matches to put a butterfly in and finding a live match in it). His parents were already concerned that he was too much on his own at Woodlands, being many years younger than his brothers and sister, and decided it would be better for him to go away to school. (Akeley Wood School was later moved to Sussex, where he went on to Lancing College, followed by Army service and a successful career as international representative for Massey-Ferguson.)

My brother, David, also went on to the Latin School from Dadford School in September, 1943, winning what were called promotion marks in the scholarship exam, allowing him to go as a fee paying pupil (fees were finally abolished in 1945, after the 1944, Butler Education Act replaced the scholarship by the 'eleven plus' exam).

An incident that took place just after David had started at the Latin School, indicative of changing social attitudes, occurred one lunchtime when we went together down to the Oddfellows' Hall in Well Street, that had been turned into a 'British Restaurant', one of many set up everywhere to serve basic meals during the War. Because of the evacuation of other schools into the area and overcrowding, a number of us were now being sent to have our school dinners there. The meal that day was boiled potatoes with some slices of beet root and a piece of cheese. When a boy sitting next to us saw what was being served, he began drumming on the table with his knife and fork, crying out, "Luvur-lee beet-root, Luvur-lee beet-root!" The master in charge told him twice to stop but he persisted, and the teacher finally exploded, shouting, "God damn you, Kline, will you be quiet!" This brought about a deathly hush—-we school children had never heard an august, authority figure like a teacher swear like that before. It must be realized that at that time, ordinary respectable parents didn't swear in front of their children (that was the province of the slums and the gutter). 'Blast' and 'damn' were the most we heard from Father, and Mother, for some reason, favoured, 'cussabianca'. Again, although there was plenty of swearing in all male or all female working groups, it was frowned on in mixed company, the miscreant being told to "wash his mouth out". However, this attitude was beginning to break down, like morality in general, with the course of the War.

The cane on the copper: After his promotion, Father left Mother with his old sergeant's 'swagger cane', which Mother kept strategically placed on the copper in the corner of the kitchen, handy for when quarrels between David and Max led to a fight, and indeed, when my intervention, on the presumption of being her 'right hand man' only made it worse. She would then seize the cane and strengthen her rebukes with a few choice cuts. This would rapidly restore order and usually led to a good laugh later.

An amusing incident of this sort happened one hot summer night. Sleeping three in a bed, we sometimes played the game in which the one in the middle tries to push one of the outsiders out of the bed. The one pushed out then had to go under the bed and get in the other side. This particular night was hot and sticky and we were playing the game in good earnest, not wanting to be the one in the middle. Mother called up several times telling us to be quiet and go to sleep and finally, her patience exhausted rushed up the stairs with the cane to deliver impartial punishment. Max and I wisely stayed in bed and pulled the single blanket up over us, which muffled the strokes, but David unwisely stayed under the bed and really caught it. It took Max and me a long time to choke down our laughter, which increased poor David's mortification. (I hasten to add that the cane was mainly used for lifting out washing from the copper.)

"Then we brought the girls in": Sometime after Father had been downgraded medically to B and joined another Ack-Ack battery, and after his unit had been warned that they were to undergo boat training in preparation for the eventual landings in France, another blow fell when he and one or two other officers were told they were to be withdrawn. He was initially aghast when he found that they were to be assigned to mixed batteries for training purposes. However, his commanding officer, Major Ridell (who had represented Scotland in the mile in 'Hitler's Olympics') told him, "Don't take it to heart: they want the brightest and the best officers. They have got to be well led and well trained." At this stage of the War, as we went on the attack in the Mediterranean theatre and the Far East, as well as preparing for the eventual invasion of Europe, there was a manpower shortage in the Ack-Ack, with most young men under thirty being drafted into the infantry (Montgomery was also concerned to keep seasoned desert soldiers in reserve). This led to a demand for young women to take over on 'static' Ack-Ack gun sites—-the Auxiliary Territorial Service (ATS). Despite his first reaction, Father, as he said, learned to have the greatest respect for these women:

"They were as keen as mustard and in all the tests we did, on getting on target, on height finders and predictors, and most importantly on the GL set, they beat the men every time; they were more dedicated in keeping on target. We also had them marching and cleaning their kit. They really tried hard, those girls. They did a most magnificent job that has never been adequately recognized."

As an illustration of the keenness of the ATS, Father recalled an amusing incident when he was commanding officer of a mixed battery later:

"There was one group of corporals that really worked hard cleaning and polishing their quarters until you could see your face in the floor boards and the stove and the buckets shone. They wanted to be the best hut when I went round on my tour of inspection. One said, 'I'm sure you won't find anything wrong'. The junior commander (woman officer in charge of the girls) looked at me and I thought, 'There's nothing for it but the old OCTU ploy used when we cadets thought our quarters were the best'. Invariably a little dust gets caught on the frame of the beds, so after looking round apparently impressed, the officer would run his finger along the top of one of the beds and say, 'Very good but you need to pay a bit more attention to the beds'. But I thought, 'If I do that they will think they have to turn the beds over and shampoo them', so I thought of the top of the door instead. So I went in, my stick under my arm, and looked round, 'Absolutely marvellous girls, it's difficult to find anything wrong, I must invite some of the chaps to see this if you don't mind'. Then on the way out, as one of them opened the door for me, I ran my finger along the top of the door, 'AH! Well. Do you think that's worth taking note of junior commander?' Then I walked out, imagining their reaction.

"When some CO's were inspecting the guns they would ask to look in the ammunition boxes and other places the men wouldn't think of attending to, 'Open up the breech, Sergeant, a little further, AH! what about this?' It didn't do to be cocky with a good inspecting officer."

The guns were always fired by the men, because the gender difference was thought to preclude women in those days, and the reason for all the 'bull' was because it helped to sustain the same level of attention and accuracy in action.

Father became very fond of 'his girls' and felt it very deeply when, as he said 'tragedy struck' at his gun site down near Southampton, where their battery was helping to guard the docks. He had a short leave one day and went into Southampton for a swim in the municipal baths, and afterwards to the cinema. While in the cinema there was an air raid and he left immediately, but by the time he got back to camp he found that an enemy bomber had scored a direct hit. The casualties included a number of the girls. (The bombers naturally often targeted search-light and Ack-ack batteries.)

MY LAST YEAR IN THE LATIN SCHOOL

More changes: As well as the changes in the regime at school, there were other changes at home in the Ridings that summer and in the winter of 1942/43. It was decided that an aerodrome should be built between Stowe, Silverstone and Whittlebury, greatly disturbing the ancient peace of the old Luffield Abbey farmlands. Chub lost his top field at the north end of Blackpit Farm and the trees at the end of Point Copse were cut down because they were too close to the projected main runway. The contractors were John Mowlem and their lorries began running backwards and forwards down the road to Dadford, carrying sand from Jack Davies' sand pit at all hours until it was hugely extended (incidentally destroying the nest holes of the old martin colony).

About this same time a family called Evans came to occupy the empty cottage adjacent to ours. Mr. Evans worked for Johnny Evans who was then farming at Woodlands (which covered the fields west of Stowe Woods and Point copse to the Silverstone/Dadford road). Mr Evans had three children, Megan, Dilys and an infant son called Ivan. We were intrigued to hear them speaking Welsh most of the time. David had previously picked up some Welsh words from his friendship with the younger son (Lyn) of the Davies family who had succeeded our Hurst relations at the Boxes in Slapton, and ever the good mimic he soon had us laughing at his renditions of the Evans's calling their children in for meals and so on. Some words entered our own vocabulary, like 'pudden reis' (rice pudding) and 'pruin nuts', (prune, or plum stone kernels) which as the children explained to us were actually edible.

Mother viewed Mr. Evans with some suspicion after he came home one evening and finding his wife talking to her across the garden fence, shouted, 'Come on Kate, where's my dinner?' However, he was kind and helpful to me with tips about growing vegetables and my growing collection of rabbits and chickens, and one day in the winter after we had a chimney fire, he advised me to use holly branches to clean it. So I cut some branches from the wood and went up on the roof with a rope, let it down the chimney and pulled them through a couple of times; it worked perfectly well.

I had bought my first rabbit that summer (1942), a black and white Dutch rabbit, from Fred (Charles Teague) down in the village, and by swapping stock with him and also with another friend, 'Jonah' (Arthur Jones), the only son of the couple who had replaced Uncle Harold and Aunt Nan at Jack Davies's Home Farm, soon built up a collection of more than twenty in various hutches and runs about the garden.

David (who was ten years old in 1943) also had a rabbit, a Belgian hare called 'Bluey', and for good measure decided to buy a ferret so we could go rabbiting with it. He got on quite well with the ferret (which had a dark coloured coat, more like a polecat) for a week or so, but then one day it locked its teeth into his thumb. Mother and I had to struggle for several minutes before we could get it to open its jaws. It was taken straight back to the previous owner, with thanks!

Late that summer, I started to build up a flock of hens with five chicks I bought from a cottager in Akeley. I also bought some in the market at Buckingham and from another school friend called Mike Corbett, whose father raised day-old chicks on his farm near Tingewick. There was an old pigsty at the end of the rustic barn in the pasture and Aunt Chubbie allowed me to covert it into a henhouse. I put an old sheet of linoleum over the roof, put up perches and made some rough nest boxes, as well as making sure it was fox-proof. The hens were allowed to range freely under the oak trees of the pasture. I fed them on tailings (poor quality grain) supplemented by household waste, including potato peelings, boiled up on the primus stove and made palatable with 'Karswood poultry spice'.

By the spring of 1943 we were getting a welcome, extra supply of eggs. The ration was only two a month, supplemented by dried eggs, which Mother used to mix with milk to make a dip for fried bread or spam and a 'quick breakfast' for us before we set off for school at 8am, an abiding memory of those days. Mother remembered that food became even scarcer during the U-boat campaign in the Great War when she was a little girl. Her breakfast then was often simply bread 'dipped-in' the fat of her father's fried breakfast; the breadwinner for the household having to come first, of course.

Scouting and other activities:

"A scout smiles and whistles under all circumstances. When he gets an order he should obey it cheerily and readily, not in a slow hang-dog sort of way. Scouts never grouse at hardships, nor whine at each other, nor swear when put out." (Scout Law no.8)

Although the entries in my five year diary petered out quite soon after we moved to the cottage in the Ridings, they started again at Christmas and continued in January 1943 (probably a New Year resolution) and are more or less complete for the first six months of that year, before being abandoned entirely. Amongst other things the diary reveals the importance of scouting during this period. At some point in the previous autumn, two public spirited gentlemen called Mr. Ross and Mr. Balls decided to set up a scout troop in Dadford after a meeting had been called in the old school. Most of our meetings were down in Dadford and in the surrounding fields, but naturally we also made good use of Stowe Woods.

8/1/43: "Went to scouts—-learnt how to break a flag. It is very cold tonight—-Mother's ear is not better yet."(One of the first things learned by the 'tenderfoot' is the right way to raise and fly the Union Jack.)

9/1/43: "The lake bore today—-David fell and hit his chin—-the ice bore in the middle but not round the edge."

During this cold spell large flocks of birds were attracted to the stack-yard at Blackpit; and my young cousin, Jeremy (then five years old) spent hours crouched by the broken window of the granary, with a long string attached to a stick, which held up a big sieve with some grain under it. He caught quite a few of the birds in this way, mainly sparrows, yellowhammers, chaffinches and bramblings, but he always let them go unharmed. An abiding memory of those days is of the clouds of finches bursting up from the stack-yard and the stubble fields in winter.

12/1/43: "We did not have football today and our Tyran (n) ical Schoolmaster made us gaze at a spot on the Blackboard for five minutes." (This was Taffy Williams, training us in the first stage of Buddhist contemplation!)

2,12/1/43: "Dad's leave cancelled—-went to scouts—-I went up Stowe pictures (afterwards) but there was none.

24/1/43: "Max and I went wooding—-the Squire saw us and told us we could cut down a dead tree. The catkins are out."

This friendly intervention by the Squire (John Robarts) encouraged me to go over to Tile House and pay him a visit, later on, when the time came for me to go in for my scouts' woodman's badge and ask if I could cut down a tree as part of the test (this was the only time I got inside Tile House). He arranged to come over and select a suitable tree and decided on a conifer about eight or nine inches in diameter near the base, not far from the big beech tree where I had first met him. So one evening, sometime later, the scout troop came up and the scoutmasters checked my axemanship as I cut the tree to fall in the direction we had selected (no safety helmets or goggles thought necessary in those days, of course!).

25/1/43: "We had domestic science instead of woodwork. We (each) made six blackberry tarts—-I'd eaten five of mine before I got home."
This was one of Dr. Foster's more reasonable 'progressive' innovations. He also made the girls alternate with us at woodwork and also to play against us at hockey (not such a good idea).

29/1/43: "Went to scouts—-had boxing afterwards—-I boxed with Fred. We shovelled coke at school."

The scoutmasters were keen to encourage boxing because of its character forming potential. I think we used my family's boxing gloves. Fred and I were vociferously egged on by the troop and it was quite exciting. Fred had been taught by his father and we were pretty evenly matched, so it was more or less a draw.

31/1/43: "One of my red chickens (Rhode Island Reds) laid an egg today. I only put the artificial egg in (the nest box) this morning. Very rough winds—70mph." (This marked the beginning of my egg production.)

5/2/43: "Went to scouts had wrestling, knots, bandaging—-windy, rainy.

8/2/43: "We played the Newtons (in a) junior house (football) match—-we won 6-1. I had (scored) 2. Sickle (Martin) had 2. Goffy (Gough) had 1. Mathews had 1.

10/2/43: "Bought two white beveran rabbits from Corbetts (Mike) 8/- for both (eight shillings) they are pure white."

I had adapted the linen chest that had housed the 'canaries' and connected it by a ramp to a big wire enclosure to make spacious quarters for the new rabbits. Unfortunately, a predator struck only two nights later. I heard the squeals from the bedroom, but by the time I got there a stoat had killed one of them and there was no sign of the other and I didn't see it again. However, I replaced this loss with a chinchilla (a beautiful, silver grey rabbit) and another white beveran from Mike and had better luck with these, and they went on to produce a large number of progeny.

21/2/43: "Had two eggs today (the chickens were now beginning to lay well) went for a walk round the gorse bushes—-they are putting up poles with lights on."

The lights were for navigation purposes and would be switched on when aircraft were coming in to land. This also led, later in the spring, to the cutting back of more trees, especially along the long riding, which was not far off the line of the NNE trending, main runway. This was to lead to me acquiring some unusual pets.

26/2/43: "Went to scouts—-had tracking—-getting the message through. At Stowe (pictures) we saw 'In the Navy'.

28/2/43: "Pulled an old ash log from the beech wood and rig (g) ed it up as a bird table—-nine swans went over Woody Park—-3 signets are down the lake.

1/3/43: "A lot of soldiers camped in the Riding. Brazier (Tom) and I were told we are to go up into the fourth form."

Up to fifteen hundred troops eventually arrived in lorries, and camped in Stowe Woods for about a week; the first contingents in the middle of the night to the great consternation of Mother, who thought the Germans had invaded! She was only reassured when two obvious British tommies came across the Riding in the morning with towels round their necks, carrying a tin bath to the well for water. These troops were on manoeuvres designed to prepare them for the eventual invasion of Europe. They had an immediate effect on our life because our well was the only water supply and after a couple of days it was drained dry, the only time in living memory! Mother complained to the Commanding Officer (who had commandeered part of the rustic barn as his headquarters) and it was quickly arranged for water to be ferried in, and the well soon recovered. Kind hearted as always, Mother let some of the men come into the cottage in the evening (on the quiet) to write letters home. She also arranged a party for some of the officers, with singing round the piano. One of them said that he hadn't realised there were places like Stowe Woods within reach of London, and that after the war he would bring his family down for a camping holiday!

One afternoon, I was pedalling off on my bike down to the village and a soldier came out of the woods and asked me to get him some cigarettes. In no time several other men also pressed money into my hands for the same purpose. When I got back with all the cartons, to my great embarrassment, one man was out of luck and the change didn't quite square. However, they soon sorted things out to general satisfaction and were very good about it. Clearly, I hadn't any money to begin with and I handed all the change back, so to my relief, they sent me on my way home with a clap on the back and many thanks.

An event connected with the manoeuvres, which gave me just an inkling of what it must be like in Europe with invading armies rampaging in, happened while I was out at the well in the Riding. With a tremendous roar a squadron of tanks came down from the highroad and smashed through the gate and fence into the long riding, and straight on down the track demolishing the gate and fence by the farm, round the lake, through the fence into the next field and away in the general direction of Whittlebury Park. Chub's cattle and other stock were scattered in all directions and the horses were eventually found several miles away. Minimal compensation was paid, sometime later, for the damage, but it didn't make up for the inconvenience, which, of course, had to be accepted by farmers, as it was in a good cause.

5/3/43: "At scouts (we) had semaphore (and) A (rtificial) Respiration. Fred has won his tenderfoot (scout's badge). It was presented (by the skipper) tonight at the end."(The badge, obtained after various tests, such as knowing various knots, and the Scout Laws, marked one's confirmation as a scout.)

15/3/43: "We are now in the fourth—-Brazier, Martin, Daniells, Annits and me. The old form (3b) has been joined to 3a and is now the third." (These new arrangements actually came into operation in the summer term, after Easter. Wendy Chivers, our clever classmate, had already left.)

This was an interesting move on the part of Dr. Foster, as it went against the prevailing ethos of the new movement of 'progressive' thought, and its horror of selection, with the idea of 'fast tracking', as we would say now, those of us generally at the top or near the top in 3b, and it meant we would be doing the School Cert. a year early (though I should add, that the anti-selection bias of the progressive movement appears not to have become dominant until after the War).

Despite my elevation into the Fourth form, the following entries show that schoolwork was hardly uppermost in my mind at this juncture.

18/3/42: "Aunt Lill (Chubbie) gave me four eggs to put under my broody hen. I shall put them down on Monday.

22/3/43: "We played Dentons (in a house football match) they won 2-1. I mated the white doe (the beveran) to the grey buck (the chinchilla) tonight. Mr. Evans (next door) made some preparations to move.

23/3/43: "Mr. Evans moved today to Gilesborough (Guilsborough) 9 mls Northants. He gave me an old iron bedstead to make a rabbit run.

25/3/43: "It rained all night and morning—-found some frog spawn down the lake—-found a blackbird (nest) with four eggs.

26/3/43: "Went to Scouts (had) semaphore, games, tug of war. I took Fred's rabbit up to my grey buck, Mustang (to be mated).

28/3/43: "Went for a bike ride with Mr. Ross our Skipper almost to Abthorpe—-passed my tenderfoot (test) all through with him." (It included a map reading exercise.)

29/3/43: "It turned windy. Mr. (Johnny) Evans moved a lot more of his stuff in (to the cottage next door) on a cart."

The sad sight of Johnny Evans moving into his former labourer's cottage with what was left of his furniture after a big sale at Woodlands, accompanied by his dark, withdrawn, only recently married wife, marked another big change in the Ridings. He had apparently taken on the tenancy of Woodlands without sufficient capital, machinery or stock and had got into difficulties that made it impossible for him to meet the exacting requirements of the War-Ag (War Agricultural Committee) which had been set up to oversee agricultural production as part of the war effort. As Jeremy puts it when describing Woodlands:

> Johnny Evans the previous occupant
> A Welshman with a high voice who would rant
> And rave at his dogs and sheep who would bleat
> As like him they had so little to eat

The War-Ag had draconian powers and after an investigation, Johnny Evans was deprived of his tenancy. Unfortunate as it was, this event provided an opportunity for our relations. The Tile House estate needed another tenant and running an adjacent farm, it was logical for Chub to take the farm over and combine operations with those at Blackpit. (Eventually, the family was able to buy the freeholds of both of the properties.)

The interventions of the War-Ag were not always sensible. One of their directives was the ploughing up of the central part of Woody Park, a heath-like tract on the ridge of glacial sands that runs along the north front of Stowe House (where Jack Davies' big sand pit is situated). The crops were very poor and it was a waste of time and money, but no doubt, as part of the campaign to 'dig for victory' it was thought 'good for morale'. At the end of the War, some expensive machinery was left lying around, including a ditch-digger that was acquired by my cousin Robert, for a song. This became the basis of a successful agricultural contracting business that expanded into general earth moving and contracting work, now in the capable hands of his son Paul. So again, an ill wind blew our relations some good.

!/4/43: "Mum went to a dance in Stowe. Barry Payne (Agger) had a rabbit from (Arthur) Jones   2/6d (half a crown).

2/4/43: "Scouts, Semaphore, judging distances—-rope-swinging-—Cock fighting (played mounted upon another boy's back).

3/4/43: "Fred (Charles Teague) came over with his dog—-we went rabbiting. Me and Graham went over Woodlands."

I went with my cousin Graham to have a look around Woodlands, which with the departure of Johnny Evans was now empty. The house is a tall, imposing, redbrick, Victorian building, with windows of a rather ecclesiastical style and high gables once occupied by servants, called by an elaborate system of bells, covering a good section of the wall in the passage outside the butler's pantry. Some years after this visit, Mother was to rent the servants quarters from Aunt Chubbie and my bedroom was one of the high gable rooms with a fine view over the fields to the south (see photos 7-1, lower right).

The house had seen grander days. It was built by the Earl of Southampton when he acquired Stowe Ridings and added them to his estate at Whittlebury, after the huge sale and sell-off of Stowe property in1848, occasioned by the collapse of the fortunes of the Third Duke of Buckingham. In Edwardian times it was occupied by a German, Count Wallach, (who, apparently, left precipitately just before the onset of the Great War, and the story went round that he had buried valuables in the garden, which led later to an unsuccessful search with a metal detector by Jose's son Terence). Since this period as a 'Gentleman's Sporting Residence' it had gently mouldered into a somewhat dilapidated farmhouse. However, it had some very attractive rooms, including a fine, miniature ballroom, with tall windows overlooking the garden, where there was a tennis court.

8/4/43: "Auntie Chub finished moving her stuff (furniture) into Woodlands. She has let me have Tim White's goldfish bowl."

Tim White's furniture that had been stored in the rustic barn at the cottage was now transferred to Woodlands and his books were put in the old ballroom, now the sitting room. I was sorry to lose the easy opportunity of delving into the books, especially T.A.Coward's *Birds of the British Isles*, but was pleased to get the goldfish bowl!

It was now the end of the Lent term and we had our junior cross country run at school, which was won by Mike Corbett (the friend who had sold me the pure bred rabbits and the day old chicks); and the main reason I did well was because of his encouragement. I was quite fit, and for the first time had trained, by running up and down the long riding. In the event, Mike and I went off in the lead, up towards the old railway station in Buckingham and out into the fields, making good time, but on the return I began to suffer from a sharp 'stitch' (cramp) in my right side and began to lag behind. We were both in the same house, Stratton, so Mike kept crying out, 'Keep it up! Keep it up!' and I managed to do so until we came down the street to the finishing line at the school gates, maintaining second place.

Curiously, I remember very little about the Sports Day, in the summer term (maybe after the sudden elevation into the fourth form and being a year younger than other 'seniors', I wasn't competing, or perhaps I had missed the heats) except for two incidents. During an interval, some of us were lying in the long grass near the track waiting to see one of the senior long distance runs, when the other lads began talking about the various film stars they would like to make love to (we were all in the first flush of adolescence). I felt myself odd boy out, because I hadn't the slightest interest in celluloid images. I didn't admit it to them, but I was generally only attracted to girls of my own age, although at the same time I was attracted to certain pretty teachers (and aunts). However, I remained romantically true to my idol, Gwen Biddlecombe. Later in the afternoon, we watched the junior girls in their hundred yards' dash, green gym slips tucked into their knickers. Gwen came storming in first, like Atalanta, and the sight of her beautiful figure was to haunt my daydreams for a long while afterwards.

10/4/43: "Went to ENZA concert up Stowe with Mr. Ross. All the chicks hatched—-1 white 1 grey/blue 2 brown 2 black." (From the eggs I had put under my broody hen. One had hatched the day before.)

After scouts we often went up to Stowe pictures or to a concert with one of the scoutmasters, because these shows were on the same night. As they were also concerned for our moral welfare, one of them also occasionally accompanied those of us that had been confirmed, which included Fred and Arthur, to Stowe Church for communion.

11/4/43: "The chicks (now a day old) began to eat today—- one learned to drink—-running about at the end of every half-hour."

This diary entry recalls an incident that happened later that spring when I had a broody hen sitting on four eggs. She smashed two of the eggs after about a fortnight (which I replaced) and went on sitting. When the original two eggs hatched I took the chicks away and raised them by hand while she continued to brood the replacement eggs. The diary is blank for this period, but a year or two later it led me to write the following notes in a nature diary I was keeping:

"I have just read a statement I do not think is entirely true, 'Chicks hatched and then reared in brooder do not recognise a hen's voice'. Two years ago I reared some chicks. The sitting hen smashed the first two eggs (which I replaced) and left two. She sat again and the first two hatched out a week later. These two I took away almost as soon as their down was dry. I reared them by hot water bottle in a warm window (in Ann's bedroom; in a wooden box with food and water and a water-bottle over them, suspended on slats, to keep them warm at night). Two weeks later the others hatched. I removed them all (with the mother hen) to a coop and (put) those a fortnight old under (the hen) with them. I then sat down to watch. After perhaps an hour the old hen called them out into the hot sunshine. The hand reared chicks were the first out. The old mother offered them food and they came at once to her call. When I moved they froze at her warning, then vanished under her wings."

These observations indicated to me that the behaviour of the chicks was inborn. However, I realized later, when I had more understanding of the phenomenon of 'imprinting' discovered by Konrad Lorenz, was that the first chicks would have been imprinted on their mother even before breaking out of the egg (which she would have encouraged) and not later, on me, when I was feeding them.

12/4/43: "Saw swallow over the lake—-chicks running about a bit more—- Lionel home at Woodlands—-I now know 13 nests."

Our cousin, Lionel (Wheeler) was home on leave. While home he lent Mother his copy of Henry Williamson's *Flax of Dream* which he told her, was his favourite book. Mother passed it on to me to read and it became a favourite of mine too; as, naturally in the circumstances of life in the Ridings near my fourteenth birthday, I found it easy to identify myself and my friends with Willie, Boney Watson and Jack Temperley in *Dandelion Days*, the second novel in the sequence. Mother's favourite novel was Hardy's *The Return of the Native,* and to a large extent, she identified herself with the wayward, darkly tempestuous Eustacia Vye.

Lionel was about to go out with his unit to Italy. This campaign took longer than was at first hoped after the initial landings in Sicily in the summer of 1943. Despite the surrender of Italy in the September of 1943, the advance of the Allies was held up by the desperate, rear-guard action of the German Army, especially after they established the defensive 'Gustav Line' based on Monte Cassino, near Naples. This line was not broken until the allies had mounted four successive attacks; the eventual total of casualties resembling those at Stalingrad. In one of his poems, Jeremy describes what happened to his brother after Dunkirk:

> Lionel survived and got onto a boat
> Managed to get home by keeping afloat
> He joined the Commandos at Loch Eilert
> Learned to cut throats, then became a pilot
>
> His skills in his Auster were legendary
> In Italy he got his D.F.C.
> For dropping a message bag on a tank
> From the Eighth Army approaching the bank
>
> Of the River Po, whose bridges were blown
> All except one, just by him known
> Auster means south wind, a plane with no guns
> Just its pilot's skill to avoid the Huns

Lionel's commendable sang-froid was already evident at Dunkirk. As one of his platoon commented when they had to spend the night on the beach, "Wheeler was determined to maintain civilisation and actually produced a pair of pyjamas to sleep in, and in the morning insisted on all of his platoon shaving!". Happily, Lionel survived the war, a testament to his skills as a pilot, and had a successful career in the Regular Army, rising to the rank of major; finally (and appropriately, considering his love of books) returning to the printing firm he had worked for as a young man, Hazell Watson and Viney, in Aylesbury, acting as their London representative.

As well as reading *The Flax of Dream* that spring, amongst the presents I had for my fourteenth birthday, was a second hand copy of Darwin's *Voyage of the Beagle'* from Mother. This exciting work, largely written from the point of view of a geologist, quickly led to reading *On the Origin of Species,* which on the basis of previous reading, especially the articles in my encyclopaedias, immediately struck home with the force of an essential, all embracing truth; especially, because I read *The World in the Past,* by Webster Smith, about this time too.

15/4/43: "Did some digging—-planted some Brussal (Brussel) Sprouts, Cauliflowers, Sunflower seed and carrots. Put in the Pea Sticks.

16/4/43: "Very hot went SWIMMING FIRST TIME (in the lake) ever so warm. Had boxing at scouts.

18/4/43: "I passed my second class cooking test, so did Fred, Arthur and Victor-went swimming-warm.

The scouts came up to Stowe Woods for the cooking test, which meant that necessarily, we had to show we could build and start a camp fire as well. As Fred and I had now passed all the necessary tests to be first class scouts, the scoutmasters now decided it was time for the troop to be divided into patrols, with the two of us as patrol leaders. We were allowed to choose our own totems and I chose the otter (not altogether surprisingly) and Fred the owl.

As the weather remained fine and warm, the scoutmasters allowed us to demonstrate our competence with a camping weekend in the woods looking after ourselves. This led to a revealing incident. I suggested a camp-site down the riding that runs diagonally across Stowe Woods down to the lake, making it easy to get water and swim. When we set up the tents it was quite late in the evening, so leaving the others to sort out the camp, Fred and I went into the wood to get logs for the fire before it got too dark. When we came out we were most surprised to see Stan Bunting, who was in my patrol, running as fast as he could up the riding, climbing over the fence at the top, silhouetted against the evening sky for a moment, before quickly disappearing in the direction of Dadford and home. When the others explained that he was too scared to spend the night in the woods we both laughed, but we also felt sorry for him, and I realized, not for the first time, how lucky I'd been to have been brought up in the country with no such irrational fears.

It also so happened, that just before my fourteenth birthday, Max and I were down the long riding and noticed a squirrel's drey in the ivy of one of the trees being cut back around the landing lights (erected to guide planes into the new aerodrome). A year or so later (when in Grimsby in June 1944) I wrote an account of the three young squirrels we rescued in a new nature diary, and it's worth repeating because it is the first piece of my own extended writing that survives. It is also interesting in that it shows how the laconic boy's style has given way to a more self-conscious, portentous, adolescent manner (often unintentionally funny!):

"Early in the spring of last year I was lucky enough to acquire three young squirrels. I reared them, after some deliberation, on a syringe. Milk constituted the main bulk of the food (to begin with). A rabbit hutch was fitted up for them with a few playing logs and the best of clean hay nests. It was surprising how quickly these fairy-like creatures lost their instinctive fear of man. Their coats were a warm sunny-grey in colour. Sloe black eyes seemed to challenge the world and their sharp faces seemed brimming with good sense. But the supreme ornament which seems to transform them from mere rodents to woodland sprites, were their silver-shot brushes (tails).
"Their first home was a gigantic entwined ball of bracken, hay and leaves. The parents had built in a well chosen spot. In the ivy covered crotch of an elm. It would probably never have been discovered if the trees had not been lopped. Climbing into the tree the day before it was going to be cut down I saw the drey in its friendly crotch. Then I decided to catch the already agile young squirrels. It took us nearly all that wet, misty, April morning. The last one was the largest and most agile. Got him! I thought. But no, with a flick of his bushy tail he was gone. At last the game fellow lost his footing and tumbled to the ground. He was prom(p)tly and gently put in the sack with the others.
"The first day the animals remained buried in the hay nest. They were fed with difficulty. The next day, however, the young animals had lost much of their fear. As soon as they had splashed milk over their noses they lapped it up eagerly. If I picked one up the others would miaow, scoldingly. Then one in sudden (jealous) rage would leap from the cage and run up my coat onto my shoulder. When drinking they place their paws in the spoon and suck and lap by turns.
"In play they put kittens to shame. The favourite joke was for one to hang by its hind legs from a log and bat the others as they raced past. Another game was racing madly up a flapping sack, as if the four fiends were after them. (I had them in the cottage sometimes and they played this game up the curtains, until Mother decided enough was enough!).
"The gnawing instinct soon grew; they began to take an interest in pine cones and nuts placed in different parts of the cage. Sadly I recall their passing. One morning dawned and all three were stiff and cold. Through what means they died, poison or otherwise, I never knew."

* * * * * * * * * * * * * * * * * * *

Although the attempt to rear the young squirrels came to an unfortunate end, I had better luck, when, some weeks later, I took two young jays from a nest of five in another of the trees exposed by the lopping back along the riding. This was also written up later in the nature diary (March '45), as follows:

"The first avian pets I ever kept were two jays, the most sagacious members of the crow tribe. Their first home was a raft–like structure in the top of a ragged hawthorn. For a long time I had wanted a feathered companion, to be kept flying round the house. I did not want to commit the sin of making a 'pet' of it. Awful word 'pet'. On hearing it I think of uncomfortable rabbits, wet and dirty, in a small, equally dirty box. To continue: The jays, after quite a lively encounter with the parents, were carried home in my brother, David's cap.

"Once home they were fed with difficulty. For the first few days they were kept in a box in a window (of the outhouse) shaded by a budlia shrub. The morning after the capture of the birds I was awakened by the harsh screams of the parents. When I went outside, one of the birds, which was fluttering at the window of the barn, flew into the apple tree uttering a low gurgling cry. This was the last I saw of the parent birds. They continued to feed the other three young in the nest, however. It is highly possible that we were followed home when we took the two young ones. The distance was only about a mile.

"The fledglings soon sprouted quill feathers and took tentative flight round the barn. Their main food was milk and bread pellets, chopped worms and caterpillars. So they could gain confidence outside, I gave them a few hours freedom each day. Soon they were so strong on the wing that I only shut them up at night. One day the main bulk of the blackcurrant crop was found to have disappeared. The jays were caught red-beaked, as it were, and condemned to imprisonment. When not eating they sat on the floor or perched in very dejected attitudes, setting up a tremendous screaming when anyone appeared. Their beaks grew raw with pecking at the wire (of their cage).

"With the passing of the soft fruit season they were again set free. They now slept side by side in the plum tree. Sometimes they flew in the bedroom window and slept on the bedrail (behind my head) to the detriment of the pillows. (This is an indication of the great tolerance shown by Mother to my activities!) Our postman, an old labourer of great age (Tommy Cadd from the Council Houses), was mortally afraid of them. They attacked his head in search of delicacies, 'Git' he shouted, telling me in quite 'good truth' that 'they'll peck out your eyes'.

"They took to the habit of wandering the woods—-they still came home to roost however." (Eventually, they took up residence in the Round Wood, opposite the cottage, but for a week or two still came to my call and I was able to impress my friends by calling them out of the woods to perch on my head and shoulders.)

"Then one day there was no reply to my rasping, 'ka-a-r-r!' They had vanished for ever into the living green haze of the woods."

* * * * * * * * * * * * * * * * * * *

The aerodrome becomes operational: An entry made in the diary towards the end of April that year, indicates another major change in the Ridings.

> 29/4/43: "Joner (Arthur Jones) brought his rabbit up to be bucked (mated with my chinchilla buck), prepared marrow bed with dung from the field. There are some planes up the airdrome."

A flight of Wellington bombers had now arrived at the aerodrome, and to begin with we would walk up the riding to see them take off, but we soon got used to them taking off in the evening for operations over Europe and returning sometime in the early morning hours. Some of the first flights were, I believe, leaflet raids on a propaganda mission, soon succeeded by the delivery of heavier and more painful messages.

The arrival of aircrew and ancillary staff caused an accommodation problem up at the aerodrome and a number of them were found places to live off the camp. After our relations had moved to Woodlands, Blackpit farmhouse became vacant and it was let to a family called Russell. 'Russ' was a sergeant instructor and he came to live there with his wife Doll and three children, Jean a girl about my age, a boy called Roy and a child of three called Rosalind (film star names). The couple were the same age as Mother and soon became friends. Russ was a handsome, fair, blue-eyed man and his wife, Doll was dark and quite like Mother in some ways. The children were soon coming with us on some of our expeditions, including Rosalind. On one occasion, later that summer, we children all went to pick blackberries over in Woody Park one morning. We lost all track of time and eventually got back, long after dinnertime, the little three-year old with torn dress and blackberry juice smeared face, quite exhausted but very happy (I don't know what her mother said, ours was used to that kind of thing).

Russ was musical and a good violinist, playing duets with Mother at the piano when he came with Doll to a party in our cottage. Often this was preceded by a walk over the fields to a pub called 'The Fox' over the fields in Lillingstone Dayrell where they used to go with our Wheeler relations. Russ also ran a dance orchestra up at the camp and Mother began to go to dances regularly with them on Saturday nights. Crowded with young airmen desperately enjoying themselves after the tension of bombing raids over Europe, these were exciting if not phrenetic occasions. For more formal dances, Mother needed a dress and she adapted her white satin ball-gown (which was of simple classic style and like all her clothes had been looked after carefully) and dyed it red in the copper (I was sent into Buckingham to buy the dye). It really was a beautiful scarlet and eye-catching, combined with her glossy black hair, such that the orchestra used to strike up *The Lady in Red* when she appeared on the dance floor.

A pilot who chose to live off the camp in a caravan in the orchard at Woodlands, was Andrew Tancred (a member of a titled Scottish family). He became a great favourite of my Aunt Chubbie, and Jeremy remembers him having tea in the farmhouse and especially, because he gave him a book called *How Birds Live,* for his sixth birthday. Sadly, his plane was eventually lost over Germany.

Other, damaged, planes that made it back to England sometimes crashed when trying to land. One just failed to make the runway and crashed in flames at the end of Point Copse. My cousin Robert was first on the scene and tried to save the men, but his efforts were in vain. Another crashed on the Whittlebury side of the aerodrome and David and Max managed to get over to it shortly after the crew had been taken out but nothing else had been removed. They found a pistol used for shooting up a signal 'Veery light' and Max fired off a round. What reaction this had on the camp, they didn't wait to find out!

German bombing raids over England were still continuing, of course; and one rather wet, misty morning in July, very early, Mother, who happened to have just got up and was looking out of the window into the riding, woke us up, shouting that she could see a German plane. Before she could hustle us all out onto the landing to get us down into the 'shelter' under the stairs, there was a loud, reverberating, multiple Curump! The plane (with black crosses on the wings) had clearly been flying down the line of the long riding and had dropped a stick of bombs, possibly aiming at the airfield, and overshooting, or at Stowe School (perhaps mistaken for a building of military importance attached to the aerodrome). The bombs fell between them, about three quarters of a mile away from us, not far from the Wolfe monument, two near Jack Davies' barn, destroying an elevator, and two in the adjacent cornfield.

Prisoners of war on the farm: Our victories in North Africa led to the capture of large numbers of Italian prisoners, and as there was a labour shortage in agriculture many of them were employed on local farms. A prisoner of war camp was built at the cross roads where Oxford Avenue, which is a continuation of the road running along the north front of Stowe, crosses the Buckingham/Brackley road, on the right hand side going on to Tingewick, (see map). An entry in my diary shows, two who came to work at Woodlands had arrived shortly after my Uncle and Aunt Chub had moved in:

5/5/43: "We had sports practise up the fields—-high jump—-with Victorio (Vittorio) one of the Italians."

We had improvised a high jump and Vittorio came and joined in. Vittorio was very dark and from Southern Italy (Naples, I think) while Gino, his companion was very fair and blue-eyed and from the north, either Milan or Turin. They came to live on the farm and were housed in the tack-room at Woodlands, the wood panelled room next to the stables where horse collars and saddles and other gear were hung up on pegs. They made it quite comfortable and we would often talk to them when they sat outside on a summer evening. David, especially, liked to try and pick up some Italian words and they could practise their English on him.

Vittorio was quiet and reserved, but Gino was more ebullient and, indeed, quite aggressive. Chub found him difficult to deal with because he refused to do what he was told and this finally led to a fight. As Jose says:

"It was deadly serious, nothing sporting about it—-it was a mini World War 2 battle which my father had to win, having had enough of Gino's arrogance, defiance and downright refusal to obey instructions. He could so easily have requested that Gino be returned to camp and a replacement sent out, but it became a matter of personal English honour and he was offered no alternative. To give Gino his due, he accepted his thrashing and afterwards treated father with more respect. Many of the Italian POWs stayed on after 1945 and forged close links with local families. Angelo who spoke not a word of English used to 'sit-in' for Robert and Doreen, and later, they used to visit him when staying with Lionel (who had married an Italian girl, Mimi) in Italy. Dante, who worked at Thatcham Ponds for the Tofields stayed on, and returned after marrying an Italian girl called Nita, to live next door (to the cottage). They still visit Blackpit and one of their daughters is called Doreen."

Later in the war, German prisoners replaced the Italians at the camp, and one day when I was walking along the side of Stowe Woods towards Woodlands, I came upon my uncle talking to a squad of them hoeing in the big field by the farm. I was struck by the poignancy of the scene, because he had been a prisoner of war himself, in Germany some twenty-five years before, and worked on a farm where he had been well-treated.

A decision 'to wonder at': The entries in the diary gradually petered out during the summer of 1943 and the last were in September, one concerning the loss of my best young Rhode Island Red cockerel, who used to lead his band of bachelor brothers farther and farther into the woods until he paid the penalty and was taken by a fox.

Part of the reason for the lack of more entries that summer, is perhaps that pressure was building up in school, where the four of us promoted into the Fourth had to catch up. Though I don't seem to have been unduly concerned about this, as on several occasions the lure of the 'living green haze' of the woods took precedence over going to school. One pearly morning as I set off on my bike for school a green woodpecker looped across the riding and disappeared into the woods with its ringing laugh; this was too much for me and I decided to spend the rest of the day in the woods as well. Another time, as I left the cottage I looked up the riding and saw a Gray Squirrel run along the top of the fence from one side to the other, which also convinced me that the day was better spent in the woods than in school. It was possible to get away with this because under the new regime of laissez-faire, you no longer had to take in a sick-note to explain your absences. However, my activities didn't go unnoticed, and Aunt Chubbie remonstrated with my mother, telling her that I wasn't 'going to get anywhere mooching about in the woods all day'.

The reason Mother was not all that worried by my absences from school was that she had long been party to my boyish desire 'to go sea', fired at an early age by Father's stories of our fishing ancestry and my big blue *Book of the Sea*. Indeed, for a time, Mother fondly harboured the idea of having all her boys 'in blue'. Some time during the previous year she had found out about entrance scholarships for the Naval College at Dartmouth and entered me for the examinations. This was against the advice of Dr. Foster, who pointed out quite reasonably that the school was very much orientated towards the sons of naval officers and that I would stand little chance without special coaching. However, he kindly arranged for me to take the examination at the school, and let me sit at a table in his office to take the papers. As he had predicted, I was able to make very little of the questions asked, except here and there in the maths and geography and history. Despite this setback, Mother continued to look for possible ways for me to get into the Navy.

After the disappointment of the scholarship exam for Dartmouth, and considering I was leading, what was for me, an ideal boy's life in the Ridings, immersed in nature, coming and going and staying out all night as I pleased, it is certainly something 'to wonder at' that I should want to leave Stowe Woods to join the Navy. One influence was reading Darwin's *Voyage of the Beagle* that summer, which described Captain Fitzroy's hydrographic surveys around South America and led me to think that I would enjoy life as a navigating officer. Another, the feeling I had that I was going to be in the War sooner or later. I now had two uncles in the Navy, Mother's brother in law Tom (Kit's husband) as well as Frank, two in the Army, Dad's youngest brother Norman, and his brother-in-law Cecil (Irene's husband), and one in the Air force, his brother-in- law Eric (Floss's husband); also, together with my cousin Jose in the Navy, I had three cousins in the Army, one of whom, Jack (the son of Mother's brother Val) was in the Commandos, who I had met in Grandmother's house in his full kit; so it seemed just a matter of time before I had to join up too. Elevation into the Fourth form had also brought the School Cert. forward a year, with the question of what I was to do afterwards. I didn't want to work in an office.

My results in the end of year exams also had an influence. As might be expected with a lot of catching up to do, my marks for class work in the summer term were mediocre to poor (except for 81 percent in history, actually the top marks in the class); but in the exams, although languages and science were again mediocre (and French poor), I surpassed myself to get 94 percent in maths, and I also got 80 percent in history and 78 percent in geography. These marks put me along with Tom (Brazier) in the top four of the class, as Dr. Foster quietly informed us. He was, of course, most pleased that his experiment in 'fast-tracking' was proving successful. However, my good results in maths and geography actually strengthened my idea that I might be able to become a navigating officer.

At some point after I had entered the Fifth Form that autumn, Mother found out about T.S. *Mercury,* the naval training ship run by Commander C.B. Fry (a famous diplomat and sportsman) and his formidable wife, Beattie, down on the River Hamble, in Hampshire. C.B. Fry had an unusual method of selecting boys for entry to his training ship. He asked the mothers for their photos, and if he approved of them he was prepared to accept their sons. Mother passed inspection (no problem there) and so late in the year, in December, I found myself down on the *Mercury* at Hamble. This was not without serious opposition from Dr. Foster, who (upset that 'the Navy' had again reared its head) argued that I should get a good education before making up my mind about what to do in life. Father (now on a gun-site at Eastleigh, quite near Hamble) was very decidedly of the same opinion, but wisely he didn't exercise his power of veto, thinking that as in his own case, I would probably soon get the romantic idea of 'going to sea' out of my system, and if not, well and good.

I was full of enthusiasm about joining T.S. *Mercury,* but it was painful for me to have to sell or give away my rabbits and reduce the size of my flock of chickens, although Mother decided to keep and look after the laying hens. I had been given a young labrador pup by Brian (Edrich) over at Tile House farm, which I used to take with me when I spent the night in one of my bivouacs and I had become very attached to it. So I was sorry to hear from Mother a week or two after I had left, that, not altogether surprisingly, she had taken it back. Oddly, also a short time after I left, my cat, which habitually hunted in the woods, went off and never returned.

SOURCES/NOTES   CHAPTER SEVEN

1) In recent reports on the natural history of the woods, nightingales have been recorded as rare, Dodds, M. 1999, Aylesbury Vale Countryside Service County Wildlife Project, *Stowe Woods* 63UO1; *Sawpit Wood* 64QO1. (The Stowe Woods report includes Medri, D., Stowe Ridings Woodland and Management Plan).
In the early Forties, the woods were still being regularly coppiced, with beneficial effects for the flora and wildlife. In the post-war period, this practice died out and the woods generally neglected. However, this has now been rectified by the management plan devised by David Medri for Paul and Patsy Wheeler (Robert and Doreen's son and daughter-in-law). To quote from the above reports: " This is one of the most impressive management plans that has been encountered during the County Wildlife survey programme in terms of the compromise between active forestry/game bird production and conservation/ecological enhancement. The production of timber is done in a sensitive and traditional manner, which enhances the ecosystem by reproducing the conditions that woodland species have evolved to exploit, over the hundreds of years that man has been the most significant influence on the woodland environment in this country."

2) This whole episode is interesting, in that it may be one of the first attempts to introduce some of the practices of 'progressive' education into a conventional secondary school. The period between the Wars was rife with educational theorists setting up special private schools, usually heavily influenced by the sophistries and destructive half-truths of Rousseau and his followers, with an emphasis upon 'creativity' and self-motivated enquiry through play. A.S. Neill at 'Summerhill' did have some success with disturbed children found uneducable at other schools. What was bizarre was the idea that undisciplined 'play' had much relevance for education in general! Some sixty years later, this movement, with its horror of physical punishment, as well as selection, appears to have reached its apogee (? nadir) with the anti-smacking bill and the suggestion that the 'problem' of boys and young men is best dealt with by bringing them up like girls! Dr. Foster left in 1945 when Toft returned, and he went on to become ordained into the Church; a good, kind and indeed, clever man (previously Senior Science Master at Aylesbury Grammar School) but with no grasp of discipline, this was undoubtedly a sensible move on his part: the effects of sentimental kindness without discipline being worse even than those of discipline without kindness.

3) The first attempt at the recovery of Burma in the spring of 1943, with an attack by the 14th Army under General Slim in the Arakan on the Assam border, was badly supplied and a 'shambles' which led to the loss of what prestige was left to the Raj, although mitigated by the success of the first raid in the rear of the Japanese lines by Wingate and his Chindits. For the rest of the year South East Asia was 'put on the back burner' by the Allies because

of the requirements of the Mediterranean Theatre and preparations for the Second Front, and further difficulties were caused by a terrible famine in Bengal. In the spring of 1944, the Japanese Army under General Mutaguchi made a final effort to break through the Naga hill country of Assam and out onto the Indian Plains, with the help of the 40,000 men of the Indian National Army under the renegade, Subhas Bose; in the hope that India would then rise up to throw off the Raj. However, our Indian troops that made up some two-thirds of the 14th Army remained loyal. Our garrisons at Kohima and Imphal were besieged but heroically held out until relieved and then the tables were turned and the Japanese suffered the greatest defeat on land in their history, with the elimination of almost an entire division (80,000 men). The 14th Army then fought on through Burma, and recaptured Mandalay in March and Rangoon in the April of 1945.

CHAPTER EIGHT

SEAMAN BOY TO FARMER'S BOY

T. S. MERCURY

"In my days we had wooden ships and iron men; nowadays they turn out iron ships and wooden men." Lt. Cdr H. F. Budden

"...the aim of the school was to cultivate initiative and leadership in boys aiming to become Merchant Navy Officers or enter the Royal Navy under the advanced class scheme. Such training is necessarily tough, and most of the time we were hungry; what boy isn't?" E.W. Clayton

"I had to learn to stand up for myself, to understand and appreciate discipline, to be proud to make a good job of anything and, yes, to enjoy the benefit of prayer. And that 'Woman of Terror' turned out thousands of boys in her time with similar attributes." Capt. G. Lindsey

"Life is a fight from birth to Home." Beattie Fry

(See note 1.)

First impressions: I arrived down at T. S. Mercury late in the year (1943) with a small party of other new recruits, ahead of the rest of the ship's company, who returned from leave a day or two later. The shore establishment consisted of a small park just upstream of Hamble village where the river Hamble flows into Southampton Water. Commander and Mrs Fry had a large, four story country house, with a parade ground adjacent, separated from the village by the sports field and cricket ground. Below the parade ground were the mess-hall and the wash-rooms. On the north side of the park, going up towards the entrance off Satchell Lane were a rustic, and quite attractive, chalet-type chapel, class rooms and a sick-bay (small isolation hospital); and at the north end of the parade ground, along the path behind the clock tower, there was a lofty, wooden building with ropes, sails and all the gear for teaching seamanship. There was also a small, perfect replica of Wagner's theatre at Bayreuth for concerts and music teaching.

My memory of actually arriving at the *Mercury* is vague. I think I said goodbye to Mother at Waterloo station before travelling down with some other new recruits. We were given tea in the mess-hall and Chief Officer Harold Fraser, apparently of Scots-Canadian origin and Mrs Fry's right-hand man, gave us a short talk about life on the ship and what would be expected of us. He was quietly spoken, that as we were to find, belied the choleric temper which went with his red hair. Afterwards, still in our civvies (civilian clothes) we were taken down to the causeway, which led through the marsh and rushes to the small-boat moorings where we watched some of the officers hauling on ropes to 'warp' in one of the whalers (a heavily built type of Naval cutter, about thirty feet long with five or six pairs of oars). It was dusk and a fresh, damp breeze was blowing up from the Solent carrying the cries of water birds, and one of the boys said, "We're gunna enjoy it here".

We had to take our shoes off to get into the boat (tying the laces together and hanging them round our necks).The officers then rowed us across to the dark hulk of the *Mercury* where we had to climb the Jacob's ladder up to the main deck. After a short prayer, we were taken down to the hold which had been adapted as a large dormitory, with rows of hammocks slung from metal lines about five feet from the deck. We were shown how to get into the hammocks, by swinging up on the lines and putting our heels in, before tucking the single blanket round ourselves. I was soon asleep (and soon grew to like sleeping in a hammock).

The *Mercury* was originally a sloop, called *Gannet,* both sail and steam powered with seven-inch guns on the main deck. After active service in Queen Victoria's Navy, she was converted to become the headquarters of the RNVR (Royal Naval Volunteer Reserve) as the *President,* with the engines and sail removed and the main deck roofed in for drill and gunnery. The original training ship on the Hamble*,* the former barque *Ilovo,* had become dilapidated by 1908 and the Admiralty agreed to provide *Gannet/President* as a replacement. However, nothing was done about it until Churchill, as First Sea Lord, in 1913, inspected the *Mercury* at short notice and was so impressed that the replacement was towed up the river within a few weeks. Although the very reverse of picturesque, the roofed-in main deck with the seven-inch guns still in place, was ideal for the purpose (see note 2).

After we had been taken ashore in the morning and had our breakfast, we were issued with our kit, our formal 'blues' with bell-bottom trousers, collar and lanyard, with cap and gold T.S. *Mercury* hatband, together with overalls for everyday wear, and a pair of boots. (Some of the lads, as soon as they went on leave, sewed wide gussets into the bell bottoms to make them even wider and more fashionable!) The boots were for the parade ground and for route marches, but were never worn on board ship or in the mess-hall, where bare feet were the order of the day (indeed, the deck in the mess-hall was scrubbed daily and clean enough to eat off). We were also issued with a huss'if (the sailor's 'housewife') containing needle and thread and other material required for Friday afternoon, 'make and mend' when our laundered kit was returned from the laundry (no hardship for me as I was already used to darning my own socks). Our civvies were put away in store until such time as we went on leave.

Following this kitting out, we were taken in batches to have our hair cut, that is, our heads were shaved. We were told this was for hygienic reasons, but it was designed as much to reduce our individuality and bind us to the rest of the ship's company; each of us being given a number at the same time, replacing our names, to the same end. My number was 358, and my two best friends, their actual names long forgotten, were 376, a boy from Kingston-on-Thames, whose father ran a boat hiring business, and 372, a boy from Rushton in Northamptonshire, who wanted to go to sea for similar romantic notions as my own. He became my particular friend. We were also medically examined and our eyes were tested, particular attention being given to our colour vision; and I was quite pleased to find that there was only one colour card, of a purplish/brown colour, in a set of over twenty, where I couldn't read the number.

When the rest of the ship's company returned we were assigned to our watches. There were about 140 boys in all, divided into four watches, port band and port watch, starboard band and starboard watch. I was placed in port band with 372 and 376. On parade and on board ship we mustered in our groups, and as the ship was moored facing upstream, port band always gathered on the port side for'ard. Each watch had a leading hand, responsible to the officer in charge (a lieutenant) and was divided into three sections of about twelve, each with a section leader. The sections sat together at trestle tables in the mess-hall. The officers' titles were purely honorary, as it appears none of them had achieved that rank in the Navy. They came into use at the time of the Great War, when the *Mercury* became renowned for the quality of its entrants into the Royal Navy, and C. B. Fry was made Hon. Commander (and Beattie received the O.B.E.). Our lieutenant was, I think, the youngest of the officers. His ambitions in the Navy had been thwarted by problems with his sight, which had led to him joining the staff on the *Mercury*. If he was bitter about that he showed no sign of it, always being very fair and amiable, and hardly ever raising his voice, except when necessary. Our leading hand was a quiet, tall, dark boy (from Southampton), very competent and well liked.

Life as a seaman boy: On three mornings a week, reveille ('Wakey-Wakey' sounded by our bugler from the main deck) was at 5.30am. This was the signal to 'lash-up and stow' our hammocks, which had to be drawn up tight with the rope on the end wound in neat half-hitches round them. On these mornings we mustered on deck to be issued with scrubbing brushes, floor cloths, soap and pails. Water was pumped up from the river onto the deck and on our knees, with trousers rolled-up we worked our way across the deck in serried ranks. On the alternative mornings, reveille was at 6am and we were mustered on deck to clean and polish the seven-inch guns. The gun ports were then swung open and we practised loading and firing dummy shells to order.

At 7am the order would be given to board the whalers, via the Jacob's ladder, to go ashore and be ushered in successive groups through the washrooms. One morning, when there was a white frost, an officer known to the ship's company as 'Chinless', because he was singularly lacking in that area, was in charge. As we were marched down the path from the causeway, some of us were putting our bare feet down on the gravel rather gingerly and in response, he made us double-march, raising our knees. No doubt it was designed to toughen us up, but it did make us look rather sardonically at his thick great-coat and sea-boots with thick, white sea-boot socks smartly turned out over them! Of course, our feet soon did toughen up.

The showers in the wash-rooms were long perforated pipes at about the six foot level, allowing a number of boys to wash at the same time. One day when Chief Officer Fraser was present, some of us held back because the water was steaming hot, and he casually booted us back under it. In fact, it was not that hot. However, on another occasion, one of the boys suffered more seriously. At that time 'cleaning the inner man' with a dose of salts was as much a fetish as the present day injunction to drink seven or eight pints of water a day. So about once a week, he gave us a dose of salts from a big pewter jug, after our shower, making sure everyone took a good draught. This boy baulked at it, and the Chief Officer made him drink all that was left in the jug. The poor lad then spent most of the rest of the day in and out of the 'heads' (loo) to the wry amusement of the rest of us.

After the showers we had morning prayers in the chapel before, finally, with our appetites well sharpened we filed in to the mess-hall for breakfast. This normally began with cornflakes or another cereal, which would often prompt Chief Officer Fraser, who naturally preferred salted porridge made with water, Scottish style, to deliver a homily on the decadence of modern times! In general, (remembering that we were at the height of rationing) the food, though plain was adequate, with plenty of bread and potatoes and fresh vegetables. A meal I particularly remember, was high-tea/supper on Saturday evenings, when I think some of the kitchen staff were probably off duty, when we were always given a big plate of finely chopped raw carrot and cabbage, with a piece of cheese or sardines, or something similar. Some of the more finicky boys disliked it, but I took to it. It's true that 'we were always hungry' but this was dealt with to some extent, by the regular issue after supper of hard-tack, one of those very hard ship's biscuits that take an age to eat.

The mornings were spent mainly in class-work. Together with the new intake of boys in my group I took maths and geography with Harold Fraser and naval history with another officer. Seamanship was taught by a very amiable, jocular Lieutenant, who had lost his arm in an earlier naval engagement but not the ability to demonstrate various knots to us with great skill, building on what I had already been taught in the scouts, but now including knots like the running bowline, important in life saving at sea. As well as semaphore, we learned how to send messages by naval flags, of the 'England Expects' variety and to tap out messages in Morse code to each other; and of course, we had to learn the 'Rules of the Road at Sea' and the various seamarks. I liked the atmosphere in the high, wooden building where we were taught, which was part sail-loft and part store, with ropes and nets hanging down and other bits and pieces of gear; and looked forward to being taught to sail, as was promised for the following summer.

In the mid-morning break we did physical exercises, in the gym or on the parade ground or the sports field if it was dry, regularly being made to scramble up and over the big nets, suspended on a wooden frame about fifteen feet high at the edge of the cricket ground, to improve our agility and heads for height. Everything had to be done 'at the double' and it is this order that still rings in ghostly fashion in my mind when I think of the *Mercury*. This was generally followed by a short period at-ease on the field and during this interval a favourite game was 'Weak Horses'. Three or four boys from one of the sections would line up with their backs to the wall of a shed, with the rest of the section packed like a rugby scrum, the front row with their heads in the hands of the boys standing. Another section of boys would then leap onto the 'scrum' one by one until it eventually collapsed under the accumulating weight; the object being to see which section could take the most. This caused great hilarity amongst the boys, and much amusement to the officers in charge, until things got rather out of hand, with too many boys leaping on and danger to the poor unfortunates trapped underneath, and it had to be curtailed.

The afternoons were generally reserved for physical activities. We were drilled in various marching manoeuvres on the parade ground, equipped with old Lee Enfield rifles. These were quite heavy for young lads and I was glad I was never 'put on a charge' because for certain misdemeanours you were made to run round the sports field with the rifle held above your head until told to stop! On two afternoons a week we went on a cross-country run and, of course, we were all taught to row (the different watches had to take it in turns in ferrying the others to and fro from the ship). I soon found rowing very satisfying, despite the weight of the fifteen foot oars used on the whalers; getting one's body behind the stroke, the stomach muscles doing most of the work, followed by the smooth, feathered return, the rhythm eventually exerting almost an hypnotic effect. Sometimes we would go well down into the Solent and it was exciting to feel the first pulse of the open sea.

On weekends we went out into the country on long route marches of up to twenty miles or so. I found it a relief to get away from the ship, especially as we usually went through woods, trampling the autumn leaves, on much of our way, and I could keep a look out for birds. Quite often we returned through the park of Netley Hospital, a big house fronting on Southampton Water, full of war-wounded at that time. Often, in fine weather, there would be convalescents in the grounds in their bright blue hospital uniforms, looking curiously at us as we marched past (perhaps wondering what our fate would be).

The main winter sport on the *Mercury* was football, and the ship's company was divided into twelve teams, all named after famous battleships. I was put in *Fighting Temeraire,* one of Nelson's ships of the line. Fortunately, our captain was a very good player, the best on the ship, and I was able to play at inside-left, as I preferred. Our team came top of the league, although we narrowly lost, 1-0, when we finally played the Rest at the end of the season.

It was not all physical activity: several times a week we attended the beautiful little Wagnerian theatre to learn to play an instrument. The theatre had all the required features, a sunken orchestra pit, so that the players were out of sight of the audience, and a balcony above the stalls arranged so that all the seats had a good view. The music teachers were former members of the Royal Marine Band and very good players. I hoped I could play a woodwind instrument, but my lost index finger ruled that out and I was put onto a trombone. I never really took to it (I should have asked to be put on the French horn) but I did progress to simple tunes, including the obligatory march from Tannhäuser, the ship's signature tune, which whenever I heard it in after days always took me straight back to the *Mercury.* The best players were picked for the school band, which put on concerts in the evening for the ship's company and also played locally. Some of these boys went on to join the Royal Marine band themselves (this included the bugler who played during my time).

Friday afternoon was also quiet, when, at 'Make & Mend', we had to make sure that our kit and clothes returned from the laundry were all in good order and make all necessary repairs. This was important because we were inspected on the parade ground with all our kit, including sports gear, boots and pyjamas, in front of us, after breakfast on Saturday mornings, by Mrs Fry and Chief Officer Fraser. For the new entrants, our first experience of this redoubtable lady was at our first Saturday inspection. By this time of her life she was elderly, but still a very upright and commanding figure, with a firm mouth and penetrating, searching gaze, generally wearing a long, old-fashioned great coat and a sort of slouch hat. Woe-betide if she found anything amiss. This is attested by the panic that ensued if, just before inspection, any boy found that one of his boot laces was broken or missing. He would immediately help himself on the quiet to someone else's, which would lead to a cascade of petty thefts, no one wanting to be the one on punishment detail! (I was only caught once in this negative version of pass-the-parcel; it certainly kept you on your toes!)

Commander Fry inspected us on Sunday mornings, when we were wearing our full dress uniforms. On the first occasion I remember thinking that he looked rather abstracted, a little sad and forlorn; also that the shoulders of his naval greatcoat were rather dusty and that it was rather odd that no one had brushed it off for him before he inspected us! This probably explained why his inspection as he passed down the line was somewhat perfunctory. Sunday inspection was quite pleasant because we had the band in attendance and marched off in tune. Another sharp memory of the Sunday inspection is seeing a goldcrest one morning, after a slight snowfall, very near too, in one of the evergreens that grew round the house. (See note 3.)

My first personal encounter with Mrs. Fry arose because during the morning break, when it was possible to get a few minutes on your own, I got in the habit of going up to the edge of the sports field to look into a garden on the edge of the village, where the owner was raising some chickens. This led me to go into some detail in a letter home to Mother about the care of the flock I'd left behind. Mrs Fry read all our letters, so I was called into her office in the House and asked some probing questions about how I was settling down and advised to put my former home life behind me and throw myself whole-heartedly into the life on the ship. Although severe, I felt that her interest was not unkind. Father had come to see me at the *Mercury* some time previously, in his uniform, and as Mrs Fry undoubtedly approved of smart, handsome young officers, this probably helped.

On another occasion, I was returning with a group of other lads on the final stretch of one of the routine cross-country runs, and with no officers in sight we were just jogging along, not making a race of it, when to our consternation, we saw C. B. and Mrs Fry standing at the gate of the football field to watch us make our final circuit before running down the lane to the school gates. As we came up she called me out and told me sharply that as I obviously had the build of a runner, to stop being a slacker and to put more effort into it, because she expected much more of me. Meanwhile Commander Fry stood quietly at her side reinforcing her words with the frown on his face. After this stinging reprimand I went off like a startled roe buck, and raced round the field and down to the school gates, passing large numbers of my bemused shipmates on the way!

This intervention of Mrs Fry, and the flea in the ear, had a good effect some time later when we had an afternoon of athletics. I had been placed last leg in the four x quarter-mile relay race. When I finally got the baton, our team (Port Band) were well behind, but I went away at a furious pace which I kept up to the finish, passing two runners and putting us in second place. Unfortunately, chiefly because Port Band had a disproportionate number of new young recruits, we ended up overall with the wooden spoon that day. However, it was a useful experience for me, to find that I could run the quarter at my fastest speed and still have a little in hand for a final burst.

Another encounter with Mrs Fry came about because, somehow, I caught conjunctivitis. As this is contagious I was sent to the sick-bay for a few days. At first I was glad to keep my head down out of the light, but as my sight improved I took the opportunity to read one of the books there (especially as we didn't have any time to read for pleasure normally!) It was a copy of Gilbert White's *Selborne*, which eventually became one of my favourite books. However, I didn't have time to get far into it on this first occasion, because Mrs Fry came to see how I was getting on, and although she seemed quite pleased to see what I was reading, she said that obviously my eyes had improved enough for me to rejoin my shipmates.

We were back on board the Ship each night at 9pm. Once a week, in the period after supper, we were allowed to write our letters home. On other occasions we had a concert from the school band and there was a weekly boxing night (and it is true that Mrs Fry did get very enthusiastic, crying out "Make 'im bleed", though she was not the first woman to do that from a ringside seat). There were also talks and readings. Particularly memorable were readings given on successive Sundays by Harold Fraser from Scott's diary of the expedition to the South Pole. He was a good, clear reader and the whole ship's company would sit in absolute silence as he recounted the heroic exploits of Scott, Oates, Evans and Bowers and their struggle over the ice in the face of ferocious Antarctic weather (see note 4).

After a strenuous day and an evening of this sort it was good to swing into one's hammock and settle down as our bugler sounded the Last Post, accompanied by the lisping gurgle of the river along the hull of the Ship. Normally I fell immediately into a dreamless sleep, not waking until reveille. However, it was now only a few months before D-day, and Southampton Water and all the surrounding creeks were crowded with naval vessels and transports. Sometimes a lone German raider flew over at night, desperate to get information about the preparations for the invasion and a barrage of guns would open up, including the pom-poms (multiple anti-aircraft guns) on a vessel anchored quite near to us on the Hamble, jolting us out of sleep.

Disquiet and disillusion: In many ways (as the reader may well surmise) I was suited by background and upbringing to life on the *Mercury,* but there was a fatal flaw: I gradually became depressed by the way in which we were constantly confined to the school, and never allowed out on our own. I also began to worry about the direction I was taking. Some former *Mercury* boys, now based nearby in Portsmouth, came to see old friends, and talked to us about life in the Navy; pointing out that after our training on the Ship, we would find it a doddle, and also that we would be 'able to lick any boy of our own size'. More seriously, from their description of our future in the Navy, which involved a further course on HMS *Indefatigable* in the Isle of Man and signing on for twelve years (seven with the colours and five on Reserve) it became clear to me that it was unlikely that I could rise from the lower deck to officer rank. Mother would have been delighted to see me become a petty officer but my mind had been set on becoming a navigating officer, and I had rather more of my father's ambition in me than she probably realized. However, the crucial issue was my sense of being confined to what began to seem like a prison ship, and the stark contrast with my former free life in the woods.

One morning during the break, I was out on the field with my friend, 372. I was in a particularly despondent mood and when I failed to hear a remark he made to me, he gave me a nudge to get my attention. As I still didn't respond he nudged me again and when I remained oblivious he gave me a hard poke. This did rouse me and I angrily poked him back. In a flash we went at each other in cold fury. He could box, and we began to land some shrewd blows on each other; and might have done serious damage if our young watch officer hadn't quickly broken us apart with the curt command 'to cut it out!' Wisely, he took it no further. We were lucky because the normal punishment for boys caught fighting was three rounds in the ring under the Queensbury Rules, which might not have improved our friendship (as you were expected to go all out and give your opponent a pasting). As it was, we were friends again by nightfall, but I've always had this spat on my conscience. Perhaps for this reason, it was the last, serious fist fight I ever allowed myself to engage in.

What the fight shows is that I was in a state of some confusion about my future and life on the *Mercury*. Some of the other new entrants, especially those brought up in over-protected, soft, town homes, reacted more severely, being unable to take the discipline or the hard strenuous life. After a few weeks two of them ran away, immediately after roll-call one evening. They didn't get far; easily recognized by their shaven heads and work overalls, they were intercepted by the police after they had got about twenty miles up the London road. The next day, these two boys had to stand in disgrace by the flagpole, until their parents came to collect them in the evening. We were sorry for them of course, but we had a low opinion of how they had just cut and run. Thinking it over, I decided that whatever decision I came to about the future, I would see things through until we went on leave in the spring, only too conscious of the shame it would bring on my parents if I didn't!

Discipline and rough justice:

> On T. S. *Mercury* we all took heed
> When Beata Fry cried, "Make 'im bleed!"
> But that's a time long gone away,
> Of England's glory, come what may.

It is ironic, that I should go straight from a school in which the attempt was being made to put the latest ideals of 'progressive' education into practice, to a naval school in which the ethos and discipline still differed little from that operating in the great days of sail and the races between the clipper ships, the century before; there couldn't have been a greater contrast.

However, it is also true that there is a tendency for old *Mercury* boys to play up the harsh side of life on the Ship, and Ronald Morris, in his book *The Captain's Lady* although reasonably objective in his account of the remarkable personal history of C.B. and Mrs Fry, cannot be said to have resisted it. He was obviously a kind soft-hearted boy and he joined the Ship's company a couple of years after me in 1945, apparently from a comfortable home, expecting it to be like attending a public school with nautical aspects. He was quickly disillusioned, and horrified by the crop-haired, bare-foot regime, the harsh punishments, relentless physical activity and, indeed, the cold: "Only those who have experienced the English climate with the minimum of protection can appreciate how brutally inhospitable it is for six months of the year, and the *Mercury* boys experienced it all at first hand, being spared only the fall of rain and snow directly onto their canvas hammocks." He also found it remarkable that Mrs Fry slept all year in an unheated room with the window open! I find this quite amusing and equally laughable, his comments about the awful food and how, "The boys were driven to the point of exhaustion every day and kept so hungry that they were not interested in anything except food and sleep." He claims this was because Mrs Fry, in puritanical guilt and over-reaction against her own irresponsible and wild sexual behaviour in youth was determined to make sure the boys had neither the time nor energy for sexual thoughts, or what Baden-Powell called 'beastliness'. In my own case, I have to say that when I eventually went home on leave, Mother was delighted with my appearance, and said she had never seen me look so fit and healthy (my black curls had also grown back), which argues that the food although plain, was adequate and the constant exercise beneficial. In the present age when we now have the 'problem' of childhood 'obesity' his criticism seems increasingly out of place.

It's true that every night I fell straight into the dreamless sleep of the 'just', and, indeed, of the 'blessed', because during the whole time I was there I never had a single sexual thought; although I was fully into puberty before I went on the *Mercury* and such thoughts soon came back into action again after I left. It taught me that Mrs Fry and Baden-Powell were right in this respect; you didn't 'have to have it' and you could put your energies elsewhere. This was useful to me later in life when it became expedient for me to do so.

Morris finds Beattie Fry's puritanical drive to domination over the boys, responsible for the harsh discipline and the constant supervision. As the headlines of the newspaper article accompanying the publication of his book proclaim:

'A WOMAN AND HER REIGN OF TERROR—-The extraordinary story of the messianic ferocity with which the wife of the legendary cricketer C.B. Fry ran a boys' training ship.' (Sunday Telegraph, July 14th 1985)

How the headline writers loved it. This is reminiscent of the 'Living Hell' suffered by the apprentice boys on the Grimsby trawlers the century before!

It's interesting that Morris illustrates the 'reign of terror', not by an account of his own experience, but by describing a day in the life of the Ship when the chief officer was the notorious Arthur 'Sharkey' Ward, a former petty officer and physical training instructor in the Navy. According to Morris, he was employed by Beattie Fry, 'to thrash the boys into submission' because, 'She was unaware of any alternative to setting man and boys at each others throats'.

Although the boys certainly suffered during the tenure of 'Starkey', who appears to have been a thorough-going sadist, this was only from the Great War into the Twenties and it is quite wrong to infer that the whole history of the Ship was one of daily sadistic brutality under Beattie's watchful eye. My experience doesn't bear this out, or indeed, that of Morris himself, who admits that in his time she had mellowed to the point of suggesting that the boys should be known by their names rather than their numbers!

Morris does bring out one detail that I (with the 'lack of imagination'—often commented on by my father) had been unaware of: many of the boys, probably including those that ran away, were 'terrified' when going out to the Ship in the whalers in the night, especially when there was a gale whipping up from the Solent, as there were no life jackets, where-as I found it exhilarating.

I only had one experience of rough justice myself. It happened one frosty January morning, when we were scrubbing the deck. The water being pumped up from the river was ice-cold, and as we worked away on our knees, with bare feet of course, I developed a cramp. I'd seen Chief Officer Fraser go below deck down the gangway and thinking we were unobserved, stood up to stretch and exercise my foot. Unbeknown to us, he had quietly come up another stairway and was standing right behind me. He gave me a swift kick up the backside and sent me sprawling face down on the wet deck. There was nothing for it except to get on with it, and the other boys, after a quick glance, carried on scrubbing away even more energetically.

I didn't feel any particular animosity towards Harold Fraser after this. I was much more annoyed at myself for not having the sense to realize that he wouldn't leave us unsupervised and I determined not to make that kind of mistake again. As for the kick, the pain didn't last long and, of course, in the days of sail, a kick and the ropes end were the normal method of encouraging laggardly lads up to the masthead. As it happened, I got on well with him in class, being somewhat ahead of the other boys in maths and geography. I never felt he was sadistic in his punishments; he was probably more often simply irritated, by what he regarded as snivelling or lubberly behaviour from a bunch of snotty-nosed seaman boys, and he did easily fly into a temper, as another incident will show.

One afternoon we had gone down river in the whalers, in four parties picked from each watch. On the way back, as we got near the *Mercury* the officers decided we should have a race upstream. Instead of our young officer, who was absent for some reason, we had Chief Officer Fraser in charge of the Port Band boat. As I have explained, most of us in our watch were younger and of rather lighter build than those in the other watches, so although we did our best we soon fell behind. This didn't please the Chief Officer, especially when the other officers waved us goodbye! He was sitting in the bows and he began to shout at our coxon, sitting in the stern, which actually confused him and made things worse. The Chief then lost his temper completely and charged down the boat, not minding where he put his boots, and we were, naturally, bare-foot, to give the coxon a box on the ear. By this time, as we had stopped rowing, we were drifting back downstream, past a naval torpedo boat at her moorings. There were a couple of sailors leaning over the rail watching what was happening with great interest, and one of them shouted, "You leave that boy alone, or we'll come over and do you!" Immediately, the Chief desisted and picked his way carefully back up the boat with a chastened expression on his face. We had to hide our smirks of satisfaction as we rowed quietly back upstream, and there was no further trouble.

These incidents have their amusing side, but there was one disciplinary episode that upset and depressed us all. Late one afternoon we heard to our consternation that our leading hand in Port Band had somehow fallen foul of the Chief Officer and was to get twelve strokes of the cane. We never found out precisely what had happened, but so severe a punishment almost certainly meant that he had disobeyed an order, or was considered to have done so, which we thought most surprising in the case of this boy. The punishment was carried out in the Gym, where he was strapped to the vaulting horse (a substitute for the gun employed in the old days).

We were all very quiet and subdued when we filed into the mess-hall for our supper that evening, and most of us just toyed with our food. Harold Fraser at his raised table just busied himself with some kind of administrative task, without raising his head. Our gloom was relieved somewhat when we heard that after his punishment the boy had been put in the sick-bay to recover from the shock and had found the opportunity to slip out and escape. He got clear away to Southampton, where his parents lived, and we didn't see him again. Thus, no doubt, a good recruit was lost to the Navy.

It took a day or two for the atmosphere to improve. This brings up an important point. In those days boys were ready to accept (when we knew we deserved it) reasonable physical correction and chastisement but we all knew when it was excessive and neither just nor proportionate. In pre-war Slapton, for instance, we village boys would discuss it with great concern if any parent was over-zealous with the buckle-end of his trouser belt. However, this was the only time while I was on the Ship that the vaulting horse was made part of the ritual of exemplary punishment, and what our reaction also shows, is that we were, obviously, not being subjected to a continuous, 'reign of terror'.

As spring came on, I began to look forward to going on leave, but I still had mixed feelings about the future. I hadn't got any ideas about an alternative career, but there were times when my spirits were lifted, as happened one afternoon, when we were at ease after an exercise on the Ship, and the sun glitter off the river sliding by was reflected through the open gun ports, and I thought, "This is the life!" I was also attracted by the thought of learning to sail in the summer and swimming everyday off the Ship (in retrospect, I wonder why we didn't swim all year!); but in general the sense of oppressive confinement prevailed and I began to look forward to resuming my old life in the Latin School and in Stowe Woods.

One morning, during what may have been a maths lesson, I remember writing the date on the top of my exercise book, 4/4/44, and wondering, rather ruefully, what I should be doing when it was 5/5/55. Easter was late that year and we celebrated it with several services in the chapel. Shortly afterwards we went on leave.

Postscript: Beattie Fry died in 1946, and C.B. left in 1950. The school continued to be run by the Navy until 1968 when it was closed and demolished, being replaced by a housing estate, leaving no trace behind, except in the minds of those who once went through the gates off Satchell Lane with such hopeful expectancy.

FAMILY BREAK-UP

A long day's journey: I travelled up to Waterloo together with a number of other London-bound lads, all of us in our dress uniforms. Mother met me at the station, accompanied by her friends, Doll and Russ (the Russells). She was proud to see me in uniform but I was a little embarrassed, especially when on our way to the Zoo in Regents Park, a squad of infantry marched past and I didn't know whether to salute the officer in command. Actually, in the War the rules were relaxed for naval ratings, but I was unsure of the protocol.

The trip home via London, the day before my fifteenth birthday would have been memorable in any case, but it was made more so by an incident at the Zoo. We had been looking at the chimpanzees and I lingered when the others walked on, saddened that such intelligent, active animals should be confined in such a small cage. Father had always extolled the virtues of Whipsnade and said that the other zoos should be abolished. There was a chimp sitting near the bars at the front of the cage, only a few feet away as I leant on the visitors' safety barrier. He looked at me and suddenly put his hand through the bars and picked up a razor blade from amongst the leaves, cigarette packets and other rubbish in the dead space between (goodness knows how it got there because it was shining bright and not rusty); then he neatly sliced down a length of straw he was holding upright against the floor with his left hand. He then looked at me again, almost as though it had been done for my benefit. I was immediately aware that he was conscious of me being conscious of him, being conscious of me. If I had not already been aware of our close relationship with the higher apes through reading, this demonstration of intelligence would have convinced me of it. It also showed that we were not separated from them by the ability to make and use tools. As I hurried to catch up with Mother and her friends, I was in an unusually thoughtful mood, quite apart from wondering how I was going to tell her that I had decided not to return to the *Mercury*.

After we got home to the cottage very late that night, I finally did tell Mother, and at first she was quite upset and annoyed. She accused me of being too soft and unable to take the life and discipline. I tried to explain, rather poorly I think, that it wasn't that but the confinement and loss of freedom (after all, cutting kale in the snow and a biting east wind with my cousin Graham on the farm, was as hard as scrubbing decks on the *Mercury* on a frosty January morning). She then asked me what I intended to do; and when I said I had thought of returning to the Latin School, she said that it would be impossible, because she and Father were splitting up and it had already been arranged that the other children would be going to relations in Grimsby. The reason for her disappointment at my decision then became clear. She had hoped, with me settled on the *Mercury* that I was out of the equation; now I was a further complication. It took me some time to get to sleep that night, wrestling with the problem of how I might bring my parents together again, and unable to understand why we couldn't all stay with Mother in the cottage in any case. My birthday, the next day was a sombre affair, not improved when Mother wanted to take a photo of me in my uniform and I, unkindly, refused.

"Oh Jess, you silly little fool!" : It was only much later that I understood, at least to some extent, what had been going on. Mother had begun an affair with Russ and while I was away had discovered that she was pregnant. She realized that she had to tell Father and unwisely (presumably led into a fantasy of unreal expectations by Russ) said that she and Russ intended to look after all their six joint children together—-not including me, of course. No mention was made of Doll's wishes in the matter. Father, naturally, was furious, and told her he must have custody of the children, which in those days the husband had the power to do, especially in the case of an erring wife. When Mother asked what was going to happen to them, he told her he would make arrangements for them to stay with his mother and sisters in Grimsby.

At some point after we had been packed off to Grimsby, Father went to see Mother in the cottage in order to settle matters. Apparently, his Commanding Officer relieved him of his side-arm (revolver) before he left the camp and gave him some cautionary advice about how he should conduct himself. There was, of course, no question of reconciliation, and by strange chance, just before Father arrived, a letter came for him and Mother read it, in case it was important, and found it was from one of the ATS (girls) in his camp. It was full of endearments and the hope that he would soon be back; (it seems he must have been up in Grimsby, prior to going down to the cottage and the letter had been sent on). Mother confronted Father with this letter when he arrived and it must have cooled him down a bit, but ever the consummate salesman, he managed to convince Mother it was for another Lieutenant Haynes at the camp, and she gave it to him! When she told her sister about this later, Aunt Chubbie rolled her eyes to heaven and exclaimed, "Oh Jess, you silly little fool!" Older and much more worldly-wise than Mother, she realized that the letter would have put Mother on a more equal level with Father in the divorce court.

Father always blamed the War for the break-up of the marriage, and undoubtedly it exacerbated the factors that tended to divide them. Apparently, during the meeting at the cottage, Father had bitterly remarked that Russ "Was only a sergeant." Mother took this as an example of his snobbery. This was unfair, because Mother had made no secret of her dislike of his promotion to officer rank, telling us children, "I liked it much better when he was a sergeant," which must have hurt his feelings. She clearly preferred to consort socially with 'other ranks' up at the RAF camp, despite the fact that when she forgot about 'class', she could happily converse at any level. (Mother was nothing if not contrary!) She was also dismissive of Father's pride in not having been unemployed during the Great Slump. Father wasn't snobbish, but he did think that someone who had had the benefit of a good school and a good university would probably be better fitted for certain positions in life.

As an 'ideas man' he believed in rewards for merit, and greatly approved of the American way of life, with its get-up-and-go and optimism. Before the War he had, rather ruefully, explained to me that he didn't have much time for reading after writing his reports in the evenings, and had caught up by reading the *Readers' Digest*, (that quintessential American publication). Quite a shelf-full built up at Slapton, and I read all of them too. Mother's approval was reserved for writers and artists, especially if they were 'good' men, on the side of the 'working-class' (as distinct from business men and Tories).

What may have been the precipitating factor was the death of Mother's father, Grand-dad Watson, the day after her own birthday the year before, on the 10th of September, 1943, and her legacy. She suggested to Father that she could use some of the money to go down and stay near him so they could spend time together. Father put her off and she suspected that there was an ulterior motive (another woman). Father then criticised her for spending the money entertaining her friends over in the Fox and Hounds Pub in Lillingstone Dayrell. Although Mother was usually most frugal with money, perhaps Father shouldn't have been surprised!

After this final meeting with Father, Mother auctioned off the household goods. It was at this time that Father's cups for boxing, swimming and tennis disappeared, and most of the books, though she preserved my diaries and school reports (as Ann and I discovered when we were sorting out her effects after her death). This drastic action must mean that she still hoped to get together with Russ. However, Father took some small revenge by getting his C.O. to contact the C.O. up at the RAF camp to have Russ transferred to another unit.

Interlude in Grimsby: We children travelled up to Grimsby some time in the middle of May. Mother came and put us on the train at Finmere station (near Tingewick, and then still open) and we went on alone up to London where we were met by Father's brother Charles and his wife Mabel. To our consternation, we found that Max (then nine years old) was to go and stay with them and not come with us. This upset him, and Ann began to cry as well. As she said later, she should have stayed with Uncle Charles and Mabel, because they had a daughter Pam near her own age, and Max should have come with me to stay with Grandmother. It appears that Father had made this arrangement because Charles had always wanted a son, but it didn't prove a very happy solution. We carried on up to Grimsby in a somewhat subdued state, but it was interesting to see the coloured strips of the bulb fields as we crossed the Holland district of South Lincolnshire, and exciting to reach Doncaster, our first experience of a northern industrial city, the rain and fog thickened by the smoke of the trains and the factories going hammer and tongs in the war effort.

We were met by our relations in Grimsby, and David went with Aunt Nora (Father's eldest sister) to go and stay with her and Uncle Bill, a trawler skipper, at 6, Garnet Street, Cleethorpes. She had two step-daughters and was happy to look after David and became very fond of him. She was a very good cook and he has always remembered her rhubarb tart and date slice. However, Uncle Bill proved a strict guardian. Just after David went to stay with them, they went out for the evening and he innocently asked them where they were going; and Uncle Bill angrily told him off, telling him he was lucky not to get the buckle-strap for being so cheeky! On the other hand he was kind, and David used to help him on his allotment and go down to the docks with him to get fish from some of his friends on other trawlers, because during this time he was suspended for fishing outside prescribed limits (like Grandfather in the Great War). They also cut up fish boxes to take round the neighbourhood for sale as firewood and Uncle Bill found him a Saturday job as a butcher's boy, riding round on a bike delivering joints for Sunday roasts from a big basket on the front. He took old bones to a local factory on the bike as well, a place that smelt much worse than the Fish Docks! (My strongest memory of Aunt Nora's house is of the big aspidistra in the bay window of the front parlour, associated in my mind with the north of England and the famous song of Gracie Fields.)

Ann and I went with Aunt Irene to stay with her and Grandmother at Wendover, 78, Clee Road, the house Grand-dad Haynes had bought newly built when he went back to deep-sea trawling in the Twenties, on the road out to Old Clee and Humberstone from Cleethorpes. Things were a little difficult for a while. Aunt Irene had been instrumental in introducing Father, her favourite brother, to Mother, and she was very critical of her behaviour. This made Ann cry, which started us all off and had the effect of bringing us together, and we got along very well afterwards (Grannie Haynes was particularly soft-hearted and kind). I had the back bedroom to myself. I could put my small set of nature books out on the window sill, which looked out over the recreation grounds, where there were often large flocks of gulls and also sheds, housing the donkeys ridden on the sands. These sometimes made a great clamour in the early morning and at night one occasionally heard the evocative sound of ship's sirens from the Humber. I was no longer keeping a diary but after a week or two I did transcribe some nature notes into a new notebook, including this entry:

> June 14th:"Having been moved up north owing to unfortunate circumstances shall endeavour to learn a few secrets of the sea-birds—-these never having fallen under my ken before. I have not been out into the country yet."

Shortly after we arrived, Father came home on leave, and as he had decided to get a divorce he took me with him to his solicitor's office to answer a few questions, because evidence of adultery was required in those days. Fortunately, or unfortunately from the solicitor's point of view, before I joined the *Mercury* I had only seen Mother and Russ engage in apparently innocent social and music making activities at the cottage, so I couldn't add anything to the case. The solicitor then put it to me that Mother had sent me off to the *Mercury* in order to pursue her affair; but I made it clear, although it looked like that and may have turned out to be very convenient for her, it had been my decision to go. This interview was a disagreeable experience, as it clearly was for Father, because he decided not to proceed with the divorce, probably influenced by Grandmother, who hoped that the two of them could be reconciled.

We now went to new schools: Ann, to Humberstone Girls' School, David and I to Humberstone Foundation School for Boys, both only a few hundred yards up Clee Road. David used to walk from Aunt Nora's house in Garnet Street and go with me. We were usually accompanied by a fair-haired boy called Kennington, who had an extremely rapid stride, difficult to keep up with. In after years, David and I would say, when one of us was walking very quickly, "Don't be like Kennington." He reminded us of the striding, red-jacketed figure on the side of the Force packet, a popular breakfast cereal at that time.

The headmaster of Humberstone Foundation School was an ex-colonel and ran it under a strict regime. When we changed classrooms we had to march along in order, without speaking, under the surveillance of prefects stationed at strategic points. This was no problem for me after the *Mercury,* but one lunch-time, I did get caught out. We were supposed to sit quietly in the dining hall, and were not allowed to talk to each other until the first course had been served to everyone; and the master in charge heard me whispering to my neighbour. He was a Welsh teacher, inevitably called Taffy. His accent reminded me of our teacher in the Latin School, "Any more tay (tea) on this table?" but I don't think the coincidence went as far as him teaching languages. He gave me an imposition for my misdemeanour: a hundred lines on, 'My Garden'. It so happened that one of my first jobs for Aunt Irene, had been to remove the weeds growing on the roof of the Anderson air-raid shelter in the back garden and plant out some annuals on it, which led me to write a light-hearted account to show that it wasn't a 'common or garden' affair. Taffy showed my lines round some of the other masters, so it did me a bit of good! The Anderson shelter was partly dug into the ground and the soil and subsoil removed were piled on the roof; we had to take refuge in it when we had a buzz-bomb (flying bomb) alert. These attacks began in June. When we arrived, Aunt Nora told David that they might have to wake him up if there was an alert in the night, to go into the air-raid shelter in their garden. When it first happened, it woke him up first and he had to wake them!

An encounter with the master who taught English to us in the fourth form was a little more fraught. He was known as Old Straw, and reputed to be 82 years old. He had been brought out of retirement because of the war-time teacher shortage. We were reading passages in turn from a Shakespeare play. When it came to my turn he let me go on for a while and then stopped me. He then went to the blackboard and wrote, "A bright light shone forth in the night." "Read that out," he said, so I did. "No, this is what you are saying," and he wrote on the board, "A broight loight shone forth in the noight," (to titters from the back of the class). After the class, some of the boys commiserated with me and said they thought he had been too hard on me, a view that many soft-hearted people have echoed since. I thank him for it. It was precisely the metaphorical kick up the backside I needed at that point in my life. I heard myself as others heard me for the first time and it wasn't long before I had a much better command of the King's (now Queen's) English; though no doubt an expert could divine my origins and history since. However, a certain irony did not escape me: to my ear the other lads would have said, "A brart lart shone forth in the nart"! I hasten to add that I have not entirely lost my 'heritage', and quite enjoy putting John Clares's poems into the vernacular, and my 'sense of identity' appears to be intact.

D-day (on the 6th of June, 1944) was only two or three weeks after we arrived in Grimsby. The morning we heard the announcement of the invasion of Europe, a group of us from my class were sitting on the grass in the playing field discussing this momentous event and then the conversation turned to another topic. One of the boys told us of his embarrassment when his mother had discovered that he had been indulging his sexual fantasies, from the state of the sheets on his bed, and we all quickly assured him he wasn't alone in this matter. In retrospect, it would seem that our thoughts took this turn because we were all very conscious that young men only a few years older that us, were going ashore on the beaches of Northern France, and that it might not be too long before we were called on to demonstrate our own manhood and virility.

We had Saturday morning classes with the afternoon off in Humberstone, and Wednesday afternoon off as well. David and I did a lot of sea swimming and went for long walks on the sands, south from the Humber mouth, as far as we could go in the time to look at sea birds. Uncle Bill took us both down to the docks and to see a late season football match, our first experience of the first-class game, when Grimsby played Hull, their arch enemies from across the Humber. At one point the referee made an unpopular decision and the crowd threw beer bottles onto the pitch (another good illustration of crowd behaviour for me). Uncle Bill also showed us a small reservoir near the Grimsby football ground where we could fish, and we also rode out on our bikes to fish in the dyke at Tetney Lock. We cycled out to Bradley Woods as well, but found that they were a poor substitute for 'Leafy Bucks'.

The end-of-year exams were held at the school early in July. I was in a difficult position with all the breaks since I was elevated into the fourth form at the Latin School the year before. However, our form master decided that although I'd only been in the class a few weeks I should do the exams. Without exercise books and sitting them 'cold' I did very poorly, but I did have one bit of luck. The history exam was on a Monday, and on the Friday afternoon I got hold of the textbook being used and read it over the weekend. I managed to get 72 percent, and was second in the class in that subject. This was the only reason I came second from bottom of the class, rather than bottom overall. When the form teacher discussed the results, I was held out as an example of someone who had made a sterling effort, unlike the boy actually at the bottom. It made me feel quite sorry for him, and I almost wished I had been bottom; at least I had a good excuse!

As I had now reached the school leaving age (15), I had to consider what to do. There didn't seem to be much point in staying on to study for the School Cert. considering how bad my results were. While I was mulling all this over, Grannie Watson wrote to me to say that Mother was in the Royal Bucks Hospital and wanted to see me, and that I could stay with her at 62, Fleet Street. So I packed up my few things, sent my bike on ahead and went down by train to Aylesbury.

After Russ had been posted to another unit, the affair petered out and Mother, having sold up, found refuge with her sister, Trix, who was divorced and lived with her young son Bobby in High Wycombe. In early July, her pregnancy ran into complications and as Aunt Trix went out to work Mother decided to go and stay with her mother, and went down on the bus to Aylesbury. Before she got there, her condition worsened and an ambulance had to be called to take her directly into the Royal Bucks.

When I went to see Mother in the hospital she looked very pale and wan, having lost the baby, but she brightened when she saw me, and showed me off to a fair girl in the next bed, who was in the same predicament as she was. During my next visits we discussed what I should do. She was going to stay with Grandmother to convalesce and I decided that meanwhile I would try and find a job doing farm work, because I was at least familiar with it. I wrote to my friend Arthur Jones in Dadford and asked him about the possibilities in the village. He wrote back and said that there was nothing going at Home Farm but that Tommy Osborne, up at Parkfields was short of labour, and that if I came down I could stay with them; so I made up my mind to go and went up to North Bucks with my things in the saddle bag of my bike. On arrival I enquired about a job at Parkfields and was taken on.

FARMER'S BOY

Problems at Parkfields: It is about a mile from Home Farm up to Parkfields and easy for me to go backwards and forwards on my bike, as well as slipping back to have lunch with the Jones family at midday (the midday meal still being the main meal of the day for ordinary people at that time). At first, although quite fit, I found the work arduous. It was still haymaking time and we were carrying hay by horse and cart from the fields to the stackyard. I couldn't match the ease of the seasoned labourers as they pitched up huge forkfuls onto the cart, for hour after hour in the summer heat. We also carried off a crop of flax that had been grown for linseed oil. The sheaves were small but their heads tended to intertwine and mat together, so you found yourself pitching up the whole shock (stook). I think my early difficulties led Tommy Osborne to think I was somewhat dilatory. This became evident early one evening, when instead of going back to Dadford for tea before returning to work late, I was invited into the farm kitchen to have some tea by his daughter. He had been away somewhere on business, and when he came back and found me there, he exclaimed, "What the hell are you doing here, feeding your face when you should be out working!" (Perhaps he thought I had designs on his daughter; she was attractive but three or four years older that me and I had no such ambitions.)

One morning, I was put to work shocking-up (setting up in stooks) a crop of oats that had been cut by the reaper and binder into sheaves. I was working with Cecil Jones, Tommy Osborne's right-hand man, a dark, quietly serious, very steady worker. (Not related to the Jones family I was staying with, he and his wife Sue had five children, all dark and hazel eyed. The oldest, Betty, who as I mentioned earlier had won a scholarship to the Latin School, but her parents had felt unable to afford to let her take it up; then two boys, Arthur, namesake of my friend in Dadford, and Edwin, both of them worked at Woodlands later; another daughter Rosemary, and the youngest child, Johnny, who was friendly with Max and our cousin Jeremy at Dadford School. They lived in the cottage at the entrance to Parkfields).

Soon after we started work, Mr. Jones had to tell me not to, "go at it like a bull at a gate," otherwise I'd never last all day. Another problem was that I was wearing shorts (as boys did then up to fifteen or sixteen); a mistake because although oats are soft compared to wheat, with its hard ears, and barley, with its scratching awns, I kept getting grains and straws in my boots. We had just reached the end of a row and before turning to go back along the field, I sat on the ground to empty them out. To my amazement, Tommy Osborne suddenly leapt up from behind the hedge and shouted, "I've been keeping my eye on you, you lazy young bugger. If you don't work harder I'll have to get rid of you!" With that he stomped off. We just carried on, neither of us saying anything.

I suppose it should have been clear to me by then that I was going nowhere up at Parkfields, but I carried on until one afternoon, Tommy Osborne asked me to cycle straight into Buckingham the following morning, and pick up a small piece of equipment from the blacksmith's. It was required for the elevator which had to stand idle until it had been mended. Elevators, in common use then, were mechanical escalators with spikes, to carry hay, straw or sheaves up onto ricks as they became higher, powered by a small diesel engine via a belt; thus saving a good deal of hand labour. I set off for the blacksmith's immediately after breakfast the next day, but I was kept hanging about and it was almost midday when they finally finished mending it. On the way back, as it was dinnertime, I snatched a quick bite as I passed Home Farm in Dadford, before going on. When I got to Parkfields, Tommy Osborne was waiting for me in high dudgeon. "Where the hell have you been? I phoned up and they said they'd got it ready hours ago!" This was gross exaggeration and I was struck speechless. Then he said, "If I wasn't so short handed, I'd sack you now!" This was too much, even for me, with my slow burning fuse. "Right" I said, "If that's the way you feel about it, I'm going now," and I walked off, got my bike and pedalled away down the lane. Before I got to his top gate, he came after me in his car and quietly paid me off, with just a hint of contrition. (I would have been getting about sixpence an hour.)

After this debacle, I went and found a job at Woodlands with my Uncle Chub. When I told him what had happened at Parkfields, he laughed, and said, "Tommy Osborne always was something of a slave-driver." Thinking it over now, it seems to me that I must have acted as a kind of lightning conductor for this propensity. It was a useful lesson that you can't expect to get on with everyone in this life. There are occasions, quite rare in my case, where on meeting someone, an immediate intuitive and visceral reaction indicates that you should part company and take care not to meet again. In the reverse case, being rather slow at 'reading' other people, I have often been puzzled by their reactions, only belatedly realizing that from the outset, they just didn't like the cut of my jib.

For balance, and to show how differently people can behave with different people, here is Tim White's description of an evening spent with Tommy Osborne, after they had been arguing about the best way to recapture his hawk, Gos:

"After a brief wrangle we proclaimed peace with honour: the company had arrived; and the rest of the evening was a symposium of this inimitable host's quite inimitable stories about arson, murder and fire in the surrounding villages for the last forty years. Mrs Osborne sat in one corner telling Tom not to shout, the rest of us egged him on, and he, carried away by the fury of his discourse, overset his chair and whirled an imaginary fox above his head, in the effort to convey the smallest particle of excitement which had prevailed when Frank Ayres of Chackmore took a living fox from the trap with his bare hands in 1900. If God, or any other observer, momentarily regretted the obliteration of our race in the near future, it would be on account of a few families." (See note 5.)

Though perhaps this does show that the temperament of the man was all of a piece!

Better days at Woodlands: Like most farms in the area, Blackpit and Woodlands were mixed farms in those days. Chub had a herd of about thirty milking cows, mostly red, dairy shorthorns, and his own bull. There was also a small flock of sheep and he had a number of pigs, while Aunt Chubbie looked after the flock of hens. At this stage of the War, an increasing acreage was being put to the plough, chiefly for wheat and oats, as well as for swedes, mangolds and kale for animal feed. Although he had a tractor, considerable use was still being made of horses for pulling carts, cutting machines, hay rakes and tedders, and for harrowing. He was lucky in the complementary interests of his two sons, Robert in the machinery that was increasingly coming into use, and Graham in the cattle and sheep; and also in the fact that although both of them wanted to join the Forces like their elder brother, they were firmly kept on the farm in a 'reserved occupation'.

When I started at Woodlands they were well into the corn harvest, which I always preferred to the heavier work of haymaking that generally took place during the hottest and longest days of the year in June and July. The corn was cut with the reaper and binder, the wooden sails going round, stroking the corn against the cutting blades, the sheaves then being ejected from the side, tied up with binder-twine. It was surprising how quickly it would be known that reaping had progressed to where only a small block remained uncut, as a shelter for animals that had been hiding in the corn. Boys with sticks would turn up, and sportsmen with guns, stationing themselves at strategic points hoping to 'knock over a bunny or two'. If there was a fox in the corn it would usually be wily enough to come out at an early stage, a red streak into the woods, and sometimes there was even a roe-deer, but most of the rabbits and occasional hares would wait until the last possible moment, providing good sport. After the corn was cut, the sheaves were set up in shocks (stooks) to dry out before being carted off and built into ricks, to await the advent of the threshing box later in the year. Shocking-up was a job that I liked, and I quite enjoyed doing it on my own. One afternoon my cousin Graham put me to work in the big field west of Point Copse. It was one of those days of high, silvery-gray cloud, and blue, unfathomable distances. One soon got into a rhythm: so many steps out, picking up two sheaves, and back to set them up firmly in the stubble with their heads together, adding two more pairs to make a tent-like structure, then another pair, one at each end for stability; so on down the field, making sure the shocks were in line; the pleasurable physical monotony of the work releasing the mind into a dream-like state. When Graham came to tell me to come for tea, he was quite impressed with the military precision of my rows (as he told me, many years later).

Working at the cart was also pleasurable, once I got over my attempt to keep up with my cousins who could fork up two or three sheaves at a time, and took it steadily, remembering Cecil Jones' advice! This was necessary, because we were then on 'double summertime' and worked late into the evenings; often well into the twilight and the play of summer lightning along the line of the Chilterns to the south. I also made a better fist of building the load when I was on the cart, than I could with the more difficult job of building a stable load of hay. When we were working on a corn rick, and I was put to fork the sheaves to the man building the rick as they came off the elevator, I was always amused to see that however well you placed them for him, he would always lift them up and put them down again, even if only in the same position, placing them was his prerogative. Rick building was a skilled job, because a stable, four–square or round structure had to be built, and then thatched, to stand the weather until the threshing box came on its rounds, which could mean several months.

Shortly after I started at Woodlands, my aunt suggested that I stay with them, which saved all the biking up and down from the village. It meant that I could help my cousin Graham, get the cows in to be milked and with other small jobs, before breakfast, though I didn't learn to milk at this particular time. (Milking the cows twice a day, of course, had to continue at the height of harvesting.) The milk was taken in churns up to the top gate to await the milk lorry. This was done after breakfast when the milk had been passed through the cooler. I enjoyed that, going with Graham in the milk float, drawn by a black gelding, usually coming back at a spanking trot. Aunt Chubbie was a good cook and we had substantial breakfasts, but one morning she saw me picking in a desultory way at a boiled egg. When I admitted that it was bad, she wagged her finger at me and said, "You mustn't be like that John, you mustn't be afraid to complain. I can easily boil you another!" I have to admit I never did quite grow out of the misguided tendency to try and enjoy curates' eggs.

When the harvest was finished and as the season progressed, we were busy with threshing and I found myself at my usual task of chaff carrying, but in October, with the more labour intensive part of the year at an end, only odd jobs could be found for me, and it was suggested that I might like the job that was going on Tile House Farm, where Mr Edrich ('Bill Senior') wanted a lad to train as tractor driver and ploughman. However, at the same time, Mother wrote to say that Aunt Kit (her husband Tom away in the Navy) had offered to let her share her house and that Ann, David and Max were to join her in Abbey Road, and that I might like to come too, and get another job there. I decided I would go, and once again, rather regretfully, left Stowe Woods and pedalled off on my bike down to Aylesbury. It seems that the two Grandmothers had been making efforts to bring Father and Mother back together and that Aunt Kit hoped to expedite this by offering Mother a home. This was very good of her, considering that she had a young daughter of her own (Vicky aged about two and a half). It meant that we three boys shared a bedroom while Mother had to sleep on the sofa; a houseful when Uncle Tom was on leave.

As Mother and Father were already in touch, when I was back in Aylesbury I decided to go and see him to discuss my future. This was made easier than it might have been because, after his promotion to Captain, he had been posted to a battery stationed in Richmond Park in London. He invited me to come and stay on the gun-site, so I went up by train and walked to it across the Park. On the way, only a couple of hundred yards from the camp there was a very large bomb crater, which Father explained to me later, had been made by one of the new V-2 rockets only a week or two before. The V-2 attacks had started in

September as a follow up to the Doodle-bugs, both continuing into 1945, when the launch sites were finally over-run by our troops. During this time there were two to three a week in the London area alone and a total of about 9000 casualties and seriously injured.

Father allowed me the use of his room while he occupied other quarters, so I had the novel experience of being served tea in bed first thing next morning by his batman, as well as joining him for meals in the Officers' Mess. He showed me the predictors and the guns and we went for a walk through the Park for a long talk about my future. He strongly advised me to go back to school, pointing out that if I did well I would be able to get a better job, and perhaps, even go on to a training college and become a teacher. In retrospect, he said, he would like to have done that himself and been a games and geography master, and he added "Think of all the time you'll have to do all those things you like doing, like bird watching and nature study." (It is only while writing about this visit to see Father, that I have suddenly realized that just as his favourite subject in school was geography, so it was of my brother David, and, of course, one of mine—-very apposite, considering the ancestral necessity of knowing all those capes and bays!)

While I occupied Father's room at the camp, I was encouraged to see he had a framed photograph of Mother by his bed, and there were further signs of a thaw when Mother, together with Ann visited him in London. I think he may then have written to George Furneaux, the head of Aylesbury Grammar School about us. He had been very friendly with Harry Deeming, the English master, since his own schooldays. Also, I have realized since reading Paul Poornan's book on the Royal Latin School that Charles Foster had previously been senior science master in A.G.S., and this probably expedited matters. Certainly, David, Ann and I were accepted as pupils without any trouble and began attendance there in the November; we were after all, Aylesbury born and mainly Bucks educated. It was rather lucky that Father had been stationed relatively close at hand at this juncture. Shortly afterwards he was promoted to Major and put in command of a battery in County Durham, which would have been much more difficult to visit.

SOURCES/NOTES—-CHAPTER EIGHT

1) The extracts quoted are from letters from old *Mercury* boys that were published in the Sunday Telegraph on July 21st 1985 in response to the publication of a summarized version of Ronald Morris's book on Beattie Fry and the *Mercury* (see below) published in the same paper on July 15[th.] The quote from Mrs Fry is from the letter sent out to the parents before we joined the Ship.

2) The *Gannet* was built in 1878 at Sheerness, one of the Osprey/Dotterel Class of operational sloops, introduced in 1875, to patrol distant waters of the British Empire and help enforce the Pax Britannica through 'gun-boat' diplomacy. This class was between the lightly armed earlier sloops and a colonial cruiser, with a complement of up to 200 men, and entitled to fly a Commander's pennant; the officer in command being considered to rank between the Lieutenant of a 'gun-boat' and the Captain of a corvette. Because it was designed for a global role and to be capable of operating over long distances for long

periods, the construction was such that the ship's carpenter and the crew could make essential repairs while at sea. She was 190ft long overall, 36ft in the beam, with 1130 tons displacement, capable of 15 knots under sail and 12 knots steaming (expedited by a collapsible funnel). She was also one of the last naval ships with a carved figure-head. Her armaments on the main deck comprised 2x7ins muzzle loading rifled guns, and 4x64 pounders.

The *Gannet* was given four major commissions between 1878-95: first, on the Pacific station, where she shadowed the 'Nitrate War' between Chile and Peru; secondly, on the Mediterranean station (Malta) on anti-slavery patrol off the Sudan coast of the Red Sea, during which she played a vital role in breaking the siege of Suakin; thirdly, at Malta, surveying the Mediterranean; and fourthly, again at Malta doing hydrographic work in both the Mediterranean and in the Red Sea. (Ironically, when I joined the ship it had been in the hope of eventually doing this type of work.)

After *Gannet* ceased active service she was converted to become the headquarters and drill ship of the RNVR (Royal Naval Volunteer Reserve) and renamed the *President,* served in this capacity from 1903 to1911 at the West India Docks. She was then replaced herself and eventually acquired by C.B. Fry in 1913, after the intervention of Churchill. (It was because the *Gannet* was entitled to fly a Commander's pennant that C.B. then became Commander Fry.)

The training school was closed in 1968, and in 1971, ownership was transferred to the Maritime Trust and she was moored at Gosport until she was finally towed to Chatham Historic Dockyard in 1987, by the Alexander tug *Formidable,* to be restored to the condition she was in at the time she helped lift the siege of Suakin, a hundred years before. (I have obtained most of these facts from the Chatham Historic Dockyard website.)

3) The remarkable story of C.B. and Mrs Fry and the history of the *Mercury* are well told in the following books:
Morris, R. 1985, *The Captain's Lady.* Chatto & Windus. The Hogarth Press.
Wilton, I. 2002, *C.B. Fry: King of Sport* 500 pages Metro Publishing, London.

To summarize these interesting accounts: Mrs Fry (Beatrice Holme Sumner 1862-1946) had aristocratic connections and was, indeed, connected with the Danish Royal House. Her father was Master of the Cotswold Hunt, but was perennially short of money, and she was brought up without any formal schooling, becoming a passionate rider to hounds and Honorary Whip to the Duke of Beaufort's Hunt (and the subject of a painting by G. F. Watts). She had a wild, ungovernable character in adolescence and fell in love at fifteen with the already married Charles Hoare, Master of the adjacent Vale of White Horse Hunt. Charles Hoare was the rich heir to the banking family of that name and had similarly avoided formal schooling and spent most of his time riding and sailing; he owned a number of yachts down at Exmouth, in which he trained some of the local boys.

 The association between these two became a scandal when riding near Charles' home in the aftermath of a hunt, Beattie engineered a 'fall' and spent several days in bed there (despite the presence of Charles' wife). The families did everything to separate the couple, and won a court injunction in 1881, which prevented Charles from making any contact with her, although they still managed to keep contact by letter. When she was 21, and the law could no longer prevent it, Beattie boldly went and lived openly him after becoming pregnant. Charles was then prosecuted in the Court of Chancery for disobeying the injunction and faced a prison sentence, but more or less got off, simply having to pay costs. (It didn't help the Sumner parents' case that while this was going on they had borrowed money from him!)

This major Victorian scandal led to attempts to remove Charles from his position as Master of the Vale of White Horse Hunt, which was finally split into two between his supporters, most of the tenant farmers, and his opponents, most of the landed gentry (this split lasted beyond the end of the century!) Excluded from polite society, Charles and Beattie now put all their energies into building on his experience in training young lads on his yachts down at Exmouth. He bought the 400 ton barque *Ilovo* and the schooner *Diane,* together with a number of small boats and set up the training ship *Mercury* to prepare boys for the Royal Navy, initially on the Isle of Wight but moving to the Hamble in 1892 because it had a more sheltered anchorage.

The emphasis was on practical skills, physical fitness and sailing. This suited Beattie, with her bold, adventurous spirit, and she took to it immediately, dressing the same as the lads, hair cut short and bare-foot at all times, showing them the way at rowing, sailing and fearlessly climbing the rigging. She also became very interested in music and when they took on James McGavin, a carpenter who proved to be an exceptional music teacher, the tradition of fine music on the *Mercury* began. This interest led the couple to visit Bayreuth to attend a performance of *Parsifal* (with its theme of redemption through suffering) which appears to have triggered a spiritual awakening. On their return, Beattie sold all her jewellery in order to have a replica of Wagner's theatre built in the grounds, and they both became seriously religious, leading Charles to build the chapel. It also led Charles to start living separately from Beattie, twenty miles away at West Meon, leaving the day-to-day running of the Ship to her. In this way, it seems, they began to try and make amends for the damage their behaviour had done to their families and to society.

Although now living separately from Beattie, Charles retained general oversight over the *Mercury* and often invited famous sportsmen down to play with the boys. About 1895, this included W. G. Grace and C. B. Fry. As Beattie put it in her diary "Charles Fry came to play cricket today. I like Fry". This led to a romance that Charles Hoare appears to have encouraged, thinking it in Beattie's best interests, and they were married in 1898.
C. B. Fry was one of the best, if not the best, all round sportsmen Britain has ever produced. In his first year (1891) in the freshman sports at Wadham College, Oxford, he won the 100yds, the 120yds hurdles, the long jump and the high jump; together with the hammer and the shot-put in the Wadham sports later. He also set up a British record in the long jump in the Varsity sports, finally equalling the World record in his third year. He also excelled in games, becoming a 'triple blue' in cricket, football and rugby, and played football as an amateur for England against Canada and Ireland. After leaving Oxford, Fry played football for the Corinthians and Southampton, appearing in their F.A. Cup final

against Sheffield United. However, he became most famous as a cricketer, especially for his partnerships with Ranjitsinhji, when playing for Sussex and England, as well as for his cricketing journalism and classic book on the art of batting. To cap all this, his friend and contemporary at Wadham, F. E. Smith (later Lord Birkenhead) described him as "a Greek God, so beautiful in face and body that he might have been wrought by the chisel of Praxiteles".

At the beginning of the marriage, while Charles Hoare was still in charge of the *Mercury*, C. B. Fry's role was largely confined to coaching the various sports, but when Charles Hoare died in 1908, and the future of the *Mercury* was in doubt, he worked through his friends in high places to secure the Ship's financial security. His petition to the High Court, to establish a school governing body with a scheme of operation, was accepted, and with all his contacts, he was also able to raise enough money from various sources to make it an educational charity. His sporting prowess made him the obvious man to run it, and he became Captain Superintendent. However, his role was largely administrative and financial, with Beattie taking over the practical side. This arrangement proved very successful, the trainees winning the approval of the Admiralty, leading to the acquisition of a new ship by the time of the Great War; also to Beattie's O.B.E. and C. B.' s honorary title of 'Commander'.

After the Great War, although still retaining administrative and financial oversight, C. B. became very busy with sports journalism and increasingly involved with politics, three times running unsuccessfully for Parliament; also serving on the Finance Committee of the League of Nations with his friend and batting partner Ranjitsinhji (which led to him being offered the vacant throne of Albania!). Beattie was thus left effectively in charge of running the Ship. However, although there has been much controversy about C.B.' s exact role on the *Mercury* it is clear that without his intervention it would otherwise have foundered on the death of Charles Hoare.

4) Later in the century, in the age of sentimental kindness, flower power and Greenham Common, it became fashionable to denigrate their iconic achievement, as in the notorious book by Roland Huntford, where Scott is portrayed as someone who couldn't do anything right, and emblematic of the entire 'officer class' responsible for the decline of the British Empire! In particular, Scott was criticized for not using dogs and skis, which ignores the fact that his route through the high Antarctic mountains meant that man-hauling was more dependable and the preferred option.

5) Pages 169-170 in *The Goshawk* by T.H. White, Jonathan Cape. London. (1951)

CHAPTER NINE

AYLESBURY 1944-46

AYLESBURY GRAMMAR SCHOOL

A schoolboy again: Once we were all back together with Mother and staying at Aunt Kit's in 82, Abbey Road, Ann, David and I began to attend the Grammar School, and Max started in Queens Park Junior Council School (which I had attended in the 1930s, as had Mother in the 1920s). The Grammar School in Walton Road was the same red brick, Edwardian building (opened in 1907) where Father had enjoyed all the sports, but chemistry and the firm discipline of the headmaster, Thomas Osborne, rather less. At the time we attended it was still a mixed school, with about 450 boys and girls, each group using a separate entrance and cloakrooms at either end. The headmaster's house was in a large garden on the right. As Father had been in Ridley House we were all enrolled in it too. The other Houses were Denson, Hampden and Phillips (after former patrons and benefactors, and also having a historical resonance, see note 1).

The headmaster in our time was George Furneaux (incumbent 1927-1951), a most pleasant and amiable man, who, like all good headmasters, had the secret of firm but relaxed discipline. There was a cane in a glass case in his study but I don't think it was used during my time in the school. It was simply there as the ultimate deterrent—none the less effective for that. The photo (9-1 top) shows the twenty teachers in post. Mr. Furneaux is seated in the centre, with his wife to his left and the senior mistress and history teacher, Miss E.R. Stewart, to his right. Miss Stewart, Mr. Deeming, Miss Avery and Mr. Lloyd-Jones were to have a particular influence on me.

It was now well into November, and a year since I'd been briefly in the Fifth Form in the Latin School. I had some catching up to do; made more difficult because I had missed a term of third year work and most of the fourth year work after that. However, things were made easier in that the Fifth Form pupils (School Cert. year) in AGS were split into a classics/languages stream, a physics and maths/science stream and a 'modern' stream for those not shining in either languages or mathematical sciences and presumed destined for a 'commercial' occupation. Geography and general science were central subjects for the modern stream. We had taken general science in Buckingham, and as I was now well behind in Latin, while geography was one of my best subjects, it was logical for me for me to be placed in this group. Fortunately, this group were taught history; and also biology, both as a separate subject, and as part of general science. This 'double dose' of biology played well to my preference for it amongst the sciences. Although I now gave up Latin, which caused some difficulties later, I was able to continue doing French.

Another fortunate circumstance was that shortly after I entered the class I was put to share a textbook with a fair-haired, lanky boy with a prominent nose, known as 'Percy'

(John George Packer). He was equally keen on natural history and we quickly became great friends, which tended to reinforce this interest. Percy, whose father was an instructor in the R.A.F. camp at Halton, near Wendover, also had a younger brother, David and an older sister, Dawn. Percy was an ebullient, out-going character, ready to speak his mind, unlike me who usually thought twice (or three times) before saying what I really thought. In this way, as in the difference in colouring between us, we were a foil for each other. Percy was slightly short-sighted and this produced some amusing, if heart-stopping moments on the rugby field. He was a good player (and became vice-captain of the school team) but without his glasses, especially when he was playing at full-back, he would really take his time peering up to focus on the high ball, tossing back his floppy hair before catching it. Then, always it seemed at the very last moment, almost languidly kicking the ball into touch, before going down under the rush of the opposing forwards.

Quite soon in our friendship, Percy coined the nickname, 'Hainoff' for me, deciding that I looked like a Russian (see photo 9-1 bottom). A little while later, another friend, Jim Symon, added the soubriquet, 'Joseph' to complete the transmogrification; not I hoped, because they thought I had a resemblance to Uncle Joe Stalin! The nick-name 'Joseph' or 'Joe' was to prove long-lasting, because of the large numbers of Johns in our age group.

Football was not played at the Grammar School, being replaced by rugby in the autumn term, the soft season, and by hockey in the Lent term, when the ground tended to be harder. This arrangement was considered safer, though one has to say that the ball flew most dangerously from end to end in some hockey matches when the pitch was frost-bound. Starting in school late in November, I missed playing any rugby, but had my introduction to hockey in the following Lent term (1945). As I didn't know how to play, I was put in goal for the first few games (in at the deep-end). I didn't do too badly and made a few good saves but gave away too many fouls by not knowing the rules. I was then allowed to play at left inside and I did well enough to go with the Second Eleven to play against a school in Oxford, where by pure luck, I happened to score the only goal! As it happened, I was never to play hockey again after that match.

Photographs 9-1 Aylesbury Grammar School

Top -: Staff teaching at Aylesbury Grammar School in 1946: The headmaster G.P.Furneaux sitting in the centre, his wife to his left and the senior mistress, Miss E.R. Stewart to his right. From the left in this row are Miss Simmonds (Domestic Science) and Miss Murray (Junior Maths) and from the right, Miss Taffs (Form 1) and Miss Langham (Latin and PT). The deputy head, Mr. Harry ('Dickie') Deeming is standing behind Mr. Furneaux and the art master, Mr. W. Harrison, is standing on the extreme left of this row. Miss J. K. Avery, the botany mistress is third right and Mr. R. Lloyd-Jones ('LJ'), the geography master, on the extreme right. The music teacher, Mr. C.A.G. Pope is immediately behind Mr. Deeming in the back row, with Mr. C.A.B. ('Cab') Bartlett to his right, and the French teacher, Mr. C.G.S. Furley, second to his right.

Bottom -: The A.G.S. Biological Society field trip to Hayling Island in June 1946: second left G. D. Ramsden, third left, 'Percy'= J. G. Packer, with his hand on my shoulder, and looking between us is Den Paton. Margaret Tucker is to my right and 'Cab' the zoology master is looking over my right shoulder. Unfortunately, I can remember the faces but not the names of the other girls, except Pat Clarke, second from the left. Miss Avery is just managing to peep over all the heads to the right of Margaret Tucker.

The relaxed atmosphere in the school and my growing friendship with Percy enabled me to settle down quite quickly and in the New Year I began to do reasonably well, though I never really picked up again in French, and after the disappointment of my ambition to become a navigating officer I lost way in maths and never did so well as previously. On the other hand, I took to the history teacher, Miss Stewart, a graduate from Edinburgh, who was always very kind to me, and to Maurice Severn, who taught geography before the arrival of Mr. Lloyd-Jones, and also to the biology lessons taken by 'Cab' Bartlett, who, it is rather poignant to recall, considering that he had an albino daughter, explained to us the intricacies of genetics.

Learning to write: Amongst my new teachers, Harry Deeming was the major influence on me at that time in the Fifth Form. He was an excellent English teacher, who had, of course, taught my father, and he took a kindly, very concerned interest in me. However, things didn't go too well to begin with. He gave us a home-work composition (essay) to write, from the limited choice offered in a previous School Cert. examination paper. I chose the only one I thought could do anything with: rubber planting in Malaya. I had no references to consult and I tried to write something from what I could remember from past reading, turning in a very poor effort, made worse by my total lack of feeling for the subject. Unusually for me by that time, there were lapses of grammar and a number of spelling mistakes, made painfully obvious to me when it came back heavily loaded with corrections made in red ink. I think I scored something like 3c-, and as I had already started to write 'nature notes' with some pretension to a literary style while up in Grimsby, I was highly mortified and resolved to do better in the future.

The following week, the choice included a topic on foxhunting, which gave me the chance to do so, because I had rehearsed the arguments for and against years before and also witnessed many hunts, especially when hounds were drawing Stowe Woods. My marks now improved to 2b+. Only the last page of this essay survives, but a sentence in my 'corrections' reads "A jay, that sentinel of the woods, broke the silence of the morning with loud harsh cries, like the brisk tearing of linen." After this, in reference to the simile, 'like the brisk tearing of linen', I had added, "horrible plagiarism—-see Tarka the Otter". So I was already aware of the dangers of over-reliance on the style of my favourite authors!

In the following spring term (1945) the first assignment included the topic, 'Fish and Fishing'. This appealed greatly to me, as it did to my friend Percy. We had both discovered Isaak Walton and I already possessed the book with a similar title by Negley Farson called *Going Fishing,* so I wrote quite a lengthy article; but to make it more dramatic, made it an imaginative account of fly fishing, rather than writing out of my own experience of coarse fishing. Nevertheless, despite its heavily derivative character, the piece showed that my writing and attitudes were developing rapidly at this time.

Mr Deeming considered this essay "Very good work", deciding that it already showed that I was "developing a style of my own", and gave me 1b for it. He had me read it out in class, and asked a few questions to make sure I understood all that I was writing about. One query concerned the Ephemeridae, and I was able to enlarge upon the ephemeral lives of the Mayfly and its relatives, entirely to his satisfaction. One thing he said stayed in my mind: he recommended to the class my sparing use of adjectives. What the essay also shows is that I had no trouble in recognizing that fish were intelligent and experienced pain and fear; also, that along with environmental concerns, I was beginning to have mixed feelings about fishing, except for the pot.

With this encouragement I went on to do quite well in writing assignments during the period up to the School Cert., generally scoring 1b or 1b+. He had me read a couple of these out to the class as well, and remarked that there were a number of magazines that would be glad to publish them. This sparked my ambition and after the School Cert. exams, I made a serious effort to bring this idea to fruition. Meanwhile Percy and I spurred each other on with our readings of nature writers. We scoured the second-hand bookshops both in Oxford and Aylesbury (Blackwells, and especially Weatherheads) for old copies of Jefferies and Hudson, and any new book by Williamson was keenly anticipated. As our funds were limited we would try not to duplicate our purchases; for instance, Percy bought *The Story of a Norfolk Farm,* where-as I bought *The Sun in the Sands.* I would also try and get hold of a copy of the *Evening Standard,* on my way home from school through Kingsbury Square, in case there was a Williamson nature article in it; and I made a collection of cuttings of nature articles by writers like Frances Pitt, Austin Hatton and F.G. Turnbull to help in seeing what kind of article was acceptable to the editors.

The Lure of Stowe Woods: After going back to live in Aylesbury, I lost no time in making regular trips back to Stowe, sometimes for the day and sometimes for the weekend, sleeping out in the woods as formerly; and I quickly introduced my new friend, Percy, to the delights of Stowe and Stowe Woods. As the entry for March 3rd puts it:

"During these last three months since Christmas I have been three or four times rambling. I have come to the conclusion it would be as well to continue my nature notes. It was tolerably fine last Saturday, so I decided to take a bus over to Stowe. I have recently made acquaintance with another fellow interested in natural history, Packer, who accompanied me.

"Stowe Avenue was full of activity. Some weeks ago the hedges rang with mating quarrels. These seem to have been sorted out satisfactorily. The Great Tits were the chief participants. Grey Squirrels were active. Rooks were well away with nest building and a Tree Creeper attracted our attention near Chackmore as it searched for early insects in the silver-grey bole of a beech.

"Ascending the track to the Corinthian Arch we surprised a Nuthatch. While watching it a strange finch-like bird flew into our range of vision. As it flew away from us we could see its white rump and olive back. The breast was rose-pink and under-parts white. It may have been a Hawfinch." (This was probably an immature cock Bullfinch.) "Jackdaws were inspecting nesting sites in the Arch as we passed and the bushes round New Inn Farm rippled with the liquid songs of Robins. There were still a few chaffinches flocking. A pussy willow was a pyramid of sulphur bloom by the old toll gate.

"We tramped past Stowe Lakes towards Lamport Lodges by the old Armoury; this is a strange Gothic looking building. Its walls were almost orange in the sunlight. Near Stowe School's museum are various beautiful pines, Douglas fir, Monkey puzzle, Sequea (sic) and spruce. Near the old music room is one of the finest Scotch Pines I have ever seen.

"Crossing Woody Park we made for Blackpit and Woodlands and tarried a little by the pond at the lower end of the Valley riding. It was here a week or so ago, that I found a squirrel in a snare. The wire was pulled tight round its belly. Needless to say, I released it. It yikkered in anger and tried to bite me as I took the wire apart.

"We continued round Four-some Oak to the Lake. The nuptial rites of the coot and moorhen tribes are already in full swing. Loud chitterings and splashes echoed among the wind-blown reeds as we watched. We disturbed Old Nog as he fished by the lakeside. With heavy lumbering flight he winged his ponderous way over the swaying willows. Over the fallow the lapwings were crying as they wheeled and seemed to drop like leaves over the old summer's stubble. We could hear the wind protesting in their stiff pinions. Pee-e-o-weet! Their plaintive cries followed us away into the budding woods.

"We had tea at Woodlands. Uncle Chub made his usual jokes. We had a look at some of Tim White's bird books. Among these books is Williamson's *Starborn;* in colloquiell (sic) language—I think this is 'darn good'."

One of the reasons for spending the day or a whole weekend over at Stowe, apart from nostalgia for my former life in Stowe Woods, was, probably, our rather crowded life at 82, Abbey Road, where my Mother and Aunt Kit had to deal with five children, four of school age and our young cousin Vicky who was a very active toddler (out of the front gate whenever it was possible). When the Easter holidays came that year, and just before my sixteenth birthday, I took the opportunity to make two visits, camping overnight in one of my quickly assembled bivouacs.

8 to 10/4/45: "I went over to Woodlands. Crossing Woody Park a stoat almost ran up to me. So intent was the bloodthirsty animal on the trail of its unfortunate prey that it heeded me not at all. It climbed like a squirrel up a fence covered with wire and leapt a clear four feet to the ground, disappearing into the undergrowth.

"Near my camp (in Stowe Woods) I was interested to notice a hawk sail into the wood. While cutting logs I heard a commotion: a rook was being attacked by two sparrow hawks. Creeping through the wood I spied their nest quite high in a tree. It may be an abandoned crow's nest rebuilt. The birds, which stood over the nest, flew away with sharp cries, Ki-ki-ki, on my approach. I did not molest their building operations.

"When I awoke in the early morning, I amused myself by identifying birds by their song. I had no difficulty with Carrion Crow, a sonorous croak, and my two nesting hawks. The others were: Robin, Skylark, Nightingale, Jay, Yellow-hammer, Willow Wren, Ring Dove, Yaffingale (Green Woodpecker); also by sight: Pheasant, Partridge, Blue Tit, Blackbird, Great Tit, Bottle Tit (Long Tailed), Song Thrush, Marsh Tit, Cole Tit, Little Owl, Wren."

By this time I was becoming quite skilled at identifying birds by their song. Indeed, in the woods it was the best way to do it. (I continued to improve into early manhood and then with less practise and gradual hearing loss my skill declined, to my great regret.) A week later, during a period of very good weather, I spent another four days in the woods:

20/4/45: "This date marks the end of a camping trip. The cuckoo was heard in the locality as early as the 15th, I didn't hear it until the 17th. Nightingales were very numerous (and in full song) in the thick copses. I foolishly left my cheese on a plate one night. It disappeared. The next day while resting in camp, I noticed two wood-mice scuttle into my bread bin. These little creatures grew very bold, coming even when I moved about in camp. On the 18th a large cock pheasant walked in a half circle right round my bivouac (in the early dawn just after I woke up). Fifty yards from my camp was a Kestrel's nest. All day long the male patrolled the area round the nest, driving all alien birds away."

I should, perhaps, point out that there was no serious game-keeping on the Tile House Estate at this time of the War and John Robarts (the Squire) had it seems, little interest in shooting. This will explain the number of predators and, indeed, how (with my uncle's permission) I was able to enjoy the freedom of the woods in the way I did.

VE (Victory in Europe) Day: A few weeks after my sixteenth birthday the long struggle to liberate Europe finally came to an end with the surrender of the German military leaders to the Allied commanders. There was a tremendous and overwhelming sense of relief and in the evening of May 8th large numbers of people poured into the Old Market Square in Aylesbury to celebrate, David and me amongst them, with many of our school friends. One teenage boy was so carried away with excitement that he hurled a thunder-flash into the crowd. He was quickly apprehended by a public-spirited bystander, who put a half-nelson arm-lock on him and frog-marched him to the nearest policeman; so further trouble of that sort was immediately nipped in the bud.

A long convoy of lorries came through the square packed with American GI's. They were greeted with wild enthusiasm by the crowds and the lorries were held up for a while by the masses of people wanting to shake hands with the troops. David (then twelve years old) was hauled up on board one of them and was carried away out of the Square, and was not able to get off until the convoy reached Great Missenden, well into the Chilterns. He then had to walk back to Aylesbury, a distance of ten or eleven miles; not getting back until the small hours of the morning, wearing the peaked, woollen forage cap one of the GI's had given him. David treasured this for many years afterwards.

A most lamentable performance: When I started in the Grammar School again and was deciding how to concentrate my efforts for the School Cert. I gave up the option of doing Art. One of the reasons for this decision (apart from my lack of training in it after the first year in the Latin School when the teacher left) was that the class was doing different types of lettering. I had never done this and I thought I would have difficulty in catching up: a mistake because it was just what I could have done with when I began map work and surveying later! Also I'd never been taught to paint.

It so happened, that Percy had opted out as well and in the spring we made use of the Art lesson period to practise on the Sports Field. We both enjoyed throwing the javelin, but he could nearly always out-throw me (later holding the school record). When we practised the quarter-mile, our positions were reversed, and he found it difficult to keep up with me.

One morning, I decided to run the full lap at my fastest speed and Percy abandoned the chase before we got half way round. This performance was watched with interest by the Art Master, who had come out for a breath of fresh air from the Art Studio, a big wooden shed that stood at the side of the Sports Field.

On sports day I proceeded through the heats for the quarter-mile without trouble. As we went off in the final I tucked myself in behind and to the right of the leading runner and we went round at easy pace (a little slow for me). When we entered the final straight I moved up to make a burst, but then noticed a girl I was quite keen on in the knot of people clustered at the finishing line. I knew she was all eyes on the leading runner and immediately made my decision. I cut in behind the leader allowing a runner to come up on my right and 'box me in', then 'stumbled' over the rope at the edge of the track, out of the race, lying on my back pretending to be blown. The race over, a boy who had been close to the incident, ran to the Art Master, saying, "Did you see that Sir? Haynes was pushed out!" The Art Master, simply pursed his lips, raised his eyebrows, and walked away. It was a good thing Father wasn't present to witness this piece of aberrant behaviour. (Fortunately, our parents never did attend our sports in those days.)

The School Cert.: A classmate called Jack Clayden lived in Abbey Road quite close to us and we often walked to school or back home together. As the summer term advanced he became worried about the apparent lack of serious study, and indeed, concern, on my part, with all my trips over to Stowe Woods; especially as he was a gifted boy, destined to get a complete string of A's (and, I think came top of the list). He didn't appreciate that by this time, to make up for my 'easy come, easy go' rote memory, which generally left me with simply the gist of things, I had learnt to reserve my main effort of revision for a final, week to a fortnight's blitz, immediately before the exams. He was pleased when I finally did get down to it, and, no doubt, he did help me not to leave it too late.

I had mixed fortunes in the exams. I didn't enjoy the maths papers. I'd missed something somewhere in the gap terms and I hadn't caught up. Similarly, in the English Grammar paper, I had to leave out an important section on 'parsing' i.e. the parts of speech, which I had missed in the Latin School, where it was done in detail in the Fourth Form. (I'm still pretty hazy in that area, once one goes beyond subject, object and predicate. As for accusative and nominative! Best to let sleeping dogs lie, I've always thought.) The other papers went quite well but I was pretty sure I'd failed French, as I hadn't done any real work on it.

Before the results came out, Percy and I went camping in Stowe Woods for a week, taking our gear on our bicycles. On the way back, we were coming down the long hill from Whitchurch towards Hardwick (where Grandmother's direct ancestors had farmed before the Civil War) when we met a boy in our class pedalling in the opposite direction. He told us the results were out and that he thought we had both done quite well. So with renewed energy we cycled on to Aylesbury and up to the Grammar School to look at the notice board. Unexpectedly, we had done well, both of us scoring four A's, including biology (with general science, history and geography in my case). I had 'credits' in both English and maths and even managed to pass in French. This was important because it meant I would obtain the certificate of matriculation for entry into London University (the London Matric.) which required at least five credits (including English and maths, or a pass in one and a credit in the other according to whether you intended to study Arts or Sciences, and had another credit). This certificate was accepted for entry into provincial universities, but entry into the ancient universities still required a pass in Latin. These restrictions could lead to difficulties. A boy in the school in our time, who had done very well in physics and maths in the Higher School Certificate, only passed School Cert. English on the third attempt.

Our results meant that we could now stay on in the Sixth Form, which we could hardly have imagined prior to the results. (No one from our respective families had ever done such a thing.) But there were difficulties because it was not clear where this would lead. University entrance was still very restricted in those days, with only a few scholarships and County awards. These went to the small number of top-flight scholars, like a boy called Scheuer, whose father (a refugee) worked in the Alloys factory down Bicester Road. He passed his Highers with distinction in applied maths and physics and also passed in pure maths and botany with subsidiary German, and obtained a scholarship while still only seventeen. As the science master ruefully told us, he had soon found that there was little he could teach him! Also, as Mother pointed out, naturally worried about the strain on her limited budget, there was no guarantee that I would get a better job by staying on and it might be wiser to leave and get established in a job sooner, rather than later. However, Percy and I with the optimism of youth were delighted to take the chance; and I was mindful of Father's advice, supposing there might be a way to teaching via the Sixth Form followed by a training college, because grants for these were easier to get. I was also encouraged by being lucky enough to be awarded the Harding Prize (for the pupil considered to have made the most progress in the year) which was, of course, the intention of the School. The Head, Mr. Furneaux, was intrigued by my choice of White's *Selborne*, with photographs by the famous, Edwardian, bird photographer Cherry Kearton. He invited me over to his house where we walked round the garden talking about birds. We also discussed future prospects and I well remember his advice of, "Anything but teaching"! (He was exasperated that most of his sixth formers seemed to have no other ambitions.)

Unlike Percy, with his mind set on natural science, I was uncertain what courses to take in the Sixth Form. His progress through to University (Leicester) and eventually to a professorship in botany, in Canada, was to be straightforward. My trajectory was to be much more circuitous. I too was greatly attracted to the natural sciences, but I was loath to give up history and also English, after the encouragement Mr. Deeming had given to my writing. At the end of term, to help make my mind up, I borrowed a copy of Borrowdaile's *Invertebrate Zoology* to read, and was completely put-off by its achingly dry 'naming of parts'. Of course it is a handbook of anatomy, not meant to be simply read, but this was enough to swing me to the Arts side. It was at this point that Percy and I went to spend the holidays at the School Harvest Camp.

The School Harvest Camp: During the war years (1942-45) the Grammar School organized a camp, with the headquarters in the village school at Steeple Claydon, so that groups of boys and girls could work, on contract to local farmers, to help bring in the harvest. The time Percy and I attended, a few months after VE day, was the last time it was held. It was organized by Cab (Mr. Bartlett) who gave up his summer holidays to do it, assisted by his wife who, together with some of the girls, looked after the cooking. To get there, the pair of us biked to Steeple Claydon on the old gated road that runs from Berryfields farm on the Bicester Road, up between the villages of Quainton and Oving. We found that we were to sleep in bunks in the school (rather than under canvas, as the boys had on previous years) so we were very comfortable and well fed.

The work involved shocking-up (setting up in stooks) the cut oats or wheat, and helping to load the carts; with other jobs like weeding and hoeing according to need and the weather. I was already knowledgeable in all these tasks, of course, and on the first day out, after we had been organised into shocking squads, needing no instruction, went away at my usual pace and was soon far ahead. Jack Clayden, who happened to have been put in charge of our squad, and had always taken me to be a relaxed, if not lazy chap, was taken aback and came across to see if my shocks were just thrown together. He was duly impressed when he found they were well made.

Boys and girls worked together, so we had a lot of fun, which comes back to memory like scenes from mediaeval life, gone for ever from the harvest fields of Bucks. Some of us spent a couple of days at a farm, digging ditches. I quite enjoyed this, getting the slope even and the sides square. Sometimes when it rained, we took shelter in hay barns and it was on these occasions that I learnt to play card games like solo whist. Often, we marched back singing in the evenings, songs such as, *Be Kind to your Web-footed Friends* to the tune Colonel Bogey.

One day, two of us were sent out to shock-up a field which the farmer was still in the process of cutting. He had just come round to our side of the field with the reaper and binder and was proceeding along when an aeroplane came over and dropped a small bomb, which landed right on the corner of uncut corn behind him. The farmer leapt off the tractor and we all vacated the field very smartly. We ran up to the farm and he rang the Police and, after a while it turned out that the R.A.F. had dropped a practice bomb 'by mistake'. Although quite small, the bomb would have made a mess of the tractor if it had scored a direct hit. (Perhaps the bomber crew were bored and couldn't resist the impulse to liven us up a bit!)

It will be understood that we generally got back to the camp very tired and after our evening meal were not disposed to much ragging and horse-play, but one day the word went round that 'a fight' had been arranged with the village boys. For me this was bad news. Until I moved back to Aylesbury I'd been a village boy and had no wish to be involved in a brawl between 'townee' toffs versus yokels. More than that, a few days before when our squad was on the way home we had met an attractive girl walking in the other direction and when she had gone by I realized that it was Gwen (Biddlecombe) my old heart-throb. On several evenings after that I went round the lanes hoping we might meet, without success. (I was too shy to enquire in the village about where she lived.) So I had good reason not to engage in hooliganism in Steeple Claydon! Quite apart from these considerations, as I had been taught how to box, I understood the dangers of an unregulated fist fight. Fortunately, the village boys, wisely, didn't show up at the time arranged, so I didn't have the embarrassment of having to appear to 'chicken out'.

It was while we were at the harvest camp, that the war in the Far East came to its final, dramatic conclusion. Early on the morning of the 6th of August, Cab roused us from our bunks to tell us that a new type of bomb, an atomic bomb, had been dropped on the city of Hiroshima in Japan. Then three days later (9th) that another atomic bomb had destroyed the city of Nagasaki and that Japan had capitulated. Cab explained how the bomb worked and how it had ended the war and perhaps all such 'World Wars'. We were all tremendously relieved and excited by the news that the war had ended at last, but unlike the unrestrained joy with which we had greeted VE day, there was a feeling of disquiet about the bomb and the great forces that had been unleashed from this particular Pandora's Box.

Percy and I greatly enjoyed our time at the camp and although most of the children stayed only a week, we stayed for several. As Harry Deeming put it, in his School Notes for the *Aylesburian* (see note 2): "In 1945 we held our most successful camp. There were two recognized shocking squads, and work was mostly carried out by contract. The shocking squads did 1/400th of the whole Buckinghamshire area and again took first place in the County for boy (including girl)-hours. The camp closed with a very successful Farmers' Dinner."

The move to no. 9 Granville Street: In the autumn of 1945, not long after I entered the Sixth Form, my father was finally discharged from the Army. As our parents were now making the attempt at a reconciliation, and the house in Abbey Road was very crowded, (Sally was born in August and Uncle Tom was already home), they rented part of a terrace house in Granville Street, just off St. Mary's Square. This only partly relieved the overcrowding, because the front sitting room and front bedroom were already let, and the kitchen and bathroom had to be shared. There were only two other bedrooms upstairs, so we had to have beds in the corners of the dining room as well as doing our homework there. (It was a good thing we didn't have television in those days, though funnily enough, Uncle Tom, who was an inveterate gambler, bought one after a big win on the horses, and large numbers of people used to crowd into the front room to see the programmes, because it was the first one in Abbey Road!)

Before Father left the Army, he had already been in touch with an old friend and business acquaintance called Peter Hoy, and they had discussed setting up a small publishing company together when the war ended. However, Cheneys, Father's former employers, had kept his job open, and hoped he would return. This made it difficult for him to come to a decision, and so one evening he suggested a walk so we could have one of his 'serious talks', but this time about his problems. We went down the Oxford Road, past Hartwell Park and Hartwell Pits (not yet built over) and he bought me lemonade so we could have a drink together in the garden of the Bugle Inn. I couldn't be much help but he used me as a sounding board, and the upshot was that he decided to join his friend Peter in the publishing venture. They set up their office under the name, Sentinel Press, in Soho, and Father went up to London daily on the train. I remember him coming home late on one occasion, and having his supper in the kitchen at No. 9, and becoming highly exasperated by the lines of wet washing hanging down in his face: not what the ex-officer had been used to, and not surprisingly, he now made strenuous efforts to recover the tenancy of our house in Kenton (rented out since the summer of 1932). This wasn't easy because there were now strict rent controls and tenancies were protected, especially long-term arrangements. Our tenants refused to leave and the matter had to go to Court. Father was able to win the case on compassionate grounds by describing our overcrowded living conditions and how he now worked in London, plus the weight given to his six years' war service. All this took some time, and it wasn't until the early summer of the following year that the tenants finally left. Meanwhile we continued to live in Granville Street and go to school in Aylesbury.

Life in the Sixth Form: I began my studies in English, history and geography (for the Oxford Higher School Certificate) that autumn, in the first year of the Sixth Form, with enthusiasm, but soon had doubts about where these subjects, in particular English, were going to lead me. I was very impressed with Mr. Deeming's exploration of *Paradise Lost* and the Romantic poets but realized after a few weeks, that at the higher level, English was largely concerned with a minute analysis of texts. This didn't appeal to me very much. Also, one hot afternoon that September, when we were discussing Wordsworth and his admonition to be outdoors studying nature and not books, it was not lost on me that we were in the stuffy Sixth Form library reading books, rather than out on the Chilterns or in Stowe Woods! (See note 3.) So, although at this very time I was actually thinking of polishing up some of my school essays for possible publication, I decided there was no future in English criticism, as far as I was concerned, despite my early efforts at writing. Indeed, it was because I wanted to try and publish articles on natural history that I was drawn back to the natural sciences.

After discussing the problem with the Headmaster I switched to zoology and botany with geography. But now I ran headlong into another problem, because I found I had no stomach for dissection. I am uncertain about the reason for my squeamishness. It may lie in my childhood experiences, in and out of hospital and the sight and smell of surgical instruments and disinfectants. Be that as it may, my final disillusion came with the second or third time the stinking dogfish was brought out from the barrel of formalin under the laboratory bench! However, another reason for me baulking at zoology, was because it was then very heavily biased towards traditional comparative anatomy. As Sir Peter Medawar says of this subject, as it was taught at Oxford in the immediate post-war period (and we were studying for the Oxford 'Highers'), it was 'deadly dull' and no longer a 'live issue', despite the 'grandeur of the demonstration of evolution'. So my reaction to Borrowdaile hadn't been entirely misjudged (see note 4). I was not the kind of boy drawn to dissect and stuff animals and birds, and who often becomes an anatomist or surgeon. My interest had been very much focused on bird behaviour and this was still hardly a subject of respectable academic study (although R.M. Lockley had already published his ground-breaking studies on the Manx shearwaters of Skokholm and David Lack his *Life of the Robin*).

I had to go cap in hand to see the headmaster again. He must have groaned inwardly, but he was very kind and he agreed that I could drop zoology, but continue taking botany, together with history and geography. He was somewhat worried as to where this mixture of subjects would lead but it turned out well. It played to my strengths and the combination of physical geography, ecological succession in plants and history would eventually lead me (after many twists and turns) to the essentially historical science of geology. There was a sharp frost the morning after I had made this decision, and when I went in via the boys' entrance into school, the conifer by the gate, crystalline with white rime against the blue sky, symbolized the clarity of science and confirmed the feeling I had made the right decision in continuing to study botany.

The cap was not entirely metaphorical. On entry to the Sixth Form, I had been made a prefect, which meant that I was now entitled (and, indeed bound by the School rules) to wear a 'halves cap'. It was half black and half scarlet, with quite a long peak, and was awarded to boys who had played for the School, and also to the prefects. We were expected to wear it going to and fro from School, which some of us older boys found slightly embarrassing (though today, it would have been a fashion statement being quite like a base-ball cap). I had some reason for embarrassment, because on my way home to Abbey Road, I normally walked down Bicester Road, past the Royal Bucks Hospital, which is separated from the pavement by a high, red brick wall. In fine weather, nurses used to come out onto a patio that over-looked the wall for a break and a chat. Not long after I had started wearing my new cap, the nurses were there when I came by and I was greeted by whistles and "Oh, who's a pretty boy then?" "Doesn't he look smart in his cap," and "Will you come out with me tonight Dearie?" and such like. My face went as red as my cap and the next time I thought that perhaps I should go down the other side of the street, but I resisted that craven impulse and put up with the whistles (and soon after, we moved to Granville Street and I went home that way no more).

The Sixth Form botany was taught mainly by Miss Avery, though Cab Bartlett did some courses, such as genetics, and they both co-operated on field courses, when we went out to study plant associations. Miss Avery was an enthusiastic young teacher who had graduated from the University of Wales, Aberystwyth (then the University College of Wales) and had been under the influence of Arthur Chater, the ecologist there, and of Lily Newton, the head of the Department of Botany and famous for her studies of sea-weed and other algae.

I was very pleased to be back doing history with Miss Stewart, a grave but sympathetic, Scottish lady I grew to like very much; (she was, at this time, living at the Red Lion Hotel in Kingsbury Square). An example of her kindness occurred one morning when we were discussing Mussolini and I pronounced Duce with an S rather than CH, which made the rest of the class hoot with laughter, and she quietly remarked, "I've often mispronounced words that I haven't heard spoken". We were studying the period from the Enlightenment and the French Revolution up to the Great War, covering the social and political history of Britain and Europe; and also for a paper on the British Empire from the American Revolution up to 1914. Two books from our prescribed background reading that particularly struck home were Milton's *Areopagitica* and Mill's *On Liberty.* The liberal principles enshrined in these works were to keep me on the straight and narrow during years when I tended to drift leftwards, affected (like most young people) by Soviet propaganda and the fellow-travelling, pseudo-liberalism of state socialism.

We were taught geography by Mr. Severn, up to the time he left at Easter 1946. He was very fond of skating and this led to an embarrassing incident. Early in the New Year a prolonged, hard frost gave bearing ice on the canal (a branch of the Grand Union, which runs to Aylesbury). Percy and I bought ourselves some old-fashioned, clip-on Dutch skates in the second-hand shop that used to be in Cambridge Street, and quickly learned how to do it without falling too often. Though there was a problem in that the screws holding the clips to our shoes easily loosened, so the skates flew off. We told Mr. Severn that the ice on the canal was bearing and the next day he came down with Mr. Deeming, another enthusiastic skater, when Percy and I were in action. We were all having a good time when the two masters suddenly stopped and engaged in serious conversation. Mr Deeming then came across and told us that we weren't allowed to cut 'free periods' and sent us packing back to school. Meanwhile they carried on skating: a lesson in the general unfairness of life! However, as soon as school was over we were back on the ice, continuing until dark, developing skills we were both to exercise more fully in Canada. (See note 5.)

Mr Severn and Mr. Deeming were also fond of dancing (which, after all, goes naturally with skating) and they were prominent at the dances that were held from time to time for the Fifth Form and Sixth Form boys and girls. There was one of these dances at the end of the autumn term (1945). Percy and I were unable to dance at that time and two of our classmates, Dug Otteridge and Ray Bourke, offered to teach us in the School Gym. They were both good dancers, and good athletes; Dug was a very good swimmer with a stylish breaststroke, and Ray prominent in the hockey and cricket teams. Ray was tall, dark, a very suave social operator, and we particularly admired his way with the girls. So during one of our 'free periods' these two taught us the basic steps. From Dug we learned the three- step routine for the waltz and the quickstep, and from Ray the six steps of the foxtrot, together with the technique required to make turns.`

Percy and I got on reasonably well at the dance (which was to gramophone records) managing to make full circuits without too many mistakes, and delighted to have this new social skill. A number of the teachers took to the floor and at one point, when they were passing each other, Mr Severn asked Mr Deeming, who was wearing a white linen jacket, why he was "Dressed like an ice-cream merchant". Mr Deeming, without losing his sang-froid, immediately replied, "So I don't get overheated". Looking back, I think dancing was one of the more important things I learnt to do in school. To underline this: shortly after the dance, I think at the instigation of the Head, Mr Furneaux, and a new teacher, Miss K. Haggerty, who arrived in January1946, a Dancing Club was set up; in response, it was said, "to the continual complaint of the girls at dances, that none of the boys could dance".

Another good friend I made when I moved up into the Sixth Form, was Jim Symon, a dark, clever, witty boy, of middle height who lived up Tring road (he came near the top in the Annual Oratory Contest held the following March, speaking on: *The Wording of Modern Songs is not Poetry*). As I had Percy, I introduced him to Stowe Woods and the three of us went over one November weekend, but by the time we got there the short day was already closing in, and we didn't have time to make a bivouac, just making do with our single blanket and groundsheet each. It was a chilly, damp night and we soon got cold, so I suggested we should borrow some sacks from the granary at Blackpit. We went over and with the light of a torch we selected three, seven-foot wheat bags, which we took back into the woods and used as sleeping bags. They were very satisfactory, but we had to make sure we took them back before milking time and first light the next morning. I wondered afterwards what Jim, essentially a town boy, had privately thought of this escapade. (He went on eventually to become a lawyer, and like Percy and me, went to Canada.)

The following spring, although now busy with Sixth Form studies, I recommenced my nature notes, with observations made round Aylesbury as well as on visits to Stowe. They show how the hard weather that had made the canal fit for skating persisted well into March, and how my powers of observation and knowledge of nature were developing:

1/3/46 Stowe: "Old snow still lies in the hollows. It was very cold along Stowe Avenue but rooks were building. Arum was flaunting her green leaves. Robins sang in liquid plaint of the bad weather. Two swans swam round and round in an attempt to keep a hole free from ice in Rufous River Lake (Woody Park). In the birch wood the melting snow from the trees was thumping down among the first shoots of bluebell and soft leaves of primrose. Tits worked among the tassels of the birches with needle-like notes: black-crowned marsh tits with white necks and acrobatic blue tits. Rooks were foraging where the wind swept across the red plough-land.

3/3/46 Aylesbury: "Snow still falling although the buds of the lilac are bursting with life. The canal was full of slush ice. A grey wagtail ran over the ice flirting its blue, grey-black tail. As we approached it flew up with a flash of sulphur yellow, alighting farther on at the edge of the ice by the frozen spear points of the rushes. We left the blue-black, sulphur-breasted bird drawing dainty tracks in the slush.

4/3/46 Aylesbury: "Still snowing, Starlings fighting garrulously in the chimney stacks.

8/3/46 Aylesbury, Hartwell: "Dunnock singing a short song where the keck (Cow Parsley) ground ivy and red dead nettle are laying the foundation for the ladders (of climbing plants) which scale the hedge in summer. Four magpies were chuckling noisily in a copse. A ball of black and white thumped down into the grass, the two uppermost birds worrying one on its back. My appearance frightened the garrulous crowd back into the trees where I left them still wrangling. A yellow hammer was singing of summer somewhere but his monotonous little catch lacked a few notes.

10/3/46 Stowe: "Rooks building in a mist of red elm buds, Jackdaws talking softly above the robin's sibilance. There was ice on the lake (Blackpit) where moorhens walked with coral beaks and white tail coverts bobbing. A sparrow hawk dashed through the spires of fir spinney. It was very warm in crowland (on the plough land) the sun drenching the red earth.

18/3/46 Stowe: "Greater spotted wood pecker in Stowe Avenue, a red capped male. Duck and drake standing on the ice at the lake (Blackpit), the ice has held for three weeks, since the last snow. A loose flock of tits slipped through the woods while we sat over a small fire: cole tits, blue tits, great tits and noisy long-tails. Their passage reminds one of leaf fall among the hazel wands. I watched them while the rain ran down my neck. (Percy was with me on this occasion).

20/3/46 Aylesbury: "The cold weather has broken and the sky is hazy and flecked with cloud. Starlings are voluble again.

25/3/46 Aylesbury: "Very hot, first tortoiseshell on celandine, Crested grebes on Willesdon Reservoir.

26/3/46 Aylesbury: "Bees in almond blossom, Brimstone and Peacock in orchard (back of house).

31/3/46 Stowe: "Weather still holding, first chiff-chaff in one of the great elms (in the Avenue), white and sweet violets by the Gothic Temple. An orange bee hummed happily in a white violet. A pheasant called in the woods above Blackpit, another chiff-chaff called in the birch wood, the summer warblers are returning to their usual nesting places.

2/4/46 Aylesbury, Hartwell Pits: "A willow wren sang of summer and the cool green places. A chiff-chaff darted furiously after insects in a pussy-palm (Goat Willow). The grass was studded with the discs of dandelions and frosted with daisies. Linnets and greenfinches conversed in low tones behind a hedge. A frog bulged up from beneath the green weed, its eyes a wink of topaz, diving again with a plop as my footsteps flushed a water hen.

3/4/46 Aylesbury: "Starlings are building in a down pipe by the window.

6/4/46 Aylesbury: "Thrush brooding her china blue eggs near the Pikell, Blackbird nesting in Hartwell Pits.

7/4/46 Hartwell: "Linnets singing in low canary-like manner. Corn bunting in Dinton Lane; a wary bird resembling a large, hen yellow hammer with a song like the shattering of glass. Aylesbury: Herons over school field.

10/4/46 Hartwell Pits: "Reed bunting fussing with a hen in a thicket, willow warblers singing in the sulphur-yellow goat willows. The frogs have left the water.

11/4/46 Aylesbury: "Starling imitating call notes of little–owl. The orchard is misty with pear and apple blossom. A chaffinch is singing in a rollicking tempo. There is an unfinished nest of pressed moss in the hawthorns. Cowslips, primroses, ground ivy, bluebells, dandelions and celandines are blooming, coltsfoot and shepherds' purse are in their seed time."

As I had done the previous year, I spent a few days in the woods over at Stowe just before my birthday:

15/4/46: "Cuckoo in Stowe Avenue. The hot weather has brought the hawthorns to full leaf. Grasshopper warblers are singing all day (in the thickets at the top of Point Copse), a secretive, mouse-like bird, striated more than the other warblers. It is a lover of the hedge bottoms, rising to a point of vantage to utter its sustained song, a ticking whirr. The milkmaids curtsy in the meadows again, with bluebells, violets and anemones in the woods, keck flowering in the hedges.

16/4/46: "Whitethroat fussing in the brambles. Two chickadees (Cole tits) conversing in low tones in a goat willow. Oaks breaking into leaf, Kestrel building its nest ten feet away from its last year's nest.

17/4/46: "The grasshopper warbler sings through more hours than the willow warbler. At sunset, blackbirds, thrushes, a robin, three willow wrens and a chiff-chaff were singing together with a grass wren. At 8.30pm as the last luminous brightness of the sun faded, only the blackbird and the grass wren were singing. At 9pm, when it was quite dark only the grass wren was singing, continuing until 10pm. It then sang briefly from 10.15 until 10.20, then stopped, recommencing at 2.30am and continuing until 11am; being joined by the first skylark at 4am."

These were to be the last of my nature notes for a while, apart from recording the first appearance of swifts over Aylesbury on May 8th. We were now busy in school preparing for the mock 'highers', and we also had a new teacher. Mr. Lloyd-Jones came in place of Mr. Severn after Easter, to teach geography, after he had been demobbed from the R.A.F. Like Miss Avery he was a graduate of the University of Wales, Aberystwyth, where he had studied under the great Welsh historical geographer, Emrys Bowen, and the geologist H. K. P. Lewis. He was young and enthusiastic, and he was helped in his task of preparing us for the paper in geomorphology (landforms) by the publication, in 1944, of Arthur Holmes's book, *Principles of Physical Geology* (which includes geomorphology, i.e. physical geography). This now classic work, beautifully written and illustrated, by one of the greatest geologists of the twentieth century (author of the first acceptable, radiometric time-scale for the earth) was to be a strong influence on me. Also, just as Miss Avery had alerted me to the possibilities of the Cardigan Bay coast for ecology, so LJ described the possibilities there were for hill-walking in the hinterland of Aberystwyth, via the numerous old mining trails that run up the valleys.

When the mock Highers were out of the way in the spring (in which I did reasonably well) our school social life continued. As well as dances there were parties in various homes, such as those of Valerie Dellow, in Church Street, just off Temple Square, and Margaret Tucker (the attractive fair girl on my right in the photo) up Tring Road. Although the parents made themselves scarce, these parties would have seemed very decorous and restrained, even childish, to today's teenagers (a category hardly known to us) involving stratagems for pairing off, like kissing games. Groups of us also went on rambles in the Chilterns, boys and girls wandering hand in hand along the Downs, perhaps to have tea in the rustic tea-house, near Coombe Hill, or in the home of Marion Lister, a dark girl I was attracted to, who lived near Wendover; whose Mother had difficulty finding enough cups for us all. Another dark girl I was attracted to at this time was Gillian Hills, who lived in

Dinton, in a cottage close to our Hurst relations (and submitted a good sonnet to the *Aylesburian*). However, I remained fancy free and this was to persist for some years. I was only too conscious that I had to find my direction in life, and, as always, was keen to avoid entanglements until I had serious intentions. This led to some unkindness on my part: I twice refused point blank to accept an invitation to a party from a girl I knew was interested in me, and another time I walked a girl home from a dance, leaving her at her door with an offhand remark that I revealed to a boy who asked me how I had got on. It was relayed back to her and she was upset—-how these arrows come back to strike us.

Percy and I also went for more vigorous walks in the Chilterns, along the Icknield Way (the prehistoric track-way) that runs along the lip of the downs. I'd passed on my liking for George Borrow and we fancied ourselves on Barrovian tramps. For a long while we used his Romany catch-phrases, such as 'Wind on the heath, brother' and 'Sun, moon and stars', as greetings between ourselves.

We also went camping over at Stowe, and going for milk at Woodlands met Tim White when he was wiping dishes for Jose in the back kitchen. I was struck by his white beard and very bright blue eyes. He asked our age and exclaimed, "I wish I was seventeen again!" He would have been amused if he had known we were practising with home-made javelins cut from the hazels, and that Percy's was 'Questing Beast' and mine was 'Pellinore'. Tim had returned after the War to reclaim his books and other effects and also to try and realize his ambition to get Jose to marry him. He took her for a holiday to a cottage in the Pennines owned by his friend David Garnett (author of *Lady into Fox*) but all his blandishments failed and she married Brian instead. "She married the cricketer" as the disappointed Tim, said in disgust.

Once in the Sixth form we could opt out of team games. As I have already mentioned, my experience of cricket was generally of too little time at the crease and too long in the outfield waiting for the high ball; so although Percy continued to play cricket that summer and was in the school team, I used to go to the open-air baths in the Vale recreation grounds to swim, with others of like mind. I was not in any way a remarkable swimmer, unlike my two brothers. I had a reasonable, but not very powerful breaststroke, and my crawl was ragged and inefficient; this didn't stop me from greatly enjoying it though. Both Percy and I played a lot of tennis, on the School courts and in the Vale in the evenings (attempting to emulate the great Australian players, like Sedgeman and Rosewall, who dominated Wimbledon during this era). Mother and I also used to play doubles with her sister Kit and her husband Tom, on the courts at his place of work. Although only a very moderate player, I developed an efficient, if unorthodox serve, getting in a good proportion of first-serve smashes down the centre line, and I also had the ability to, quite often, retrieve the apparently, out-of-reach, un-returnable ball. I particularly liked doubles and playing up at the net.

School Field Trips: For me, perhaps the most influential part of the botany course that first year in the Sixth, was the fieldwork (now being organized again after being suspended during the War) especially two trips that took place early in the summer. The first was a full days' excursion by bus across the Weald, down to Hayling Island, in Hampshire. We went down over the Chilterns and through the beech woods on the Chalk; crossed the Thames at Marlow and made our first stop on Bagshot Heath, to look at the acid heath developed on the Tertiary sands and gravels. Here we were shown how to calculate the percentages of plants within a yard-square, wooden frame (quadrant) and found some of the typical species, like Heather, Cotton Grass, Sundew and the peculiar parasite, Dodder. We got to Hazlemere at lunchtime and went into the Natural History Museum there, which has a good geological section that had benefited from the attention of Sir Arthur Ramsey, a former Director of the Geological Survey, who had lived nearby in his retirement.

We spent the afternoon on Hayling Island, collecting plants from the sand dunes and from the salt marsh. I was not to forget Cab intoning the rolling English and Latin names for some of the plants, *Atriplex portulicoides* = sea purslane; *Carex arenaria* = sand sedge; *Sueda maritima* = sea blite; *Honckenya peploides*= seaside sandwort; *Spergularia marina* = sea spurrey; mixed with the cries of seabirds. This was the beginning of my love for the wild freedom of estuarine salt-marshes.

On the way back we stopped briefly on the South Downs to look at the low, almost prostrate, dark, blue-green junipers, which grow naturally there on the Chalk; a fitting end to the trip, which brought home to me for the first time, not just the beauty and interest of plant associations and successions, but also their close relationship to the underlying soils and geology.

Later that June, we had an afternoon trip to collect plants on the Chilterns at Whiteleaf Cross, near Princes Risborough (where there is a large cross cut out in the Chalk). There was a prize offered for the pupil collecting the most kinds, and Percy and I set to vigorously, hoping we might win it. But at the final count, two of the girls came out well ahead, one of them with over 120. Percy managed about 110 and I had just over 100 (this would not be the first time that Percy and I would have to admit that there were certain pernickety tasks that girls could manage better than mere males). Of course, the purpose of the trip was to introduce us to the remarkable diversity of the Chalk-down flora; also to orchids, and both Bee orchid and Bird's nest orchid were found, though I was already familiar with Butterfly orchids, which grow in Stowe Woods. (See note 6.)

LONDON AGAIN

The move back to 28, Alveston Avenue, Kenton: We finally recovered 'Ridley', the Kenton house, in the summer of 1946, and moved in towards the end of the summer term, the three of us children continuing at the Grammar School, going down by train to Aylesbury. As is often the case where tenants have been forcibly removed, the house was left dirty, full of rubbish and in disrepair. The husband had been a radio ham and the concrete patio in the back garden was completely covered with discarded equipment and other bits and pieces in a pile about ten feet high. Father had to get some contractors to clear the rubbish before we could start cleaning and decorating, Mother and I going up at weekends from Aylesbury to do this until we could move in. Late one evening, I think in early July, I was painting the frames of the upstairs windows, leaning out to do the outside, when a gathering storm forced me to close them, against one of the most spectacular thunder storms I've ever experienced.

One of the reasons for the three of us children continuing in Aylesbury Grammar School until the end of the term, was that Mother liked Kenton no more the second time round than she had the first time in the early Thirties. So despite 'Ridley' being very convenient for Father in his new business, they decided to sell it and buy a house somewhere else. It might have been thought 'sensible' to stay in Aylesbury, but I don't remember that being considered. As it happened, Father decided we should celebrate the end of the War (using part of his gratuity) with a long holiday in Cornwall, and for Mother, with her romantic love of Cornwall and the West Country, this was to have an important bearing on the issue.

We rented a bungalow about a mile behind the village of Coverack, on the Lizard in Cornwall, for six weeks. Mother's sister, Aunt Trix, came to stay with us for the first part of the holiday and Father for the final two weeks. We went down by train, delighted to cross the Tamar Bridge and once again experience the unique smell of the Cornish heaths. The bungalow belonged to the Cowles family and Ann became very friendly with the daughter, Virginia, who was about her age. Mr Cowles took us out in his rowing boat mackerel fishing and David very quickly learned how to imitate his Cornish accent, and his often repeated phrase about the plot in front of the bungalow, where he considered that there was "anuff room fer a thousand cabbages". We quickly discovered the grand cliff walks, with their view of the sinister 'Manacles', a dangerous reef, and exposures of beautifully coloured and textured rocks (which I was to learn later, belonged to the Lizard Complex). David and I also walked over to Kynance Cove and also to Mullion, when on the way back we were caught in mist on Goonhilly Down and went for two hours in the wrong direction. On fine, sunny afternoons we all walked a mile or so westwards to a small sandy cove (Llankidden Cove) approached by a steep path down a narrow valley with a farm at the head, to swim and sunbathe and dive off the rocks. We were generally the only people there, but on some occasions there was also a party of wounded service-men, still not fully recovered and requiring assistance to come down the path and while paddling in the water. Seeing them watching our boisterous antics, I was very conscious of the debt we owed to them, the generation just before my own. Afterwards, we used to have tea in the farmhouse at the head of the valley, a boiled egg, followed by scones with jam and Cornish cream: then the walk back, pleasantly tired, often seeing a white owl quartering the heath, spectral in the dusk.

While we were on holiday, Mother got hold of a copy of the property magazine *Dalton's Weekly* and found the particulars of a cottage in the Blackdown Hills of Somerset that caught her interest. When Father came to join us on holiday, they discussed it together and decided it was worth investigating. Leaving us behind, they took the train up to Taunton, then a taxi to Buckland St. Mary and went to see it. It was a thatched, stone cottage, with an orchard, and a fine view eastwards into the Dorset hills and the Somerset Levels (see photo 10-1). It turned out that it had been the property of an elderly lady called Miss Moulton-Barrett (great niece of Elizabeth Barrett Browning) who had recently died. The situation and the literary associations pleased Mother, as did the view down towards the Levels and Glastonbury Tor (because as well as the Hardy novels, one of her favourites was

The Glastonbury Romance by John Cowper Powys). By the time they returned to Coverack, Mother was full of what it would be like to live there. Father's attitude was more equivocal; it meant he would be spending the week in London and commuting to Taunton, a two-hour train trip, at weekends. I think Mother hoped that the change to a new life in Somerset might help the marriage, and that Father might even take a job travelling in the West Country, underestimating his commitment to his new publishing venture.

Shortly after we arrived back in London after the holiday, our parents put in an offer for the cottage, which was accepted, and we went ahead redecorating 'Ridley' so it could be put up for sale. This took some time and we were not able to move to Somerset until mid-December. This meant that we children continued to go to school in Aylesbury for most of the autumn term.

Getting nature articles published: Early in that year (1946) after I had finally decided what to do in the Sixth Form and settled down, I carefully rewrote the last essay I had written while in the Fifth Form, *Summer Afternoon,* in my best longhand. I had discovered an interesting and well–produced nature magazine, entitled *Animal Pictorial* edited by Peter Shaw Baker. Linked with the magazine, Joy Shaw Baker had set up the *Young Naturalists' Association* which you could join by submitting a publishable photograph, drawing or nature article to the advisory committee, which included the writer, Frances Pitt, Oliver G. Pike, a naturalist and photographer, and the writer H. M. Tomlinson, as well as the Shaw Bakers. My article was accepted and I was sent my membership card (which I still have with its sketch of a wren and quotation from Ruskin). This was in the February. The article was not published that spring or summer, being put aside until a convenient slot could be found for it.

When we returned from our holiday, enthused by the sights and scenes of the West Country, I altered another essay that I had written while in the Fifth Form, called *Wild Weather*; after having had the benefit of experiencing a gale down in Coverack, as well as the severe electrical storm in July. I gave it a new introduction and a new title, *Old Year's Leaves,* as well as an ending from another essay on autumn. I submitted this to the magazine, and to my surprise it was accepted immediately and published in the next issue, prior to *Summer Afternoon,* both coming out in the following year (see note 7.)

The editor did me proud, because although the magazine was otherwise entirely illustrated by black and white photos, he had arranged to have a painting of a seascape at sunset placed across the top of the first two pages, above the title. It shows a rocky cliff and estuarine sandbars with waders and seabirds and the view of a distant island. It was in perfect sympathy with the spirit of the article, which I give below, because it conjures up the 'dreaming youth' otherwise so difficult to recall. As all writers say, "I wouldn't (couldn't) write like that now!" (I should perhaps add that even a scientist is a kind of 'writer').

Old Year's Leaves

"How long ago was it when the warblers first sang of summer and the cool green places? A long time counted by sunlight and cloud shadow. Yet it seems but a moment ago when the swifts screamed about the old thatched cottages and the partridge chicks ran through the poppies, so quickly does the leaping mind count the hours of the year. Now the dry chuckle of leaves in a corner of the garden wall tells of autumn's painted days.

*   *   *   *   *   *

"As the year grew old I went down to the sea, obeying a primitive urge as old as the flighting of migrant birds. One owl-light, when Venus, the morning and evening star, burnt dully over the rim of the hills I came to the estuary. Since the sun had set, the tide, which had moved like oil in the old river bed had ebbed away again.

"A dwarf pine stood on the headland and as I took the cliff path I heard a dry wind in its branches. Five score times since the winged seed had blown from the deck of the Scandinavian schooner and lodged in the cliff, had the gulls nested, the grass grown knee-high, and the leaves fallen from the wild cherry trees. The tree was gnarled and twisted by the salt winds which were never still in its branches. It was September, at the equinox, when the first migrant birds flock south-wards, the savage gales of the Northlands following hard upon their invisible flightways. On the moorlands, under the sky, the cotton grasses were in flower. In the valley orchards the apples hung like scarlet lamps on branches shaggy and grey with lichen. A white owl quartered the silent stubble fields.

"Wane of summer…but since the sultry dog days the countryside had lain under quiet skies. In the tide-race the estuary salmon were waiting for the freshet—the spate of turbid brown waters that would ensure them a safe passage to their spawning redds in the gravel of the high moor.

"A trip of waders stood motionless on a sand bar dissolving in their own shadows. As I crunched across the shingle they flew away with broken, fretful cries. In echo, the mud flats left by the retreating tide grew delirious with the mellow pipes of redshank, whimbrel and plover. Three birds rocked over on hooped wings, and the twilight was made eerie by the sad plaint of the curlew.

"For a while the sunset's afterglow was mirrored in the shining mud. Then a dark cloud shadow blotted out the last luminous brightness in the western sky. Wandering clouds stole before the stars. The air grew sultry and the clouds massed together until the whole earth seemed held in their thraldom. The sullen wash of the ebb-tide intensified the almost living silence. To the imaginative mind the atmosphere suggested the troubled brooding of the water spirit.

"At last the muttered grumbling of thunder told of the storm's passage. Suddenly the clouds were ragged with lightning. A moment of even greater silence and the air was heavy and unbearable with the shock of thunder. Black sheets of rain fell, whipping the waters of the bay as the wind went snorting through the heather. The pine crouching in the cliff bent before the terrible blast. It was alone except for a few withered handfuls of thrift and two old thorns, whose branches shrieked and howled as the wind pulled their beards of lichen. The cliff was the playground of wind and water, and the twin hammers of the weather-god had split and riven the crags. As the storm rose the cliff-face became scarred by sliding rock. Suddenly the hammer of Thor dealt the pine a shattering blow. For a moment it rocked, fibres screaming then fell into the sea. Somewhere a gull laughed the struggle of wind and water embodied in its satanical cadence.

"The thunder rolled on into the hills but the gale lost nothing of its former fury. Under the shadow of the cliffs the lights of the fishing-village sparkled in the wind like guttering candles.

"The tide turned and the gale blew green combers into the estuary. As I crouched in the bracken of the hillside, under the wind, I heard the gale-blown piping of the redshanks disturbed by the inundating onrush of the tide. Such was the fury of the storm that soon the foam-flecked cavalry of the water spirit were pawing resentfully at the foot of the cliffs. With glorious thunder they flung themselves against the rocky ramparts of the coast.

"So great was the tempo of the gale that it soon grew less. The wind tore the rain shrouds from the bright disc of the moon, a golden coracle putting for shelter in cloudy harbours. The last rain drops pattered in the marram grasses and drained away into the wind-pared dunes.

"A salmon leapt in the tide-race. The first dark flood-waters of the brimming moorland streams were staining the bright surface of the estuary. The turbid waters of the freshet, sparkling with oxygen, brought to the waiting salmon memories of river life. Again the salmon leapt; eager to win immortality by the perpetuation of its kind.

"The moon set and the sky grew wan as old lead. At half light, I watched the wildfowl flighting to the estuary. From a great distance, I heard a sibilant whisper, the protesting cry of air beneath taut pinions. It was two swans flying towards the sea, snow-white barbs against the darksome sky. As they swung over the estuary, the whisper became a deep-throated bay. Slowly they dwindled into the grey immensity of sea and sky. A strange longing came over me as I stood on the wind-swept saltings, that I the earth-bound, could also go a-journeying down the trackways of the stars.

*　　*　　*　　*　　*　　*　　*

"After the harvest moon has worn away it is October, moon of the painted leaves; the cold touch of frost in the night, and the woods flame with colour. It is as though the trees and rooted things had drunk too deep of summer's wine and their leaves were splashed with its tawny drops.

"The first trees to colour at the hint of winter are the hazel and the maple. In August when the hum of the reaper rises and falls on the windless air, the lower leaves turn yellow. As the days go by the colour rises through the trees. Soon the limes and birches shimmer in pale gold, the wild geans flame in scarlet and vermillion, and the

271

buckthorns smoulder in deep purple. The air sharp with frost fires the blood. October, the mad moon, when the enquiring whistle of the migrant bird bubbles down from the night sky. Then for a brief season the summer seems to come again and walk hand in hand with autumn. The air loses its sharpness and becomes that soft blue only seen during an Indian summer.

"At this time the beauty of the world becomes almost too poignant. I long for the scent of blue twitch fires and damp woods until towns and the habitations of men become hated prisons. At last I am compelled to break the shackles which bind me to the plough of civilisation and go into woods where Orion the hunter shakes his starry spear.

"When I go into the woods my caravan is an ancient beech tree. On many still autumn nights my ceiling has been the sky a-shiver with stars. As mists steal up the lonely woodland rides my only companion is a wood fire. As the flames dance and the sparks leap into eternity I dream back into the firelight of ancient days. Fire was man's first friend. The tall white savages of Cro-Magnon sheltered in its glare, when lions roared in the Mendip hills and the grey wolf coursed the red deer beneath the oaks of the forest. These things live again in ancestral memory when the ashes fall, soft and thick as the plumage of owls.

"To me, autumn seems bound to the song of the robin. The October hedgerows ripple to the liquid notes of this bird whose breast burns like a dying dogwood leaf. The robin seems to take an interest in man for its song is full of the pathos and sorrow of the world, as though it would lead him away from his household gods. How many have heard the sibilant pipes of Pan?

"The golden days of autumn are melancholy because they are so transient. One day the dawn breaks grey and blear eyed, as a bitter wind huddles the branches of the wild cherry trees. The painted leaves are weary of wintry strife and a drift of scarlet and amber is gathered to the forest floor. Chestnuts thump down amongst the hazels to lie side by side with the acorns dropped from the oaks. There is a simple truth to be found among these old leaves where the life spirit slumbers in the seeds of summer's hope. In spring the alchemy of the sun will awaken the plants that will thrive in the leaf-dust of centuries, for nothing is lost and nothing ever dies. If you are groping for reality, go down where the wild apples are garnered to the earth. Here, where the sunlight clasps the fruit with fingers of warm colour you will find immortality."

*   *   *   *   *   *   *   *   *   *   *   *

Naturally, I was greatly encouraged by the publication of this article (I'd been too diffident to show it to my parents before sending it off). It shows how my style was developing: with a smoother flow and better paragraph construction, though, of course, full of the fine writing and emotional intensity that is so dear to the heart of adolescence. It was to take me a while, helped by the struggle to write accurate, clear, concise scientific descriptions, to refine my style. (The essay does include some mistakes e.g. It is unlikely that there were oaks in the Mendips contemporary with the Cro-Magnon hunters.)

The London experience: My romantic identification with nature did not prevent me from enjoying the chance I now had to explore London, a simple trip by bus and tube-train. David and I went regularly to the skating rink at Wembley, though the hired skates never fitted very well, and also watched the greyhound racing and motor bike races there. I soon found these races rather too predictable and the bookshops in Charing Cross Road more to my taste, especially Foyles, where I could spend an hour or two amongst the second-hand books. I also found my way to the Natural History Museum, going a number of times, usually heading straight for the bird collection. (Percy and I were already familiar with the excellent collection in the museum at Tring.) Not that any of this would have reconciled me to the prospect of living permanently in London.

Sentinel Press was now becoming well established at 44, Gerrard Street, and so when visiting Father at his office, I was able to explore the surrounding area of Soho. Among the publications that were produced about this time, was a successful series called *New Knitting,* an illustrated *Baby Diary* and a handbook for women called *Handywoman in the Home,* which must have been commissioned with Mother in mind, because it included all the jobs she used to try and tackle herself, all those tasks usually left to the 'man in the house'. This sold quite well. Another good idea that Father had was for a series of pocket booklets, one for each club in the Football League, covering the history of the club and famous players, photographs of the current team and prospects. When these were produced, he thought that the best way to sell them was at the various grounds, but here he ran into a problem with the clubs, who wanted a cut of the proceeds that would have creamed off most of the profits. To get round this he organised sales outside the grounds. David (then thirteen) was roped in to help as one of the vendors. He remembers selling twenty-five copies outside Highbury, the Arsenal ground, at 2s/6d each, getting sixpence on each copy sold, i.e. 12s/6d. I think he also sold some outside the Tottenham Hotspurs' ground, which became his favourite club, which he still follows from out in Australia! After this the sales went through the normal channels of newsagents and bookshops. The firm also published illustrated books for young children (Father didn't get round to his own verse stories, unfortunately) and also a crime novel called *The Admiralty Murders,* by Michael Adam, a pen name for a lady novelist. (This was printed by Hunt Barnard's, his old employers in Aylesbury.)

To attend school in Aylesbury every day we travelled down by train from Harrow-on-the-Hill, which involved a bus journey with a change midway to get to the station. We soon got used to the journey and enjoyed the colour changes in the Chilterns that autumn. I even made a few nature notes from the train, e.g.

25/9/46: "Brimstone (butterfly) at Wendover - Starlings hawking gossamers over Amersham."

One foggy evening in late autumn, I was late coming home from school, and as we approached London the fog, turned to smog by the smoke of coal fires, got thicker and thicker. I just managed to get home by bus, but the traffic was now practically at a standstill. I had difficulty finding our street and the smog was so dense that I couldn't see the street lamps until I almost reached them. I had to walk along, running my hand along the privets and counting the gates to be sure of finding our house (it reminded me of getting lost in Kenton as a small child).

I had another disconcerting London experience, this time on the way to get the train. There was a short walk over a railway bridge before catching the second bus. There had been about an inch of snow overnight and the pavements were slippery. I had just reached the bridge when an elderly man in a black overcoat, walking towards me, slipped and fell on his back and couldn't get up. Two people walking in front of me quickly stepped round him and another even stepped over him. I helped him up and made sure he could carry on without difficulty, before I went on myself, quite taken aback by the contrast between the concern that would have been shown in a village or small town, compared with this example of metropolitan indifference (or perhaps one should say, fear of involvement).

Last days at the Grammar School: It will seem that my brother Max has vanished from the narrative: this is because, when our parents decided to buy the cottage in Somerset, they found Max (now eleven years old) a place in the prep school in Chard, a small country town a few miles to the south of Buckland St. Mary, and he went away to school for the autumn term while we were still in London. They also made enquiries about places for us in the nearest grammar schools (single sex), which were at Ilminster, four miles to the east. The schools had places for Ann and David in the New Year, but there were problems for me because the Sixth Form in the boys' school was studying for examinations run by a different board and they did biology, rather than botany and zoology as separate subjects. I decided that as, in any case, I'd had enough of changing from one school to another I would simply study on my own, and present myself back in Aylesbury as a private student when the time came for the exams. I put this to the Headmaster and he agreed and then (most nobly, it seems to me in retrospect) my teachers offered to send me the essay questions they set for the classes and mark my answers by post.

My final term at the Grammar School was not without incident, as I did not entirely miss out team games while in the Sixth Form. At the beginning of my second year, I was made Ridley House captain, and to my consternation I found that I was expected to captain the House rugby team as well, as part of my duties. As I hadn't played before I had to make a quick visit to the town reference library (then in Pebble Lane just down from St Mary's Square) to get some idea of the rules (what made it more embarrassing, was that D. H. Dykins, who had been the previous captain, was an excellent player). In the competition, any necessary directions to the team had to be made by the vice-captain, and I was more or less a passenger in the forwards, not at all sure of my supposed role. It was because of, rather than despite, my ignorance of the game, that I actually managed to score three tries, by doing the unexpected. I wasn't at all clear even about what was meant by a forward pass, so when the ball came to me, or I grabbed it from the loose, my one idea was to head for the line by the shortest and quickest possible route, disregarding the shouts of "Pass man, pass!" The most memorable of these tries was in the match against Phillips House. Percy was their captain, and he was getting a bit annoyed as the game went against them. When I gathered up the ball and went for the line, as he knew very well I didn't really know how to play rugby, he shouted with some exasperation to his team, "Gash him! Gash him!" However, his team failed to 'gash' me and I went over for a try in the corner, close to a knot of masters on the touch-line, who were vastly amused at this incident (and the current schoolboy slang). As it was then thought that I must have some aptitude for the game, I was asked by the captain, Den Paton, to play for the School team. Unfortunately, this meant playing on Saturdays, and as I was travelling down daily by train in the week and helping to get the Kenton house ready for sale at the weekends, I had to turn the offer down. I rather regretted it later, especially when they played Stowe School and although they lost, performed very creditably. (My cousin James Robins played for the Old Boys in the first match after the War opposite Den Paton at fly half; and also played cricket with my contemporary G. Ramsden in the Town Cricket Club. By coincidence he worked with both their fathers in the Council Treasury Dept.)

That autumn, Harry Deeming revived the School magazine, *The Aylesburian,* and asked me to contribute a short article. It was the last of my schoolboy essays, entitled, **The Granary,** and may stand as a farewell to boyhood scenes:

"Trudging through a litter of old leaves and straw, already being churned to mud, I walked towards the granary. As I passed the ricks, snug under their yellow hoods of straw, I turned over memories like old, beloved coins. It was ten years since I had first seen the wind tugging the branches of the cherry tree. Even yet it had not lost the habit of snatching straw from the top of every loaded cart. I opened the heavy door and escaped the wind's cold breath.

"A solitary beam of light pierced the friendly gloom. Darkness, full of beckoning mystery shrouded the cobweb corners and the great vault of the roof. A mountain of grain occupied the centre of the concrete floor. Ever and again a dry whisper came from the piled grain. Like the restless dunes of the sea-shore, the wheat seemed shaken by continual motion. Behind, tier on tier of bulging sacks rose into the indefinite confines of the roof. Bins of corn, hard, polished beans, and dry, puckered peas lined the walls. I thrust my arms elbow deep into the golden grain and felt it stream coolly through my fingers, gold more precious than any metallic ore, treasure wrested with great labour from the earth. As I climbed the cliff of sacks, I saw a round, feathered head following my movements. The owl left its perch and floated silently round the beams and out of the window.

"Two old ladders were laid over the beams, bending beneath a pile of old implements accumulated through the years. Waggon wheels, planks and corn bins were inextricably mixed with broken hay forks, a water trough, old ropes and a splintered axle. As I looked down from my seat on the beam, the walls resembled a museum, being hung with an old flail, a reaping hook, several scythes and numerous appurtenances of the carter's trade.

"As time passed finches flew to and fro between roof and rick, and mice stirred in the wall. The scratch of claw and prick of questing feet sounded strangely loud under the roof. Suddenly, a robin way-wise about the farm appeared in the hole cut through the door to allow the passage of cats. It flew up into the barn and perched on the handle of the chaff-cutter. An arrow of light struck colour from its breast, which burnt like a dogwood leaf. Spilling a ripple of liquid song, it flew through into the cattle shed.

"This red-brick barn with its slate roof and broken window, its jungle of nettles and lonely cherry tree, is no uninteresting place. It is beloved by birds, by robin, owl, swift, swallow and cheerful finch. In summer the sun beats on the red walls and the swallows fly up from the eves. In autumn the wind sweeps the vermillion leaves from the cherry tree, splashing the roof with colour, and the painted butterfly and drowsy bee find warmth in its friendly crannies. In winter the mice flee the ice spirit and shelter in its cities of straw and sack, as the rains drift up over the sodden fields and the barn is full of the wind's rune.

"Generations of hobnailed boots have stumped on the concrete floor. As children, men have played amongst the sacks; as men they have pitted muscle against shifting straw and immovable wheat bag; as old men they have stirred the golden grain with their hands and pondered the beauty of seed-time and harvest. The granary is an epitome of human life and has, above all buildings other than home, an atmosphere most friendly to man, being full of happy ghosts."

****

SOURCES/NOTES—-CHAPTER NINE

1) Mead, W.R. *Aylesbury Grammar School* 1598-1998—-*A Commemorative Volume* 1998, Peterhouse Press, Brill, Aylesbury.

2) *The Aylesburian,* Vol. 3, New Series No. 1, 1946, Ed. H. Deeming. This was the first number of the school magazine to be issued, after it had been suspended during the War.

3) More seriously, I was uncomfortable with the central Romantic tenet, derived from Rousseau: natural child /noble savage, expressed in Wordsworth's description of himself at four years old as a "Naked savage in the thunder shower", and the idea that we come into the world 'trailing clouds of glory' which are dissipated in the adult 'light of common day'. It didn't square with my own experience of a growing delight in nature. Eventually, I came to see that it was a poetic conceit projected back onto childhood rather than arising from it (and related, no doubt, to the early loss of his mother). Still less could one put any credence in the idea that 'Nature' could 'teach us' anything in the realms of morality or ethics; except perhaps about their evolutionary origins. We are here very much in the world of Paley's watch and God as the Great Designer! Nevertheless, *The Solitary Reaper* and the lines *Composed upon Westminster Bridge* remained amongst my favourite poems. I also came later to respect his mature reaction to the French Revolution. He had witnessed the Terror at first hand (during his affair with Annette Villon) and unlike Hazlitt and some of his other friends who remained permanent adolescents in their revolutionary enthusiasm, realized that social change had to be a process of education and gradual amelioration.

4) Medawar, P. *Memoirs of a Thinking Radish,* 1986, Oxford University Press.

5) Maurice Severn had been a noted athlete in his time and had represented British Universities as a sprinter. My cousin James was one of a number of boys that (pre-war) he encouraged to join Wycombe Phoenix Harriers, to which he belonged, taking them to meets in his car.

6) These two trips were written up as minutes of the School Biological Society in the issue of the *Aylesburian* noted above, under the initials B.H.T. Unfortunately, I don't know who that might be (though it could be the dark girl who preceded me to study botany in Aberystwyth).

7) *Animal Pictorial,* Quarterly, Winter 1946/7, vol. 4, No. 1, pp18-22. Ed. P. Shaw Baker. The second article, although submitted first, appeared in the volume for Spring/Summer 1947, Vol. 4, Nos. 2 and 3.

CHAPTER TEN

GREEN HILLS OF SOMERSET

HARVEY'S COTTAGE, DOMMETT, BUCKLAND St MARY

The move to the West Country: We went down to Somerset about ten days before Christmas (1946). Father stayed on in London while we travelled down by train with Mother, after the furniture had been loaded into the van at 'Ridley'. This meant we arrived in Chard very late on the branch line connection from Shepton Mallet, but at the George Hotel they had very kindly kept a meal ready for us, although it was nearly midnight. Next morning the van met us at the Hotel and we all piled into it to go round to the cottage. It turned out to be one of a scatter of isolated cottages and farms in the Dommett Valley about a mile east of the village of Buckland St. Mary, which is at the eastern end of the Blackdown Hills (see map). We could see that the valley was well wooded, especially at its head, where we came down through the beeches on the ridge from the highroad, and on the south side; and that there were many trees, mostly oaks, in the hedgerows round the little fields. My first impression when we arrived at the cottage was of the loud music of running water, because a stream (called the Ding) ran along two sides of our new property and there was also a rivulet running down the lane opposite to the cottage; the moist air was full of country smells. I was delighted with the situation; so was David, as Mother no doubt assumed we would be.

The cottage is stone built and thatched, including many pinkish-brown 'Buckland Flints' (photo 10-1). These flints occur as concretionary masses in the softer lower part of the Greensands that makes up the Blackdown Hills. Broken across, they are arranged flat face out to make quite a pleasing effect. There were two rooms upstairs, and two down, the living room with a fine, open fire-place against the end wall of the cottage, capable of taking very large logs. This fire-place was also remarkable for housing a cricket that used to perform in the evenings, the only time I've ever heard one; and quite often, when I was reading late by the fire, a mouse would come out and sit by the hearth, washing its face. Mother arranged the piano against the wall opposite the fire-place, and one could look out through the open door of the porch whilst one was playing it in summer, down the valley towards the Dorset hills and the Somerset Levels away to the north-east. In addition to these rooms there was a long, lean-to back kitchen with a coal-burning range and oven at one end, and a sink with a water-pump. There was a bath, but this had been installed in another lean-to addition on the end of the house, and it could only be entered through a door from the front garden (on the left side of the cottage in the photo). There was no electricity and the loo was the usual wooden seat with a bucket under it, in an outhouse. There was as much cleaning up and re-decoration to do as there had been in Kenton. Worse, Miss

Moulton-Barrett had kept a number of Pekingese dogs. These had clearly been allowed the freedom of the house and there was even straw in the oven—-perhaps she had been drying it for bedding? Because water had to be carried round to the bathroom, she had not used it but housed the dogs there. It was about a foot deep in straw matted with faeces. David and I had to steel ourselves to dig it all out and shift it by wheel barrow to the orchard to rot down. The first structural alteration Mother had done was to put doors between the kitchen and a rear outhouse and from thence into the bathroom. After that you didn't have to face west gales or an east wind when you went to the bathroom, carrying your buckets of hot water!

We managed to get the cottage into a liveable state by Christmas, when Father came home late on Christmas Eve with a turkey he had managed to get hold of at one of the London markets late that afternoon. We children had never had turkey before, so this was a great boon at a time when strict rationing was still continuing after the war. (What we had looked forward to during the War years was roast chicken at Christmas, relatively much dearer then than now.)

There were about three acres of land attached to the cottage, including a large orchard at the back, mostly old cider apple trees, but also plum trees and eating apples. In front of the cottage there was a walled garden with a small field, 'Goose's Plat' adjacent to it, running down to the Ding; then down the lane on the other side of the entrance to this field another walled garden largely gone wild. At that time there were a number of elm trees in the hedge of the little field and three down the side of the second garden—-one for each of us boys, as Mother said.

One of my first jobs, over Christmas and continuing into the New Year, after we had acquired a good ladder, was to prune the old fruit trees. This was a job I enjoyed, conscious of the fact that Grandad Watson had travelled for the Taunton Cider Company, and there were few days when I didn't spend some time in the orchard. It had been planted beyond the memory of the inhabitants of the valley on the land which slopes from the cottage to the tiny river. Many of the trees had since died and their place taken by others now also grown old. Some of the trees had ripened apples in the sun of sixty summers. Generations of cattle had rubbed smooth their iron bark and the weight of the fruit, the westerly winds and the slip of soil to the river had caused the trees to lean at all angles. Their knotted branches were shaggy with grey-green lichen.

The following autumn, we found that hardly any two trees were alike in the taste and colour of their apples. Those from the cider trees were the most beautiful, but also the most bitter until the oak beam of the cider press squeezed out the summer-sweet juices. The apples were left on the trees until they fell, heavy with ripeness in October. As you plucked down a brown russet or pulled down a hazel nut from the hedge the lamp of their colour in the grass refreshed the eye. Red admirals, drunken with the juice of rotten plums, sometimes settled on them for a moment. Sad to say, in after years the orchard was grubbed out, like most of the cider apple orchards that used to beautify the valley in spring, their rose-pink blossom, and exotic names like Sunset, Bloody Butcher and Slack My Girdle, fading beyond recall.

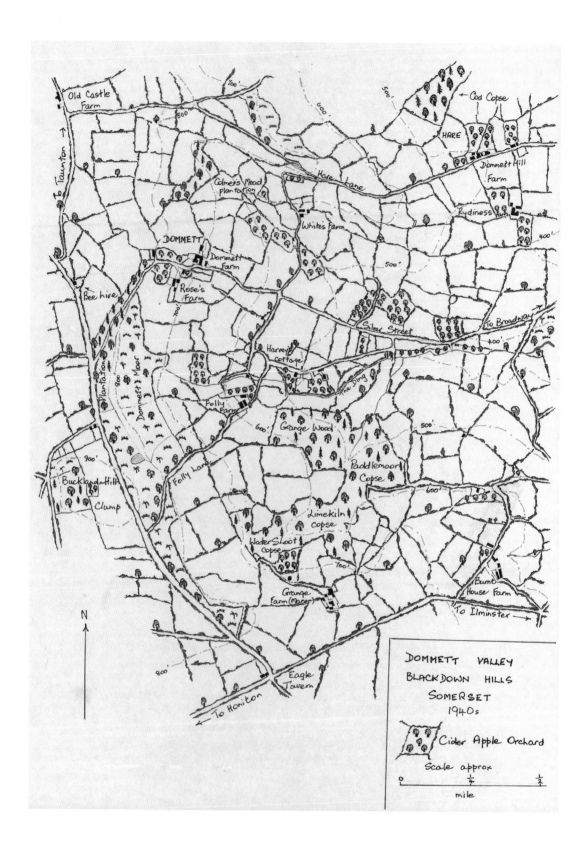

Old Castle Farm

← Cod Copse

To Taunton

HARE

Dommett Hill Farm

Colmer's Mead Plantation

Hare Lane

White's Farm

Rydiness Farm

DOMMETT

Dommett Farm

400'

500'

Silver Street

To Broadway

Bee hive

Rose's Farm

400'

Harvey's cottage

The Ding

Folly Farm

Grange Wood

500'

Paddlemoor Copse

600'

900'

Buckland Hill Clump

Folly Lane

Limekiln Copse

600'

Water Shoot Copse

700'

Burnt House Farm

To Ilminster →

Grange Farm (Manor)

N

900'

Eagle Tavern

To Honiton ←

DOMMETT VALLEY
BLACKDOWN HILLS
SOMERSET
1940s

Cider Apple Orchard

Scale approx

0   ¼   ½

mile

In the New Year, we also cleared the front garden and made a lawn in front of the porch and I created a new vegetable garden at the far side behind a rustic fence I erected for roses. There were also some galvanized iron sheds at the back that I painted green and as the backyard had become overgrown, I had to clear it.

The valley was mainly occupied at that time by small family dairy farms, run by the farmer with the help of his sons, or a boy or young farm servant, often living in (and generally held on tenancy from Colonel Pringle of the Manor/Grange farm). Most of the fields were under permanent pasture with some arable devoted to root crops and oats. Pigs, chickens and geese were also usually kept. I now got the milk from one of these farms, 'White's Farm', over on the north side, which had been taken by Bob Palmer and his wife Peggy. Bob was a former glass blower from up North, who after the war had decided to try his luck as a farmer. His 'boy', Ron Gilpin, was a lad from Malden in Essex who had got the job by answering an advert in a newspaper. The farm immediately adjacent to Harvey's Cottage, on the west and south side is Folly Farm, then run by Richard ('Dick') Smith, a former butcher (photos 10-1 bottom) whose wife Fern (née Strawbridge) was from Stockbridge, just over the border in Devon; and they had two small sons, Richard and Clifford. David began doing weekend jobs for Dick at Folly, and this led eventually to him leaving school at fifteen and going to work there full time. These details will show that although we had come to live in quite remote 'deep country' it could hardly be described as having remained unchanged 'since time immemorial'.

Long distance learning: In the New Year, Ann and David began to attend their respective Grammar Schools in Ilminster, going as weekly boarders, which meant that they left on Monday mornings, walking to catch the school bus at the village of Broadway, and returned on Friday evening. As Max went back to his prep school in Chard after the holidays, this meant that during the week I was left on my own with Mother to get on with my studies for 'Highers'.

Studying by correspondence was unusual in those days, especially for the Higher School Certificate, and in my case was considered eccentric by my school friends in Aylesbury. As Jim Symon wrote in a letter to me that January, "Dear Joseph... I was greatly amused by your 'correspondence course' idea, which struck me as being a particularly lunatic Haynish idea!" Percy was a little more sanguine in his letter of January 2nd, "Dear Hainoff....I had more or less taken it for granted that you would be coming back, though I knew the odds against you getting settled (with relations) were great. It hit me hard when I realised that the fun we had, camping, skating had ended....have you got a wireless to keep in contact with the rest of the world, you might as well be with Byrd's Expedition from the point of view of remoteness!....Your idea of a correspondence course with the school, is excellent, though not very practicable. The staff with the exception of Miss Stewart would not take the trouble, and Cab, you know as well as I do that he couldn't teach you much. In history it would be good, for you could send essays, and seeing that you can do botany and geography on your own it's not so impracticable after all....I'll inspect a microscope as soon as I can." (There were some, second hand, in a shop in Aylesbury.)

In the event Miss Stewart and Mr. Lloyd-Jones worked very hard marking my essays and answering my letters. In botany, as in science generally in those days few if any essay topics were given out. The problem there, was that I now had to rely on my memory and notes for the experiments we had done. I never did acquire a microscope, and as, in any case I had no reagents, I couldn't do any more section cutting of plant tissues. I knew that in the practical, a good proportion of the marks were given for the floral diagram and plant identification and I resolved that I would make sure that I could analyse all the flowering plants I could find in the valley that spring, as I had a copy of the famous flora by Bentham and Hooker and several other flower books. This didn't work out as well as I hoped, but I certainly found out a lot about the flora of Dommett!

The list of books I made when we were living in Harvey's reveals that I had the main set text books, but lack of further reading was now a problem, alleviated by borrowing from Jim and Percy. Jim told me that after I had left, I was blamed for taking all the missing books in the Sixth Form library, which rather upset me, as I wouldn't have dreamed of such a thing! Considering my heavy reliance on the post it was fortunate that the relative cost, especially for packages, was much less in those days. It required a regular walk to the post office in Broadway. Another indication of the relatively low cost then is indicated by the amount of lighter literature that we exchanged, revealed in Jim's first letter, "I have just obtained vast quantities of Penguins—-the books not the Antarctic curiosities. One in particular, which should appeal to your distorted sense of humour, called *Literary Lapses* by Stephen Leacock, which is extremely funny. I will send same to you as soon as I've finished it." In return, I sent him *Boule de Suif,* a collection of short stories by de Maupassant.

So with a little help from my friends and the kind attention of my teachers, I settled down to a regular routine of study mixed with work in the orchard and garden and walks in the valley and surrounding hills. Mother and I also used to go down into Taunton once a week on the local bus, where we could buy goods not brought round by travelling vans, visit the library and have a meal, or, something she liked to do, have tea and toasted tea-cakes in the restaurant by the river, where you could look at the swans.

Despite the difficulties, my studies probably benefited from the lack of distraction. In his letters, Percy told me about his latest heart-throb, and how he'd "Got it bad" and wondered if there was "A comely, Somerset maid" amongst my neighbours, and if so, "With your intellect you may get hitched to the 'Belle of Dommett', so watch your step!" Fortunately, or unfortunately, there were no young people of my age in our close neighbourhood. The nearest I came to distraction of this sort was when Mother sent me on an errand to Chard and I called at a little dress and materials shop in the main street not far from where Max was at school. There was a dark, pretty girl serving at the counter and it was one of those moments of instant attraction, a rush of blood to the head and tongue–tied confusion. For some time afterwards I thought of various reasons for going to Chard and calling into the shop on some fictitious errand, but resisted the impulse and got down to study again.

The Great Snowfall of 1947: The weather was deceptively open and mild over Christmas and into the New Year with no hint of the dramatic change to come. This is shown by entries in my nature diary:

30/12/46: "A grey showery day with splashes of blue, painted the sheds all day, buzzards flew over late in the afternoon, wren singing and unidentified finch, (also) bullfinch in hazels.

31/12/46: "Another mild, showery day, painted sheds all day, except when wiring a gap in the hedge. The stream became a different thing when the sun burnished the water. Two cole tits worked the shaggy lichen of the apple trees. Dave and I left at home the rest going to Taunton and later I toasted bread before a roaring fire while Dave amused himself by drinking Dad's sherry and smoking his cigarettes. He tried a cigar but was unable to stomach it.

1/1/47: "Max's birthday, I presented him with *Rolf in the Woods* once my favourite book, another showery day. I finished painting the big barn and uprooted the last of the (redundant) fence posts in the orchard. Found a gravel foundation beneath the mud of the yard and attempted to clear off the wet, matted grass—-deuce of a job!"

The mild weather continued through the middle of the month:

19/1/47: "Today the bright sunshine deceived the birds with its spring–like warmth. Three robins sang together in the orchard, a stormcock (mistle thrush) in the copse, a linnet somewhere unseen, a great tit in a hawthorn and a flock of ten goldfinches worked the long grass. Birds seen (until then) in the orchard in January: common—-blackbirds, chaffinches (all cocks), dunnocks, robins, tits (blue, oxeye, long tailed, cole, marsh), wrens; also bullfinches (two cocks), goldcrests (always in pairs) and flocks of goldfinches and linnets; single jay and single magpie." (Original brackets)

The weather changed towards the last week of the month, with extreme cold and heavy snow, that lasted through the whole of February well into the beginning of March. In contrast to the winter of 1963, which was even colder, there was more snow, causing severe problems, especially in the upland areas, with some places cut off for weeks, and large numbers of sheep were lost in England and Wales. We were cut off from time to time and I had to walk down to Broadway for bread and basic supplies. However, we had plenty of coal and paraffin for lamps and the primus stove. Also, luckily, I had bought the top of a wind-blown oak tree from Dick Smith soon after we had arrived. It was down the end of the field the other side of the brook. When the snow came, I went down each morning after breakfast to cut off some logs, bringing them back on a sledge I made from old planks, with runners made from the iron hoops of an old water butt. There were a number of long, dead branches, which were good for burning, together with 'apple sticks' from the orchard. This job was very pleasurable, of course, made more so by the opportunity to study fresh tracks of animals that had passed through the field: rabbits and hares, a fox or badger and sometimes the slot of a deer coming down from Grange Wood. (David and I also greatly enjoyed tobogganing down Folly Lane on a bent-up length of corrugated iron—-sometimes shooting clear over the bank when taking the bends!)

After cutting the wood it was also pleasurable to settle down by the kitchen stove (sometimes with my feet up on it on really cold days) to get on with my reading. I soon got some of my texts, for instance Maximov's *Plant Physiology,* almost by heart. In the event there was only one question where Maximov came in useful. This illustrates one of the difficulties of my isolation: not knowing what questions were likely to come up and over–emphasizing certain topics. This was certainly the case with plant ecology. In the Sixth Form I'd devoured Tansley's great work on British vegetation and made copious notes and I was hoping a question would come up on the S ('scholarship') paper, but it didn't (not that all this did me any long-term harm).

There was a curious occurrence late one evening during the Great Snow: Mother and I were reading by the log fire in the living room when we heard a loud pattering from above the wooden ceiling of the kitchen. We were used to hearing mice running about there at night, but this was louder than usual, and then they began squeaking. This gradually rose to a song-like crescendo before abruptly dying away to complete silence. I'd heard about mice 'singing', but this was the first (and only) time I ever heard it. It was rather eerie, because it made one think that there must be more to the lives of mice than we imagine from our position of lordly condescension.

There was also a remarkable weather phenomenon during the long cold spell. One day there was a slight thaw with the temperature hovering near freezing and it began to rain, but the rain froze as it fell, gradually covering everything, trees, bushes and grass and the cottage roof until they were mailed in ice. There was a six-foot high fence of half-inch gauge chicken wire at the back of the cottage and rain drops steadily congealed until it was a solid sheet of ice about one inch thick with the wire embedded in the middle. After some hours of this, hedges were bent over and branches of trees, especially on some of the oaks, began to break under the unbearable weight, with a frightening noise, like cannon. Even after the rain had stopped and when I went for the milk that evening, branches were still falling, and I had to cut across the fields because it was too dangerous to go by the lanes. Although I thought then that the ice-storm was confined to the Blackdown Hills, it also affected high ground west to Dartmoor, which remained below freezing while warmer air at a higher level brought rain that froze on contact; remembered by the oldest inhabitants there as making a 'winter wonderland'.

A 'Young Naturalist's' Spring Nature Diary: When a slight thaw encouraged some birds to start singing again at the end of February, I recommenced my nature notes and these were eventually accepted by the editor of *Animal Pictorial* as a 'Young Naturalist's' contribution. They are of interest, not just because of my developing powers of observation but because they were made before the biochemical revolution in agriculture and the changes that have ensued. I took particular note of chaffinches as the following will show:

> 28/2/47: "A cock chaffinch sang in the orchard for the first time. The cocks are still in flocks but I have observed no antagonism between them. It has been the first warm day after a month of almost arctic cold, loud with the drip of moisture and the black rushing of the river Ding under its tunnel of snow.
> 1/3/47: "The snow has melted in the vale but still remains on the higher parts of the Blackdowns. The Polypody ferns are rusted by the frost. Robins are singing again and today I heard the saw-like note of a great tit. This morning two chaffinches fought amongst the hazel poles in the hedge, white feathers flashing. When fighting the cocks puff up their feathers and expand their white epaulets. They also have the

habit of pressing their plumage to their bodies giving themselves a slim war-like appearance.

9/3/47: "The thaw continued only briefly. The wind recovered his arctic breath and snow fell on most days in the first week of March. Although the birds crowded our sheltered dooryard for food, they seemed conscious that Winter having once relaxed his cold grip would soon lose his hold, and in the warmer hours stormcocks, robins, chaffinches and great tits were provoked into song. Today I walked into the orchard to find the wind in the west, a thick mist cloaking the grey apple trees and the Ding pouring in a brown flood over the waterfall. A grey wagtail ran over the slush and then with a flash of sulphur yellow alighted farther on where snow still bridged the stream. Chaffinches sang boldly again after the further week of snow——-alarm note = Whit! Whit! —-- taking no notice of the females which have now appeared in the orchard. The increasing warmth later, also brought out a tortoiseshell butterfly from its cranny to sun itself on the garden wall.

10/3/47: "Chaffinch song now general. A cock chaffinch ('Calypso') has taken possession of a territory stretching to an indefinite distance from the large apple tree near the barn and sings almost all day. He has two other song perches in other apple trees within this territory but his most constant perch is a high, dead branch free of twigs in the large central tree.

28/3/47: "First chiff-chaff, singing from an orchard elm in the afternoon.

29/3/47: "Dunnock singing short, bold song revolving round one note, Chaffinches courting in the large apple tree. Calypso perched on his favourite branch facing the female, then singing his usual territorial or challenge song, his plumage tight against his body, and wings drooping loosely, white epaulets showing, he hopped towards the female. When close his fervour increased, and swaying his body from side to side he uttered a prolonged rattling gurgle. She made no response.

1/4/47: "Chaffinch pair now mated.

6/4/47: "Chiff-chaff singing in the wood where the wind blew the catkins one way, like a golden rain.

13/4/47: "Chaffinches nest building in the beech hedge——-female searching the wall for moss, very bold.

14/4/47: "First swallow flying over and first willow wren singing.

16/4/47: "Courtship display of male willow wren, he flew over the garden with his wings cocked high over his back and alighted on the wall with a gasping chirp. The initial notes of the song recall the opening bars of the chaffinch, though pitched in a melancholy key. The song then drops down in a liquid cadence so beautifully measured as to appear effortless. The song of some cocks is ragged and unfinished—-immature?

17/4/47: "Failed to discover whether the greenfinch has other notes apart from its long-drawn, husky pleading. The major song of March was the chaffinch's bold flourish. In April the song of the chiff-chaff, if not the loudest is the most insistent—-the spirit of spring. Swallows are now general.

19/4/47: "First cuckoo.

20/4/47: "Marsh marigolds open in the bog (a few hundred yards down the lane).

21/4/47: "Chaffinches' nest finished. Male song now more subdued.

22/4/47: "The dunnock is a mysterious bird. It is rather mouse-like and creeps about the hedge bottom as does the grasshopper warbler. The tail is depressed while singing, and when in flight it hardly ever rises higher than the hedge top.

23/4/47: "Cowslips out and milkmaids; also my favourite flower, the Veronica (speedwells) in bud; heard the whitethroat's stuttered warble for the first time.

25/4/47: "Nightingale suspected in thicket at bottom of Goose's Plat.

26/4/47: "Nightingale confirmed. I have had difficulty in distinguishing between the song of the blackcap, which I can now recognise because it recalls some of the notes of the blackbird produced at a hurried tempo, and that of the garden warbler. The whitethroat's song is a harsh warble. Veronica and Nepeta (mint) out, bugle in bud, coltsfoot seeding; rattling twitter of a greenfinch in the evening."

There was, of course, no mistaking the song of the nightingale. They were abundant in the valley, although we were not far from the Devon border, which was then their western limit. As an indication of their abundance, one evening at dusk, I was returning from Broadway, and as I came along 'Silver Street' I heard a nightingale singing and I heard six more, each marking their individual territory, as I walked the last mile or so home—-an uplifting experience. The present occupant (Melanie Tufnell) of Harvey's Cottage told me (2003) that she had never heard one during her time there.

27/4/47: "Song-thrushes are rare in this valley but a pair are nesting in the fir copse.

28/4/47: "Stitchwort in flower.

29/4/47: "Very cold and blackthorn out.

30/4/47: "Still very cold = 'Blackthorn Winter'.

1/5/47: "The chaffinches now have an egg and the round nest of the wrens in the copse has eight.

3/5/47: "Warm again. The chaffinches have two eggs, cock with indrawn whistle and alarm note = 'Too-oo-oo'; song interspersed with rattling note during mating in small hedgerow elm. First eave-swallow (house martin) seen.

4/5/47: "Observed curlews on Staple Hill (high Blackdown north of Buckland). I crouched in the brown heather stalks and watched their rocking flight and very swift gliding. Besides their bubbling song they have an alarm note which is almost a bark, if it wasn't so mellow. In the evening I watched a cock greenfinch near the Roman Camp, Castle Neroche; it took no notice of me although I was within three yards: call note 'whe-eet' interspersed with a twitter. After a while it began a soft, low twitter ending with a sweet indrawn whistle. This was repeated several times until a hawk raced over. This indrawn alarm note is also common to chaffinches and is used by the cocks when courting.

5/5/47: "Lesser spotted woodpecker in the orchard; heard the water–clear, gong-like note of a (great) tit. Fifteen to twenty swallows flocked over in a south-westerly direction and disappeared in the direction of Buckland. The woodpigeon's nest in the apple tree leaning over the stream in the orchard contains one egg. The raft-like nest is so thin that the egg can be seen through it. The jackdaws nesting in our chimney will fly in only if you look away from them. All birds seem to dislike the human face, which is, of course, the most animated part of the body. Small wandering bands of linnets and goldfinches are passing through, sometimes mating. Herb Robert and lilac cardamine (milkmaids), red dead-nettle, yellow archangel, bluebells and jack-by-the-hedge are in flower; striped bees working in currant bushes and plum blossom.

6/5/47: "First swift over Chard.

7/5/47: "Tree pipit in orchard. Many striped bees in the plum blossom but none with red tails. Three species of butterfly out: red admiral in the plum blossom, tortoiseshell and small white in the wood. Birdsong included the wistful, indrawn alarm notes of the willow warbler, jackdaws crooning in the chimney, the full song of the great tit; Calypso making rattling notes in elm. This elm is now more popular with the chaffinches than the old apple tree, which was perhaps too popular with climbing boys (Max and David).

8/5/47: "Linnets lisping amongst the beautiful, olive-yellow leaves unfurling from the buds of the sycamore.

12/5/47: "The swifts are now back in our valley, sickle-circling and screaming with reptilian glee; red clover out and wrens in full song.

13/5/47: "Stitchwort flowers bell-like with dew

15/5/47: "Apple blossom out and the laggard walnut and ash now coming into leaf. Whitethroats nest building and the garden warbler making a low, sweet song in the hazels by the stream.

> The oak is out before the ash
> So we shall only get a splash.

16/5/47: "Larks dusting themselves in the lane outside the cottage gate; lesser whitethroats singing all day. Red campion, tufted vetch and the evil smelling ransoms (wild garlic) now out.

17/5/47: "Today I collected the following wild flowers: orchids, ramsons, yellow archangel, stitchwort, marsh marigold, daisy, celandine, buttercups, milkmaids, bugle, ground ivy, cowslip, tufted vetch, bird's eye, Herb Robert, dandelion, keck (cow parsley) red campion, primrose, bluebell, violet, apple blossom, plus two others identified as woodruff and marsh valerian. The whortleberry is also out on the hills and bird's nest orchid (?) in bud in the woods. Coltsfoot, shepherd's purse, moschatel, wood sorrel and anemone are seeding. A linnet came to the dandelion clocks with blood red breast—-a study in scarlet and gold. Still no red tailed bees, only the striped ones and some pure bronze."

My investigation of the floral structures was difficult without a hand lens, but my sight, like my hearing, was good in those days. I also never possessed binoculars until I was earning a good salary at twenty-five: the advantage here is that one learns to employ careful woodcraft, and in particular, to sit quietly and allow wildlife to come near to you.

20/5/47: "Charlock and Forget-me-not out. The blackcap which sings in the hollies at the end of the orchard appears to be blind in one eye. I managed to creep within three feet of the bird (for this reason). The holly overhangs the stream and I sat under the leaves for a long time while the polished water ran beneath the pebbles and the blackcap sang like an impassioned blackbird. The winged seeds are already discernible in the flowers of the field maple; hop trefoil now in flower, and also the greater celandine, *Chelidon*—-lovely name!

21/5/47: "Walked at sunrise to Buckland Hill to hear tree pipits in the beeches of Buckland Clump—-wren-like flourish.

The following weekend was the Whitsun holiday, and my school friends, Jim and Percy came down on the Friday, by car with my father, after they had found their way to the Gerrard Street office. Over the long weekend we tramped over the Blackdowns, and also went down to the coast, as the nature diary reveals:

25/5/47: "Went with Percy and Jim to Culmhead (in the valley of the Culm at the south-west end of the Blackdowns), found milkwort, tormentil and needle-whin out." (NB. In earlier times milkwort was made into garlands to be carried in procession on the 'Rogation Days' before Ascension Day and Whit-Sunday.)
26/5/47: "Silver flash of trout in the gin-clear Yarty (a stream that rises near Staple Hill and runs down west of Buckland St. Mary to join the Axe at Axminster).
27/5/47: "Hard cries and white sweep of gulls in Lyme bay."

After my friends had gone back to Aylesbury my nature notes continued:

29/5/47: "A very good day for hawks: a passing sparrow hawk was being mobbed by swallows and starlings and then a few minutes later a peregrine went over, followed at a respectful distance by a crowd of swifts——peregrines quiver with power like a thrown lance. As usual there were buzzards over all day.
30/5/47: "Goldfinch daintily plucking seeds from a dandelion clock. Two swallows running in the lane; bird's foot trefoil and moon daisy out.
31/5/47: "Kestrel hunting near Yarty. They are rare here compared with Bucks, more pastoral and less mice?
1/6/47: "Great tits still in song; ragged robin and John-go-to-bed-at-noon out.
3/6/47: "Mouse-eared hawkweed and sow thistle out.
8/6/47: "Wood avens, self heal and meadow pea out.
14/6/47: "Foxgloves in profusion lifting their purple spires.
17/6/47: "Two mollherns (herons) flew over—-shades of Blackpit!
18/6/47: "Cat's ear, sorrel, pig nut, spotted orchid, honeysuckle out, together with moon daisies, hop trefoil, foxglove, campion and self heal making a wilderness of flowers. The jackdaws have now flown from the chimney. A little owl comes every afternoon and sits watchfully on a post in the orchard.
Saw an orange underwing (?) on a fern, and painted lady, heath fritillary and five-spot burnet on the wing.
19/6/47: "Stonecrop and nipplewort out.
20/6/47: "What is the daylight flying moth which flies swiftly like a bee and broods on the gravel of the lane with which its colours merge completely——fawn brown and mottled like a hawk and with orange underwings——soft reddish yellow body, I think" (Possibly a bee hawkmoth.)
22/6/47: "White comfrey on the banks of the Isle."

The Ding flows down through the village of Broadway to join the river Isle near Ilminster, which flows north to become in turn tributary to the river Parrott that drains the Somerset Levels. That summer David and I went regularly on our bikes to swim in the Isle at Isle Abbots, where the river runs deep below sheer banks cut back into the water meadows, and you could dive into it safely. An incident on one of these trips is revealing of David's quick temper. We were biking back and his chain kept coming off. Tired of constantly having to stop and wind it back on, he finally picked up his bike by the frame and heaved it into the hedge, deciding to walk home and abandon it. When I saw what had happened, I went back and began pushing both bikes home, and of course, for shame's sake Dave had to join me. But he had another problem because there was a slow puncture in one of his tyres, so when we got home he decided to mend it. The usual business, the bike upside down in the orchard, and the inner tube out and inflated so that when immersed in a bowl of water the minute chain of air bubbles would reveal the tiny puncture. David persevered for quite a long time, but finally, becoming completely exasperated he grabbed a screwdriver and attacked the inner tube, shouting, "By God, if I can't find it, I'll soon make one!" Mother wasn't very amused because he now needed a new inner tube as well as a couple of links taken out of his chain, but his cruel siblings had a good laugh. David had inherited Mother's quick temper and contrary nature, so, although very fond of each other they often clashed. (Considering this episode, it is perhaps not surprising that David went on to have a lifelong admiration for that social theorist commemorated with a bust in Highgate Cemetery, and the epitaph, "It is not necessary to understand the world, only to change it"!)

23/6/47: "Found a milk-white spider devouring a fly on the purple head of a knapweed.
24/6/47: "Young larks walking amongst the beet leaves in the garden. I can see a buzzard now as I write on the window ledge—-the glorious sweep of its pinions."

My entries into the nature diary came to a stop at this point, conveniently more or less coincident with the summer solstice, the astronomical beginning of summer, and were in abeyance until the late summer. This was because I now had to prepare myself for the coming 'Highers' in Aylesbury that July; however, I kept up-to-date my chart of the incidence of bird song (fig. below). A conspicuous feature of the chart is the absence of the song thrush as well as the blue tit; also, I inadvertently left out the wren, probably because it only sang intermittently. This, incidentally, was the first of many 'distribution charts' I was destined to draw up in my life!

Incidence of birdsong in the orchard, Harvey's Cottage, Dommett, 1947

289

An interesting occurrence that summer, which might otherwise have been reported in the notes, happened because I put a small dam in the brook. The Ding came under the hedge on the long west boundary of the orchard and ran down on our side. It is not far from its source here and about four feet wide with stretches of gravel and small pools. I built an embankment to enlarge the pool below a little waterfall, and a pair of water shrews took up occupation. It was a pleasure to sit quietly watching them diving for small prey organisms, their coats silvery with trapped air bubbles.

An article published: In the spring, the day after my birthday, I had the pleasant surprise of receiving the winter edition of *Animal Pictorial,* which contained my article *Old Year's Leaves.* I made this comment in my nature notes, "It was written two years ago and displeases me now in its immaturity, even compared with my present callow, juvenile efforts." Then I added, "(False modesty!)" which it was because I had reshaped it only the previous autumn, though perhaps it felt like two years. Jim Symon's reaction, when I wrote to tell him about it, was more humorous, "The idea of one of your immature efforts nestling next to that of Joy Baker gives me a sense of great deeds being done (Byron style); and your not being paid for it adds the supreme touch, fumings of the thwarted prodigy!" Jim, then studying *Northanger Abbey* with Harry Deeming, probably thought my romantic nature writing contrasted ill with Jane Austen's dry irony. The issue of payment is part of a long story I shall recount later.

When I showed my father the article he was very enthusiastic. He immediately saw possibilities and showed it to his partner Peter Hoy, who also liked it, and they decided that if I went on to produce a series they could publish them as a book. This gave me the idea of writing a series of descriptive articles describing the wild-life of the valley through the year, combined with a general study of nature in the Blackdown Hills. For a number of reasons that will gradually emerge, this grand project failed to materialize, but I did write a number of the intended articles.

A quickening interest in geology: An entry made in my nature notes shows that by the April of that year I was beginning to build up a collection of fossils:

17/4/47: "I now have a number of fossils typical of the Lias (lowest Jurassic) including *Nautilus truncatus* and various ammonites taken from the stream."

Although I became interested in geology very early it was largely from the point of view of the evolution of life. In childhood I became familiar with Jurassic building stones but neither at Slapton nor Stowe were there exposures near at hand, other than glacial sands, so I was never a boy fossil collector. Then in Aylesbury Grammar School I became aware of the connection between geology, soils and thus plant associations; and at the same time acquired a background knowledge of geology through physical geography (= physical geology). Now translocated to the West Country we were in an area of abundant exposures of fossiliferous rocks, especially down on the coast (now the Jurassic World Heritage Coast). More than that, fossils could be collected from the stream in the orchard.

The sands of the Blackdown Hills constitute what is called an 'overstep' of early Cretaceous rocks, laid down as the Cretaceous sea advanced onto an eroded Jurassic landscape, in this area, clays representing the lowest subdivision (i.e. Lias). The small streams running off the hills have cut down through the sands, so that the valleys, as in the case of Dommett, are floored by the clays. The Ding springs out from below the sands at the head of the valley and flows down across the clays, washing out fossils, which can then be found in the stream bed or on the gravel banks. After the floods following the snow melt, I found a large number, even in the orchard. These included the 'Devil's toenail', a well-named, thick-shelled, incurved oyster, and vertebrate bones, especially large spinal vertebrae of marine reptiles, as well as the ammonites and nautiloids. Another thought-provoking find there was the core of a Buckland flint, which had clearly had blades struck off it (for tools).

On my birthday, at the time of the above entry about my fossil finds, Father gave me a copy of *This Strange World*, a very good general introduction to geology, based by Sir Arthur Trueman on his introductory lectures, first at University College Swansea and then Glasgow. Trueman had been instrumental in encouraging geology as a school subject in South Wales in the inter-war years, because of the importance of the mines. It was then rarely taught in schools, outside London and the industrial north.

During the spring and early summer, when Father was home for a long weekends we went by car down to the coast, to Lyme Regis, and especially to the small sea-side village of Charmouth, which Mother particularly liked going to, with its great Liassic cliffs. I also went down alone by bus, involving changes at Chard and Axminster, and it was on one of these jaunts I first walked west from the Cobb at Lyme Regis towards Pinhole Bay and Culverhole and saw the spectacular displays of Lias ammonites in the limestones of the beach platform.

When I returned to Lyme, on that first occasion after walking westwards along the cliffs, I discovered a bookshop near the Cobb and while browsing there, by happy coincidence, found a copy of Lyell's *Student's Elements of Geology* (a first edition of 1871). It is a stratigraphical treatment working back in time to illustrate geological principles, and is beautifully illustrated. Although many of the generic names are now out of date, many of the species names survive. It was this that allowed me to pronounce so knowledgeably that I had found *Nautilus truncatus* in the brook (the first fossil I ever identified to species level). In addition, on a trip to Seaton (Devon) I saw the marked fault that brings down the chalk and greensand against the red marls of the Triassic, a much earlier system, evidence of profound earth movements. Even if I hadn't already been interested in geology, these experiences would have brought me to it.

Family problems: Relations between my parents were becoming increasingly strained that summer. The painful past could not be forgotten and made full reconciliation impossible. Father was immersed in the new publishing business, doing his best to get it established in the difficult, immediate post-war period when paper was rationed. The big firms had an allowance based on their pre-war production, while small, new businesses had to share the small amount that was left; this made it difficult to expand and was most frustrating. He began to come home less often and finally it was only once every month or so. When he came home he found it difficult to settle down and relax. After six years in the army it was hard for him to fit in to our family life, especially as he found me in charge of the garden and orchard and jointly making decisions with Mother about the cottage. This is what partly led him to take us out on trips to the coast when he did come home, and some were awkward because of the underlying tension between them. One very fraught occasion was a trip over to Ilfracombe in North Devon. It doesn't look very far on the map but in those days just after the war, the roads were in very bad condition. Father had acquired a second-hand car, at a time when they were difficult to get and it was something of an old banger with deficient springs. The journey back seemed endless. Mother was fretful and every time the car hit a bump, making a bang, she cried out, until Father, normally a most patient man, but now tired and worried, completely lost his temper and shouted at her until she fell into tearful silence. We children wished we were anywhere rather than in that car.

It appears that by this juncture, Father had already met Edith, the young woman who was to become his second wife. She joined Sentinel Press as a secretary, and as she told me later, it was a case of love at first sight for both of them. We were not to know of this for a year or so, but it meant that Father was suffering the inevitable conflict between passion and conscience.

It has to be said that I was not a great deal of help to Father at this time, and as many will have found, it is difficult from a later standpoint to forgive the upstart, big-headed, know-all that was one's adolescent/teenage self; but my father can certainly be forgiven for becoming irritated by my attempts to re-invent various political wheels for his edification. When Percy and Jim came to stay at Whitsun, we talked into the small hours late one evening, and Father who had heard it all from downstairs (as well as all before) complained bitterly to Mother, who remonstrated with him, saying, "Go on Ro, they're only boys!"

My developing views were nothing if not contradictory of course. On the one hand I still clung to my early Liberalism (and, indeed, innate conviction that liberty and equality are mutually exclusive) but at the same time was increasingly influenced by the strong leftward swing of society as a whole, with the new Labour Government taking over the 'commanding heights of the economy' under the delusion, as it proved, that it could run industry and services better than private individuals. I had also recently read a well-written, and plausible, Marxist interpretation of art and found it difficult to refute in its entirety (by John Cornford, an ex-Stowe boy, who was killed in the Spanish Civil War on his twenty-first birthday).

This confusion of ideas is brought out by a comparison of two essays that I wrote earlier in the year. In one, for the history course, we were examining the necessary requirements for democracy. I based my answer very much on the principles of Mill's *On Liberty*, and on those of the founding fathers of the American Constitution, particularly the practical/utilitarian philosophy of Ben Franklin; concluding that widespread ownership of property was essential. Miss Stewart was quite pleased with my efforts (although another colleague she showed it to, clearly more left-wing, didn't like it and thought it too old-fashioned). The other essay concerned the regional geography of certain Asian countries.

Here I was influenced by the Continental School of geographers, especially in Germany, who regarded the region as a unique response to historical and geographical factors (Le Pays of the French). I developed this idea quite strongly in my essay. Mr. Lloyd-Jones found it interesting enough to read out to the class, where it led to a lively discussion, the opposition being led by my friend Jim, as he informed me in his next letter. Jim was right because I had taken historical and environmental determinism too far (as has been well-said, 'People do not map geographically'). This idea is useful in moderation but taken as an overwhelming factor puts you on the dark road to the myth of the nation springing from the soil itself (with the individual reduced to a corpuscle in its 'blood consciousness' as D.H. Lawrence put it with enthusiasm!); or, to its mirror image, the international communist state, which is welcomed because the individual is 'vague and unreal, only the state is real' (Stephen J. Gould, Harvard science writer and Marxist, again accepting personal extinction gladly!). Both these authors made the fundamental logical error of supposing that abstractions such as the state and the nation are 'real things out there'. They may be real enough as ideas in the mind, but they do not exist as real entities in the external world.

It is not surprising that my immature mixture of ideas at this stage irritated Father, considering that he was trying to run a new business under a government and in a political climate antithetical to private enterprise. One evening when I was alone with him in the cottage, he lost his temper with me and went for his walking stick and I just got round the bend in the stairs as it hit the wall behind me. I think he only meant to give me a scare, and in the morning we passed it off with rueful grins, but it shows how difficult he found me at that stage. To emphasize this I should point out that he was generally most equable and urbane in argument, rarely losing his temper; and a favourite device, when he became bored with winning the argument too easily, was to change tack and argue the opposite case.

Another occasion when I earned a sharp rebuke was when out on a walk with him and I made a remark about something and he retorted, "Don't think you're the only one who can see things and feel like that!" Although he admired my knowledge of natural history he obviously felt that I was inclined to patronize 'townees' and romanticize country life. He needn't have worried too much on that score. I had been partly brought up in towns and I had also worked on farms from the age of eleven, which although enjoyable in many ways did not dispose me to idealize life, 'Close to the soil!' Although I preferred an isolated life in deep country and had been greatly influenced by writers like Henry Williamson and H.J. Massingham, I had little sympathy with the idea of a general back to the land movement, or an art and crafts return to mediaeval guilds. Already, through my studies, I was too well aware that town and country are interdependent and of what we owed to our industrial and mercantile success, and the advance of science. It must also be understood that this was prior to the operation of the 1947 Agricultural Act, which because of fears of food shortages, led to the long period of over-intensive farming in the late 20th century, with its damaging effects on the environment and wildlife.

'HIGHERS' AND THE AFTERMATH

The examinations: Early in July, after Father had been home for a weekend, he drove me up to Aylesbury in the car to sit for the Oxford Higher School Certificate, at the Grammar School but as a privately entered student (for which there was some kind of fee). We drove up through Ilminster and over Salisbury Plain, stopping for lunch at a pub in the village of Wylye where we went for a short walk and I was impressed with the chalk-stream clarity of the little river Wylye (a tributary of the Hampshire Avon) flowing over its long tresses of crowfoot. On the Plain we stopped briefly at Stonehenge, simply getting under the wire on the side of the road and walking over to admire this spectacular megalithic monument (not something you can do today, of course, owing to pressure of visitors and vandalism). It was of particular interest to me at the time because I had been reading about prehistoric Britain in books by authors such as Jacquetta Hawkes and Gordon Childe.

While in Aylesbury, I had arranged to stay at the home of my friend Percy in Walton Way. It was very kind of his parents and I think his elder sister, Dawn, moved out of her bedroom so I could occupy it. As Percy was also taking botany and geography it meant we could discuss the coming exams and, of course, post-morts! In the exams, perhaps inevitably because of my rather restricted preparation during the final year, I found it difficult to find enough questions on some papers that I could answer really well. This was certainly the case on the history S-paper (scholarship paper) where you had to extend yourself on three questions over the three hours. I managed two reasonably well, but had difficulty choosing a third, and when I had got into it I realised it was really an alternative to the first question that I had answered (about the development of the British Empire in the nineteenth century) and I had to use some of the same arguments; so ending very lamely. Miss Stewart, who looked through the papers before they were sent off, agreed that I had slipped up, because you had to score an A in this paper to get a distinction in the subject overall.

As was to be expected, I had a particular problem with the botany practical, racking my brains to remember precisely how an experiment had gone the year before; and unfortunately, for the floral analysis we were given a plant that was, I believe, a species of knotgrass (*Polygonum)* with exceedingly small pink florets. I found it difficult to make out the arrangement of petals and anthers, even when I borrowed a hand-lens, and I failed to classify it. For these reasons I returned to Somerset somewhat chastened.

Walking in Williamson Country: Through the year, I had discussed with Jim and Percy, various possibilities for a walking tour when the exams were over, ranging from the Lake District and Cornwall to Aberdeenshire, where Jim had family connections. We intended making use of Youth Hostels (Jim had no intention of sleeping on the ground in damp woods!) and found those in the Lake District were fully booked in the period we wanted, and finally, because we were all short of money, and not least because of the Williamson connection, we decided on Exmoor.

Towards the end of July, Jim and Percy came down with Father from London one weekend and we set off, walking up from Minehead over Dunkery Beacon and the high moors to spend three nights in the hostel at Simonsbath, the maximum allowed. It was while there that we walked down the river Barle and saw the clapper bridge at Tarr Steps (photos 10-1 top). We then went down the Lyn from Watersmeet to Lynmouth and west along the coast, finally ending up at Barnstaple and the wide estuary of the 'Two Rivers' Taw and the Torridge. At that time we were under the impression that Williamson was still on his Norfolk farm and we didn't know that he had returned to the village of Georgeham in North Devon where he had begun his writing career. Even if we had known about Georgeham and gone to have a look, we wouldn't have had the nerve to disturb the great man in his famous 'writing hut'. My last memory of Barnstaple, as we began the trek home, is of the crowds of swifts circling over the roof tops (noted in my nature notes later as the last sighting, 'about August 9th'). My memories of the various youth hostels we stayed in are largely confined to the very basic (although adequate) facilities provided so we could cook the food we carried with us, and sweeping out the dormitory between the bunk beds each morning before we left.

The results: The main reason for the extreme pressure to do really well in Highers in those days arose from the paucity of scholarships and County Awards. On enquiry, I had found that in the year 1946-7 there was only one county award available in the whole county of Somerset! This was to some extent alleviated by the grants given by the Ministry of Education for intending teachers, but they came with the requirement to teach for five years after graduation and I was reluctant to follow this route.

During 1947 there were government moves to increase the number of County Awards, and living in hope, I had, like most of my former class-mates applied to various universities. They mainly restricted themselves to London or near-by provincial universities such as Leicester and Nottingham. I was keen to go further a-field. After what Miss Avery and Mr. Lloyd-Jones had told us about Aberystwyth, looking at its location on the map and finding a photo of the road to it over the mountains showing it still unfenced, I applied. I was further encouraged to discover that they still ran a four-year course (as in Scottish universities) and that in my first year I could pick up geology as a first year course ('intermediate') while studying botany and geography at second year ('subsidiary') level. It was also possible to study a combination of arts and science subjects at the lower levels.

However, I was still considering other lines of study. Percy and I had often discussed our future over the camp fire and the possibility of following botany with a career in forestry, so I applied to Bangor where they ran a forestry course, but found I would need an extra year to pick up basic sciences, including chemistry and physics. At the same time, I had been impressed by Gordon Childe's books (written, incidentally, from a Marxist viewpoint) and thought of studying archaeology in his department in Edinburgh. This turned out to be impossible because I didn't have the necessary Latin at School Cert., then still required in the older universities for those intending to graduate in Arts and Humanities. I therefore settled on an application to the University College of Wales, Aberystwyth, and waited for the results of 'Highers', but more in hope than expectation.

On the morning the postman brought the results to the cottage, I was playing the piano. Mother gave me the long brown envelope and returned to the kitchen where she was talking with Father. I discovered that I had scored 'Good' in all three subjects. The grades available then were: Fail, Pass, Good and A, so I had done quite well, but not very well in them all;

and it certainly meant that there was no chance of any sort of scholarship. As, after my experiences in the exams, I had already become resigned to the idea that I should probably be going on to do my two years' National Service by the autumn, I just threw the papers up on top of the piano and carried on playing. This brought Father rushing in, exclaiming, "Alright John, how have you done then!" (Poor man, he did have quite a lot to put up with, especially my 'lack of reaction', in addition to my 'lack of imagination', as others have had to, since). He was very pleased when he looked at the results, and I realize now that, in the circumstances, he had naturally been afraid that I might fail altogether.

I had become eligible for National Service when I reached eighteen, but this was delayed until I had sat 'Highers'. I then received a summons and travel warrant to attend a medical examination in Exeter. What chiefly stands in my memory about this event is the question of my lost index finger. Mother had always hoped that it would mean I wouldn't be called-up for Army service, because regardless of the branch in which you served, as a medical assistant or in the cookhouse, you had to be able to use firearms in emergency. A couple of the doctors discussed my case privately for a minute or two during the proceedings and then when I was getting dressed again I realized that they were paying me close attention to see how I managed. It half crossed my mind to play it up a bit, but at the same time the last thing I wanted was to be turned down on that basis (especially as my friends and schoolmates were being called up too) and when it came to doing up my shoes I did this with great dispatch, at about twice my normal speed; and, of course, passed A1.

As it happens, I did have mixed feelings about National Service. Like many young people I had been strongly affected by the massive destruction and death toll caused by the atom bombs dropped on Hiroshima and Nagasaki, and for a while it seemed to make pacifism not merely morally, but practically, the only sensible course: an attitude and time personified by the young American, Gary Powers, who went to Europe and publicly tore up his passport and declared himself a 'World Citizen'. Gradually, I came to understand that this attitude was hopelessly idealistic. It turned out, true to Cab's prediction at the School farm camp in Steeple Claydon, when the first bomb was dropped, that the balance of atomic weapons between the major conflicting powers would inhibit an international war; but 'small wars' continued to be fought. It was clear, that in the nature of things, we would still have to resort to conventional arms to defend our interests when necessary. One could only preserve a pacifist stance if one sincerely believed that to take part endangered your immortal soul. As this required standing aside while your family and friends faced destruction, I found this impossibly solipsist. I couldn't subscribe to it, or to what we might call the pseudo-pacifist, anti-war stance, which conveniently pretends that Britain and its allies are the parties always in the wrong (assiduously promulgated by various Communist front organizations); so despite my misgivings, I knew that when called-up, I would have to go.

Photographs 10-1 Green hills of Somerset
Top-: John on Tarr Steps, the clapper bridge over the river Barle, when walking in Williamson Country.

Bottom-: Richard (Dick) Smith, the local farmer, and David's onetime employer, in front of Harvey's Cottage some years after we had left.

Waiting to be called-up: During the two months or so that I now had to wait before being 'called-up' for National Service, I was able to enjoy working in the garden and orchard, and what I liked most, 'mooching about' in the woods and fields. I also busied myself completing the writing-up of nature articles, to go eventually towards the possible book. I also continued my nature notes into late September, as some examples will show:

28/8/47: "The clouded yellow is very common this year, probably a result of the fine anti-cyclonic weather that has characterised this summer. Cabbage whites, heath browns, meadow browns, silver-washed fritillaries, red admirals, and tortoiseshells have also been in great abundance—-though the painted lady has been rare. The fine weather has also given a golden harvest of ragwort, tansy and fleabane. August has not been entirely silent and robins are in song again with chiffchaff and yellow hammer, also great tit once—unusual." (Another interesting plant that I found abundant in some of the damp fields was the Dyer's green weed, once collected for the purpose indicated.)

2/9/47: "Returning from Broadway village I saw a family of partridges in a stubble field. They disappeared and I stalked them, finally putting them up in the middle of the field. The mother bird trailed a wing on the ground and ran away uttering a creaking cry; meanwhile the cock and the young ones flew a few yards and plumped down again. Although I knew the hen bird's action was a trick, she held my gaze until the young ones had hidden themselves and I searched for a quarter an hour without finding them. It reminded me of the very long time it took me and Arthur Jones (my Dadford friend) to find some young lapwings in the Crouch field at Stowe.

11/9/47: "Swallows and martins flying around excitedly all day, chiffchaff in elm.

23/9/47: "Swallows still here.

25/9/47: "Three woodlarks singing at once outside Broadway, chiffchaff in pussy willow near cottage.

27/9/47: "The swallows appear to have gone."

My call-up papers arrived in mid-September, before the final disappearance of the swallows. I was told to report to Taunton Barracks in ten days' time, with instructions on what I was to bring with me. I was quite pleased to find that I would do my initial training only a few miles from home, making it easy to get back on short leaves, and to continue collecting information in my spare time towards the nature book on the Blackdowns. I wasn't particularly looking forward to the initial three months' 'square bashing' but after the *Mercury* I knew I would manage it without too much trouble.

As happens to best laid plans, my preparations to get ready to join the Army were almost immediately disrupted when the postman delivered another important looking envelope. To my surprise it was the offer of a place at University College Aberystwyth, to read for honours in botany, together with geography and geology. It was quite unexpected because I had heard nothing since I sent in my application months before, and as I had not been called for interview, I assumed it had fallen by the wayside. Undoubtedly, good references from Aylesbury Grammar School had induced the offer, especially those from the two Aberystwyth-trained teachers.

I was at first disposed to simply write and tell the College that I had been called-up, and in any case had no means of support, but Father was home for the weekend and we discussed it. He was favourably impressed when he found that the fees were very low, about thirty-five pounds a year. This was because the College had originally been set up on subscriptions, which included 'pennies' from the slate miners, and fees had been kept at an historical low figure so that poor students would not be barred from study. On finding this out, Father said he would pay the fees and help as much as he could, but I would have to find other sources of support.

I had recently heard from Percy, who had done well in 'Highers', getting an A in botany, that he would be getting an award to study at Leicester, but also that some pupils with results similar to mine also hoped to get grants, which meant that their military service would be deferred. This encouraged me to think I could also get some kind of grant and that by working in the long vacations, supplemented by getting articles published, I would be able to manage financially.

After making this decision, I contacted the local recruiting office and was referred to the chief recruiting officer for the Southwest of England in Bristol. When I spoke to him on the phone and explained my position, he chuckled and said, "My son is in the same position as you." So, despite the lateness of the hour, I was given further deferment there and then. For this reason, one bright morning in early October, instead of jumping to attention on Taunton Barracks Square, I caught the train in Taunton Station and set off to start a new life over the Severn Sea beyond the 'Misty Mountains of Wales'.

Epilogue: If I'd had any idea of the difficulties ahead, I might have thought that the simplest course after all, would have been to have gone into the Army at that juncture in my life (like my friend Jim Symon who served in the British Army of the Rhine, and took up Law afterwards). When I applied to the Somerset Education Committee for an award, they replied saying that although domiciled in the county, as I had sat the exam elsewhere, they weren't responsible for my further education, and suggested that I write to the Bucks Education Committee. When I did, their reply was that although I was Bucks-educated and had sat the exam in Bucks, it had been as a private student when actually domiciled in Somerset, so I wasn't their responsibility either—-a nice example of falling between two educational stools!

My attempts to earn money from my writing also failed. The week after I arrived at college, I sent off an article I'd written in September, followed by another written later. In the following year these were eventually returned, together with some sent earlier that had been accepted. The little firm had gone bankrupt and I was never paid for the two that had been published. Father was very annoyed, saying that happening right at the beginning, it was likely to put me off writing completely. However, I did continue writing articles for a while and looked for other outlets, but it did bring home the uncertainties of the freelance writer's life and confirm my decision to find a life in science if it were at all possible; and of course, eventually the pressure of my degree studies largely precluded other writing. These monetary problems meant that I was much more financially dependent on Father during my first year in college than either of us had hoped. It was only at the beginning of the second year that I managed to get the Bucks Education Committee to advance me a loan (£50 a term, which paid out over the following three years amounted to £450—-about £10,000 today).This, together with vacation work, saw me through.

Fortunately, I was quite unaware of these problems ahead when I set off that morning for college, or, that matters would be further complicated by the final collapse of our parents' marriage in the spring of the following year (1948) when they decided to sell the cottage; nor, therefore, that when I went home for the Christmas vacation, I would not be returning to the cottage again but would spend the following Christmas with Mother back at Woodlands in North Bucks, and that eventually she would return like a homing pigeon to live in Aylesbury. During that last Christmas holiday at Harvey's Cottage I wrote an article towards the projected book on nature in the Blackdowns, which I append here, as it shows what the book might have contained, and more particularly, how my writing style was developing and would now, over the next few years, be applied to descriptive science instead:

WINTER IN THE BLACKDOWNS

"Indoors the ash falls softly from the great sticks of oak and apple. Fragrant flame-flowers blossom and die, brightening the open hearth. Outside the pale sunlight shines obliquely through the branches of the bare trees, picking out the beautiful symmetry of stag-headed oak and towering elm. The slanting rays assert the mellow wintry colours of the countryside.

"The bracken lies in rusty heaps on the slopes of the Blackdowns. Brown streams brim their banks and mists shroud the pink-barked pines and moss-boled beeches of Dommett Moor. The west wind is a prolonged hiss about the ancient tumuli of Browndown, wry music in the blackened heather and broken bent grass. It is winter in Somerset.

"Leaves crackle tersely beneath my feet as I leave the cottage for winter has long since pierced the bronze armour of the trees. Only an oak here and there and the beech hedges that line the lanes, still retain leaves. Behind the buff-headed oak trees the clear winter sky is very blue. The mist has lifted from Dommett Moor and seen between the branches of the dark beech trees it is, by contrast, a seemingly even more intense blue.

"A jackdaw flies from one of the trees set about Goose's Plat, our little field; it is probably one of those that nested in the disused chimney of the cottage in the spring. The sun shines on its wings and ash-grey poll. A bullfinch pipes wistfully in the brambles and a blackbird shuffles amongst the leaves in the hedge bottom. When the wind first tugs them from the twigs the oak leaves are buff-bronze above and parchment coloured below, staining mahogany with the autumn rains. Those leaves which the ebon thrush rakes from the wet ditch are dull black, already merging with the earth again.

"As I pass on my way down the valley a cloud of finches burst from the hedge, fly up and away. Chink! Chink! Cries the blackbird, Chink! Chink! A sound to winter twilight as the abrupt barking of dog foxes and the far melancholy hooting of owls is to December moonlight. Animal cries, like the stars are more beautiful in the longer, darker, more brilliant nights.

"There is a long low wall farther on, opposite a beech hedge, which as usual in the West Country, crowns a double mound. In the crevices of the wall, pennywort, maidenhair, spleenwort and harts' tongue find shelter. Sere grasses bow stiffly to the wind where sometimes squirrels leap from stone to stone along the top. Beyond, a bunch of Polypody ferns grows in the crotch of an old cider apple tree.

"Tap! Tap! Sounds from the top of the tree which leans on the wall, bent with the weight of years and many seasons of red cider apples; a yaffingale or oddmall had not seen me sitting on the wall. I see his light blue-green eye and scarlet crown as he sidles round the trunk, his eight toes hidden in the shaggy lichen. He shoots away without uttering his joyous laugh; he still hasn't seen me.

"At the bend in the road, by a copse where the woodlark sang when gossamers glinted in the September sunshine, a lane wanders away into the fields. Tall hedges border a track-way, which is poached by hooves because at dawn and dusk cattle are driven along it. The ruts are drifted with leaves and the pools reflect sky, bare branches and arching briers. The bracken by the hedge is bronzed, the grasses are white and sere, but the giant bromes are yet unbroken by the wind and water-drops entangled in the pendant awns flash back the light. Green bunches of rushes grow in the wet patches, some cut short by the cattle as they pass. The fluted columns of the gix (hogweed) and pig-nut are blackened by the rain, as are the nettles and thistles, many lie broken on the ground. The willow herb is dead having loosed its plumed seeds, thus fulfilling its purpose and rain has rusted the massed ranks of hemp agrimony to which the peacocks and fritillaries came in July. The fleabanes which were yellow suns in the blazing August noon still bear a few seeds, although brown and dry. Life has not quite gone for on the bank are some sprays of keck (cow parsley) and in one place a ragged campion holds a solitary red flower.

"Walking quietly I surprise a flock of felts (Fieldfares) pulling haws from the topmost sprays of the hawthorns. Chuck! Chuck! They gather in an oak and watch me silently until I have passed before flying down again. Just here the lane opens out into a glade such as gypsies like to camp in. Across the throat of the valley a party of rooks oar silently through the still air. Behind, the purple-brown of the winter woods, the yellow-green of the pasture lands and the red-brown of the arable fields, melt into the far blueness of the Dorset hills. The sunlight slants warmly through the hedges, falling yellow on the autumn stained roseleaves, scarlet on hip and haw, purple on privet leaf and pearly on snowberry.

"The patch of snowberry fringes a small field where there are a few apple trees. Above a stone linhay (barn) in the corner of the field, a buzzard drifts and brings up against the wind, then drifts on over the ploughlands where the winter wheat is pushing through the clods. The grasses sway and return and the wind brings back his forlorn crying.

"Beyond the glade the hedges almost meet overhead and it is easy to see the nests of old summer against the light, the rafts of pigeons and the bowls of thrushes filled with haws by mice. Lichen like the flattened horns of fallow deer, clings to the twisted blackthorn the castle of the nightingale in May. Something rustles in the hedge and looking through a gap I see a rabbit darting zig-zag through the rough tussocks of the field.

"The lane runs on, crosses a road and winds down a slope to a stream flowing beneath oak trees. It is the river Ding which springs from a bog under Dommett Moor, bubbling up under old leaves and rushes, the haunt of snipe. Rushing by orchard, wood and tiny field the dark waters curve about root and boulder, making sharp music on the yellow Buckland flints. At the margin I disturb a woodcock, a bird with the drab hues of the leaves which thickly strew the banks. The strange woodcock, with its elusive flickering flight, is the spirit of that hour of the day which fades into dusk, the most beautiful time in the winter woods. It seems almost imperative to wait beneath the oaks until Orion hunts in the southern sky and the wind seems to burnish the red eye of the Bull, whilst the stream runs with secret sounds and sudden silences beneath the gloomy hollies and lolling hart's tongue."

* *

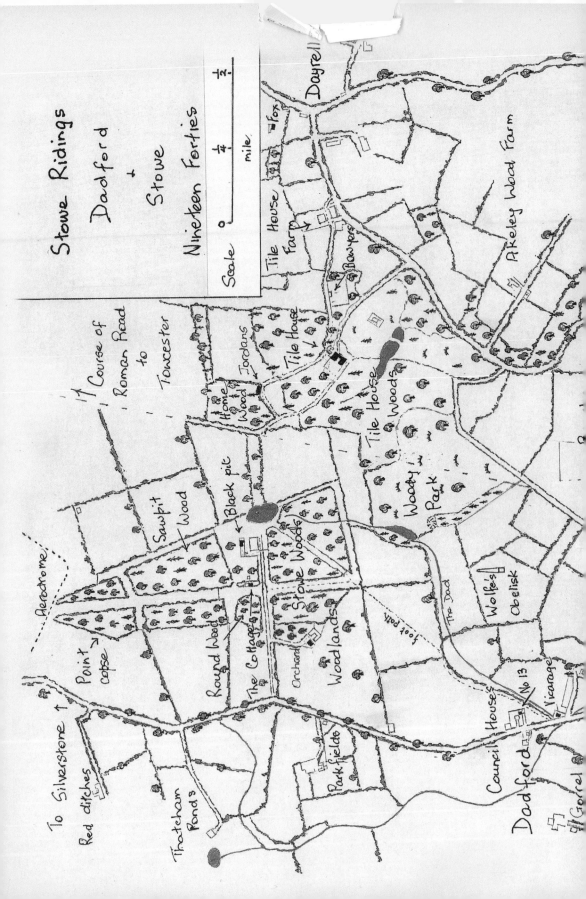

Stowe Ridings

Dadford + Stowe

Nineteen Forties

Scale 0 — ¼ — ½
mile

To Silverstone ↑

Red ditches

Point Copse

Aerodrome

Thatcham Ponds

Sawpit Wood

Round Wood

The Cottage

Orchard

Black pit

Home Wood

Jordans

Course of Roman Road to Towcester

Tile House

Tile House Farm

Fox

Bowyers

Dayrell

Akeley Wood Farm

Tile House Woods

Woody Park

Stowe Woods

Woodlands

Foot Path

The Dad

Wolfe's Obelisk

Park Fields

Council Houses

No 13

Vicarage

Dadford

Gawcot